MI IB1B41405

Economic Literacy

A Comprehensive Guide to Economic Issues from Foreign Trade to Health Care

by
Orley Amos, Jr.

CAREER PRESS
180 Fifth Avenue
P.O. Box 34
Hawthorne NJ 07507

1-800-CAREER-1
201-427-0229 (outside U.S.)
FAX: 201-427-2037

Economic Literacy
A COMPREHENSIVE GUIDE TO ECONOMIC ISSUES FROM FOREIGN TRADE TO
HEALTH CARE
ISBN 1-56414-135-7, $14.95
Cover design by The Gottry Communications Group, Inc.
Printed in the U.S.A. by Book-mart Press

To order this title by mail, please include price as noted above, $2.50 han-
dling per order, and $1.00 for each book ordered. Send to: Career Press,
Inc., 180 Fifth Ave., P.O. Box 34, Hawthorne, NJ 07507.

Or call toll-free 1-800-CAREER-1 (Canada: 201-427-0229) to order using
VISA or MasterCard, or for further information on books from Career Press.

Library of Congress Cataloging-in-Publication Data
Amos, Orley M., 1954-
   Economic literacy: a comprehensive guide to economic issues from
   foreign trade to health care/by Orley Amos
   p. cm.
   Includes index.
   ISBN 1-56414-135-7: $14.95
   1. Economics. 2. United States—Economic conditions—1981- I. Title
   HB171.A63   1994   94-34074
   330.973—dc20   CIP

TABLE OF CONTENTS

ACKNOWLEDGMENTS v

AN INTRODUCTION TO GET YOU STARTED vii

**Section 1   The Seven Facts of Economic Life That Everyone
Should Know**   1

Number 1   Our Limited Pie   3
Number 2   Our Subjective Values   10
Number 3   Our Unfair Lives   17
Number 4   Our Monopolized Markets   26
Number 5   Our Necessary Evil   35
Number 6   Our Unknown Economy   45
Number 7   Our Circular World   53

**Section 2   The 38 Most Intriguing, Confusing, or Controversial
Issues in Our Economy**   61

My sales pitch on advertising   63
Those astronomical athlete salaries   67
Business as usual   71
Charging up your credit cards (aka plastic money)   76
Stealing a few moments for crime   80
What do you have against discrimination?   84
The crystal ball of economic forecasting   87
Pumping up the economic growth   91
Learning all about education   94
Trading some ideas on exchange rates   98
Getting your share of farm subsidies   101
Taming our beastly federal deficit   106
Borrowing through the financial markets   110
A translation of foreign investment   114
The wide, wide world of foreign trade   118

The odds on gambling   122

The sick state of health care   127

In the neighborhood of immigration   131

Keeping the lid on inflation   135

The risky business of insurance   139

Some prime stuff on interest rates   143

The business about investment   147

A tycoon of the mutual funds   152

Conserving our natural resources   155

The economics of dueling political views   160

Scraping up the pollution   165

A somewhat defective look at product safety   170

A perfect picture of profit   175

On the lookout for a recession   180

Laying ground rules on regulation   185

Planning on social security   189

Playing the stock market   193

Paying taxes   197

An altogether look at unions   202

Creating wealth   205

Collecting welfare   209

A careful view of worker safety   212

Getting the most out of working women   216

Section 3 A Whole Bunch of Economic Terms and Definitions   219

Section 4 Index   295

Acknowledgments

Help Along the Way

My casual stroll through our economy has been assisted by helpful comments and useful suggestions from many tour guides. At the top of my list are the three people who share my residence. I am referring, of course, to Pamela (aka "Pam"), my long-time partner in marriage, financial obligations, and household remodeling, and our two suprisingly well-behaved teenage offspring who are popularly known as Chris and Holly. They have laughed at the humor, critiqued the grammar, and provided valuable fashion tips.

Indispensable directions along this pedestrian path of enlightenment were also offered by Ann Amos, Rick Amos, and Rann Amos. Sheer coincidence cannot explain why they share my last name. They are, in fact, mother, brother, and brother. I want to add a big assist to the in-law side of the family ledger, as well, with thoughts and comments coming graciously from several Angelos, especially Patti Angelo.

Others who deserve a nod of the head, a wink of the eye, and a pat on the back include a cluster of colleagues residing within the academic ivory towers of Oklahoma State University, and a flock of faculty at my alma maters—Wichita State University and Iowa State University. As a group they fostered (often unknowingly) instruction, inspiration, and introspection that led to this book, actually a "pedestrian's guide" to our economy.

My biggest thanks goes to Betsy Sheldon, Ron Fry, and all of the good folks at Career Press who made your purchase of this book possible.

To dad, who taught me how to jaywalk

AN INTRODUCTION TO GET YOU STARTED

Through undaunted determination, sheer luck, or a missed turnpike exit, you have happened upon *Economic Literacy*. You'll find hours of reading pleasure contained within these pages, with more entertainment value per calorie than most office memos. *Economic Literacy*, a "pedestrian's guide," however, is more than a recreational supplement. As a handy reference book, it provides answers to many of the most-asked, a few of the least-asked, and some of the never-asked questions about the economy.

What's a pedestrian's guide?

The best way to begin our excursion through the economy is with a simple question: What is a "pedestrian's guide," anyway? Let's resort to the time-tested technique of analogy.

Consider how you might embark on an exploration of the American heartland. You'll easily detect that Kansas has fewer mountains than Colorado and more vegetation than New Mexico. A car, by contrast, gives you more insight into the terrain. You'll not only see Colorado's mountains, you'll also experience them first hand as your 1972 Volkswagen Beetle strains to reach higher elevations.

But if you really want to discover America's heartland, then throw a couple of granola bars and an extra pair of sweatsocks into a backpack, and take a stroll across the Kansas plains, the Colorado mountains, and the New Mexican desert. A pedestrian's trudge across the country will give you insight unattainable by car or plane.

In terms of the economy, most of us have a pedestrian's knowledge of our own neighborhood but only see the rest by car or plane. This book tries to fill in those sightseeing gaps with a more leisurely pedestrian's stroll.

Who should read this book?

Economic Literacy has been specifically formulated, designed, and engineered for the overworked, underappreciated members of the third estate. "What's the third estate?" you might ask, and "How do I know if I'm part?" Both are excellent questions. A little explanation is in order.

Back in the days of yore (when knights, castles, and the like were popular), people were usually lumped into one of three "estates." Religious leaders and the clergy were the first estate, nobility the second, and the common folk (everyone else) made up the third. (Later on, journalists—bless their hearts—added their occupation as the fourth estate.) Most importantly, the educated, powerful leaders of the first and second estates made the rules that the uneducated, uninformed peasants of the third estate were supposed to follow.

A great deal has changed since those bygone days of yore, but then again much remains the same. The clergy and nobility aren't all that important now, but new versions of these estates have arisen. Our modern first estate is populated by a handful of government leaders who spend the majority of their adult lives running for an elected office, holding an elected office, or resting in appointed government positions until an elected office is available. Our modern second estate consists of a select few business leaders who run major corporations, sit on the boards of major corporations, or own gadzillion (a handy term meaning "a whole bunch") shares of stock in major corporations. Like their counterparts of yore, members of the new first and second estates—government and business leaders—make the rules and control the information. (Of course, our fourth-estate journalists try to keep a close eye on the nefarious doings of our leaders, but they often end up working for, rather than watching over, the first two estates.)

That leaves us with our modern third estate. Like the peasants of yore, our third estate includes the vast majority of common, everyday folk, who do their work, pay their taxes, and quietly follow the dictates of the first two estates. If you're a consumer, worker, and taxpayer, then you're part of the third estate. Even though you might work for a big corporation, are in the employ of our government, or run your own small business, if you don't set the rules, then you're in the third estate. And while you're certainly more educated and informed than your hardworking, overtaxed third-estate counterparts in the days of yore, you can never learn too much about the world.

That's where *Economic Literacy*, a pedestrian's guide, enters the picture. Most books on the economy are written by economists for economists (who are well-known henchmen for the first two estates). Occasionall, economists will pen a volume or two directly for politicians or business leaders. I suppose both of these have a place in the grand scheme of things. But what if you don't have a Ph.D. in economics, run for reelection every few years, or head a Fortune 500 company? What if you're one of the gadzillion overworked, underappreciated, taxpaying consumers who form the backbone of our economy? What if you're a member of the third estate? Well, this book, *Economic Literacy*, is for you!

Why do I need this book?

If you're like most overworked, underappreciated members of the third estate, you get information about the economy in three ways:

• *College.* Because you whiled away the early years of your adult life in college, you were maneuvered into an economics course—usually by an economics professor seeking job security. You bought the textbook; spent a few hours a week listening to endless lectures on prices, costs, and "gross something or other"; took a few exams; and sold the textbook back to the bookstore. Then you forgot as much as you could except"gross something or other" and the fact that the instructor usually had one of the following: (a) a hair out of place, (b) a nervous eye twitch, or (c) unzipped pants.

• *Nightly news.* Because your television remote control was mailed to Aunt Helen with last year's Christmas packages, your TV is left untouched between *Oprah Winfrey* and *Wheel of Fortune.* As a result, once a night, Dan Rather, Tom Brokaw, or Peter Jennings introduces a news story that uses the term "economy" at least twice and contains a quote from a noted government economist. You suspect that portions of the news event affect you, but you're not quite sure why.

• *Life.* Because you have a job, pay taxes, frequent your local grocery store, and have more bills than unmatched socks, you recognize the existence and importance of this thing we call the "economy." While you may not know that economists have created sophisticated, mathematical economic theories that use every Greek letter that exists, you do understand, through the miracle of plain old common sense, that the economy affects your life.

Wouldn't it be nice if you knew a little more about what affects what—without the Greek letters?

Everyone has occasional questions about the economy, such as: What are those leading economic indicators that Dan Rather joked about last night? One way to answer your questions is to get a Ph.D. in economics, which then forces you to learn all sorts of stuff that can only be written with Greek letters. Another option is to befriend an economist and subtley pose questions such as: What the hell is a leading indicator? This, however, can have serious side effects, such as an excruciatingly painful bout of boredom.

A third option is to keep this book handy. It gives you a reference guide to the more intriguing, important, and confusing aspects of the economy while omitting the Greek letters and sophisticated mathematical economic theories.

How should I use this book?

Economic Literacy is divided into four sections—"excursions" into enlightenment—not including the table of contents and this introduction. If you like, you can read all four in sequence, from cover to cover, one right after the other, and become very, very knowledeable about the economy all at once. A second, highly recommended option is to read only the stuff that seems to be the most interesting or relevant to your own situation. A third alternative is to leave it unread on the table for the sole purpose of impressing visitors. This, however, will cause problems when your guests, who have read this guide, begin spirited but one-sided conversations. You'll then get a stiff neck from constantly nodding in agreement to perpetuate your charade.

Here's an overview of our four sections:

1. "The seven facts of economic life that everyone should know" tours seven fundamental features of the economy that most of you probably, sort of, know, but then again may not. Because it gives you a working start into the economy, this journey is best taken before moving on to the more detailed topics in Section 2.

2. "The 38 most intriguing, confusing, or controversial issues in our economy" journeys into economic issues that are often dis-

cussed but seldom fully understood. You can read every issue, beginning with Advertising and ending with Working Women, or you can pick and choose them in any order. Each is cross-referenced to provide you with something more than a random walk through the economy.

3. "A whole bunch of economic terms and definitions" has detailed definitions of economic terms commonly flung through the media by the fourth estate—yet no one tells you what the stuff really means. Use this glossary section as a reference source to check out these terms.

4. An index of everything in this guide, like any index, has page numbers for every topic and key term, except for those in the glossary of economic terms, which are already alphabetized for your ease of reference Because it helps you avoid the paper cuts that often occur from needlessly thumbing through undesired pages, this is often a good place to begin a quest for economic knowledge. (Issue chapters follow "See also" in text.)

A SPATTERING OF PEDESTRIAN TIPS

Sprinkled throughout Sections 1 and 2 are an assortment of tips that give bits of advice and recommendations. They're intended to assist your walk through the economy as a consumer, homemaker, citizen, worker, voter, or taxpayer. Some of the tips are obvious, but some are not.

The not-so-obvious tips come from one of the most important facts about the economy, ones that can't wait any longer. Because of its overwhelming importance, let's call this Fact #0.

Fact #0: A multitude of primal economic forces. Our economy contains many diverse, pervasive forces, some that are easily controllable and others that are not.

Because this book helps you identify the often obscure forces of the economy, especially the ones that are most controllable and the one that aren't, I would be remiss if I failed to note how you can act on the information. Consider these three options:

1. *Individually.* You can often improve your lot in life with the right information. Many of the tips offered in this guide suggest things to do, questions to ask, and warnings to heed.

2. *Collectively.* No man (or woman) is an island. In some cases life can be improved only by joint efforts of a neighborhood, community, city, county, state, nation, or the world. Several tips note what you should consider before casting your vote, writing letters to politicians, or otherwise jumping into the collective decision-making waters of the government.

3. *No action.* Occasionally you find economic forces so powerful that nothing can be done. In this case, it's best to sit back, grab a granola bar, and check the television listings for your favorite programs.

Valuable time can be wasted with individual efforts on collective problems, collective solutions where individual actions are best, or pursuing either when the primal forces are insurmountable. Please note, though, that these tips are only tips—mere suggestions. The ultimate responsibility rests with you. (This, by the way, is probably the most important tip that you'll get.)

A last note before getting to the important stuff

Your pedestrian excursion through the economy will not go unrewarded. Of course, you'll be the proud recipient of economic knowledge that's even beyond the grasp of many members of the first and second estates. But that's not all. You'll get the opportunity to keep pace with our fast-paced pedestrian economy through "Pedestrian Footnotes"—a monthly newsletter on the most current, pressing, and controversial topics stampeding through political debates and the news media. And there's even more. On completing your trek through *Ecomomic Literacy*, you will have also satisfied the requirements for the Doctor of Pedestrianism (Pe.D.). There's no reason why pointy-headed economists should be the only ones with fancy certificates. For a free, official-looking Doctor of Pedestrianism diploma (it's suitable for framing and bound to impress family and friends), simply write to: Ambling Institute of America, P.O. Box 2045, Stillwater, Oklahoma 74076.

It's now time to lace up our jogging shoes, grab some extra granola bars, and begin our little pedestrian trek through the economy.

SECTION

THE SEVEN FACTS OF
ECONOMIC LIFE THAT
EVERYONE SHOULD KNOW

OUR LIMITED PIE

The first stop for any pedestrian on a leisurely stroll through the busy economic streets of Shady Valley is Scarcity Stan's Ye Olde Bakery Shoppe and Confectionery Palace. The most noted pastry on Scarcity Stan's list of delectables, wedged between his mouth-watering apple danishes and scrumptious jelly donuts, is economic pie. My mouth waters with the thought.

Economic pie isn't like other donuts, cakes, and confectioneries with their gobs of sweetness but very little nutritional sustenance. In fact, given that it refers to the sum total of the economy's resources and productive activity, economic pie is filled to the brim with sustenance. Unfortunately, Scarcity Stan and the congregation of people we call "society" have only one economic pie, and while it's pretty large, it's never quite as big as we would like.

Scarcity Stan's economic pie resides at the source of the first of the seven facts of economic life that we'll encounter on our economic stroll:

What is this economic pie and why is it limited?

> ### Fact #1: Our economic pie is limited.
> The economy has a finite amount of production, income, resources, and wealth at any given time.

Scarcity is one big problem

Scarcity Stan's conceptual namesake—scarcity—lies at the heart of our limited economic pie. An extended discussion of scarcity is presented with all of the other definitions in Section 3; however, for our current purpose a shorter definition will do. "Scarcity" simply means that there is not enough "stuff" for each and every one of us to get everything we want. It's a problem because all members of society want or need an unlimited number and variety of products. But here's the catch, the resources and means to create these products are limited.

So, you say that you want beach-front property, an expensive sports car, and a private jet? You're not alone. Can our economy provide you, me, and everyone else

A PEDESTRIAN ...

with beach-front property, expensive sports cars, and private jets? No! And not because you, I, and the other 5 ½ billion people on the planet are undeserving. The problem, quite simply, is that we don't have enough resources to produce beach-front property, expensive sports cars, private jets, and a gadzillion other products—way too many to list here—that we all want.

Our economic pie begins with resources

Limited resources lie at the root of this problem of scarcity and are ultimately responsible for the limits on our economic pie.

What are these resources?

- *Natural resources.* Any listing of society's resources needs to start with natural resources: land, water, air, wildlife, vegetation, sunshine, mineral deposits, fossil fuels, and everything else that comes with the planet. This is the "stuff" from which everything is made. (See "Natural Resources" in Section 2 for more on this topic.)
- *People.* Of course people and their labor are another important resource. This includes factory workers, clerical staff, executives, managers, accountants, educators, legislators, auto mechanics, and, well, basically anyone who puts forth the

mental or physical effort to transform natural resources into the products we all want and need. (It's often useful to isolate a special type of human effort—entrepreneurship—which does the job of getting production started.)

- *Capital.* The last, but by no means least, of society's resources is capital, which includes the factories, buildings, machinery, and equipment used to transform natural resources into products.

It's probably evident that without these resources—all of which are limited—we wouldn't be able to satisfy our wants and needs. Whenever we eat food, watch a movie, visit a doctor, or warm a house, we use these resources. Here's a challenging exercise for you. Think of something, anything, you consume that doesn't use these three resources.

Resources beget production, which begets income, which begets wealth

If we stopped with resources, we would have a pretty good grasp of our limited economic pie. However, our limited pie only starts with resources. Because resources are limited, a whole bunch of other stuff is limited, too. Here's why.

Limited resources—natural resources, labor, and capital—also limit our production of goods and services. Once our factories are cranked up to capacity and labor is working to the point of exhaustion, then we have pretty much reached the limit on production. You've probably come across the official term that newsguys and government types use when talking about production: "gross domestic product." Its status is reported regularly, creating major headlines if it goes up a bunch or down even a bit.

Limited production also limits our income. As we explore further in Fact #7, Our Circular World, the income we spend comes from producing stuff. If our economy produces less, then we have less income to spend. Even though some people are occasionally given income, there would be no income to give without production by others.

Our limited production and income also restricts our wealth: the stockpile of stuff we own. As your personal wealth is the amount of assets and things of value that you own, the wealth of our economy is the assets and productive resources that we all own. And as you're able to accrue wealth by saving some of your income, our economy's wealth goes up by saving part of our production and income. Because production is limited, our accumulation of wealth is also limited.

No matter how we label our economic pie, it's limited. A limited economic pie is the source of some of our more interesting economic, political, and social predicaments. Let's explore of few.

Everything has a cost

Contrary to many advertisements and promotional "give-aways," nothing is truly "free"; everything has an opportunity cost. A slice of pie consumed by one person can't be consumed by another. For example, when our resources are being used to make you a sweater, they aren't being used to make me a sport coat. The cost of making your sweater is not necessarily the price you pay for it, but the satisfaction that I don't get from the sport coat.

This is, unfortunately, an often-overlooked fact of economic life. Special-interest groups, lobbyists, and others who are inclined to seek favors from the government have a tendency to champion the benefit of their pet program without fully disclosing, or even recognizing, the opportunity cost.

For example, car companies, farmers, veterans, teachers, lawyers, or _____ (fill in your own favorite group) might lobby Congress for a tax break, subsidy, or other benefit. *But* (and here is an important *but*), whatever they get, someone else loses. Because our pie is limited, what one person gets, another one doesn't.

This is important for any card-carrying member of the third estate. As we see in Fact #3, Our Unfair Lives, the third estate includes those who don't have as much wealth and control over resources as the first and second estates. The political and economic power of the first two estates often allows them to gloss over opportunity cost—especially when it's paid by the third estate. For that reason, you need to keep your eyes peeled, your ears opened, and your mouth ready to ask questions about any undisclosed opportunity cost.

You might get some help uncovering opportunity cost from the fourth estate journalists, who have long held the self-proclaimed role as watchdog over the first two estates and protector of the third. Unfortunately, though, the fourth estate tends to be eaten by the first two. (Ask yourself if a journalist who was once a high-level presidential advisor and now makes 20 times the salary of an average worker can be truly considered a watchdog for the third estate?)

In Section 2, we'll see how and why opportunity cost enters into many ongoing public debates. For the time being, however, let's ponder the widespread use of the word "free," "Free," "FREE."

When a "free" good isn't

Because nothing is truly free, you need to be on guard anytime the word "free" appears within a hundred miles of your purse, wallet, or checkbook. Every "free" give-away has a cost somewhere along the way. That "free" Captain Amazing decoder ring in the bottom of the Frosted Honey-Coated Super Sugar Junks cereal box, that "free" car wash given with a tankful of OmniGuzzle gasoline, and those "free" steak knives provided to hearty travelers willing to consider a time-sharing summer retreat cottage along the banks of the Cheatemifucan Lake are anything but "free": Someone pays.

The question, however, for those with limited incomes and wealth is who does the paying. The cost of "free" goods are paid in one of three ways:

- *Higher price.* The price you pay is high enough to cover the cost of the desired good (Frosted Honey-Coated Super Sugar Junks) and the "free" good (Captain Amazing decoder ring). Businesses can't remain in business very long if they give away too many "free" products.
- *Subsidization.* Someone else wittingly or unwittingly pays the opportunity cost of the "free" stuff—a subsidy. Unwitting participants often include other customers of the same business who pay higher prices but don't get the "free" stuff. A witting participant in this alternative is often the government (but with unwitting taxpayers). Government is well known for subsidies—a theme we'll encounter frequently on our journey.
- *Promotional investment.* The stockholders or owners of a business might willingly pay the opportunity cost when they give "free" stuff to customers. This, however, is best viewed as an investment, not charity. Businesses see "free" promotions as an investment in future sales. Like a business invests its profit in a factory to increase future production, it invests in "free" samples to increase future sales. We'll return to this investment idea in a few pages.

What does this mean for anyone trying to get the most out of a dollar?

CONSUMER TIPS FOR "FREE" GOODS

- If the cost of the "free" good is part of the purchase price, then don't be fooled by the promotional propaganda into thinking that you're getting something for nothing. Ask yourself if the price you pay—your opportunity cost—justifies all products included in the package.

- If your "free" good is subsidized by other consumers or taxpayers, then enjoy their unwitting good nature. Be careful, though, that you're getting the subsidy and not giving it.
- If your "free" good is part of an investment promotion by business, then lay back and enjoy their hospitality. However, once more you should recognize the underlying intent of the business. They aren't giving you a "free" good out of the kindness of their altruistic heart; they expect greater sales in the future. If you like the "free" product enough to buy it, then do so; if not, don't.

But how can you know why a particular good is "free"? Many businesses are pretty shrewd in their ability to disguise who pays for "free" stuff. Other businesses might not even know. The best advice is to ignore the word "free" entirely. When you make a purchase, compare the benefits that you get from the stuff with the opportunity cost you pay.

Pies are made to be shared

One of Scarcity Stan's biggest problems—and ours as well—is slicing up the economic pie. Distributing our economic pie has always been, and probably always will be, one of our (that is, human beings) most interesting and controversial topics. The reasons for the controversy are pretty simple:

- Everyone needs a slice of our pie to perpetuate the phenomenon we call "life." If you don't eat, you die!
- Everyone does not contribute or cannot help contributing to our pie. The very young, the very old, the very sick, and the very disabled are all often relegated to the economic sidelines when others do the producing.

As such, while some get the same amount of pie they make, others get more, and some get less. As a general rule, though, it's pretty clear that those who create most of our economic pie get out less than they put in. In other words, we have our "worker bees" with the awesome responsibility of producing

enough for everyone. Those who don't contribute to the creation of the economic pie are therefore dependent on those who do.

Let's take the familiar case of small children. They're entirely dependent on their parents when born. Parents usually (not always, but usually) willingly redistribute some of their own slice of the pie to their children. Without the "worker bee" efforts of their parents, children would go wanting.

Children, however, are not the only consumers who contribute little or nothing to our pie. The elderly, disabled, and poor, have a similar dependency on the economic-pie creators, receiving a share only by the kind-hearted (or government-encouraged) actions of others.

Many of our more controversial government programs (see Social Security and Welfare in Section 2) deal with redistributing our economic pie from some consumers to others. Because redistribution through these and similar programs are handled by the government, dependency becomes most important when selecting political leaders and evaluating their proposed policies. Before we get to specific voting tips, consider these three points:

- *Net benefits.* The first question we need to ask is whether redistribution from the haves to the have-nots gives us a net gain. If recipients benefit more than givers lose, then society has a net gain. An example of this would be if you are well fed and share the last bite of your food with a starving person. This bite of food is likely to have a very small opportunity cost to you, but just as likely provides ample benefits to the recipient.
- *Growth.* A second question is whether redistribution helps or hinders future economic growth. It might be, metaphorically speaking, better to redistribute food from the hungry to the well fed, if the well fed can use the food today to produce more food tomorrow. This is an ongoing controversy, because wealthier people tend to invest more in productive resources (such as capital) than the poor.

A redistribution of our pie from the poor to the rich might not give us a current net gain, but it might promote a future net gain by creating a bigger pie. (Check out Investment and Economic Growth in Section 2 for more on this.)

- *Waste.* We not only need to consider the cost to the givers and the benefit to the recipients but also the cost of redistribution itself. That is, many resources—including thousands of workers in government and business—are used to redistribute our pie and thus do not do anything to help create it. While the government is often singled out for wasteful redistribution, many areas of private business are also redistribution-oriented, including some (but not all) of the efforts of lawyers, stockbrokers, and real estate agents (see Wealth). We need to add in the redistribution cost to see if we really get a net gain.

Like it or not, our limited economic pie will be redistributed. Of course, those who like it least are those who have the most to lose: They've contributed the most to the pie. And those who like it a bunch are on the receiving end and have made little or no contribution to our pie. (Here's a good place to direct your attention to Political Views.)

As voters, taxpayers, and consumers, you should consider three tips when evaluating government redistribution programs.

REDISTRIBUTION VOTING TIPS

- Consider the benefit acquired by the recipients of the redistribution and the cost of the givers. Don't be fooled into thinking that there is only benefit or only cost. The beneficiaries of redistribution can make a strong case that their programs will be costless to society. We know that this can't happen. Likewise the disgruntled givers will try to make a strong case for excessively high cost and no benefit.

- Consider the long-term effects of any redistribution program. Does it promote or limit economic growth? When the benefits of greater growth or the cost of reduced growth are included with today's net gains (or losses), is the program justified? Once again, don't listen to just one side.

- Consider the cost of actually doing the redistribution—taking from one and giving to another. When this cost is included, are we really better off?

The most intriguing part of redistributing our economic pie is the complete and total lack of absolutely correct answers. Should income be redistributed from the rich to the poor? Should wealth be redistributed from the elderly to the young? Should production be redistributed from the workers to the idle? Yes, of course it should! And no, it shouldn't! Both are right, but neither one is. There are no right answers for all times and all situations.

Ah, the sort of controversy that warms your heart!

A slice of investment, please

While our economic pie is limited today, it need not remain the same size forever. Economic growth—the process in which our economic pie is increased—is accomplished with investment in productive resources (much more on this thought can be found in Investment). In its simplest terms, investment is giving up a little bit today to get even more tomorrow. Unfortunately, like all activities, investment is not without cost. The ability to move the economy two steps forward tomorrow usually requires one step backward today.

Investment surfaces in many arenas, including the most obvious example in which businesses make factories or other forms of capital. Other equally important forms of investment are in the areas of education, work, and household chores (see Education). For example, students attend college and forego income that could have been earned from 4 to 5 years of productive work in the real world because they hope to increase their income-earning capacity with their newfound knowledge (also termed "human capital"). A mechanic spends several minutes laying out tools to make an engine tune-up less time consuming. Homemakers spend a few hours organizing kitchen cupboards to facilitate future meal preparations. These are investments on and all: Give up some now, get more later.

Investment, in its many varied forms, is perhaps most intriguing because of the uncertainty of the future. You give up a known "something" hoping that you'll get "something better" later on. But you might not! For example, a student who's after an accounting degree when entering college would be sadly disappointed if accounting salaries dropped through the floor 4 years later. All investments are necessarily risky propositions because the opportunity cost is paid today, but the benefit comes sometime later. Those who guess right make bundles of money (gadzillions or more). Those who guess wrong, lose out. (At this point, I'm inclined to refer you to Fact #6, Our Unknown Future, for further insight into uncertainty. If you jump to Fact #6, however, you'll miss a lot of neat stuff in the four facts that come first. Remember: Patience is a virtue.)

AN INVESTMENT TIP

- Ask yourself if the anticipated *future* return justifies the *current* opportunity cost of the investment.

Without investment our economic pie remains unchanged and, in fact, is very likely to shrink if an increasing number of people devote an increasing share of the pie to wasteful redistribution.

What does it all mean?

Most consumers, voters, taxpayers, business leaders, and politicians recognize somewhere deep down in their economic souls that (1) our economic pie is limited, (2) we can't have everything that we want, and (3) there simply isn't enough to go around. But actions often belie rationality. The first step on the path to an economic consciousness, which frees the repressed economic soul inside us all, is to recognize the limitations of a finite economic pie. Then, and only then, can we begin to address our more schizophrenic economic neurosis, including, but not limited to, an understanding that every activity has an opportunity cost. Once accomplished, we can divide our pie in a reasonable, rational way, noting that every distribution, by helping some people and harming others, is inherently subject to criticism. But our pie can be enlarged if the distribution process includes a slice set aside for investment, making the hurt less painful and the critics less strident.

While our pie has been quite tasty, it's time to continue our sojourn through the economy. As luck would have it, Scarcity Stan's Ye Olde Bakery Shoppe and Confectionery Palace is located in the same general geographic confines as the next stop on our pedestrian's stroll: Shady Valley's low-priced wonderland, Mega-Mart Discount Warehouse Super Center. After dodging a few distracted motorists across a newly paved parking lot, we can enter the expansive automatic doors of the Mega-Mart Discount Emporium, pausing only momentarily to soak in the grandeur of 20 gadzillion square feet of merchandise under a single roof. A long loiter, however, is not possible, because there's stuff on sale. Out of My Way!

See also: Advertising, Gambling, Health Care, Insurance, Stock Market, and Taxes.

2

—————————————— **NUMBER** ——————————————

OUR SUBJECTIVE VALUES

On leaving Scarcity Stan's Bakery Shoppe and Confectionery Palace, our pedestrian's excursion drops into Mega-Mart Discount Warehouse Super Center. A quick tour of this mecca of mass production—lasting no more than 3 days—is likely to reveal within the 20 gadzillion square feet of floor space a number of salesracks, shelves, and tables filled with merchandise marked down for clearance. A prominently displayed sign on one salesrack boldly declares that the regular $24.99 price has been drastically reduced, for this week only, to $3.98. What a bargain! What a sale! We have the chance—"for a limited time only"—to get stuff valued at $24.99 for only $3.98! With a bargain like this, how can we lose?

It's easy to lose, if you don't understand the concept of value. Most of us have several "bargains" stored away in the attic, closet, or garage that never have seen, and probably never will see, anything resembling use. What seemed like a great "bargain" at the store does nothing but occupy space at home. (By the way, does anyone have use for a distributor cap for a 1949 Ford?)

The posted price of any product is only the first step in understanding this notion of value. To see why, consider the second basic fact of economic life:

> ## Fact #2: Value is in the eye of the beholder.
> The value of a good, service, or resource is subjectively determined by the satisfaction of wants and needs that it provides to consumers.

The operational term here is "subjective." As far as you are concerned, the value of a good depends exclusively on how much satisfaction it provides to you. If a good is worth $24.99 to you, then it has a value of $24.99. If, however, you are willing to pay only $3.98, then its value to you is only $3.98.

Scarcity and exchange can be bloody

Let's return for a moment to that nasty scarcity problem from Fact #1, Our Limited Pie. It tells us that society doesn't have enough of everything for everyone—a prob-

A PEDESTRIAN ...

... finds a bargain

THIS IS PERFECT! I'VE BEEN LOOKING FOR ONE LIKE THIS FOR YEARS!

HOW MUCH?

TEN CENTS

NOW THAT WOULD MAKE A GREAT NEST!

SALE

WHOA! TOO RICH FOR ME!

lem if ever there was one. What can you do about a predicament like this?

For example, suppose that you and I are browsing around Steroid Steve's Athletic Footwear for the Physically Adept in search of a pair of size 10 Steroid Steve cross-trainers. At precisely the same instant we both spy the very last pair of size 10 Steroid Steve cross-trainers on a display rack. We both want the shoes. We both have the cash on hand to make the purchase. We both reach for the shoes and make contact at exactly the same time. What do we do?

We have three options. All three have been tried by society at various times, but only two are generally deemed acceptable

in civilized society. (By "civilized," I'm excluding, of course, rush-hour traffic, rock concerts, and professional hockey matches.)

- *To the death.* One of us could extract the cross-trainers from the grip of the other, using whatever force is available, a good old-fashion free-for-all. Taken to the extreme, this will result in one death, an unappealing alternative for the shoe store, not to mention for one of us. This is also the alternative that's generally not acceptable in civilized society.
- *Parental coercion.* Much like a parent who settles a backseat territorial argument between siblings on a cross-country car trip, an all-powerful Steroid Steve clerk

could take charge of the situation to determine who receives the cross-trainers. This can be done arbitrarily or through some predetermined rule, such as height, weight, sex, previous purchases, country club membership, etc. Wait just a second! Who does this Steroid Steve clerk think he (or she) is—the government? In a word: Yes! More on this when we get to Fact #5, Our Necessary Evil.

- *Voluntary exchange.* Both of us could peacefully and voluntarily negotiate over who best deserves the right to buy the cross-trainers. We could start a bidding process in which each of us determines the price we would be willing to pay for the shoes. This alternative illustrates the common method of voluntary market exchange that occurs millions of times each day in our economy (and it's less painful than a battle to the death).

Although survival of the fittest does surface occasionally, most exchanges are conducted either voluntarily through markets or involuntarily by the government. Fact #5 considers the government's role in involuntary exchanges. Here we explore voluntary market exchanges and what this means for value.

All those in favor say "buy"

"Market" is the term economists use for voluntary negotiations that exchange commodities, resources, goods, services, and other such items. You've undoubtedly come across this term many times. For example, you run to the supermarket for a loaf of bread and gallon of milk, note that the stock market has dropped 600 points since yesterday, or browse through the want ads of the labor market because your boss is a jerk and you want a new job.

These are but a few of the common uses of the term. What they all have in common, although some are more obvious than others, is that buyers and sellers are exchanging stuff. Because buyers

want stuff and sellers have stuff, it seems natural that they would somehow get together and work out an exchange. That's what a market does.

The key, however, is that markets are voluntary. As a seller, you sell stuff that you want to sell. If you don't want to sell, then you don't sell. As a buyer, you buy the stuff that you want. If you don't want to buy, then you don't buy. The end result of these negotiations—the consequence of this buying and selling—is that the price of the stuff exchanged is agreed on by both buyers and sellers.

- Because the price is agreed on by both buyers and sellers, it reflects their preferences. This is the price that they voluntarily accept.
- Because the price is agreed on by both buyers and sellers, the value placed on the good by buyers is the same as that of the sellers.

The two sides of value

The value of any commodity–whether it's retail merchandise, military weapons, national parks, or inane television programming–ultimately depends on how well it tickles the fancy of those willing and able to pay the price. The road to value, however, can be a long one, filled with many twists and turns because the prices of goods depend not only on the buyers but also on the sellers. The paths of demand and supply go in seemingly opposite directions but ultimately end at the same source: subjective values. Let's consider these two sides of a market.

- *Demand,* the buyers' side of the market, depends directly on the consumer satisfaction generated in the course of consumption.
- *Supply,* the sellers's side of the market, depends on the opportunity cost of production, which, as we see shortly, is also dependent on the satisfaction obtained from consuming stuff.

Demand begins with consumer satisfaction

Here's the scene. You've just entered your local Master Sprocket's convenience store, where you notice a counter display for Master Sprocket's Universal do-it-yourself all-purpose spark plug tool and ice cream scoop. You don't personally own a Master Sprocket's Universal do-it-yourself all-purpose spark plug tool and ice cream scoop, but you know several people who do and they speak highly of them, usually with a glint in their eyes. Do you buy it? The first order of business is to check the asking price. It's scrawled on the cardboard display: $4.99 (plus tax).

A series of additional questions are likely to switch the neurons in your brain off and on like the lights in Times Square on New Year's Eve.

- *Income.* Can you afford the $4.99 (plus tax) with your available income? Moreover, if you wanted to buy two or three, perhaps as gifts for family and close friends, can you afford the expense? Checking your purse or wallet, you note that income is not a constraint at this time. Several Master Sprocket's Universal do-it-yourself all-purpose spark plug tool and ice cream scoops could be purchased without exhausting your available cash.
- *Substitutes.* You recall, though, that Captain Car Hop a mile or so up the highway has its own brand of spark plug tool and ice cream scoop (which also doubles as a dog whistle), but has an asking price of $5.50 (plus tax). Should you buy the Master Sprocket's or pick up the Captain Car Hop version? Is the addition of a dog whistle worth the extra 51 cents (plus tax)?
- *Satisfaction.* Do you really want to spend your cash on the Master Sprocket's Universal do-it-yourself all-purpose spark plug tool and ice cream scoop? This might require a little soul searching. On the one hand, you already have a spark plug tool hiding somewhere near the spare tire in

your trunk. And your ice cream scoop is still in working condition, although slightly bent from that half-gallon of very frozen tin roof sundae you bought last month. On the other hand, you don't have anything that can serve as both a spark plug tool and ice cream scoop. Through this deep introspection, you might even begin to wonder if you want a do-it-yourself all-purpose spark plug tool and ice cream scoop at all. Although you have the cash, hundreds of other items could be purchased for $4.99 (plus tax) that could be more useful, pleasurable, enjoyable, or desirable.

This last introspection is perhaps the most important. Your decision to purchase the Master Sprocket's Universal do-it-yourself all-purpose spark plug tool and ice cream scoop ultimately depends on the degree to which it's expected to fulfill one or more unrequited need. You buy the instrument because you want it, need it, or expect that it will somehow make you better off. Let's ponder the heart of what motivates buyers: wants and needs.

Wants and needs

It's occasionally useful to distinguish needs from wants.

- *Needs.* A need is generally thought of as a biological requirement to sustain existence. Some of the most basic needs include water, oxygen, food, and protection from temperature extremes. Needs, therefore, come with the basic biological package we call "life."
- *Wants.* A want, in contrast to a biological need, is usually considered a psychological desire. You really don't need it to continue your existence, but having it would make you a little happier. Wants, thus, depend on psychological conditioning and can vary widely from one person to the next, depending on culture, childhood experiences, or whatever.

Both wants or needs provide us with the motivation to demand products. Goods that do a better job of satisfying our wants and needs have a greater demand. *But* (and this is an important *but*), no two people are likely to have the same wants and needs, nor derive the same satisfaction of wants and needs from a given product. The value that you derive from a good need not be equal to the value I derive from the same good. Pretty subjective, eh?

Supply also begins with satisfaction

Let's return to our Master Sprocket's Universal do-it-yourself all-purpose spark plug tool and ice cream scoop. Instead of buying this wonderful utensil, we're now talking supply. If you want, we'll even make you the chief executive officer (CEO) of Master Sprocket, Inc. (which also means that you are a card-carrying member of the second estate.) In fact, let's go back a few years, when Master Sprocket's Universal do-it-yourself all-purpose spark plug tool and ice cream scoop was nothing but a idea in the mind of a junior (hoping-to-be-vice-president) executive. The junior executive, CEO (that's you), and other members of the management team are exploring the possibility of producing and selling the Master Sprocket's Universal do-it-yourself all-purpose spark plug tool and ice cream scoop. What do you need to consider?

- *Technology.* You might consider if producing this instrument is possible. Does the technology needed currently exist or can it be readily developed? If production of a do-it-yourself all-purpose spark plug tool and ice cream scoop is not technologically feasible, then you'd better direct your attention to something else, like a combination pizza slicer-paint scraper.
- *Competitors.* You need to evaluate the competition. Industry scuttlebutt says that Captain Car Hop is planning to develop a spark plug tool and ice cream scoop that can serve as a dog whistle. You'd better keep a close eye on it.

- *Production cost.* And last, you certainly need to consider the cost of producing this wonderful instrument. For example, you have the cost of the factory, equipment, electricity, workers, and raw materials (a titanium alloy developed by NASA scientists) just to fabricate the utensil. Then there's packaging, distribution, and marketing expenses. You also need to add administrative salaries, overhead, and dividends to appease your shareholders.

After evaluating all production cost, you establish your retail price, which in this case is $4.99 (plus tax). If buyers are willing to pay this price, then the junior executive becomes vice president. If not, then the junior executive becomes a mail clerk.

But let's not leave production cost just yet. Because in conjunction with the willingness of buyers to pay for the instrument, production cost helps determine the market exchange price, *and* value.

The opportunity cost of foregone satisfaction

As the CEO of Master Sprocket, you calculate the retail price of $4.99 (plus tax) to cover production cost for all parties concerned, plus to generate an acceptable profit (see Profit). Let's consider production cost more carefully? Wages to workers is an easy one. Others follow a similar logic.

Suppose that Master Sprocket hires 50 workers, paying each one $10 per hour. Why is Master Sprocket willing to pay each worker $10 per hour and, equally important, why is each worker willing to produce the combination spark plug tool and ice cream scoop for $10 per hour?

Here's why:

- *Contribution to production.* As Master Sprocket's CEO, you're willing to pay each worker $10 per hour because you've determined that each worker contributes at least $10 per hour to the production of the combination spark plug tool and ice cream scoop. Any business that pays workers more than what they add to production is losing profit.

- *Value of foregone production.* Each of your workers is willing to produce the combination spark plug tool and ice cream scoop for $10 per hour because this is equal to, or greater than, the wage they could receive in another job. But note that the other job, whatever it may be, also sets the wage based on what their workers contribute to production.

Aha! Here is where satisfaction enters supply. To produce one good, a worker isn't producing another good. The cost of production is nothing more than the value of goods that are not produced. When you make the spark plug tool and ice cream scoop, your workers and other resources are not making other stuff. Consumers are therefore losing satisfaction equal to their subjective value of those other goods.

The bottom line, literally, is that value is totally subjective. We might like to think that price and cost are hard and fast numbers with a rigorous, quantifiable, objective dimension, like height and weight. But they're not.

If Master Sprocket's Universal do-it-yourself all-purpose spark plug tool and ice cream scoop is traded for $4.99 (plus tax), then some buyers are willing to pay $4.99 (plus tax) because that's the amount of satisfaction this indispensable utensil generates for them. And Master Sprocket is willing to sell it for $4.99 because that's the amount of satisfaction the buyers of other products give up so that the resources can be used to produce the do-it-yourself all-purpose spark plug tool and ice cream scoop.

Most importantly, the price can change because some of the parties involved change their mind. If buyers don't get as much satisfaction now as they did earlier, then the price will drop from $4.99 (plus tax). If workers, other resource owners, or consumers decide that the goods not produced are more valuable, then the price of the do-it-yourself all-purpose spark plug

tool and ice cream scoop will rise from $4.99 (plus tax).

This provides us with a few useful shopping tips:

THREE TIPS ON VALUE

- Value is what you think it is. Don't let advertising fool you into thinking that a product is more valuable that it really is, *to you.*
- Because someone else places a high value on a product does not mean it's equally valuable to you. Their value is, well, their value, not yours.
- Because a product is costly to produce doesn't mean it's valuable to buyers. Cost is only part of value. The ultimate source of value is your own satisfaction.

Those annoying television shows

This notion of subjective valuation might put your mind to rest the next time you're forced to catch a glimpse of some really stupid, inane, or otherwise idiotic television show because your remote-control battery is too weak for a rapid channel scan.

Unfortunately, many of those shows, as "bad" as they may be, are "valuable" to someone. Sure, your tastes may run more in line of hard-hitting dramas like *Brace Brickhead, Medical Detective,* but you can't stand the sickening sweetness of the *Cutsey Kids Sit-Com Hour.* Meanwhile you do (or do not) like the continuing saga of *Lustful, Tormented Lovers in Madeup Town, USA,* while your significant other can't stand (goes crazy over) the live prime-time coverage of *Big Guys Hitting Each Other Over a Ball.* And of course you've never met anyone who enjoys *The Egotistical Comedian Show,* although it's been rated in the top ten for the past 5 years.

What applies to television programs applies to every other good that's voluntarily exchanged in markets. You may not understand how anyone, and I mean anyone, could possible drive that model of car, wear that brand of perfume, or live in that style of house, but they do.

Is the world crazy? No, people simply have different wants and needs and place a different value on goods. The next time you see (a) someone younger than you wearing really ugly clothing or (b) someone older than you wearing really ugly clothing, and you start to say "I don't know why they make clothes like that," feel free to slap yourself in the face as a reminder that value is in the eye of the beholder. Then be thankful that voluntary exchanges allow you the choice of wearing your own really ugly clothing.

What does it all mean?

Market exchanges help society address the problem of scarcity head on. While they can't eliminate the problem, market exchanges help improve our lives by getting us stuff that we wouldn't otherwise have. A few points follow from this:

- *Negotiation and competition.* The exchange process works best if a lot—gadzillions—of potential buyers and sellers are able voluntarily to negotiate prices and exchanges. As we see in Fact #4, Our Monopolized Markets, control of the market exchange by a few participants can really screw up the process. However, if this doesn't happen, market exchanges let us get the most satisfaction from our available, limited resources.
- *Consumer sovereignty.* Buyers generally get what they want because sellers are out to make a profit. If buyers value one

good more than another, then sellers are prone to accommodate the buyers and supply more.

- *Advertising.* Because value is subjective and depends on buyers' tastes and preferences, tons of profit can be made by anticipating or controlling buyers' wants and needs. That's one reason you see so much advertising around. It's also why you need to be on guard for any would-be "mind controllers."
- *Incentives.* Ample opportunity exists for behind-the-scenes manipulation. Government, for example, can restrict the exchange of goods like tobacco and alcohol with taxes. This raises the prices to buyers and lowers the prices to sellers. Alternatively, something like education can be encouraged by lowering the price to buyers and raising the price to sellers.

While we could spend more time in the Mega-Mart Discount Warehouse Super Center, 3 days is all we can spare for now. Our shopping bags are filled with valuable bargains, every one of which was priced just right. I think it's time that we made a (hopefully) briefer stop across the interstate at the Shady Valley Central Town Sprawling Hills Shopping Mall. Yes, yes, I know that we'll have to fight the overflowing crowds that populate this self-contained suburban city. But without the crowds, we wouldn't have much to talk about over the next several pages.

See also: Discrimination, Exchange Rates, Farm Prices, Foreign Trade, Political Views, Pollution, Stock Market, and Unions.

NUMBER

OUR UNFAIR LIVES

Across the interstate from the Mega-Mart Discount Warehouse Super Center resides the Shady Valley Central Town Sprawling Hills Shopping Mall—a prime example of our economy's climate-controlled, suburban shopping phenomenon. Our pedestrian's ramble through the economy would be totally inadequate if we did not spend at least one day strolling past the endless rows of stores with their displays of clothes, shoes, electronics, clothes, luggage, clothes, cheese pretzels, and, of course, clothes. Our pedestrian trip, however, is not concerned with the products exhibited beyond the stylish glass windows. No, our jumping-off point is the gadzillions of people who pass us by, bump into us, get in our way, and generally make our shopping experience comparable to a commuter train ride during the rush hour.

Those who comprise the shopping crowd are short, tall, young, old, fat, thin, black, white, happy, and sad. More important for our present discussion, however, is that some are rich and some are not so rich. A few of the wealthier shoppers actually buy the products framed by the picturesque win-

dows that line the air-conditioned quaint midway of Shady Valley Central Town Sprawling Hills Shopping Mall. Others must be content to ogle the prominently displayed products or perhaps buy an occasional cheese pretzel.

Is it fair that some people can afford to buy stuff, while others can't? The gadzillion people, some rich and some poor, who meander the midway of the Shady Valley Central Town Sprawling Hills Shopping Mall suggest our third basic fact of economic life:

Fact #3: Life is not fair.
Resources, production, income, and wealth are not equally distributed in our economy.

We've already seen with Fact #1, Our Limited Pie, how limited resources, production, income, and wealth translates into a limited economic pie. It's now time to see how our limited economic pie is divided, which is often bandied about in the media as the "income distribution" or, occasionally, "wealth distribution." The bottom line,

the conclusion that we will reach, the whole point of this walk through Shady Valley Central Town Sprawling Hills Shopping Mall, is that none of the items—not even one—comprising our economic pie is equally distributed. Some people have more resources, production, income, and wealth, while others have less. This is a fact of economic life. Is it fair? That's a matter of opinion. But fair or not, there is some good and bad with an unequal division of our pie. Before the mall crowd gets too rowdy, let's see why.

Everything begins with resources

Resources beget production, which begets income, which begets wealth. Everything in the economy begins with resources: natural resources, labor, and capital. To see why some patrons of the Shady Valley Central Town Sprawling Hills Shopping Mall have more income and wealth than others, we also need to begin with resources.

It's a fact of life that some of us have larger (or smaller) slices of the economy's resource pie than others: Resources are not equally distributed. Here are my two favorite reasons for this:

1. *Quantity of resources.* Some of us just have more resources—a larger quantity. For example, you might have nothing but your labor resources. Your neighbor, on the other hand, might have labor plus ownership of a factory

and an apartment building. There's a real good chance that this greater quantity of resources also gives your neighbor more income.

2. *Quality of resources.* Some of us have better or more productive resources—a higher quality. By more productive, I mean that the resources either (1) produce a larger quantity of output or (2) produce output that's more highly valued by society. Therefore, if your measly little labor resources produce stuff that a lot of people want, then you're likely to have more income, even though your neighbor has capital and natural resources plus labor. If you doubt this, compare the adjusted gross income of almost any professional athlete, who sells only labor, with any hardworking farmer, who also owns a bunch of land, farm equipment, and other productive resources.

Perhaps it goes without saying that income comes from ownership and control of resources. Maybe it's obvious, but it needs saying. Your income is directly tied to Q and Q, the quantity and quality of resources over which you have ownership and or control. The more productive resources in your control, the more income you'll have.

Ownership *and* control

What does it mean to have ownership *and* control? The ownership part is pretty straightforward. You buy something; you have it; it's yours; you own it. Most of our nation's resources are under our individual ownership and control, and we're generally free to do with them as we see fit. Our legal system and the courts spend a lot of time making sure that this continues. For example, if someone stole the eight-track cassette tape deck out of your 1968 Pontiac Bonneville (why they would want to is another question), you could have that person prosecuted. Moreover, you're also free to sell this eight-track cassette tape deck and keep the money. In general, you're free

to keep the income from the sale of any of your productive resources. Ownership, holding the legal title to a resource, also implies control: the ability to use it as you see fit.

Ownership *or* control

In some cases, however, ownership and control don't go together. You might own a resource, but not control it. Or, you might control a resource without legal ownership.

• *Ownership, but no control.* Government both enforces private ownership and control and can take it away. (More on this thought with Fact #5, Our Necessary Evil.) An example of ownership without control is given by income taxes. For most of us, 2 to 4 months of our labor efforts each year are used to pay taxes, the use over which we have no direct control.

• *Control, but no ownership.* Government can also give people control over resources, and the income generated, without giving them legal ownership. Some examples include social security, welfare, and unemployment compensation. These entitlement programs give the legal right to the income without legal ownership of resources. In other words, your social security check ultimately comes from the efforts of someone else's labor. (More on this under Social Security and Welfare.)

The politics of ownership and control

Our government of the first estate is ultimately responsible for determining ownership and control, ownership without control, and control without ownership. That, in a nutshell, is a large part of what it does. Wait a second! If I want ownership and or control over resources, and the income that comes with it, then government is the place to go. If I own resources, then government can help me keep control. If I don't own resources, government can help me gain control.

Hmmm! This sounds like the source of some interesting politics. Stay tuned for further developments (or you can turn to almost any of the issues in Section 2, especially Political Views). But first, let's get down and dirty over why the quantity and quality of resources give us our unequal distribution of the pie.

We are what we are, except when we change

We know that income is not equally distributed, because some of us own and/or control different quantities and qualities of resources. The next question to ask, therefore, is: Why do we have different quantities and qualities of resources?

Two thoughts come to my mind. These thoughts have been the source of debates since our ancestors first dropped from the trees and were puzzled by their lack of tails. These two thoughts have sparked controversies in almost every human endeavor, from politics to science to religion.

1. *Nature.* One side of this raging debate is that the quantity and quality of our resources are guided by a natural predisposition—it's in our genes. In some cases, this is obvious; in other cases, however, the argument becomes questionable. There is little doubt that actors, athletes, and scientists are genetically blessed with natural talents and abilities that form the basis for their productive resources. However, it's questionable whether someone like Winston Smythe Kennsington III, a well-known Ivy Leaguer with a social pedigree dating back to the Mayflower, has more income because he's genetically superior to anyone who ever attended a state-supported university (ugh!). On closer inspection, we see that Winnie's income is attributed to the fact that Winston Smythe Kennsington II and Winston Smythe Kennsington I owned several Fortune 500 companies and most of Rhode Island.

2. *Nurture.* The other side of the debate is that we're "all created equal," and thus the quantity and quality of our resources depend on the actions we take. You acquire more productive resources than I do because you work harder, take acting lessons, study for a college degree, scour the financial pages, or painstakingly search out unseen employment opportunities. The drawback with this interesting little argument is that everyone doesn't have the same opportunity to take dancing lessons, attend college, or "do lunch" with the personnel officers of Fortune 500 companies.

When you get down to the bottom line, it's evident that both of these thoughts are important. Sure, many great athletes have been blessed with natural talents, but the best ones have also spent gadzillions upon gadzillions of hours practicing, studying, and improving their abilities.

A word of warning is in order at this point. Be careful about taking either reason to the extreme. This suggests two timely tips:

A FEW TIPS ON POSSIBILITIES AND REALITY

- Don't attribute the success of others exclusively to their natural talents. Some people may have a head start because of their genetic makeup, but effort can often compensate for the lack of natural ability. A number of athletes who have been honored by a sports Hall of Fame once had slow, uncoordinated bodies that were improved by years of hard work.
- Likewise, be very cautious of those who promise unqualified success in areas where you might be, uhm, genetically deficient. Hard work can't always compensate for the lack of natural abilities. Some people are born with the looks of a fashion model and others aren't.

Nature and nurture have a great deal to do with the productivity of labor resources.

What about the other two resources, natural resources and capital? Like our genetically configured bodies, there are some things we can change about the ownership and control of productive natural resources and capital, and some that we can't.

This land is your land, this land is my land

On the nature side, our planet has been "genetically predisposed" to a certain configuration of natural resources. In particular, natural resources are unevenly distributed across the planet. Some areas have abundant water, mineral deposits, fertile soil, and/or a pleasant climate, and others don't. For example, water drops from the sky as rain, runs down the slopes of hills and mountains, and accumulates at the low point of the land. Geological forces of the past have tended to create huge pockets of fossil fuels from prehistoric dinosaurs and vegetation. Because of the rotation of the planet, the configuration of the continental land masses, and the tilt of the planet's axis, some areas have abundant warm sunshine, others get a lot of rain, still others see more than their share of cold temperatures and snow. There's not a whole lot anyone can do about this.

To illustrate the importance of this predisposed geographic configuration, suppose that we have two sod-busting wheat farmers, around the beginning of the twentieth century, toiling away their hours tilling the soil in western Kansas. Both are barely eeking out minimal but roughly equal livings from their ownership and control of 160 acres of rolling prairie land. Then, one morning, one of the farmers—let's call him J. D. Goodluck—discovers that his 160 acres sits atop a pool of crude oil. This is the same crude oil that Henry Ford and his associates have found increasingly useful for those new-fangled horseless carriages.

You probably know how this story ends. J. D. and his descendants buy up most of Houston, Texas, and each morning drive to the toilet in brand-new Cadillacs. The other farmer—let's call him Hapless Herb—and his descendants continue eeking out their lives in the quiet solitude of the western Kansas skies.

Because of the geographic concentration of the natural resources that came with the planet, there's obviously a bit of luck involved in ownership and control. Being in the right place, at the right time, can give you control over productive natural resources—kind of like being blessed with great facial features or quick reflexes. This also means that millions of people around the globe can only dream of walking past the glass-fronted stores of the Shady Valley Central Town Sprawling Hills Shopping Mall because they lacked the foresight to be born in a country with abundant natural resources.

This land is now my land, too

The creation of the universe billions of years ago might explain some of our control over productive natural resources. But it doesn't explain it all. We can also improve upon nature's gifts.

Let's consider Hapless Herb and J. D. Goodluck again. Sure J. D. had the fortune of homesteading 160 acres of land that would eventually produce wealth-creating oil. But was Hapless Herb destined to remain hapless? Perhaps he could have, with a little effort and foresight, kept up with the latest technological developments, performed a few geological tests on his land and that of surrounding farms, then buy J. D.'s farm before oil became a highly valued resource. In that case, whom do you think would be driving to the toilet in a new Cadillac?

Nurturing our capital

Thus far very little—in fact nothing—has been said about capital and its role in the income distribution. Capital is a resource produced from other resources, meaning there is absolutely nothing natural about it.

Factories were not, I repeat *not*, formed with the universe billions of years ago. Every factory, building, oil well derrick, mine shaft, and interstate highway in our economy is as artificial as many of the body parts seen on the movie screens.

Speaking of artificial body parts, it's useful to ponder the difference between physical capital, the sort of capital that's exemplified by factories and buildings, and human capital. Human capital is the learned, or produced, side of productive labor resources. The term "human capital" is appropriate because it is the nonnatural or artificial component of labor produced by other resources. Much as we can build a new, automated factory, we can build a new, more attractive face. We can also build physical skills, knowledge, and a warm compassionate demeanor. Training, education, and experience are the primary methods used to produce human capital. (For more on this, check out Education and Wealth, both worth the effort.)

Because of its artificial nature, capital (human and physical) can be either a great equalizer or a great unequalizer.

- *The great equalizer.* A small, unattractive, uncoordinated person with a large factory can be just as wealthy as a hulking quarterback, handsome actor, or really tall basketball player. Of course the same can be said for a small, unattractive, uncoordinated farmer who owns 160 acres of land with a pool of crude petroleum underneath. Capital, unlike land, can be produced, increased, and expanded. If I build a factory with nothing but my bare hands and the sweat from my brow (not that this is on my list of top ten things to do before the universe collapses), I would have control over not only my labor resources but also some capital resources. This would help equalize the income between me and someone who may be blessed with greater natural abilities.
- *The great unequalizer.* Because capital is produced using other resources, the more control you have over other resources,

the more capital you can produce. Recall that our farmer from a few pages back, J. D. Goodluck, was able to use his oil-rich farmland to buy most of Houston, Texas. In essence, J. D. used his resources (oil) to buy more resources (buildings, factories, etc., in Houston). Hapless Herb had hardly a hope of having even half of Hayes, Kansas, because his 160 acres were less productive. The more you have, the more you can get.

Nurturing capital with investment

Because capital (physical and human) is not part of the natural configuration of us or our planet, it must be produced. Producing capital, however, incurs an opportunity cost from lost consumption. The more limited resources we use for investment in physical or human capital, the less we have available for consumption stuff.

Once again, Hapless Herb could have been less hapless by buying another 160 acres, improving the 160 acres he had, building a Hapless Herb Museum and Tourist Attraction ("See how Herb harvests wheat with nothing but a combine! Witness, first hand, the daring exploits of planting season! Marvel at the use of irrigation equipment! All yours, for one low price of $5!"), selling the farm outright, and buying into a proposed shopping mall in the Sprawling Hills section of Shady Valley, or spending 8 years in medical school to become a plastic surgeon.

This brings to mind a few tips worth considering for anyone who would like to increase his or her annual incomes and accumulate more wealth:

INCOME AND WEALTH-CREATING TIPS

- Society pays the highest incomes for resources that it values most. If you want more income, determine what society wants, then get the resources to produce it if you can.

- Everyone has different degrees of natural abilities. Often we're unaware of how much value society places on the natural abilities we have. A (potentially) wealthy artist may languish behind an accountant's desk. Or a (potentially) successful accountant may starve to death as an artist.
- Productive resources can be acquired, especially capital (physical and human), but not without sacrifice. By sacrificing current consumption you can invest in the stock market, go to college, start your own business, or buy rental property, and thus receive more income tomorrow from an increase in your productive resources

Shall we specialize?

The unequal distribution of resources, both natural and acquired, can be good and bad. Is it fair that some people enjoy higher living standards because of the happenstance of their birth? History is filled with examples where the less fortunate—who thought that such a situation wasn't all that fair—beheaded the more fortunate. An extremely unequal distribution of resources, production, income, or wealth has never been a very stable political situation.

But (and here is one of those important "buts") an equal distribution of resources, production, income, or wealth is not good either. One important benefit of inequality is specialization. Let's see why.

Suppose that two ordinary, everyday people (call them Becky and Phil) are both capable of growing vegetables and making furniture. If Becky decides to devote her entire energies to furniture crafting, rather than dividing her time between china closets and tomatoes, she will become quite proficient at furniture making. Phil can attain a similar proficiency in vegetable production, if his time is not torn between two different activities. Specialization by Becky and Phil will let them produce and consume more furniture and more vegetables. By exchanging the good that each produces for the good that each does not, Becky and Phil can have more of both goods.

This little fact of economic life explains why few people in our current complex economy are self-sufficient. If I pick one thing to do, and do it really well, then I can earn enough income (hopefully) from my efforts to buy things that other people specialize in doing.

Comparative advantage—the savior of all

Specialization and exchange is an obvious course of action when people begin with a natural talent for one activity or another. Becky is likely to choose carpentry over gardening, if she is blessed with a natural woodworking affinity. Phil will probably choose gardening if he has the proverbial green thumb. But what if Becky is not only a great carpenter but is also an excellent gardener? In fact, Becky may be extraordinary at everything she does. You know the type of person: class president, lead in the school play, valedictorian, athlete/cheerleader, good looks, rich family. Phil, on the other hand not only has absolutely no gardening abilities but is also a complete dreg when it comes to carpentry. Is there any hope for Phil?

Actually there is, thanks to the notion of *comparative advantage*. Even though Becky is great at everything she tries, she's better off specializing in the production of one thing and buying other stuff. Becky needs to figure out what she's relatively best at doing, then specialize in it. The same is true for our apparently worthless Phil. Although he may be extremely "not good" at a lot of different things, he needs to find that one thing he is least not good at.

Here's some simple numbers to illustrate. Let's say that Becky—our class president extraordinaire—can make five chairs or grow ten tomatoes a week. Phil—our dreg of society—can make one chair or grow four tomatoes a week. Even though Becky the great is better at both, she should specialize in one.

If Becky spends a week making five chairs, she doesn't grow ten tomatoes. The opportunity cost of each chair is therefore two tomatoes. Phil the dreg, on the other hand, can spend a week making one chair, but in so doing gives up four tomatoes, an obvious cost of four tomatoes per chair. Becky is a relatively better carpenter: Her cost per chair is two tomatoes, while Phil's cost per chair is four. Phil, however, is a relatively better gardener: His cost per tomato is one-fourth of a chair, while Becky's cost is one-half chair. Let's pause to reflect on this: Phil the dreg can produce tomatoes more cheaply than Becky the great. He's found something he can do relatively better than Becky.

As such, Becky is better off making chairs and trading them to Phil for tomatoes. She can make five chairs and trade one of them to Phil for tomatoes. Phil can grow four tomatoes and trade three of them to Becky for a chair. By specializing, both Becky and Phil can get more chairs and tomatoes than if each produced both.

Here are a couple of career tips, one that's pretty obvious and another that may not be:

SPECIALIZATION CAREER TIPS

- Differences in natural and acquired abilities mean you're better off by specializing in one career, then buying goods from others. The trick, of course, is finding that one specializing career. This can be discovered through trial and error, but can be found more easily by (1) carefully cataloging your natural and acquired skills and (2) determining the value society places on the stuff produced with those skills.
- Comparative advantage tells us that everyone can specialize in something. Even if you have no apparent skill or talent, and seem to be mediocre at everything, there's always something that you can do relatively cheaper than others.

A word or two on the three estates

You may have already reached the conclusion that resource ownership, control, and the slice of the pie that follows is somehow related to the three estates. If not, you will now. The degree to which you can be classified into one of the modern three estates—government, business, and consumers—depends on your degree or resource ownership and control.

Most of us fall into the third estate because our income is derived primarily from labor resources. Sure you may own a few stocks, have a share in some rental property across town, or even run your own small business, but your slice of the pie probably depends mostly on labor.

The other two estates have significantly more ownership and/or control over resources—labor plus. Proud members of the first estate, government, have lots of control over resources, although they may have little or no ownership. (Yet, the way our system works, resource control obtained as a member of the first estate often enhances resource ownership. In other words, a lot of politicians get rich by feeding at the public trough.) The even prouder members of the second estate, business, have extensive ownership of resources and usually the control that goes with it.

A word of caution is in order. Because the government is ultimately responsible for determining resource ownership and control, a close association between the first and second estates, usually spells trouble for the third. In fact, if the first estate takes over the second estate or the second estate takes over the first, the economic pie is usually sliced in such a way that leaves nothing for the third estate.

What does it all mean?

An unequal distribution of the nation's economic pie is clearly a bad thing. It's unjust! It's unfair! It's the result of luck, chance, and happenstance. We as society (through our elected officials) should do everything we can to promote a more equal distribution of the pie. If the elected officials won't do it, then we may have to rise up and do it ourselves, by force if necessary.

No, wait a second! An unequal distribution of the nation's economic pie is a good thing. It means that hard work pays off. If you work harder or sacrifice consumption to produce capital, you're rewarded for your efforts. These activities, because they promote progress for our entire economy, are worth rewarding. If you never could get more than the average income, as many in the former Soviet Union can attest, you would have no incentive to do a little extra. Without that little extra, our economy would stagnate. And because extra reward for extra effort creates an unequal distribution of the economic pie, that's one price we pay for progress.

Whichever side of this argument you're on, you may be spurred on to action. If so, keep in mind that there is no ideal distribution of the economy's pie. Any distribution will be good for some and bad for others. Moreover, changing the pie's distribution in any way has its pluses and minuses. The question that must be asked, therefore, is: What goals do we seek?

- *Economic growth.* If the goal is progress, or economic growth, then an unequal distribution of the economic pie is not only unavoidable but also desirable. An unequal distribution is essential to growth.
- *Equal opportunity.* A problem, however, of an unequal distribution is that the rich get richer and the poor get a lengthy

rhetorical discourse from politicians. Our economy also suffers when a well-qualified person is prevented from pursuing an opportunity because of the lack of income or resource ownership. How many of the nation's Fortune 500 companies are being staffed by those whose primary qualifications are a sizable family bank account while better workers languish in the mail rooms? How many potentially great governors, senators, or presidents never made it past the city council elections because they lacked the personal wealth needed?

I don't know about you, but the gadzillions of people wandering around the Shady Valley Central Town Sprawling Hills Shopping Mall are beginning to get on my nerves. They seem to be meandering aimlessly about, never really buying anything, but always managing to stop just in front of me. I've got to get out of here!

This might be a good opportunity to pay a visit to the cable television office. I have a small, trivial, insignificant question about last month's bill. I hope they don't get mad and disconnect my service. Maybe I shouldn't go. After all, it's only a minor, minimal $3,569 charge. Perhaps I should just pay the bill. I don't want to cause any trouble.

Well, okay, we can walk by the office. But I'll have the checkbook handy, just in case they ask me to pay the $3,569. It's best not to get them upset.

See also: Crime, Discrimination, Foreign Trade, Immigration, Unions, and Welfare.

4

OUR MONOPOLIZED MARKETS

Our pedestrian's jaunt through the economy is not, unfortunately, an unrestrained shopping spree for confectioneries, spark plug tools, and Houston, Texas. We have other important errands to run. At the moment we need to hike over to Shady Valley's exclusive provider of cable television services, the Merciless Monolithic Media Masters Cable Television Company, Inc., to inquire about a mysterious fee that appeared in last month's bill.

The good news is that the Merciless Monolithic Media Masters (the 4M people) Cable office is a mere 2 miles (3 kilometers for the metrically inclined) from the Shady Valley Central Town Sprawling Hills Shopping Mall. A hop, skip, and a moderately long jump later, our excursion through the economy takes us to the front door of the 4M Cable Television Company where I hope to discover why last month's cable bill included a $3,569 charge for something called "The Vacation Channel." I didn't even know I had a vacation channel. (But I'm sure it's a great channel, and if I don't have it, then I will certainly subscribe. Please don't disconnect me.)

Of course, because this is an afternoon workday, the doors of the 4M office are locked. I can almost make out, through the expensive stained-glass windows, what appears to be several employees, with champagne bottles in hand, dancing on expensive mahogany desks. Let's not disturb them. As they say in the cable business, an upset worker is a disconnected customer.

Besides, the $3,569 is most likely a legitimate charge to cover the vacation expenses of the 4M president.. I'll mail them a payment; we can forget about this little visit to the 4M office and focus instead on the fourth basic fact of economic life:

> ## Fact #4: Monopoly is more than a game.
> The benefits of voluntary exchange depends on the relative market control of each participant.

This fact tells us that the prices of the stuff we buy or sell depend to a great degree on whether the buyers or the sell-

A PEDESTRIAN ...

ers have relatively more control over the market.

Buy low and sell high

Because buyers would rather pay less than more, and sellers would rather get more than less, here's what market control leads to:

- When buyers control the market, the price tends to be relatively lower—good for buyers, bad for sellers.
- When sellers control the market, the price tends to be relatively higher—good for sellers, bad for buyers.

(You don't suppose that 4M Cable controls the market for cable television in Shady Valley? Would that have anything to do with their lousy customer service and high prices? Let me think about that and get back to you later.)

But what if neither the buyers nor the sellers have any market control? Or what if buyers and sellers have equal control? And what do we mean by market control anyway? More importantly, how do you go about getting market control? (You might see a few possibilities with this market control thing, most of which lead to a beach in Acapulco and a sizable balance in a Swiss bank account.)

To work up satisfactory answers for these questions, let's dig into the nuts and bolts of the market—especially demand and supply.

A moment or two pondering demand

Let's think about the demand side of a market exchange. In general, demand is your willingness and ability to purchase a good. Suppose, for example, that you want an acoustical guitar and are willing to trade some hard-earned income for it. How much are you, as a buyer, willing and able to pay for an acoustical guitar?

It depends. It depends on how much you want it—your willingness. If you're thinking of forming your own folk/rock group to record the always popular Slim Whitman favorites, then you probably really, *really* want an acoustical guitar. However, if you only intend to play a few of the Slim Whitman favorites for family and close friends during the quiet, restful evening hours, then your desire for an acoustical guitar may not be as pressing. Perhaps an accordion would work as well.

Your acoustical-guitar demand also depends on how much you can afford to pay—your ability. It doesn't do you much good to really, *really*, Really want an acoustical guitar if you can't afford one. Your family and friends might be anxiously awaiting your rendition of the Slim Whitman top ten, but if you've already exhausted your income on the gold medal collectors' edition of Richard Burton reading the U.S. constitution (on three digitally enhanced CDs or a handsomely packaged set of ten cassettes), then you can't buy an acoustical guitar.

This means two things about demand.

- As a buyer, you have a maximum price that you're willing and able to pay for a good, if for no other reason than when the price is too high, you simply can't afford to buy it. Let's call this maximum the "demand price."
- As a buyer, you would rather pay a lower price than a higher one. You might be willing and able to pay $100 for an acoustical guitar, but you would rather pay $75. In fact, you would be just as happy if you could buy an acoustical guitar at a price of zero, zippo, nada, nil, nothing.

And a moment with supply

Now, let's have a brief visit with supply. Usually, sellers are willing and able to supply a good—like an acoustical guitar—if the price is enough to cover their production cost. We can call this minimum the "supply price." In general, if the price is too low and does not give sellers enough revenue to cover cost, then they can't supply the good. Of course, suppliers will occasionally sell goods at a price less than cost, and eat the loss. This practice, however, won't keep them in business very long.

Sellers are more than thrilled, and I mean more than thrilled, if the price is above the production cost. The higher the price, the more ecstatic are the sellers. In fact, there is no limit as to how ecstatic sellers would like to be—$10 gadzillion (plus tax) for an acoustical guitar is none too high.

A balance of primal forces

Market exchanges work when we throw the buyers (who want lower prices) and sellers (who want higher prices) into the same room, then see who wins. Okay, so we don't actually need to "throw" buyers and sellers into a room to get a market exchange going. We could push them gently with an electric prod and get the same result. In fact, with modern telecommunications they don't even need to be in the same time zone, let alone the same room.

Getting back to this confrontation between buyers and sellers might bring to mind visions of sweaty, muscular, Roman gladiators engaging in battles to the death—only the strongest survive. This analogy is a little gruesome, but it does help to illustrate the basic nature of markets. In markets, like gladiator battles, the strongest wins. If buyers are stronger than sellers, then buyers win and push the price down. If sellers are stronger, then they win and the price goes up. If both sides of the market have taken, so to speak, equal amounts of muscle-enhancing chemicals, and neither is more powerful or better able to control the market than the other, then the two gladiator forces balance out. Neither can take advantage of the other.

Are there really some "muscle-enhancing chemicals" that buyers and sellers take to increase their market control? Actually market control doesn't result from the exciting world of pharmaceuticals but from a more mundane source: the number of competitors in the market.

- If buyers have fewer competitors than the sellers, they tend to have relatively more market control.
- If sellers have fewer competitors than the buyers, they tend to have relatively more market control.

To see why this happens, let's scamper through the workings of a market in which neither side has any market control.

A bunch of buyers and a bunch of sellers

What if a market has so many buyers and sellers, falling into the gadzillion category, that each is nothing but a nameless, faceless entry on a sales receipt? What if none of the buyers has ever met? Or what if there were so many sellers that, even if they knew each other, it wouldn't make any difference?

This situation is what economists like to refer to as a *competitive market*. It's competitive in the sense that no one—none of the gadzillion individual participants—has any control over the market—none whatsoever, zippo, nada, nil. The buyers can buy as much of the good as they want at the market price. The sellers can sell as much as they want at the same price. None of them is willing or able to buy or sell at any other price. How so?

It works because both sides have so many participants that everyone always can find a trading partner. For each buyer, there are a gadzillion potential sellers. For each seller, there are a gadzillion potential buyers. You can always make an exchange at the going price—if you're willing and able. There's no reason to trade at any other price. There's

also no way to trade at any other price.

To see why, let's say that you're selling dirt. Nothing fancy about this dirt. It's just plain dirt. It's great for potted plants, landscaping, mudpies, keeping your feet firmly planted in, and dozens of other uses. It's also, however, quite plentiful, and offered for sale by a gadzillion suppliers—leading to a bunch of competition on the supply side. There's also a bunch of competition on the demand side with a gadzillion buyers willing and able to pay the market price of, say, $5 per bag. Competition among your fellow suppliers means that there's no way to sell dirt for more than $5. Competition among buyers means that there's no reason to sell for less. You're stuck. You sell your dirt for $5—no more, no less.

The same thing, in reverse, works for a buyer. You never need to pay more than $5 for a bag of dirt, because there are a gadzillion sellers offering their dirt for that price. If you offer one of the sellers less than $5 for their dirt, they'll laugh in your face in the most unkind way (and probably dump a bag of dirt on your head), because they have a gadzillion potential buyers who are willing to pay $5. Take it or leave it.

Dreaming about competition and efficiency

When we have a market with gadzillions of buyers and sellers, we end up with efficiency in the allocation of our limited resources. Recall from Fact #1, Our Limited Pie, that scarcity exists because we have unlimited wants and limited resources. We want to use our limited resources to get the most satisfaction possible. Competitive markets do a pretty good job of this. Here's why.

When the dust clears from the room, with our dirt buyers and sellers doing their dirt buying and selling, the dirt is traded at the final take-it-or-leave-it price. This is pretty darn important because:

1. The demand price is the value or satisfaction the buyers get from consum-

ing the dirt. (Of course, I don't actually mean consuming the dirt as in eating it. Consuming is when we satisfy our wants and needs with a good. Thus, consuming includes watching television, driving a car, or receiving a penicillin injection. Yet, if you actually wanted to eat dirt, then I suppose that would also be consuming.)

2. The supply price is the opportunity cost of the resources used to make a good, which is the satisfaction that other buyers don't get from other stuff because our resources are being used to supply dirt.

In that a competitive market equates the demand price with the supply price, the value of the dirt is equal to the value of stuff not produced. If we tried to make and exchange more or less dirt and less or more of other stuff, we would not get as much satisfaction of our unlimited wants. With competitive markets we have efficiency.

In fact, competitive markets squeeze the most satisfaction from our planet's limited resources that we can possibly squeeze. Not a bad deal. Unfortunately, most markets aren't all that competitive. Few if any have a gadzillion buyers and sellers. As such, many markets have some degree of control by one side or the other, or both. Okay, let's get down to the nitty-gritty. Let's see how the lack of competition lets one side of this market win the game of market control.

One monopoly seller and many buyers

Consider what would happen if a market, such as that for shoestring straighteners, has only one seller—OmniStraight—but a lot of buyers. Here's the story on shoestring straighteners. They are, of course, an essential product for anyone with a pair of shoes, and OmniStraight is the company—the only company—that sells this handy little utensil. The key for any seller who aspires to

market control is to find a product that is not only highly demanded but is also unique.

While OmniStraight has a gadzillion customers, the buyers have only one source of shoestring straighteners—OmniStraight. (Say, does this sound like cable television?) The buyers obviously don't have a great deal of choice.

This sort of market, with one seller and a gadzillion buyers, is what economists have long referred to as a "monopoly." In fact, the best-selling, ever-popular board game Monopoly is based on the goal of controlling the real estate market. You win when you own it all.

Complete control of the shoestring straightener market by OmniStraight lets it control the market price. Because OmniStraight prefers a higher price to a lower one, it will seek to raise the price. It won't, however, raise the price in a haphazard fashion. Rather, it keeps a close eye on its profit. That's because if OmniStraight pushes the price too high, then no one will buy shoestring straighteners. With no sales, OmniStraight's profit will also be very low— as in zero. The trick for OmniStraight, and any other monopoly, is raising the price just enough to keep people buying, and to rake in as much profit as possible (see Profit).

What can the gadzillion buyers do when OmniStraight raises its price? Nothing, or almost nothing. They either pay the price set by OmniStraight or do without shoestring straighteners.

A consequence of OmniStraight's shoestring straightener monopoly is that the price of shoestring straighteners will be pushed up to the buyers' maximum demand price. This price, however, will be nowhere near the minimum supply price that OmniStraight needs to pay production cost. Because the buyers' price is greater than the opportunity cost of production, we don't have efficiency. Monopoly is an example of inefficiency at its best—or rather worst.

One monopsony buyer and many sellers

Let's reverse the tables now, and see what would happen with one buyer and a gadzillion sellers—a sort of market economists refer to as "monopsony." In a monopsony, the buyer controls the price and the sellers must take it or leave it. In contrast to a monopoly, the monopsony price is equal to the sellers' minimum supply price that covers production cost, but not even close to the buyers' maximum demand price—yet another glaring example of inefficiency.

Most professional sports operate like monopsonistic markets when they hire athletes. There's really no competition among buyers, but there's a lot of competition among sellers. The National Football League, National Basketball Association, and Major League Baseball are the employers of football, basketball, and baseball players. A gadzillion high school and college athletes willingly sacrifice their knees and other fragile body parts for the chance to supply their services. While you might think that athletes are overpaid, their wages are actually lower than they would be if professional sports were more competitive. (Let me direct you to the entry on Athlete Salaries, for further explanation.)

One monopsony buyer and one monopoly seller

What if we have but a single seller and a single buyer in the market? What happens to price in this case? Is it high? Or low? Let's say that our shoestring straightener seller, Omni-Straight, sells its shoestring straighteners to a single buyer, Mega-Shoes, Inc. Neither side has any other options. Mega-Shoes must buy its shoestring straighteners from OmniStraight, and OmniStraight must sell its shoestring straighteners to Mega-Shoes.

In this case, market control and price depend not on the number of competitors but on other factors, such as negotiation skill or who has the best information. If the buyer, Mega-Shoes, is a better negotiator

than OmniStraight, then the price is likely to be closer to the OmniStraight's minimum. Or, if OmniStraight has better information about such things as Mega-Shoes' willingness to buy shoestring straighteners, then OmniStraight is likely to get the price closer to the Mega-Shoes' maximum.

This is pretty much the one-on-one situation you face when buying a house or car. When you're to the point of haggling with a car dealer over price, it's you (the monopsonist) versus the dealer (the monopolist). The same thing occurs when a house is sold: One buyer and one seller negotiate the price. Before we consider some consequences of market control, here are a few practical tips worth considering:

CONSUMER TIPS ON MARKET CONTROL

- As a buyer, you should search for markets with more competition among sellers and less among buyers. For example, try traveling during the off-season when possible. Surprising as it may seem, the lines at Disney World are incredibly short on Thanksgiving Day. Other bargains can be had if your timing is right—and you avoid the competition.
- The converse for a seller is to search for markets with more competition among buyers and less among sellers. For example, when selecting a career or pursuing a job, you're better off if you're the only seller with a number of buyers. You can do this—as people like Michael Jordan and Arnold Schwartzenegger have discovered—if you have a unique talent or skill.
- Consider the benefits of being contrarian—one who buys when others are selling and sells when others are buying. For example, try to sell your house when everyone else is buying, and buy when everyone is selling. Contrarians, however, need to be careful. If houses are for sale because their owners just discovered the ground is saturated with toxic chemicals

or because the town's largest employer is closing its doors, then buying might not be a good idea.

- Also, be wary of nationally broadcast financial information. If everyone in the country knows that Omni Conglomerate, Inc., is the best buy on the stock market, the price will rise because of competition among buyers. If you aren't among the first to act, then it's probably too late to take advantage of the information.

Why markets aren't competitive

Markets in the real world are seldom as competitive as economists would like. A big reason for this can be found with the basic scarcity problem and the unequal distribution of the economic pie. Here's why:

- Because we have limited resources and unlimited wants and needs, resource ownership tends to be more concentrated than wants and needs. There are usually fewer competitors on the supply side of most markets for consumer goods than on the demand side—market control by the producers. For example, most of the 5 1/2 billion people on this planet probably want a car, but limitations on resource ownership and control put the number of car suppliers in the range of 50 or so.
- Natural resources and capital tend to have more concentrated ownership than labor. Most of the 5 1/2 billion people on the planet have labor (potentially at least), but the natural resources and capital tend to be owned by a much smaller share of the population. This means the demand for labor tends to be much less competitive than the supply—market control by the factory and resource owners. There are 50 or so car companies in the world that hire the services of gadzillions of autoworkers. (Check into the stuff on Unions for more on this.)

When we combine the markets for consumer goods with those for labor, what we see emerging is a pattern of market control

that favors the second estate over the third. The business leaders of the second estate have greater ownership and control of our economy's productive resources. Most can count their competitors on a single hand. The third estate, however, has thousands, millions, or even billions of competitors in most markets for consumer goods, labor, or whatever.

If the topic of market control were nothing more than the inspiration for a board game, played to while away the hours, then this discussion would end here. In fact, it would have never started. Market control, however, is intertwined with the economy and, most importantly, the politics of government.

The politics of market control

Market participants often look to the government for greater control. As we see with the next fact of economic life, the government has the ability to control the economy in a wide variety of ways. Government laws have, well, the force of law. If one seller can get the government to make it illegal for others to sell and thus limit competition, then market control is, shall we say, greatly enhanced.

Of course, few participants come right out and say that they want greater market control. They usually have other "valid" explanations, some that even have a small grain of truth. The bottom line, however, is fewer competitors.

Let's consider a few examples:

- *Foreign trade.* One of the more patriotic proposals any red-blooded American business can make is to ask the government to keep those no-good foreign companies from selling their American-job-destroying products within the boundaries of this great land of ours. Unfortunately for the red-blooded American consumers, restricting imports reduces the number of competitors in a market and thus gives more market control to domestic firms. Domestic firms then respond in a typically patriotic way by raising prices. (See Foreign Trade.)

- *Health care.* The provision of health to the ill and infirm is not to be taken lightly. We need the best and the brightest, the most skilled and the most highly trained professionals to administer health care. So goes the line given to the government by doctors and their professional groups, such as the American Medical Association. This ensures that only those professionals licensed by the government are allowed to practice medicine. But restricting the number of licensees means there are fewer suppliers, and each one has more market control. (Check out Health Care for some details on this complex topic.)
- *Professional sports.* The major professional sports leagues in the United States have a recognized monopoly status that is even sanctioned by the U.S. Congress. Citing the unique nature of professional sports, such as the need for organized on-field competition among the different "firms," professional teams have gained market control over resources (hiring athletes) and over their output (selling tickets and broadcast rights to the networks). The consequence, however, is higher ticket prices and lower athlete wages.

Our list could go on, almost indefinitely, because virtually everything the government does affects the number of competitors, and thus control, in one market or another. Some of this is unintentional, but it's often designed to benefit the constituency of an elected official.

But (and here's another one of those important "buts"), whenever market control is increased through political action, the whole country suffers the slings and arrows of inefficiency. The members of the third estate, we might note, tend to suffer most.

The market control of politics

Politics and market control work in both directions. Wealth and income are generally redistributed from those with little or no market control (third estate) to those with a great deal of market control (second estate). In a monopoly market, sellers extract higher prices from buyers, and thus get a portion of the buyers' income. In a monopsony market, buyers force a lower price on sellers, and thus get a portion of the sellers' income. Wealth and income tend to accumulate in the direction of greater market control. And politicians, surprising as it may seem, tend to respond more readily to those who can contribute large sums to reelection campaigns. (This seems to be a good place to recommend a look at Political Views.)

What does it all mean?

Our economy makes extensive use of markets to allocate resources and to voluntarily satisfy some of our unlimited wants with limited resources. Under some circumstances—some of which are more realistic and reasonable than others—markets do a pretty good job of accomplishing this goal.

There is, however, a strong tendency for participants to seek and attain control over a market. They often do this with the cooperation and blessing of our first estate—the government. Businesses of the second estate that supply goods to the consumers of the third estate have the greatest ability to seek and gain market control. Because resources are unequally distributed, those with a greater share of our pie get more market control. This contributes to an even greater concentration of wealth and resources.

The third estate—the consumers, workers, and middle-class taxpayers of our economy—are seldom in a position to gain market control. But that's what this book, *Economic Literacy*, is all about: to inform you of the potential dangers and hazards that lurk behind the smiling faces of the first two estates.

There is, however, some hope. The government does, on many occasions, try to reduce market control and increase competition. Various government agencies, at both federal and state levels, devote their full-time efforts to promoting competition and reducing market control using antitrust laws. A few of the more notable agencies are the Justice Department, the Federal Trade Commission, and branches in most state attorneys general offices. This, however, is an ongoing process. In that government is subject to the tugs and pulls of different political views, it offers more protection against the abuses of market control for consumers, taxpayers, and workers during some periods than others.

This sounds like the government plays a key role in the economy's allocation of limited resources. Perhaps I should forget about my 4M cable bill and head over to the Shady Valley City Hall where we can check out the government's part in the economy. Besides, my semiannual property tax bill is due. I really hate to pay taxes: sales taxes, income taxes, property taxes, excise taxes, park fees, turnpike tolls; and the list just seems to keep growing. Wouldn't it be nice if we could just eliminate taxes? Let's explore that possibility.

See also: Advertising, Business, Financial Markets, Insurance, Regulation, Wealth, and Working Women.

OUR NECESSARY EVIL

It's time to give up our attempts to enter the Merciless Monolithic Media Masters Cable Television Company, Inc., office and take care of other pressing business: taxes. The next stop on our excursion through the economy is the Shady Valley City Hall, where we need to pause, momentarily and begrudgingly, so that I may pay my semi-annual property tax bill. This is the least enjoyable stop—at least for me—on our journey. Grumble. Grumble. Grumble.

Of course I hate to pay taxes! But then again, who doesn't? Taxes are one of those annoying and evil necessities of life that simply can't be avoided.

Or can they? Do we *have* to pay taxes? A quick visit to a bookstore will produce dozens of books telling you how to avoid taxes by investing here or buying this or doing that. Better yet, if we could rid ourselves of the inefficient, bloated, incompetent, do-nothing government, then you and I wouldn't have to pay taxes. Right? We could use our hard-earned income to buy stuff that we want, rather than letting the inefficient, bloated, incompetent, do-nothing government spend it on stuff that we

don't want, don't know anything about, and will never need. Right?

My disgruntled disposition on the subject of taxes and government gives rise to the fifth basic fact of economic life:

> ## Fact #5: Government is a public good.
> A number of highly valued activities that benefit the public are best produced with the coercive powers of the government.

Here's the bottom line: As members of society, we involuntarily pay taxes to the government because the government provides us with stuff that we can't get in any other way. In particular, the voluntary actions that make markets work sort of okay most of the time, don't work for all goods at all times. We want goods that can only be produced by the government. Therefore we are willing (and let me stress the *willing* part) to allow the government to *force* us to pay taxes so that we get the stuff we want.

If, bright and early today, we decided to eliminate the government completely—state,

A PEDESTRIAN ...

... visits city hall

PHMMM MMPHH MMMPH MMPHM?

RELAX! I AM WITH THE GOVERNMENT

AW RIGHT! AN ACORN SUBSIDY

local, and federal—wiping out all traces of the concept of government from our collective memories, then by early tomorrow morning we would reinvent government. (Although we might call it something else, like "plothgim.") This is a sure bet, because government—as incompetent and inefficient as it may be—is the only thing we've got that can provide us with some really, *really* necessary stuff.

So, what is this really, really necessary stuff that government, and only government, can do?

What the government does

Here's a short list of well-known activities that we wouldn't have without government.

- *National defense.* One of the best reasons (that comes to my mind) for government is defense. The centralized, coercive powers of government are the only way to effectively protect the entire country from foreign attack. A private business could not do what is needed to defend the nation.

- *Legal system.* The government also needs to be in charge of our system of laws—including writing the laws and enforcing punishment for those who don't abide. This is also pretty important if we want markets to operate efficiently. It's very difficult to exchange stuff voluntarily without laws against property theft, assault, murder, etc. (More on this topic under Regulation.) You can probably make up your own story in which a market exchange is disrupted because one party bludgeoned the other with a baseball bat. My personal favorite involves an annoying vinyl siding salesman.

- *Transportation*. One of the more important, but sometimes overlooked, functions of the government is transportation—including city streets, interstate highways, airports, and municipal bus service. Because resources and products are geographically concentrated and thus not evenly distributed, we need transportation to move stuff to where it will do the most good. For example, a ripe, juicy pineapple in Hawaii provides very little satisfaction if you're in Topeka, Kansas.
- *Education*. Government also tends to be very big on education, ranging from local grade schools up through state-supported universities. The federal government has a hand in education at all levels—even for private schools—through various policies, such as scholarships, research grants, and lunch subsidies. (We also have an appropriately labeled discussion on Education in Section 2.)

Most of what government does falls into one of these categories, or something very close. However, we can probably bet donuts to dollars that anything the government does draws criticism from someone. Some people say that the government shouldn't do education or transportation at all. Others strongly suggest that much of the government can and should be privatized—letting private businesses take over. (I hope this sets off some warning lights in your head about unhealthy cooperation between the first and second estates.)

To see if these critics of government are right or wrong, let's see if we can figure out why government does what it does, and whether or not it's overstepping its bounds by doing things it shouldn't.

Not all goods are created equal

One nice thing about being a human being, as opposed to a kumquat or other such veg-etable, is that we derive satisfaction from a variety of different goods and services. Lest I resort to a litany of television commercials ("sometimes you feel like a nut, sometimes you don't"), suffice it to say that we have a multitude of different wants and needs that can be satisfied in a number of ways. If we didn't, then this discussion would be a heck of a lot shorter, millions of government workers would be employed elsewhere, and a gadzillion critics of government would have to find other pressing social problems to debate.

Here's the line on goods that we, as consumers, would like to have because they satisfy a few of our unlimited wants and needs: The stuff we consume has two features that can be mixed and matched to give us four different sorts of goods.

- The first is what we call "excludability," which is how easily you can keep people from consuming a good. If you can keep people away, then you can also charge them for consuming. If you can't exclude them, then you can't charge them.

For example, if you don't pay for a candy bar, shirt, or airline ticket, then you can't eat it, wear it, or fly. Or if you try to eat it, wear it, or fly without paying, then the sellers of the candy bar, shirt, or airline ticket will be able to seek redress through the legal system—that is, have your tail thrown in jail.

Alternatively, if you don't pay for a good like national defense, you can still benefit. Once a country is protected against aggressive foreign parties through the procurement of weapons and the deployment of a military force, then all parties—let me reiterate, *all parties*—within the nation are protected. Those who pay for the defense are no more protected than those who don't. You can imagine how much anguish right-wing military hawks go through knowing that left-wing, antimilitary, peacenik doves are also protected. But, that's the way national defense works: Nonpayers cannot be excluded from enjoying the benefits of the good.

Of course, like much of life, this is a matter of degree. Those who don't pay could be excluded if they're deported to another country. Moreover, if the citizens of, say, the state of Nebraska don't pay for defense, then they could be refused protection against missile attacks, enemy invasions, or whatever. The bottom line is that excludability ultimately depends on the difficulty of excluding those who don't pay.

- The second feature is rival consumption—which is whether consumption by one imposes an opportunity cost on others. A rival good can only be consumed by one person at a time. A nonrival good, in contrast, can provide benefits to several people simultaneously. For efficiency, consumers of rival goods should be charged, but consumers of nonrival goods should not.

Candy bars are a good example of a rival good. If you eat a candy bar (an Almond Joy), then I can't eat it, too (but I really, *really* wanted it). When the price of the candy bar—the value to buyers—is equal to the opportunity cost imposed on others, we have achieved efficiency.

Alternatively, a star-filled night sky that can be gazed upon in wonderment by a billion separate pairs of eyes gives us an example of a nonrival good. The view enjoyed by one pair of eyes does not hinder the view enjoyed by the other 999,999,999 pairs. Total satisfaction for our economy is greater when more people view this twinkling wonderment. If we charge anyone for the view, and they don't consume, then total satisfaction is less and efficiency is diminished.

Two by two gives us four

If we mix and match excludability and rival consumption, we have four different sorts of goods. They are:

1. *Private goods.* Exclusion is easy; consumption is rival. Let's see . . . we have a good that can be consumed by only one person at a time, and we can charge people who want it. Hey, we could trade this thing in a market. Anyone who wants the good badly enough would have to pay to get it. In fact, private goods, such as candy bars and shirts, are exactly that: privately owned, controlled, and traded through markets. Moreover, competitive markets do a pretty fair job of efficiently producing and exchanging these goods, if participants don't gain market control.

2. *Public goods:* Exclusion is hard; consumption is nonrival. Here we have the exact opposite of private goods: Any number of people can consume the good simultaneously, and we can't charge any of them. We might find it very difficult to trade these goods in the market. In fact, they are called "public goods" because they are publicly (read that as "by government") produced and made available to the public. National defense is the penultimate example of a public good. We've already noted that nonpayers—including left-wing, antimilitary, peacenik doves—can't be excluded from national defense protection. Moreover, safety of left-wing, antimilitary, peacenik doves doesn't keep right-wing, promilitary hawks from being protected.

3. *Near-public goods.* Exclusion is easy; consumption is nonrival. Our third sort of good is almost a public good, but not quite. Any number of people can benefit from it at the same time, yet consumers can be charged. Television broadcasting offers us a very good example. Microwave television signals indiscriminately reach all households as they bound from overhead satellites. My reception doesn't prevent your reception. I can enjoy the same signals you do, and neither one of us loses anything. Yet, broadcasters can scramble their signals such that only those who pay get a coherent picture. It's really a waste when you have to pay for a near-public good.

4. *Common-property goods.* Exclusion is hard; consumption is rival. Here we have a group of goods that's free to all comers, yet the use by some prevents the use by others. This sounds like it could be a potential problem. A common-property good can be "used up," like a candy bar, but you can't charge anyone for it and you can't keep anyone from getting it. The best examples of common-property goods are lakes, oceans, the atmosphere, and other similar natural resources. While everyone can use the air, some uses impose an opportunity cost on others. For example, dumping pollution into the air tends to keep people from breathing. (See Pollution.)

With the exception of private goods, the other three cry out for government. The first primitive governments were undoubtedly formed among our primate ancestors to: (a) provide common protection from saber-toothed tigers, agitated mastodons, and neighboring clans who had just invented spears and (b) ensure that no members of the clan took more than their fair share of berries from the nearby forest or dumped decaying, unwanted mastodon remains into the communal watering hole. I'll even go as far as to say that if it were not for public goods, near-public goods, and common-property goods, then we wouldn't need anything called "plothgim"—that is, government.

Our modern governments produce a lot of different goods—some they should and others, perhaps, they shouldn't. When you're in the voting booth, trying to decide between candidates, public-spending referendums, bond issues, or other such democratic muscle flexing, there are a few things that you might want to consider:

VOTING TIPS FOR GOVERNMENT GOODS

- First, consider the inherent nature of any government function under debate. Based on excludability and rival consumption,
how are the functions best classified?

- If the government is trying to get involved in a private good, then just vote No! (Or Yes, depending on how the ballot is worded.) We are best served as a voting public by letting private businesses produce private goods for private consumption. You should raise serious questions if the state government wants to get in the business of selling candy bars. (For some reason the topic of state-run lottery comes to mind.)

- If someone is trying to get the government out of the production of a public good, then we're on a quick route to disaster. I'm sure foreign powers would favor private provision of our national defense—because we would have none. Thoroughly question the ulterior motives of anyone wanting to privatize public goods. Perhaps they just don't want the good produced—period!

- Near-public goods are the most controversial, because they can be privately or publicly produced. Private producers can charge a price for the goods, even though efficiency suffers when they do. Here you have to balance efficiency with other things that private or public provision would do. For example, the government needs to fund education, but is private education better? Unfortunately, there are no one-time answers for all near-public goods. Each is unique.

- We must also consider common-property goods, especially most of what goes on with the natural environment. The question is: How do you keep people from using too much? Government can pass laws, but often the lack of excludability prevents control even by government. How do you keep people from using the oceans, streams, and atmosphere as a waste depository? Like near-public goods, there are many options because each common-property good is different. (See Natural Resources and Pollution for more.)

How the government gets its money

Because we need the government to collectively do the things that can't be done individually, we have to pay for it. How? Obviously through taxes—those involuntarily, coercive payments that we make as taxpayers. (See Taxes in Section 2.) There are, however, some tricks to getting taxes, about which most shrewd leaders of the past and present are aware. You too need to be aware.

- *Tax the goods that everyone needs.* Any city commissioner, IRS auditor, state legislator, or millionaire senator knows that the best way to fill the government's coffers is to place taxes on goods that people can't do without. That's why you tend to see taxes on such goods as cigarettes, gasoline, alcohol, and food. Face it, if you're addicted to smoking, driving, drinking, or eating, a tax of a few extra pennies (or perhaps dollars) isn't going to change your behavior much. You're likely to grumble a lot, but you'll buy the good and pay the tax.

- *Keep the taxes hidden from voters.* Because voters don't like to pay taxes (grumble, grumble, grumble), it's best for the political careers of those doing the taxing to keep them as hidden as possible. The government makes it appear that someone else is paying the taxes. For example, businesses often play a major role in the collection of obvious consumer income taxes and sales taxes. Sure, your grocery receipt has that sales tax entry between the subtotal and total amounts, but you don't actually write a check to the government. You pay the store, and the store pays the government. Likewise, you're probably more concerned with the difference between your W-2 withholdings and your tax liability, come April 15th, than you are with your total tax liability. While you're paying $43 gadzillion in income taxes, you're actually pleased because your employer withheld $97.12 more than your tax liability—so you get a refund!

There are also a few things that government should, and occasionally does, consider to make the collection of taxes as fair as possible.

1. *Horizontal equity.* The first of these is the idea that everyone who has the same ability to pay taxes should pay the same amount of taxes. This seems incredibly fair, and it sometimes actually happens. For example, if I make $20,000 a year and pay $5,000 in taxes, and you make $20,000, then it's only fair that you also contribute $5,000 to the operation of government.

2. *Vertical equity.* The second idea is that people with different abilities to pay taxes should pay correspondingly different taxes. Going back to my $20,000 income and $5,000 taxes, it would be very unfair if your income were $40,000, but you also paid a mere $5,000 in taxes. A $10,000 tax would be more in line with fairness. The lack of vertical equity is often a source of political revolutions. This is especially true when the first and second estates have more income than the third but pay the same or less in taxes. Off with Their Heads!

TAX-RELATED VOTING TIPS

- Be wary of politicians who promise lower taxes and more government services. In spite of what you think about the waste in government, the provision of government services carries a price tag. While we would all dearly love to have the government do its job without taxes, it just can't happen. If a politician promises to lower your taxes, ask yourself, or the politician, whether services will be reduced, and if so, which ones. By the same token, if a politician promises more government services, better find out who's going to pay.

- Be wary of hidden taxes. Some of the taxes we pay are obvious; others, however, are buried in layers of business production. Businesses "pay" the taxes, but pass along the extra cost to consumers as higher prices.

- Be wary of the vertical and horizontal equity and fairness of a tax. Does the burden of a tax fall equally on people with equal incomes? Do people with more income pay more or less in taxes? (You really should check out Taxes if any of this tax talk interests you.)

Necessary, but imperfect

While we can't get along without government and the stuff only it can provide, that doesn't mean government is the answer to all problems. Like everything in our imperfect world, our government is imperfect.

This fact would not be such a bad thing if we recognized it fully. Unfortunately, many of us look to the government to solve all of our problems. How many times has a small town passed a law making it "illegal" to rain during the Founder's Day picnic. Sometimes we ask government to do more than it can or should.

Here are some reasons why government screws up.

Those faceless bureaucrats

Unresponsive, monstrous bureaucracies that have taken on lives of their own tend to come to the top of most lists of government problems. Because government workers and government agencies are protected by layers of legal mumbo jumbo, they often lack the incentive to satisfy their consuming public. Government employees don't have to appease each individual complaining customer, because their jobs don't depend on appeasing each individual complaining customer.

Yet, government is not the only victim of monstrous bureaucracies. Profit-motivated corporations also have large, unresponsive bureaucracies. You might have as much trouble getting the defective disk drive in your brand new Omni Conglomerate, Inc., OmniTurbo 6000 computer satisfactorily repaired as you are getting a straight answer about your income tax from the Internal Revenue Service (IRS). Each has layers of protection for individual workers that can make efficiency an unreachable goal.

This is a problem of government, no doubt, but it's really more of a problem of bigness and a complex economy. The only real solution is to eliminate about 90 percent of the economy—an unappealing option.

Those ignorant voters

Most voters are basically ignorant when it comes to politics—and I mean that in the nicest way possible. There's a great deal of information floating around during an election about the candidates, their ideologies, their positions on major issues, their clandestine affairs, etc. The problem is that voters just don't have the time to find out everything there is to know about each of the 10 gadzillion candidates on a ballot during an election. How does the Democratic candidate for state auditor feel about NATO? And do you really care? Like most voters, probably not. In other words, voters choose rational ignorance; they choose not to learn about the candidates because they have better things to do with their time. As we'll see in Fact #6, Our Unknown Economy, this occurs in all parts of the economy.

Our decision to remain ignorant, as reasonable as it may be for us individually, often leads to the election of candidates whom we might not necessarily want in office. If we really knew all of the facts, we would have voted for the other candidate. Consequently, some candidates, perhaps most candidates, who are elected don't represent those who voted for them. This is why you tend to see candidates hedge and waffle as much as they can on the issues before the election. They have to be careful that voters don't find out who they are and what they really want to do.

Those special-interest groups

Although some voters lack interest, others might be very, very interested. You might personally care little about how candidates for the state auditor position feel about NATO; your next-door neighbor, whose son is stationed at a NATO base in Germany, might be very interested. In fact, your neighbor might get together with others who have a similar interest in NATO and form a group that solicits the NATO-related positions of every candidate on the ballot, just to make sure they don't vote for a state auditor with the wrong view.

This is how and why special-interest groups are formed. Not only do some people choose to remain ignorant about candidates and elections, others choose to become very, very informed and even to seek active participation in hopes of influencing the outcome. They do this because they have a great deal to gain or lose and, unlike others, really don't have anything better to do with their time. (Not that they don't have anything to do, they just don't have anything better to do. The issues are just that important.)

Special-interest groups have seemingly come out of the woodwork in recent decades to lobby the government about everything it does. These groups pour gadzillions of dollars into the election and reelection campaigns of every politician, tugging and pulling them in every way except the way the voters apparently want. If the politicians want to be elected to office, which requires gadzillions of campaign dollars, they need the money and support of special-interest groups. This is bad, right? There are two sides to the story.

1. Side one is the potential good that special-interest groups can do. Whether actively involved or not, virtually everyone is a member of one special-interest group or another. Most of our varied interests are represented by a special-interest group. If you're a female, gun-toting teacher who runs a dairy farm on the side, then your interests are represented by the National Organization of Women, the National Rifle Association, the National Education Association, and the National Dairy Council—although you're a member of none. There are so many different interests in our modern complex economy that almost every interest has an association that lobbies the government for favorable treatment. If you're pro-this or anti-that, then someone is likely to be on your side. This is good. This lets your feelings be known.

2. Side two is the potential harm created when these groups try to get government to pour money into their own special causes (read that as "personal bank accounts"). And while there are a large number of special-interest groups, not all are equally powerful. Recall if you will that resources, income, production, and wealth are not equally distributed. The most influential special-interest groups are backed by those who have the greatest share of the economic pie. The economic pie talks, and politicians listen. As such, special-interest groups are prone to enhance our already unequal distribution of economic pie.

Those greedy politicians

If the problems of incompetent workers, ignorant voters, and powerful special-interest groups aren't bad enough, we also have politicians trying to line their own pockets at the public's expense.

Now, before I get too many nasty letters from our elected officials, or have my taxes audited for the last 20 years, let me state that many seek government office to serve the public. However, the goals and aspirations of even the most public-spirited elected officials need not be the same as those of the voting public. The number 1 reason for this difference is that elected officials are elected officials only if they get elected. Their overriding goal is to get elected and then to get reelected, a task that can only be accomplished with a majority of the voters casting ballots. This translates into one voter more than 50 percent.

Clearly, then, an elected official can have an extended career at the public trough, excuse me, in public service, by satisfying only 50 percent (plus one) of those who vote. The remaining 50 percent (minus one) might be completely unrepresented.

Considering that voters tend to remain ignorant when there's no immediate indication that an elected official's actions have any direct bearing on their lives, it's in the elected official's best interest to remain pretty quiet about some of the things he or she is actually doing. If you, as an elected official, can sneak off on a fact-finding junket to the vacation mecca of Cancun, Mexico, during the bitter cold winter months, then it's best that voters remain uninformed

VOTING TIPS ON FIGHTING GOVERNMENT INEFFICIENCY

- First, note that government will never be flawless, efficient, and free of imperfections. The critics of government who've made a comfortable living pointing out government flaws will always be able to pursue their chosen career path.
- Improvements, however, can be achieved. Humans are imperfect, too, but we can improve. The same is true of government.
- A few ways to improve government include reducing the complexities of the bureaucracies, giving voters more information about issues and candidates, reigning in the unrepresentative power of special-interest groups, and making politicians' reelection more attuned to voters' interests.
- As a member of the third estate, be wary of any unification between the first and second estates. The marriage of wealth and power is invariably the death toll for those who have neither.

What does it all mean?

Like it or not, government is with us and will be for a long time to come. I can't even imagine a society that would not involve some form of government (or plothgim). In that numerous needs-satisfying goods are produced only by government, we have no choice but to keep it around. And because we have it, we have to pay taxes. The question then is whether our taxes dollars are spent wisely. The simple answer is: No! They aren't and they never will be, because government is incredibly inefficient and incompetent! Whatever the government seeks to do, it's probably going to screw it up because bureaucracies are unresponsive to the public, voters don't care, special-interest groups have too much influence, and politicians pursue their own agendas. The problem is that if the government doesn't perform its duties badly, then they aren't performed at all.

There are some things, however, that the government (the first estate) does badly, that it should not be doing, and that could be done better by businesses (second estate) or consumers (third estate). One of the problems with government is that it tends to perpetuate itself. Once a government agency is created to address a pressing problem, it never seems to die—even when the problem has been solved. To justify its existence an agency looks for other problems to solve. In some cases, the problem falls within the domain of what the government can do better than the markets. In other cases, it's simply a matter of the agency feeding on the economy, like any B-movie monster run amuck.

The message for pedestrians of the third estate is to keep a close eye on government. We need it, but as many peasants of the Middle Ages, citizens of the former

Soviet Union, and other members of the third estate can fully confirm, the potential abuses of the government are many. Government can do a lot of good things for the economy, but it has a tendency to oppress the people, confiscate resources, and abuse power for the benefit of the few who are in charge. Like fire, government is a tool that can be beneficial or deadly destructive.

Okay, let me sign the check for my property taxes so that we can be on our way. Our next stop is a mini-mall next to city hall. While we're in the area, I thought I might stop off and pay a visit to my dentist, Dr. Nova Cain. She wanted to talk to me—something about a root canal!

See also: Farm Prices, Federal Deficit, Health Care, Political Views, Product Safety, Social Security, and Welfare.

NUMBER 6

OUR UNKNOWN ECONOMY

Dr. Nova Cain, D.D.S., has her office in the mini-mall just north of city hall. You know the sort of mini-mall. It has a branch of Interstate OmniBank, Smilin' Ted's All-Comers Insurance Agency, an auto parts store, a branch of the public library, and four chiropractors.

Dr. Cain's location near the Shady Valley City Hall is most fortunate. One of my back molars is beginning to shoot sharp pains through my eyeball, into my brain, and out the back of my head. I've been meaning to stop by for a cleaning and checkup, but, well, the thought of sharp needles and high-speed drills grinding away large portions of my teeth convinced me that other activities were more important.

Now, however, just as we're trying to trek through the complexities of the economy, that back molar has decided to throb incessantly. It's best if I stop in and let the kind and (hopefully) gentle Dr. Cain check it out.

Guess what? *Root canal!*

If only I had *known* the seriousness of my inaction. If only I had known the consequences of eating so many donuts (or perhaps it was the whipped cream on the economic pie). If only I had known the value of a cleaning and checkup. If only I had known . . . .

> ## Fact #6: More than meets the eye.
> Every action has more than one consequence: some that are direct and easily observed and others that are indirect and difficult to detect.

I didn't know that overlooking an annual checkup or two, and eating too many extremely mouthwatering donuts would lead to a root canal. But let's not dwell on my eminent pain and suffering. Let's think about the importance of information to the economy.

It's what you know that counts

I wouldn't be guilty of exaggeration to say that information is the key to a healthy, efficient, and productive economy. Efficiency in the use of our resources to satisfy our needs would be close to impossible without information. Two points illustrate this:

1. To get the most satisfaction, consumers need to know what products are in the marketplace, their location, and their prices. It's hard to satisfy any need if you can't find the good to do the satisfying. The good that will satisfy a really, *really*, Really pressing need might be in the room right next to you. But if you don't know about it, then your need goes unquenched.

2. To do their producing, producers need to know the prices of the inputs and where they may be found. Producers also need to know where the potential markets are and whether or not it would be worth their effort, profitwise, to produce the goods.

The more information we have and the more accurate that information is, then the better we're able to direct our limited resources to the most pressing needs. This is what makes our economy efficient. It's also what makes consumers happier, gives businesses more profit, creates more income, and does a lot of other really good things for the economy.

Unfortunately, information is not only very valuable, it also tends to be limited. If it wasn't, then you would already know everything that I'm about to say in this chapter. In fact, you would already know everything in this book and every other book ever written.

In spite of the vast amounts of information that's floating around via newspapers, magazines, books, and cable channels, we never seem to have enough of the right information at the right time. Sure, you may know what Liz Taylor had for breakfast every day last week, but do you know how often that used car that you're thinking about buying had its oil changed (if at all) in the past decade?

I've got a secret

Like other stuff, limited information isn't just limited, it's also unequally distributed. You probably recall that nothing in the economy—resources, income, production, or wealth—is equally distributed. This applies to information as well—which means you know stuff that I don't, and I know stuff that you don't. Some people have a lot of information and others don't. This creates some interesting problems in our economy. One example is illustrated by the used-car market, which, as most used-car buyers know, contains nothing but lemons (cars in serious need of mechanical therapy). Unequal information is one reason that so many previously owned cars are better used as lawn decorations than transportation.

Let's say that you're thinking about buying a used car, a 1990 OmniMotors XL GT 9000 to be precise. Now, OmniMotors XL GT 9000s are fine automobiles, but used cars are used cars. You can't know for certain how well this particular 1990 XL GT was maintained. Did it have regular tune-ups? Was its oil changed on schedule? Was it involved in any accidents? So many questions, but so few answers. As a buyer, you're not likely to have all of the information that you would like about the history of this XL GT 9000.

So, what price will you pay for this car? Let's say that a 1990 XL GT 9000 that's in really great shape, "a gem," sells for $5,000, while one that's in dire need of remedial work by an auto mechanic, "a lemon," sells for $3,000. If you have a 50:50 chance of getting a gem or a lemon, your best price is $4,000. Your chance of paying too much for the lemon is offset by your likelihood of paying too little for a gem. Because other buyers feel the same, $4,000 would be the going demand price for an XL GT 9000.

A $4,000 price might be okay for you as a buyer, but what about the sellers—they who know a great deal more about their cars than you? How do you think the owner of a well-maintained gem of a car is going to react when you offer a mere $4,000? "No deal," is my guess. This owner knows for certain that the gem is worth $5,000 and would not be willing to sell it for $4,000. The not-so-proud owner of the lemon, in contrast, would jump at the offer.

You, therefore, will be able to buy the lemon, but not the gem. In fact, the gem owners probably won't even put their cars on the market when they realize the going price is $4,000. The only cars you're likely to see for sale in this case are a bunch of lemons. The good cars just aren't sold.

The challenge of information search

The right information at the right time is not easy to get. In fact, it can be downright costly. Fortunately, Dr. Cain's office is located in the same mini-mall as a well-stocked branch of the public library. Before my anesthetic wears off, we can saunter past the auto parts store, the insurance agency (quickly, because Smilin' Ted has spotted us), and two of the chiropractors to reach the public library where we can uncover any information about any conceivable subject. All it takes is a little time and effort on our part.

For example, after a mere 6 or 7 hours of reading, we might discover that the University of Ibadan is a Nigerian university that was founded in 1948 and has about 12,000 students. The usefulness of this information is unclear. But we can find it, and much, much more, with a little effort on our part. Okay, maybe a great deal of effort on our part.

Unfortunately, this information about the University of Ibadan is pretty costly to obtain. And more than likely, the cost of obtaining the information is a great deal more than any benefit we're likely to get from it. Perhaps we should be a little more careful next time when searching out information. In fact, some sort of guideline—such as making sure that the potential or expected benefit of the information is at least as much as the cost of getting it—would seem to be useful. This is a good rule to follow for anything we do. For example, if you're about to buy an electric sander, you'd better weigh the anticipated benefit against its price. Will you be sanding a lot of wood or just knocking an occasional rough edge off your big toenail?

Information isn't free

Getting information is much like producing any good that you care to name. We use limited, scarce resources to acquire information, much like we use limited, scarce resources to produce frozen waffles, table lamps, or aircraft. Because the resources have alternative uses, using them to acquire information has an opportunity cost.

More specifically, the cost of acquiring information includes many of the following: our time and effort, the cost of travelling from store to store, telephone expenses if we decide to let our fingers do the walking, or the purchase price of information sources such as magazines, newspapers, books, and cable television.

But it can be useful

While information is costly to get, it also provides benefit, otherwise we would never bother to know anything. We could probably run through a litany of really philosophical benefits of information, such as fulfilling our souls in search of inquiry, but the bottom line is, well, our bottom lines. The benefit of information for consumers is what we can save on purchases. If we can save a few bucks here or there

on stuff, then we have an important benefit—a few bucks.

Here are a some things that affect the benefit of information search:

- *Price differences*. If you suspect that an item has a range of prices in different stores, then it's in your best interest to do a little bit of searching for the lowest price. For example, because of some interesting government policies, milk prices vary little from store to store in any town. It's probably not worth the effort to drive 30 miles across town to save 2 cents on a gallon of milk. Car prices, on the other hand, are likely to differ greatly among dealers. A little search effort in this case will probably generate big savings.

- *Total expense*. There's another reason why searching for the lowest price on cars is likely to be more beneficial than searching for the lowest price on milk: the amount spent. Because milk is a relatively small fraction of your household budget, price differences are also going to be a relatively small fraction of your budget. Cars, however, are big-ticket items and a big part of your household budget. While you might be able to save a few pennies on the milk, you stand to save thousands on a car.

- *Frequency of purchase*. How often you buy stuff can also help determine the benefit of information search. If you buy the same good often, then a few pennies of saving on each purchase will add up to big savings over a longer period. In this case, identifying the store with the lowest milk price might be worth the effort.

- *Price volatility*. With seasonal sales, closeouts, assorted discounts, etc., the prices of some products tend to fluctuate a lot. The more prices fluctuate, the greater is the potential benefit of searching. For example, you might be able to save 10 percent on the price of a sofa at one store, but the clearance sale at a competing store next week may let you save 40 percent on the same sofa.

INFORMATION-SEARCHING TIPS

- Because you can't know everything, you should be selective about the information you seek. Try to determine the potential benefit of information and its cost.
- Look for ways of reducing the cost of information. Handy reference books like this one are a good place to start. A few moments spent organizing search efforts can save a great deal of search time and cost. It's easier to find a book at the library by going through the card catalog than by randomly searching the shelves. Likewise it's easier to find someone who already has the needed information. For example, if you're pondering the possibility of purchasing a powerboat, find a friend who made a similar purchase.
- The telephone can be a tremendous information search cost-saving device. A few inexpensive minutes on the telephone can save the time and effort of trips to stores.

The hazards of soothsaying

One area where information is really critical for consumers, workers, and taxpayers is the future. Very few people, with the exception of the psychics who write for newspaper tabloids, know what's going to happen in the future. The future is, shall we say, fraught with uncertainty and risk. (A brief note here: In spite of the well-documented fact that the future is unknown, many economists have made it their lifelong pursuit to forecast the future condition of the economy. Sometimes they get it almost right, and sometimes they really screw up. If you want more insight into the perils of economic forecasting, check out the entry on Economic Forecasting.)

While a lot of different things could happen tomorrow, today—right now, at this very moment—you don't know which one it will be. For example:

- Ed McMahon could knock on your door and present you with a $10 gadzillion check.
- The sun could explode, killing all life on the planet.
- Elvis Presley could land in your backyard aboard an extraterrestrial spaceship, steal your peanut butter and banana sandwich, sing a few bars of "Jailhouse Rock," then leave for a planet in another solar system.
- You could wake up to the sound of your alarm clock, get dressed, eat breakfast, and go to work.

While each of these events could occur, their likelihood is not the same. Economists, scientists, statisticians, and others who spend a lot of their adult lives doing funny things to numbers, like talk about the probability, or chance, of an event occurring. Of the different alternatives given here, the probability is greatest that you will wake up, get dressed, and go to work tomorrow. (If my speculation concerning your activities for tomorrow turns out to be wrong, especially the one about Elvis, please, *please* let me know.)

This probability is based on your historical experience, what is known about the laws of physics, the life expectancy of the sun, the existence of extraterrestrials, the life and death of Elvis Presley, and the functioning of contest give-aways. Yet, even though we're very certain that the waking up/work scenario will happen tomorrow, we don't know and can't know for sure. This uncertainty not only helps the sales of supermarket tabloids, it also keeps our lives interesting. One interesting part is how different people react to this uncertainty.

Scaredy cats and gamblers

Some of us hate the idea of an uncertain future, while others revel in it, and some really don't care one way or the other. We can affectionately refer to those who don't like an uncertain future as "scaredy cats," and those who do as "gamblers."

What makes a scaredy cat a scaredy cat? They prefer certainty more than uncertainty, and are willing to pay for it. Before you start to ridicule scaredy cats, you should know that most people are scaredy cats most of the time in most circumstances. That is, we are all generally happier if we know what's going to happen. *And* (this is an important *and*) we are willing to pay for that certainty. This, in fact, is what the entire insurance industry is based on. (Let me direct your curiosity to the adventures of Smilin' Ted in the Section 2 entry on Insurance.)

We willingly buy health insurance, car insurance, and homeowners' insurance, knowing for certain that our future income and subsequent satisfaction will be less by the amount of the premiums. But we avoid the uncertain losses in income and well-being created by illness, accidents, natural disasters, or whatever.

Let's throw together a few simple numbers to illustrate this idea. Suppose that you have $10 to bet on the flip of a coin. If it's heads, you get another $10 for a $20 total; if it's tails then you end up with nothing, zero, zippo, nada.

If you flip the coin and make the same wager hundreds of times, how much money do you think you'll have at the end? Most likely $10. Because the coin has an equal chance, probability, of coming up heads or tails, the number of times you win $10 will cancel out the number of times you lose $10, leaving you with $10.

But it's not the money itself that's important, it's how you feel about the money you win versus the money you lose. That is, how much satisfaction do you give up from losing $10, and how much satisfaction do you gain from winning $10? Some people place an equal amount of satisfaction on the winnings as on the losings. Others actually get more satisfaction from the money won than from the money lost. Most of us, however, are more personally attached to the losses than we are to the winnings. Therefore, even though we might end up with the same $10 that we started with, after a hundred or so flips of the coin, the pain from our satisfaction losses outweighs the satisfaction gains of

our winnings: Each time we lose hurts more than each time we win.

The reason for these differences is how we view extra income. If each extra dollar of income is worth less than the previous dollar, then you value the lost $10 more than you value the won $10. If, in contrast, each extra dollar is worth more, then you value the lost $10 less than the won $10.

The three types of people (pick your own from the list) that we can identify are:

1. *Scaredy cats* (risk averse). Those who value extra income less and less are going to be reluctant to undertake any type of risky proposition. They would rather have a guaranteed amount of income than an equal amount of income that involves some uncertainty.

2. *Gamblers* (risk loving). Those who value extra income more and more are going to enjoy the prospects of a risky situation. They would rather have an uncertain income than an equal amount of known income. (See Gambling for more.)

3. *In-betweeners* (risk neutral). Those who value all extra income the same are indifferent about a guaranteed income and an uncertain income. They could go either way. It really doesn't matter to them. They don't care.

At one extreme, scaredy cats are those who buy insurance, take secure jobs at lower pay, stay in the same unexciting jobs for years on end, plan trips well in advance and down to the detail (if they take any), and generally try to remove uncertainty from their lives. Is this bad? No, because scaredy cats gain more satisfaction from certainty than from uncertainty.

Gamblers, at the other extreme, are those who speculate in the stock market, buy products from mail order catalogs, tell their boss in no uncertain terms where the latest efficiency memo can be filed and then quit without having any other employment prospects, begin a new business on nothing but a whimsical idea, and generally seek out risky situations. This lifestyle is not necessarily bad, either, because gamblers gain satisfaction from uncertainty. They wouldn't have it any other way.

Please note, however, that scaredy cats and gamblers are two extreme positions. Most people have a mixture. You aren't necessarily a gambler or scaredy cat under all circumstances. Today you might hazard the unknown with great bravado, but tomorrow you could tend to be a little more cautious.

UNCERTAINTY TIPS

- Make sure you know your own preferences. If you're a scaredy cat, don't let a gambler talk you into a risky situation. You'll only regret it. Remember, many of us are scaredy cats in most circumstances. Carefully select those situations in which you're a gambler.
- Likewise, if you're a gambler, don't let scaredy cats avert you from the risk you crave. However, a word to the wise: Make sure that you recognize the degree of risk and uncertainty involved. Don't let your desire for uncertainty enter into wagers that can't be won. For example, make sure that you're not waging on the flip of a coin with two tails.
- Get as much information as you can about the risk of winning or losing in an uncertain situation. Even a scaredy cat would be willing to enter a wager, if the winning is great enough to compensate for the loss. A scaredy cat might be willing to wager on the flip of a coin if the potential loss is only $5 dollars and the potential gain is $20 dollars.

A quick jog through the financial markets

Uncertainty, risk, and the future have a big part to play in financial markets. These are markets that trade legal claims on resources or goods, such as corporate stock, government securities, and foreign currency, to name a few. The key with financial markets, unlike product markets, is that you're buying and selling promises. For example, if you buy an Omni Conglomerate, Inc., OmniChef 7000 waffle iron, then you have an OmniChef 7000 waffle iron, with all of the satisfaction it provides. If you buy a share of Omni Conglomerate, Inc., stock, then you have a piece of paper that represents a legal claim on the assets of Omni Conglomerate, Inc.

Uncertainty and risk enter the picture because a gadzillion things could happen to keep you from exercising your legal claim on Omni Conglomerate, Inc. The company could fold, the president and CEO could head for the Cayman Islands with the company's profits, or a rival competitor (Tech-Bake Industries) could come out with a new, improved waffle iron (one that uses lasers) that takes away OmniChef's market. Because you don't know what's going to happen, uncertainty runs rampant.

In fact, a great deal of the reward investors hope to get when entering the financial markets is a reward for uncertainty and risk. I might guess that the price of Omni Conglomerate, Inc., stock is going to rise, while you guess that it's going to fall. If I'm right, then I stand to get gadzillions of dollars because I bought the Omni Conglomerate, Inc., stock before the price went up, and you didn't. I win, you lose. (A great deal more information on the workings of financial markets can be gathered by reviewing Section 2 entries on Financial Markets, Mutual Funds, and Stock Market.)

What does it all mean?

The efficiency of our economy is limited by the information we have. The more information we have about the present and the better our prognostications are of the future, then the more efficient our economy will be. While information is costly to get, all information is not equally costly. And therein lies some potential pitfalls.

Some information is readily available and immediately known. It is directly observable and pretty darn obvious. If you jump into a lake, you know that you're wet. You can feel the water-saturated clothing next to your skin, and you can see the water droplets on your fingertips.

Other information, however, is not so obvious. The lake might contain infectious bacteria that enter your system and in a few days make you sick. However, maybe your illness wasn't caused by the lake bacteria but an improperly washed water glass at the restaurant where you had lunch before jumping in the lake. Such is the problem with information. Our economy is so complex that it's impossible to know what's happening right now, let alone what might happen in the future.

With this in mind, you need to be wary of the information purveyors, especially those who stress the obvious and promote only one side. Information is a commodity that's produced by our limited resources. Moreover, those limited resources are not equally distributed throughout the economy. Those same people who have more ownership and control of the economic pie—the first and second estates—also have greater control over information. (See Adver-

tising for more thoughts along this line.)

Those who control the information can make the information that benefits them more readily accessible to the public. If I own a cardboard factory and a television station, I'm not likely to let the station broadcast a news story about defective cardboard from my factory. I might not prevent the broadcast, but I'm not going to encourage it either. What I will encourage, if I can, are glowing accounts of the wonderful uses of our friend: cardboard.

As members of the third estate—the estate with limited ownership and control over resources—you need to heed the tired but true warning to consider the source of any information. Be especially suspicious of any information from the first two estates.

My tooth is feeling better now. In fact, if you're willing, we might spend an hour or two walking around Shady Valley's amusement park. It's only a few blocks away. And I'm sort of ashamed to admit it, but I'd really like to ride on the merry-go-round.

See also: Credit Cards, Discrimination, Education, Health Care, Political Views, Product Safety, Regulation, and Workers Safety.

OUR CIRCULAR WORLD

Our little excursion through the economy has had, thus far, its ups and downs. My cable bill remains permanently confused, and my checking account has a large property tax-created imbalance, but at least the pain in my tooth stops before hitting my toes. I think we deserve a little rest and relaxation at the Shady Valley's own tourist mecca, Happy-Time Gala-World Fun-Land Extravaganza Amusement Park. Let's take a brief respite from our pedestrian trek and give the soles of our jogging shoes a well-deserved rest.

The Happy-Time Amusement Park has the world-famous Monster Loop Death Plunge roller coaster, guaranteed to make riders yearn for the pleasures of a Siberian forced-labor camp. There's also the Enchanted Haunted Horror House filled with serial killers, chainsaw murders, and IRS auditors. For the more timid and, fortunately, for those more interested in the workings of our economy, the merry-go-round is the ride of choice.

Two familiar faces are enjoying the circular trip on their fiberglass ponies. The slender guy with the bushy mustache is Dan Dreiling, the drywall man. I had him repair a hole in my living-room wall caused by an overexcited vacuum cleaner a few months back. The disgusted look on his dusty face tells me that I must have overlooked his $100 bill. The other recognizable rider is Pollyanna Pumpernickel, a precocious pet store owner who has somehow neglected to pay me the $100 due for hamster-sitting services I rendered a few weeks ago. Her furtive glances suggest that she is well aware of her liability.

As dusty Dan Dreiling passes by, closely followed by precocious Pollyanna Pumpernickel, it occurs to me that I could easily pay the drywall bill, if only I were paid my hamster-sitting fee. Perhaps I can work this out before the merry-go-round ride stops. While I consider the options, let's think about the seventh basic fact of economic life:

> ## Fact #7: What goes around comes around.
> Consumers and producers are interconnected through a continuous circular flow of buying and selling.

A PEDESTRIAN...

... stimulates the economy

Many of the more interesting complexities of the economy arise because one person's expenditure is another's revenue. Any of the hard-earned income that you spend on stuff ends up as income for those who produce and/or sell the stuff, which they spend on other stuff, which then becomes income for other producers, and on and on and on. It sounds like this could continue for awhile. It does.

Transforming gobs of gooey resources

Our economy is blessed with a bountiful, although limited, amount of resources.

These resources are important because they satisfy our unlimited wants and needs. You probably recognize this as our oft-encountered problem of scarcity.

Motivated by this ever-pressing problem of scarcity, we humans have discovered that our planet's natural resources can satisfy a whole lot more wants and needs if they're modified, transformed, or changed in one way or another. While a gooey pile of mud might satisfy some sort of desire, it can provide more satisfaction when formed into rectangular blocks, dried, then fashioned into a structure that offers protection from the elements. As useful (or useless) as naturally occurring resources might be, they're more useful when transformed.

Consumption and production make life liveable

The benefit of transforming natural resources into satisfying stuff gives us two fundamental activities in the economy, production and consumption. While production is the transformation of resources, consumption is the satisfying of our wants and needs with resources or the stuff produced from the resources.

Most people in the economy—not all, but most—do both of these things on a regular basis. For example, remember that peanut butter and jelly sandwich you made when you were 8 years old? You first produced the sandwich, with a little help from the bakery, the peanut butter company, and the jelly processor, then you consumed it. Most of us do a lot of producing and consuming without much thought. Producing is usually done in the employ of a business, and consuming is regularly accomplished in the privacy of our homes. At times, we transform and enjoy simultaneously, either at work or at home.

Our economy's ability to address efficiently the problem of scarcity is enhanced through production. The more we produce, the more we consume.

Getting markets into the act

We've already seen that markets can do a pretty good job—with a few important exceptions—of directing resources into the production of the most goods that best satisfy our needs. In other words, production from resources and our consumption of this production is a lot easier because of markets. There are two sorts of markets that we can think about: One mainly assists consumption, and the other is most helpful for production. You might want to note who does the supplying and who does the demanding in each market.

- *Product markets* make it easier for consumers to get possession of goods. Consumers are the buyers in product markets, while businesses are the sellers. This is probably the sort of market that most of us think about when the term arises. If you head to a grocery store, shopping mall, or car dealer to make a purchase, you're in a product market.
- *Resource markets* let businesses get the resources used for production. In these markets consumers, as resource owners, do the supplying, while businesses, as producers, do the demanding. The most common sort of resource market is that for labor. There are, however, markets for capital and the whole spectrum of natural resources, as well.

The circular flow

This whole economic process of trading goods, services, and resources through resource and product markets takes shape through the circular flow. Consumers and producers interact in a circular fashion with each other through these markets. This circular flow works like this:

- The revenue that producers get from their sales in the product markets is used to pay for the resources employed through the resource markets.
- The income consumers get from the sale of resources in the resource markets is used to buy stuff from the product markets.
- In short, the revenue of the producers becomes the income of the consumers. And the income spent by the consumers becomes the revenue of the producers. The money just keeps circulating around between producers and consumers through the product and resource markets—just like a merry-go-round.

A simple example, taken from the annals of the Shady Valley Central Town Sprawling Hills Shopping Mall, will illustrate this process. Let's pick up the story with Edgar Millbottom, an employee of Waldo's

TexMex Taco World located at the south end of the mall.

The cash register of Waldo's TexMex Taco World has just received $1 in payment for one of Waldo's Super Deluxe TexMex Gargantuan Tacos (with sour cream and peppers). The creation of this Gargantuan Taco—skillfully accomplished with the caring hands of Edgar Millbottom—and its sale are but one part of the many transactions through our economy's product markets.

What, however, happens to the dollar bill used to purchase this Super Deluxe Taco? It's used to pay the wage of our own Edgar Millbottom, whose only reason for working at Waldo's TexMex Taco World is to earn enough money to expand his compact disk collection of Live Headless Squirrels (not the animals, a rock band). When Edgar collects the wage payment for his diligent taco preparation, we have a transaction through the economy's resource markets.

Where do we go from here? Edgar takes this picante-sauce-stained dollar bill (with a dozen or so others) to Musical Sound CD Emporium—at the north end of the mall—where he purchases the latest Live Headless Squirrels CD, featuring the title song "Screech . . . Rumble . . . Crunch (Oh, Baby)." When the picante-stained dollar bill enters the Musical Sound CD Emporium cash register, it has now gone through another of our product markets.

The crumpled likeness of George Washington doesn't rest for long. It's next used to pay the wage of Alicia Hyfield, a faithful and hungry employee of Musical Sound CD Emporium. It has become part of another transaction through our resource markets.

How long can this continue? How many transactions will this dollar bill see? At least one more, because Alicia Hyfield wants nothing more from life than the succulent taste of a Waldo's Super Deluxe TexMex Gargantuan Taco.

I think we can see what's bound to happen. This dollar bill will be stained again with picante sauce and help Edgar add to his ever-expanding collection of Live Headless Squirrels. Around and around and around it goes.

More than CDs and tacos

Of course, as the title of this section indicates, the economy has goods other than Live Headless Squirrels CDs and Waldo's Gargantuan Tacos. Alicia and Edgar, moreover, are only two of the millions of consumers and producers in our economy. The circular flow works the same for gadzillions of products, gadzillions of producers, and gadzillions of consumers as it does for two. The revenue that producers get from selling stuff becomes the income of the resource owners. This income is then used to purchase stuff that satisfies wants and needs, which then ends up as producers' revenue once again. Around and around and around it goes, just like a merry-go-round.

Which reminds me: I've plucked the necessary payment from Pollyanna Pumpernickel for hamster-sitting services, and I'm passing it along to Dan Dreiling for his drywall repairs. From the queasy look on Dan's face, I'd say that our own little circular transaction has been completed none to soon. As Dan recovers, let's look into this circular flow business in more detail.

The multiplicative, cumulatively reinforcing interaction of the circular flow (whew!)

When one person spends a dollar on production, it becomes a dollar of revenue for a business, which then uses it to pay for resources, meaning it becomes a dollar of income for someone else. That someone else buys more production, which becomes yet another's income. Even more production ensues. Over the period of a year, a single dollar might be used to buy $6 or $7 dollars worth of production.

This creates what we can call a "multiplicative, cumulatively reinforcing interaction of the circular flow" (whew!). Once the circular flow is set in motion, it continues in a multiplicative, cumulatively reinforcing manner (whew!) for some time. If businesses, for example, decide to build several new factories here and there, the resources that make the factories get more income. This then triggers our multiplicative, cumulatively reinforcing circular flow (whew!) into more production and income. The same sort of thing is bound to happen if the government spends more on public goods, or if foreign types buy more stuff.

This whole multiplicative, cumulatively reinforcing interaction of the circular flow (whew!) is like a bandwagon once it starts rolling, with everyone jumping on. When consumers buy more, businesses need more factories to produce more goods, and governments get more tax dollars and consequently spend more as well. Everybody buys. Everyone spends. More production. More income.

Our bandwagon, however, rolls in both directions. When a few buyers stop buying—it could be a business here, a government there, or consumers—then others stop buying, too. This forces some labor out of work and reduces income. With less income, there's less consumption, less production, less investment, fewer tax dollars, and the bandwagon heads rapidly down a steep slope.

When things go good, they go really good, and when things go bad, well, watch out for falling stockbrokers.

Business cycle booms and busts

This multiplicative, cumulatively reinforcing interaction (whew!) means that the circular flow has more production and income coursing through its veins during some periods, and less during others. This tends to cause what pointy headed economists refer to as "business cycles."

Business cycle gyrations and turbulence in the circular flow are a normal part of not only the U.S. economy but also most other nations. The shrinking of the pie, or decline in the economy, is referred to as "recessions," "depressions," "downturns," "contractions," "busts," or some similar term. Increases in the economic pie are noted as "expansions," "recoveries" (early on, at least), "booms," "growth periods," "prosperities," or some other flowery term designed to entice voters to reelect the incumbents. (This intriguing boom and bust aspect of our economy is explored in depth in Section 2 under the headings of Depressions, Inflation, and Recessions. Feel free to explore any one or all of them at your leisure. If you want to do it now, I'll wait for you until you get through. In fact, I've been tempted to try the Monster Loop Death Plunge since we first entered the amusement park.)

While I ponder the Death Plunge, let's consider this circular flow pulsation. We've a picture of our economic pie oozing through the circular flow in a big surge, after which it contracts a bit, ready for another big surge of ooze. But here's an important point: With each surge, the size of the flow, the size of our pie, grows bigger and bigger and bigger. . . .

You might want to get some popcorn and a soft drink during our intermission because the circular flow is about to devour the once-peaceful town of Shady Valley. Recall that our pair of young teenagers, Edgar and Alicia, has been desperately trying to warn Mayor Thurgood, Sheriff Morralis, and other town leaders of the impending doom. But no one seems to care. The circular flow, however, continues to pulsate, growing ever closer to a small child, little Mary Jane, who is innocently picking daisies in her backyard. It's growing bigger, it's getting closer. . . .

Oops! Just a moment. That's not our circular flow. That's a space creation. My mistake.

The circular flow, however, does grow larger and larger over time through its pulsation. During most expansions, lasting 2 to 3 years (sometimes longer), our economic pie is bigger, much bigger than it had been during the previous expansion. When our pie shrinks into a recession of 6 months to 2 years (seldom longer), it loses some of the growth found during the expansion, but not all. Our whole process of economic growth, the improvement in our standard of living, and reduction of the ever-present problem of scarcity is accomplished through this circular flow pulsation. Could we grow without the pulsations? Possibly. Yet, we've never had the chance to find out. Business cycle gyrations go back as far as recorded time.

The good, the bad, and the political

All is not good with these booms and busts, ups and downs of the circular flow. Then again, all is not necessarily bad either.

First, the good. We already noted that the booms of each circular-flow pulsation help add to the size of our economic pie. There's no question that this is good. What about the busts?

- During a recession, resources are temporarily unemployed, then reemployed when the boom starts up. The benefit lies in which resources are unemployed. Businesses keep the more productive ones around and get rid of the less productive ones. Moreover, a lot of the businesses themselves go belly up, or bankrupt, during recessions. The businesses that fold are typically—not always, but typically—the least efficient ones in an industry. A downturn helps weed out the less productive or least efficient resources from an industry.
- This weeding-out process would appear to be good for much of our economy—more efficient production and all but what about those resources that get "weeded-

out"? They too might see some good. When the next expansion occurs, these resources have the opportunity to find a more suitable line of endeavor. They're likely to be more productive—and receive higher incomes—in the next expansion than they would have otherwise.

In the same way that your heart pumps a surge of blood through your bloodstream, then momentarily pauses, the economy expands for a few years, then takes a brief respite to recoup its resources and prepare for another surge.

Second, the bad. With each boom and bust, the economy experiences two of its more critical problems: inflation and unemployment.

- Inflation can be pretty deadly, because prices usually don't rise equally. This means some people pay higher prices for goods, but the income they get for selling their resources doesn't go up as fast. Others receive relatively higher prices for the resources they sell, and thus higher incomes, but the prices they pay don't increase nearly as fast. This causes the economic pie to be redistributed, from those who aren't getting the higher prices to those who are.
- Unemployment can be even worse, because resources are left idle and unused for production. This in itself may not seem all that bad until you recognize that production lost today can never be recouped tomorrow. Sure, we could get everyone working tomorrow and have the production that results, but we've still lost today's production. Unemployment is also an obvious problem for those who aren't working. While many unemployed workers get unemployment compensation when temporarily without work, the payments are low and last only a few months.

Third, the political. The immediate and readily apparent problems created with each boom and bust make it very difficult for any politician hoping for a lifetime of public service to avoid corrective action. When unemployment is up during a downturn, politicians pass laws to rectify the situation. If we have high rates of inflation, rest assured that your favorite elected official will seek immediate redress.

Now, don't take it wrongly that the government should not do anything to combat the adverse consequences of inflation and unemployment. There are short-term problems of inflation and unemployment that the government can help correct. However, the surges and pulsations of the circular flow have many benefits that accrue over the long run that may be lost if the short-run problems are avoided entirely.

Here's a simple analogy to illustrate the situation. A 3-year-old child often needs to suffer the pain of a scolding or mild spanking as a lesson against crossing the rush-hour traffic of a busy street. A child who does not experience this short-run pain may in the long run suffer more pain, or even death.

The economy also needs an occasional swift kick in the tail to keep it from suffering major setbacks. An occasional recession can prevent an "unexpected" but debilitating cardiac arrest. Recessionary pauses from an expanding pie are often the short-run kicks needed to ensure long-run growth.

A FEW BUSINESS-CYCLE TIPS

- The good times don't last forever, but then again neither do the bad. Enjoy the prosperity while it lasts, but don't be fooled into thinking that all of the economy's problems—such as unemployment—have been solved. Likewise, when a recession seems to be dragging on forever, keep in mind that none has lasted forever yet. We always seem to find a way to prosperity.
- Don't let the government be too overprotective of the economy. A little pain and suffering can be good for the economic soul. Of course, how much pain and who does the suffering (usually the

third estate) has been and always will be a source of heated debate. The government can best ease the problems of a recession by redirecting unemployed resources into more productive areas as quickly as possible.

- Above all, be cautious of political candidates who promise the easy, quick-fix solutions to the ups and downs of the circular flow. We have short-term problems and long-term problems. More often than not, correcting short-term problems creates or worsens long-term problems. Make sure that you give a political candidate or elected official with the guts to address long-term problems the chance to see proposed solutions through.

What does it all mean?

Our economy is a complex, dynamic system that keeps moving with very little regard for what any one of its members (for example, the President) may do. Our economy does its thing, because that's what's best for the people with unlimited needs and limited resources. Sometimes it performs very well, with the economic pie oozing through the circular flow, expanding rapidly and giving (almost) everyone a greater access to needs-satisfying goods. At other times, the circular flow pauses to regroup.

Like most activities in the economy, there's more to the circular flow than first meets the eye. The apparent problems of short-run downturns may turn into opportunities for long-run efficiency and expansion. The size of the circular flow in the long run depends on what happens to it in the short run, and vice versa. For example, we can get a bigger economic pie in the long run by diverting portions of the circular flow between consumption and investment in the short run.

The things we do, intentionally or not, can have magnified consequences through the circular flow. For example, the government might decide, after all these years, to eliminate the federal deficit; businesses might decide there are fewer investment opportunities that remained to be pursued; or consumers might groan a collective sigh of disgust as they cut their own spending—any and all of which would start the economy into a multiplicative, cumulatively reinforcing interactive (whew!) downturn.

Historically, all of our downturns have ended with an upturn. But there are no guarantees. Throughout our lives, every pulse of blood sent surging through our veins is followed by a brief rest, then another surge. Every rest is followed by another surge. Every rest, that is, but one!

See also: Economic Growth, Economic Forecasting, Federal Deficit, Foreign Trade, Interest Rates, and Political Views.

SECTION

2

THE 38 FACTS OF ECONOMIC LIFE THAT EVERYONE SHOULD KNOW

my sales pitch on
ADVERTISING

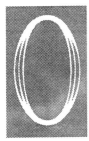

Our extended sojourn through the winding complexities of the economy has worn the soles from my jogging shoes. For the best bargain on a new pair, let's consult those annoying flyers stuffed into the Sunday newspaper. We're in luck. The Mega-Mart Discount Warehouse Super Center is having its monthly "once in a lifetime" sale on jogging shoes. Without this Mega-Mart Discount Warehouse Super Center advertising supplement, I might have unknowingly paid a higher price for my brand new Fleet Feet Footwear jogging shoes. Isn't advertising wonderful?

It's everywhere, it's everywhere

Let's not draw any hasty conclusions about the wonderfulness of advertising until we know more about this beast. As a start, we do know that advertising is very, very widespread. Advertising splashes across newspaper and magazine pages, blurts out from radio broadcasts, comes with the daily mail, interrupts television programming, and invades the landscape on signs and billboards. It's seen on high-flying blimps, sewn onto the clothing of professional athletes, and embedded in major motion pictures with as much subtlety as a blow to the head with a sledge hammer.

Advertising is thrust upon us by the biggest multinational conglomerates, the smallest "mom and pop" stores, and everything between. *Profit*-seeking businesses don't have a monopoly on the advertising deed either. Private charities, churches, universities, government agencies, and even the military have all been known to allo-

cate a few dollars of their respective budgets to advertising.

Let's put the full extent of advertising into perspective. A gadzillion dollars is spent each year (actually about $200 billion, but growing) just to pay for advertising space in magazines and newspapers, commercial airtime on television and radio, and other assorted media outlets. Gadzillions more are spent on the actors, photographers, models, advertising executives, copywriters, and everyone else who produces commercials and advertisements.

Our economy allocates a bunch of resources to advertising each year. Is this doing us any good? Would we be better off using those resources for something else? These are the questions that product-buying, television-watching pedestrians need to ask.

The greatest thing since sliced bread?

Before we jump into the bad of advertising, let's try to be optimistic. Let's look for

A PEDESTRIAN ...

... gets informed

SINCE I LOST THE REMOTE, I GET MORE INFORMATION THAN I REALLY WANT!

ON SALE!!!

NEW AND IMPROVED!!

BUY NOW! AT YOUR DEALER

O M Amos

the good. There really is some good. For example:

- *Advertising works.* Businesses advertise because it increases the demand for their products. Fleet Feet Footwear would sell fewer jogging shoes if no one knew Fleet Feet Footwear made jogging shoes. Advertising helps get the word out. I'd say that this is pretty good for business.

Advertising has benefits, though, that go beyond business profits:

- *Advertising helps efficiency.* Recall from Fact #6, Our Unknown Economy, that information is essential for efficiency. When businesses advertise information about product availability and prices,

overworked, underappreciated consumers, like you and me, have a better chance of buying the products that we really want.

- *Advertising finances goods.* Without advertising, our economy might lose some stuff that we enjoy, including television, sporting events, newspapers, and magazines, that are near-public goods. In fact, advertising can be thought of as a tax handled by businesses rather than by the government. Much as the government collects taxes to pay for public goods, businesses charge a little extra for the stuff they sell, which is then used for advertising. Without some sort of indirect financing, advertising or taxes, these goods might not be produced. Consider this thought: Television entertainers, newsguys, even athletes, get the lion's share of their multigadzillion dollar salaries indirectly from advertising.

To a lesser degree, advertising is sort of good because:

- *Advertising is a source of entertainment.* When you get down to the nitty-gritty, television commercials and other advertisement can be quite entertaining. How many times have you dozed off through a less-than-enjoyable television show, only to wake up for a clever commercial?

Or the slimy underbelly of our economy?

Everything in advertising land is not necessarily brighter and whiter. Advertising has a few chinks in its armor that make critics recommend an aerial bombardment of Madison Avenue. For example:

- *Advertising is wasteful.* Gadzillions of dollars are spent each year on advertising that may do little more than offset the effect of other advertising. Pepsi advertises to prevent Coke from getting a larger share of the market. Neither company actually sells more soft drink; they advertise to keep from selling less. If both stopped advertising, they would cut their expenses and free up our economy's resources for something more useful.
- *Advertising restricts competition.* As we saw in Fact #4, Our Monopolized Markets, markets with a large number of competitors tend to be more efficient. Advertising cost can prevent new firms from entering into a market. While advertising has made Coke and Pepsi household names, who would even consider buying a new entry called Tasty-Cola? To achieve equal footing with the well-known Coke and Pepsi, Tasty-Cola would need to do some heavy—and very, very expensive—advertising.
- *Advertising is brainwashing, maybe.* Psychologists and others who spend their days dissecting our brains suspect that advertising might exert undue influence over our behavior. For example, suppose a commercial for Hot Mamma Fudge Ice Cream Bananarama Sundae appears on your television screen at 9:00 in the evening as you're preparing for bed. By 9:15 you're at the Hot Mamma Fudge Ice Cream Parlor ordering a Bananarama Sundae. Is this coincidence? Were you really wanting a sundae, but just didn't know where you could get one at this late hour? Or were you unduly influenced by the commercial? The jury of brain dissectors is still out on this one, but the possibility is real enough to consider.

A one-sided story

A word or two (really five) about the control of information through advertising is in order.

1. From Fact #6, Our Unknown Economy, we know information is a scarce good that's costly to acquire. As such, those with greater control of our economy's resources also have greater control over information—including advertising. If you're keeping track, business leaders of the second estate and government leaders of the first are the ones controlling most of the resources and thus information. Very few workers, consumers, and taxpayers of the third estate have this luxury.

2. Advertising contains only information that advertisers want known: It's a one-sided story. For example, OmniCut will advertise durability and cutting power of it's OmniChopper 3000 lawnmower, but not that it tends to back up over the operator's foot—separating said operator from some valuable toes.

3. Advertising contains the other side of the story only if forced to do so by the government. Much like cigarettes contain warning labels, the government could force the OmniCut, Inc., to warn potential buyers about the Omni-

Chopper 3000's propensity to chop more than grass.

4. Sometimes government works for consumers and sometimes it works together with businesses. When the first and the second estate get together, then you had better kiss you toes good-bye.

5. Consumers can be saved if the fourth estate of journalism rides to the rescue, uncovering nefarious deeds of cooperation by government and business. This, unfortunately, assumes that the fourth estate remains independent of the first and second.

The bottom line on one-sided advertising can be summed up by a few tips for wary consumers:

ADVERTISING TIPS FOR THE WARY CONSUMER

- There's little doubt that some businesses use advertising for short-run, trick-the-consumer profits. Many others, though, go for long-term customer loyalty that can only be had from honest, informative advertising. When you find this valuable information, use it to reduce your search efforts.

- However, you should never lose sight of the fact that advertisers want to sell you something: a product, a political candidate, a religious ideology, or whatever. They provide only one side of the story—the good side. Their flashy commercials, catchy slogans, and witty jingles won't advertise the bad.

- Take all advertising claims with a large, very large, grain of salt. When it comes to advertising, "Don't believe everything that you see and hear." And "If it sounds too good to be true," it probably is.

See also: Business, Investment, Education, Political Views, Product Safety, Pollution, and Regulation.

those astronomical
ATHLETE SALARIES

 *It's a great day to take in a ball game, don't you think? With our hustling, bustling jaunt through the economy, we probably deserve a relaxing afternoon of hot dogs and peanuts with my favorite baseball team, the Shady Valley Primadonnas. Of course, the hot dogs and peanuts are overpriced, and you might need a second mortgage on your house to buy the ticket, but the expense is worth watching the finest athletes in the world display their world-class athletic abilities. We might even coax an autograph from the Primadonnas all-star centerfielder, Harold "Hair Doo" Dueterman.*

Are these guys worth it?

While we thoroughly enjoy the game—the Primadonnas come from behind to win in the bottom of the ninth—our favorite player, Hair Doo, strikes out four times and commits an error in centerfield. This raises a really, *really* important question in the grand scheme of the universe: Is Hair Doo worth his $10 gadzillion salary? Should Hair Doo get 100 times the salary of an average, overworked, underappreciated member of the third estate?

Hair Doo's salary really raises another more general question: Why does anyone get paid what they get paid? Any questions we ask about Hair Doo Dueterman's salary could also be asked about the wage of any average, overworked, underappreciated member of the third estate; Hair Doo's numbers just happen to be bigger. Because wages and salaries are nothing more than

prices, the best place to look for answers is the *market*.

If you're randomly thumbing through this guide, you might want to thumb carefully through Fact #2, Our Subjective Values, and Fact #4, Our Monopolized Markets. Both deal with markets and give you a good basis for looking into this earth-shattering question of highly paid athletes.

The market says: yes!

Let's first ponder the *supply*-side of the market. Hair Doo performs his athletic prowess before thousands of adoring fans—supplies his labor—because he's willing and able to take on his designated duties for a mere $10 gadzillion. If Hair Doo weren't willing and able to play baseball for $10 gadzillion, then he would do something else.

Hair Doo's willingness and ability to play our nation's past-time depends on his *opportunity cost* of other activities, such as deep-sea diving, coal mining, ballet dancing, or game show hosting. By selecting baseball, Hair Doo has given up a paycheck plus any other job-related satisfaction that could have been had from those pursuits. He's decided that his $10 gadzillion salary and the nonmonetary enjoyment of playing baseball outweigh his next best alternative. We should have little problem with this decision by Hair Doo, because we all make a similar choice. We pursue a job or career that gives us the most benefits.

But . . . (this is a good place for a dramatic pause) *someone* also must be willing to pay Hair Doo Dueterman $10 gadzillion to do what he does so well. This is the *demand*-side of the process that we affectionately call the "market," and it deserves a little more thought.

The someone who's willing to pay Hair Doo's enormous salary, the guy who signs Hair Doo's paycheck, is the owner of the Shady Valley Primadonnas, D. J. Goodluck. You might remember D. J.'s grandfather from Fact #3, Our Unfair Lives, a wheat farmer on the Kansas Plains who had the good fortune homesteading 160 acres with a *big* pool of crude oil beneath.

Why on earth would D. J. and his Shady Valley Primadonnas baseball organization pay Hair Doo this astronomical $10 gadzillion salary? D. J. must have a pretty good reason. Let's consider D. J.'s position.

Hair Doo's statistics are pretty impressive. In the past 5 years he's led the league in umpire arguments, souvenir foul balls for adoring fans, product endorsements for nonbaseball-related items, and instigator of bench-clearing fights. All of these have made Hair Doo an all-star, number-1, fan attraction.

While Hair Doo may or may not help the Shady Valley Primadonnas win the championship, he *does pack fans into the stands*. And he's packed fans into the stands for the past 5 years.

"Fans in the stands" translates into tickets for the Shady Valley Primadonnas, national television broadcasts, and revenue for D. J. Goodluck. D. J. is willing to pay Hair Doo $10 gadzillion to perform his daring-do because Hair Doo's daring-do generates at least $10 gadzillion in revenue for the team. If Hair Doo failed to generate revenue equal to or greater than his $10 gadzillion salary, then D. J. would trade him to the Oak Town Sludge Puppies (the perennial last-place, cellar dwellers in the league), send him to the minor leagues, or just release him from the team.

The bottom line on Hair Doo's salary is the same for any average, overworked, underappreciated member of the third estate: *An employer is willing and able to pay a wage up to the employee's contribution to production.* If your job is making $20 worth of Hot Mamma Fudge Bananarama Sundae's each day, then your boss, Hot Mamma Fudge, would be willing to pay you $20 a day.

Many are worth even more

As entertainers, athletes are paid for fan satisfaction. The more fans who want to see an athlete perform, the more an athlete is paid. In fact, most athletes, even those who make gadzillions of dollars for each flubbed fly ball, dropped pass, and missed free throw, probably deserve even higher salaries. The reason is *competition.*

As we discovered in Fact #4, Our Monopolized Markets, the degree of competition on each side of the market can make the price too high or too low. If suppliers have little or no competition, then the price tends to be too high. If buyers have little or no competition, then the price tends to be too low.

In the market for athletes, competition is usually less on the demand side than on the supply side. The supply of athletes tends to be pretty darn competitive. Of course,

Hair Doo is an all-star player, but he faces competition from hundreds of others who can argue with umpires and hit foul balls into the stands.

The demand side, however, is less competitive. In most cases, a particular team, like the Shady Valley Primadonnas, has exclusive rights to a player. They can trade those rights to another team, like the Oak Town Sludge Puppies, but the two teams usually don't compete with each other for a player's services. There are a few circumstances—one example is "free agency"—where two or more teams try to hire the same player, but that's the exception rather than the rule.

With little competition among buyers, the price tends to be on the low side. This means that Hair Doo Dueterman's $10 gadzillion salary could be even higher. It means that the Shady Valley Primadonnas probably get more, much more, than $10 gadzillion from ticket sales and television revenue. It means that D. J. Goodluck would probably be willing and able to pay more, much more, than $10 gadzillion for Hair Doo Dueterman's athletic services. The only way to find out how much Hair Doo is worth to the Shady Valley Primadonnas is to force them to compete for Hair Doo's services with other teams.

This is a good place to insert a little note on the three estates. Most owners of professional sports teams, almost by definition if not by heritage, tend to be full-fledged members of the second estate. The players, in contrast, usually spring from the ranks of the third. The idea that one team owns the "rights" of a player stems from the perverse, although changing, notion that the third estate exists for little reason other than to provide second-class servants for the first two estates.

Colleges are worse

If professional athletes who get gadzillions of dollars to do their daring-do are underpaid, how do college athlete's, who get almost nothing, compare? It depends on the sport.

Big-time college sports, especially football and basketball, are highly profitable entertainment industries. Millions of spectators spend tons of money each year for entertainment provided by their favorite college teams. Star college athletes can pack the fans into the stands as well as star professional athletes. With packed stands come overflowing bank accounts for the colleges.

What do the athletes get out of this? What are their "salaries?" Being amateurs, college athletes aren't paid an "official" salary. They are, however, compensated for their efforts with a college education, including tuition, books, living accommodations, and a small monthly stipend. While a college education isn't small potatoes— $100,000 plus at many places—this compensation tends to fall far short of the revenue generated for the school. The bottom line is that big-time college athletes, like the pros, are usually underpaid.

The reason is very similar to that of the professional athletes. College athletics has limited competition among the "employers" but a great deal of competition among the "employees." Many more high school athletes hope to play big-time college ball, than ever realize that dream. And while different colleges may try to hire—oops, I mean recruit—the same athlete, the collegiate governing bodies—most notably the National Collegiate Athletic Association—limit the degree of competition and fix the "wage" athletes can receive. You often hear about the NCAA penalizing a college because it went "too far" in its recruiting efforts. This means that the college paid an athlete "too" much to play, such as new cars, bogus summer jobs with high wages, and cash payments from alumni.

Underpayment is most often a problem for big-time football and basketball revenue-generating sports. Athletes in sports with less spectator interest—such as tennis, gymnastics, or lacrosse—actually may be over-paid based on their contribution to their colleges' entertainment revenue.

Here's a tip to keep in mind in the high-priced world of athletics:

A CONSUMING TIP ON ATHLETE SALARIES

• Athletes are paid based on their contribution to fan satisfaction. If you think ath-letes are paid too much, then don't contribute to their salaries by attending games or watching them on television. If, however, you enjoy their daring-do, and are willing to pay the price of admission, then worry not about their pay.

See also: Business, Education, Profit, Unions, Wealth, and Working Women.

BUSINESS
as usual

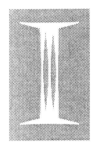*n the same mini-mall with Dr. Nova Cain's dental offices and Smilin' Ted's All Comers Insurance Agency resides Manny Mustard's House of Sandwiches, one of those small, out-of-the-way, off-the-wall sorts of restaurants that has great food, excellent service, and plenty of atmosphere. Manny, the proprietor, is a good friend of mine who's struggling to turn his dream of restauranteering into reality. His restauranteering dream doesn't stop with one small, out-of-the-way, off-the-wall restaurant with great food, excellent service, and atmosphere. No, Manny is shooting for a nationwide chain of Manny Mustard's House of Sandwiches. He wants to go from being an overworked, underappreciated member of the third estate to a member of the second estate who overworks and underappreciates others. To help out my good friend Manny, let's take a long, hard look at the differences between small business and the larger, Fortune 500 kind.*

All business is not created equal

Let's start with the basics. In our economy, the primary task of business, is to produce stuff. They combine *natural resources, labor,* and *capital* in such a way that the goods coming out the front door are more highly valued by consumers than the stuff that goes in the back door. Of course, businesses aren't the only ones to produce consumer-satisfying goods. This enormous task also falls onto the shoulders of government, as it's produce assorted public goods. Consumers are prone to do a lot of production themselves, such as preparing meals, washing clothes, painting houses, and the like. Businesses, though, do it as their, well, as their business. We consumers of the third estate are willing to pay businesses to produce and supply consumer-satisfying stuff.

If we had a century or two, we might be able to list the wide assortment of goods and services that result when businesses do their production thing. However, because we don't, let's just note that they produce a wide, and I mean extremely wide, assortment. Businesses also require a wide, and I mean extremely wide, assortment of different production techniques to produce their goods and services.

For example, some businesses, like those that generate electricity, need a lot of capital, machinery, tools, and equipment, but not much labor. Other businesses, like home construction, use significantly less capital (oh sure, they need their hammers and saws) but relatively more labor.

A PEDESTRIAN...

... does business

When we throw these observations together, stir gently, then warm over a low fire, we come to the conclusion that business firms come in a wide, and I mean extremely wide, assortment of sizes. Some are very, *very,* Very small, while others are humongously large.

Within this variety, though, we also find two sorts of business that can best be classified as *big business* (the big boys) and *small business* (the little guys). While about half of our economy's pie is produced by a small number of large companies like Omni Conglomerate, Inc., the other half is produced by a bunch of small businesses like Manny Mustard's House of Sandwiches.

As a consumer, you probably buy the same amount of stuff from the little guys as you do from the big boys.

My good friend Manny Mustard is one of the little guys who runs a restaurant. His problems are only beginning, though, because the megalith of conglomerate corporations, Omni Conglomerate, Inc., is set for a grand opening of another one of it's OmniSandwich Villa restaurants. This one is across the parking lot from Manny Mustard's House of Sandwiches. It looks as though we're in for one of those David and Goliath confrontations. Let's see why my money is being bet on the Omni Conglomerate Goliath.

Taking stock of ownership

A business, like Manny Mustard's House of Sandwiches, has a choice between one of three methods of organization: proprietorship, partnership, and corporation.

- *Proprietorships.* A whole bunch of businesses—that is, the producers and suppliers of our economy's output—are owned and operated by one person, a proprietor. Any afternoon-pedestrian-stroll around our economy is likely to turn up dozens of proprietors in areas like retail stores, farming, and home repair services. The important thing is that a proprietor makes all decisions, takes all risks, and gets all rewards. In particular, a proprietor has what the legal types refer to as "unlimited liability." That means there really is no difference between the business and the person running the business. For example, if you slip on the sidewalk in front of Manny Mustard's House of Sandwiches, then Manny Mustard is responsible for any and all damages. Manny's personal belongings, in addition to business assets, can be confiscated to pay the damages resulting from a lost lawsuit.

- *Partnerships.* The only real difference between a proprietorship and a partnership is the number of owners. A partnership has two or more owners, while a proprietorship has one. Everything else, though, is pretty much the same. The partners share the decisions, risks, and rewards. That nasty legal thing about unlimited liability also holds for partnerships. If Manny Mustard takes on a partner in his House of Sandwich—a guy by the name of Hopeless Harv, a descendent of our wheat farmer from Fact #3—then both partners are responsible for any civil damages. Manny Mustard could lose his personal possessions even if a lawsuit resulted from some horrific act on the part of Hopeless Harv.

A really big problem with proprietorships and partnerships is their size. A pro-

prietorship is only as large as the amount of wealth one person can accumulate. Partnerships can be bigger in that several people pool their wealth. But the unlimited liability thing has always meant that you really, *really*, Really need to trust your partners.

- *Corporations.* That's where corporations enter into the grand scheme of economic life. The most important thing about corporations is that they're considered legal entities by the government, meaning they are separate and distinct from the people who own or run them. This also means that the owners have what is legally deemed "limited liability." Unlike proprietorships and partnerships, the owners of corporations are only liable for the amount of their investment—no more. This lets a corporation acquire a lot of funds by getting a little bit from a lot of different people. In fact, for good or bad, the gargantuan companies like Omni Conglomerate, Inc., could not produce the vast array of goods that are part of our industrialized lifestyles if they were not corporations.

As a general rule, small businesses tend to be proprietorships or partnerships, while big businesses tend to fall under the heading of corporation. This doesn't mean that Manny Mustard will become a huge megalith like Omni Conglomerate simply by changing from a proprietorship to a corporation. It only means that his House of Sandwiches is unlikely to find its way on the Fortune 500 list as a proprietorship.

Organization, though, is only the beginning of what separates the big boys from the little guys. Read on.

Competing like the big boys

Let's consider some notable and not so notable differences between big businesses and smaller ones.

- *Competition.* Big companies compete in a different way from smaller ones. For example, when Omni Conglomerate talks about competition, it's concerned about the actions of its chief rival in all sorts of conglomerate-type business: Mega Industries. Omni is always keeping a close eye on Mega Industries. The reverse is also true. Both companies know that they can sell their products, make a profit, and be successful if they satisfactorily best the other. This is much like a foot race, where it matters very little how fast you run as long as you run faster than your competition. So much the better if your competitors happen to trip. A small business, like Manny Mustard's, doesn't have just one or two competitors; he has dozens, or even hundreds. Manny can't worry about each and every competitor. He's better off just doing the best darn job of sandwich production that he can.

- *Market control.* The size of a business and number of competitors translates into market control, the ability to control or substantially influence the market price. The big boys usually have this control; the little guys don't. The control applies to the stuff sold as well as the raw materials, intermediate goods, and even labor that's bought. Manny Mustard, for example, has very little say over the prices he charges for his sandwiches. He needs to charge about the same price as everyone else. Nor does he have much control over the prices he pays for mustard, bread, and other essential ingredients: Take it or leave it. This isn't the case for Omni Conglomerate, Inc. For example, its OmniMotors division ultimately faces one-on-one negotiation with each person buying an XL GT 9000 sports coupe. Likewise, OmniMotors negotiates prices with the tire company, steel company, labor union, and other input suppliers.

- *Cooperation.* The best way to know when a small business has become one of the big boys is the inclination to cooperate with the competition. The thought of trying to organize some sort of cooperative pricing with all 5,000-plus restaurants in Shady Valley probably never crossed

Manny Mustard's mind. Even if it did, it would be hard to accomplish. However, Winston Smythe Kennsington III, the CEO of Omni Conglomerate, Inc., has probably considered cooperating with Mega Industries more than once—each day, every day. It would be relatively easy for Omni and Mega to cooperate, raise prices, cut production, and do all sorts of other things that would create more profits for both. More than likely the only thing keeping them from actually cooperating is the fact that it's illegal, because of antitrust laws. Many of the big boys have tried the cooperation route; some have succeeded, most have been caught.

- *Political power.* The journey from market control to political power is a very short one. This road has been extensively traveled by most of the nation's big businesses on a regular basis. Big businesses have a great deal more control over resources, production, and wealth than smaller ones. Even in a democracy such as the one we have in the good old U.S. of A., wealth is power. The big boys have the wealth and power, and they're not afraid to use it to increase their market control, often through the political system, by smothering politicians with campaign money that's bound to produce helpful laws, subsidies, or restrictions on competitors.

- *Risk.* The last difference between the big boys and the little guys is risk. Small businesses, more so than their bigger counterparts, are subject to the uncertainty of the future. Small businesses are usually on the verge of bankruptcy every morning of every working day. All it takes to slip over the edge is a tax miscalculation, a disgruntled customer (one who knows a good lawyer), or an unfavorable government regulation. In fact, most small businesses close their doors within a few years after starting. In contrast, most of the big ones, like Omni Conglomerate, are so big and well known that they have to really, *really,* Really screw up before they lose enough sales to go bankrupt.

The second and third estates

Let's close this entry by clearing up a potential misconception. Our pedestrian's trek through the economy has sent, and will continue to send, signals warning consumers about the perils of the high-powered leaders of the second estate. These warnings, though, don't apply to all businesses. If the lack of control over the things that affect a small business sounds like the plight of hardworking, underappreciated, taxpaying consumers of the third estate, it should. That's because small businesses are very much a part of the third estate. The blue-blooded, certified, card-carrying members of the second estate are the ones who populate the corporate board rooms and upper management positions of our nation's big businesses.

The battle between Manny Mustard's House of Sandwiches and Omni Conglomerate's OmniSandwich Villa is on. I'm pulling for my long-time friend Manny, but the prospects aren't good. Omni has the resources, negotiating power, and political connections to squash Manny like a bug on the wall. I think I'll buy one of Manny Mustard's Deluxe Club Sandwiches. It may be my last chance.

See also: Advertising, Athlete Salaries, Investment, Political Views, Pollution, Profit, Product Safety, Regulation, Stock Market, Unions, Wealth, and Worker Safety.

charging up your
CREDIT CARDS
(aka plastic money)

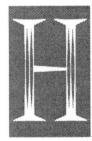*Here's the scene: You've made your monthly stop (for the second time this week) at the Mega-Mart Discount Warehouse Super Center for a few essentials: cashews, soap, licorice, garden hose, peanut clusters, color television, and a large inner tube for whitewater rafting. Do you pay with a check or whip out your Interstate OmniBank Platinum Diamond Express credit card? Credit card? Good choice. You don't actually have to pay for the stuff that you're buying—at least not right away. Your bank account is safe.*

The wonders of plastic money

Are credit cards one of the greatest inventions of humanity, or are they the devil's evil plot to suck our souls into eternal servitude? Perhaps a little of both. Let's consider the possibilities.

As you probably know, credit cards are those 2 1/8" by 3 3/8" pieces of plastic that every bank in the nation and many of our larger corporations beg you to get on a regular basis. If you're like most consumers, the mail brings at least one credit-card application each day.

While they've acquired the cute nickname "plastic money," they really aren't—money, that is. They actually represent a standing line of credit, or loan, from a bank or similar institution. The credit-card issuer has somehow determined that your credit is good enough that it's willing to lend you any amount up to a predeter-

mined credit limit. This arrangement certainly makes it easy to buy stuff—just like money—but it isn't money.

Here's why:

- Money is an asset, or something that you own.
- Credit cards, however, create a liability, or something that you owe.

When you make a purchase with money, you're trading one asset (money) for another asset (the stuff you buy). When you make a purchase with a credit card, you're creating a liability, or promise to repay a debt, in exchange for the stuff you buy. Eventually, however, you have to repay the loan by giving up an asset (money). A credit card does little more than let you postpone the inevitable payment. Credit cards fall into the same category as a car loan, mortgage, or home improvement loan, all of which have to be repaid at some point.

A PEDESTRIAN ...

... goes on vacation

AND I CHARGED IT ALL TO MY CREDIT CARD!

MAKE HIM GIVE BACK THE SUSHI

SIR! THE BANK'S ON THE PHONE! THEY'D LIKE THEIR MONEY **NOW!**

O M Ames

Credit cards, though, are widely used in our economy because they have a useful purpose. Sometimes, even the most prudent, thoughtful, budget-conscious consumer needs a quick loan. In fact, if you consider the assorted stuff that we buy with borrowed funds, you quickly realize that most of us could not enjoy our current living standards without borrowing. (More on this interesting topic can be found under Financial Markets.)

Preapproved, $10,000 credit limit; apply now!

Many banks are eager to issue credit cards to all comers. The reason is quite simple: That's what banks do. While you might have thought that banks were in the business to protect your life savings, this is only partly right. Banks offer protection for your savings, certainly, but they do so to get their hands on it. When they get it, however, they lend it to others. And they don't make loans out of the goodness of their hearts but in return for an interest payment.

Banks make a lot of different loans to businesses, consumers, foreign governments, and even other banks, but the loans they really like to make are to consumers in the form of credit cards. The reason is that credit card-interest rates tend to be relatively higher than other interest rates.

For example, suppose Interstate Omni-Bank makes a $100,000 loan at 5-percent interest for Mega-Mart Discount Warehouse Super Center to expand its auto parts department. Interstate OmniBank Platinum Diamond Express credit cards, in contrast, carries a 20-percent interest. You needn't reach for your pocket calculator to see $100,000 in OmniBank Platinum Diamond Express credit-card balances with 20-percent interest generates more revenue than a single $100,000 loan at 5-percent interest.

So, what's the deal with the high interest rates?

Credit-card interest rates tend to be among the highest interest rates in the economy for a couple of reasons. The first is risk. (A more thorough exposure to interest rates is found under the conveniently titled entry Interest Rates.)

- Any interest rate depends partly on what we can term a "basic interest" and a little extra that's tied to the riskiness of the loan. The basic interest rate is what a bank needs to make it worthwhile to lend. It includes a real interest rate, an inflation premium, and administrative expenses. Like any supplier, a bank needs to cover its costs and earn some profit.
- Some loans, however, have more risk than others. This risk occurs because banks stand a chance of losing revenue when loans aren't repaid. Credit cards are among the riskiest loans made by banks, and thus carry a big risk premium. Loans to larger businesses like Mega-Mart Discount Warehouse Super Center tend to be less risky and have a smaller risk premium.

Let's say Interstate OmniBank needs to receive a basic interest rate of 5 percent on a loan; when it lends $100,000 it needs to get back $105,000. Any lesser amount means that it can't pay its expenses, earn a profit, and stay in the business of being a bank. If it issues 100 credit cards at $1,000 a pop, and all credit-card balances are repaid, then Interstate OmniBank can charge 5-percent interest.

What would happen, however, if one credit-card holder charged the $1,000 maximum, then flew to the Cayman Islands without paying? The bank now has only 99 honest, paying credit-card holders with balances of $99,000. To remain in business, Interstate OmniBank needs to recoup enough interest from the other 99 card holders to cover the money lost from this one slimeball.

The interest charged on the 99 remaining $99,000 credit-card balances needs to be high enough to reach the banks required $105,000 total. The rate that achieves this goal is 6.06 percent; that is, 6.06 percent of $99,000 is $6,000. The 1.06 percent over and above the banks basic 5-percent rate is the risk premium. The risk premium is roughly 1 percent, because 1 percent of the credit-card holders left for the Cayman Islands without paying.

If two credit-card holders stiff Interstate OmniBank and head for the Cayman Islands, then the honest people are charged an interest rate of 7.1 percent. While this may seem unfair, it's necessary for the bank to stay in business.

Because a loan to Mega-Mart Discount Warehouse Super Center has less risk and is more likely to be repaid in full, it has a lower interest rate than OmniBank Platinum Diamond Express credit cards.

A little market control doesn't hurt

While risk explains some of the higher credit-card interest rates, it doesn't explain it all. Recall from Fact #4, Our Monopolized Markets, that the degree of competition helps determine price. Interest rates, like prices, depend on the degree of competition among borrowers and lenders.

- Competition among borrowers (card-holders) is relatively greater than it is among lenders (banks) in the market for credit cards. Even though there seems to be a gadzillion banks offering credit cards, there are a million gadzillion potential credit-card holders. Lenders, as such, have greater control over the interest rates than do the borrowers. The banks have little pressure to force them to reduce their interest rates. If one potential cardholder goes to another bank, a gadzillion others remain.

- Competition for business loans, such as that to Mega-Mart Discount Emporium, in contrast is not as great. There may be only a handful of businesses borrowing $100,000 from a handful of banks lending $100,000. In this case, a fair amount of negotiation is likely to take place. If Mega-Mart Discount Warehouse Super Center can't negotiate a satisfactorily low rate from OmniBank, then it will probably go to the Mammoth National Bank down the street.

CREDIT-CARD TIPS

- Consumers who want to keep the bank from nailing foreclosure notices on their front door should be aware that credit cards are *not* money. They are loans to be repaid. You should borrow with credit cards only if you can pay it back.
- Banks issue a lot of credit cards, some to

consumers who are a poor credit risk and won't be able to repay. This contributes to higher interest rates. All banks, however, are not equally willing to lend to deadbeats. The banks that are a little more careful in evaluating their potential customers also offer lower interest rates. Shop around.

- For this reason, be wary of "preapproved" credit-card applications received through the mail. Banks that use this shotgun approach hope to get enough paying customers to offset the deadbeats. But the paying customers often pay more. Try to go with a credit card that has the most paying customers you can determine. These cards impose a lower interest rate.
- And while you can't change the number of competitors in the market, and make credit-card borrowing more competitive, you can allow more competition into your own little part of the market. That is, don't confine yourself to selecting credit cards only from banks in your city or state. Let the banks throughout the country compete for your business. This will help keep interest rates lower for you and everyone else.

See also: Business, Gambling, Insurance, Investment, Mutual Funds, Profit, Stock Market, and Wealth.

stealing a few moments for
CRIME

*ike most consumers, workers, and taxpayers, I enter exchanges for a lot of stuff: food, labor, shelter, entertainment, and confectionery products. But as I wandered through the peaceful community of Shady Valley, U.S.A., I entered a "market" that I would have rather avoided. That's right, as the title indicates, I "exchanged" some crime. I was mugged—relieved of several valuable possessions—right in front of the Shady Valley police station. I did the selling, and my mugger did the "buying." While my part in the exchange was involuntary, the mugger's part was quite voluntary. In fact, the perpetrator of this crime acted pretty much like any consumer headed to Natural Ned's Nursery and Garden Center in search of a creeping juniper. Let's see why?*

Buying a little crime

To beautify the landscape surrounding your abode, you might consider purchasing a nice, decorative bit of shrubbery. Without getting too deeply into the neuro-pathways of your brain, let's consider this decision.

On the one hand, you think about the beautification factor: how much nicer your landscape will appear once you've planted and nourished your creeping juniper. You'll enjoy the beauty. Your neighbors will enjoy the beauty. Family and friends will enjoy the beauty. Even unknown passersby will get a glint of beauty when passing by. And let's not forget the few extra bucks you're likely to get if and when you choose to sell your more-beautified abode.

On the other hand, your pride, joy, and monetary remuneration must be compared to the price of the creeping juniper. Is a $16.95 price tag worth the myriad of ben-

efits to be had from this perennial plant? That's the question any prospective creeping–juniper planter must answer.

Weighing the cost on one hand with the benefits on the other is pretty darn fundamental to economics, the economy, market exchanges, our good old scarcity problem, and, well, when you get right down to it, life itself.

Crime is no different. The deed is done if the deed doer thinks that the benefit exceeds the cost. While we will focus our attention on the premeditated stuff (robbery, extortion, blackmail, illegal drug sales, gambling, prostitution, and similar nefarious exploits), I'm not sure we need to exclude "abnormal" or emotionally driven acts (kleptomania, sexual perversions, or one enraged spouse murdering another). Even in a fit of rage, the rager likely thinks that the benefit exceeds the cost.

A PEDESTRIAN...

... gets mugged

HAVE YOU REALLY CONSIDERED THE COST AND BENEFIT OF THIS CRIME?

YEAH! I CAN TURN A PROFIT IF YOU GOT FIVE BUCKS

OOPS!!

GIVE ME YOUR MICE!!

911! 911!

© M Ames

Adding the pluses and the minuses

Let's ponder the benefit and cost of crime.

- *Benefit*. The benefit is the easy part. For such acts as robbery you get possession of valuable stuff that can be used or sold for cold hard cash. The benefit of other crimes—especially those like gambling, prostitution, and drugs that have legal counterparts—should also be pretty obvious. "Buyers" (criminal types) expect some sort of satisfaction from the associated good or service.

- *Cost*. Unlike more traditional stuff traded through legal markets, the cost of crime is a little more involved. Of course, for many crimes you have a significant employment of scarce resource. After all, a bank doesn't rob itself, now does it? Given that crimes are illegal, there's also the potential punishment cost. A year spent in jail means a year that a criminal must forego the benefits from perpetrating other crimes, a clear example of *opportunity cost* if there ever was one. Of course, for some potential criminals, the opportunity cost is the more mundane loss of wages or income.

The cost side is particularly tricky because of our law enforcement and judicial systems. If you're a criminal, you don't really need to consider the *full* opportunity cost of being locked up, because you might not be apprehended and, if apprehended, you might not be convicted. A thoughtful criminal is likely to adjust the opportunity cost of jail time by the chance of being caught and convicted. A 5-percent chance of serving 10 years in jail is about the same as a 50-percent chance of serving 1 year in jail.

The bottom line for criminals is that crime is profitable. *If crime wasn't profitable, then it would cease to exist.*

The business of crime

Anything that's profitable will attract highly organized businesses. Crime is no different. It's not the exclusive domain of your run-of-the-mill mugger who's looking for a few extra bucks. Just like proprietorships exist alongside the likes of Mega-Mart Discount Warehouse Super Center and Omni Conglomerate, Inc., much of the crime we see today is perpetrated by highly structured, wide-ranging "business" organizations. A great deal of the illegal drug sales, prostitution, gambling, car thefts, and home burglaries are perpetrated by businesses that would list "crime" as their primary product on income tax returns—if they actually filed income tax returns.

What about morality?

This somewhat antiseptic view of crime, with a bunch of crooks sitting around their calculators and personal computers (all of which are stolen) crunching the numbers on the cost and benefit of their crimes, might be troublesome to some of you. You're concerned about morals, aren't you? How can we put crime into a cost-benefit computation when the *real* problem is our decadent society and lack of moral values? If only we would teach our kids the difference between right and wrong, then we wouldn't have any crime, right? Not necessarily.

Morality is a part of our calculation of the cost-benefit, but *only* part. Morals affect what we can call the "psychic benefit" of doing the "right" thing and the "psychic cost" of

doing the "wrong" thing. Morality, religious upbringing, the difference between right and wrong, can enter into a prospective criminal's benefit-cost consideration. For example, a prospective car thief might compare the value of a stolen car against a 10-percent chance of spending 10 years in jail *and the possibility of spending eternity in hell.*

To some potential crooks the cost of eternal damnation is too much to overcome. For others, it's not. But for all, it's only part of the equation. While a strong dose of morality might reduce crime, there will always be profit in criminal pursuit.

Cleaning up this crime-infested town

While stringent morals, knuckle-cracking nuns, and intensive religious training might reduce some crime, are there other options? Once more, let's consider the benefit and cost of crime.

First the benefit side:

- *Less valuable crime.* A number of programs that seek to reduce the value of stolen property have been tried with some success. For example, many stores have dye packets attached to clothing that do nothing more than stain the garments if not removed with special equipment. The logic is that no one will steal a shirt that's going to end up with a big stain. Other crimes, such as drug sales, could also reduced through the benefit side. Ironically, drugs are valuable largely because they're illegal. Making them legal would lower their prices and decrease drug dealer profits. Dealers would then redirect resources to something that's more profitable, maybe even legitimate production.

Second the cost side of crime:

- *Better enforcement.* More police, more stringent judges, and more prisons will increase the probability of a crook's being caught, convicted, and sent to jail. Unfortunately, the vast majority of crimes (probably around 95 percent) go unpunished. It's not clear how many more resources we would need before we get a significant increase in the probability of a crook's being punished. The specter of an extremely, big-brother-type, authoritarian society lurks large on the horizon before crime is reduced.

- *Higher incomes.* There is, however, another possibility. A big part of the cost is what convicted criminals give up while in prison. This cost is directly related to income, wealth, and standing in society. A bunch of crimes are perpetrated by poor people because they have very little to lose if caught and convicted. For many, prison life actually gives them a higher standard of living. Reducing poverty and increasing the income of potential criminals will go a long way to prevent crimes. Why steal a television when you already have two?

While the whole criminal arena is in the hands of the government, there are a few things that you can consider as a consumer:

TIPS FOR THE CRIME-AVOIDING CONSUMER

- It probably goes without saying that you should do your best to screw up crooks' cost-benefit calculations. Make it harder for them to steal your stuff, and do what you can to make the stolen stuff less valuable. Most communities have crime prevention programs that are worth a look.

- From a public-policy perspective, you should consider the alternatives that can reduce crime. Of course, there is your standard law-and-order (more police, stricter judges) option. But you should also consider some nontraditional avenues that educate, train, employ, or otherwise increase the incomes of potential criminals. Even such alternatives as legalizing illegal drugs might do the trick.

See also: Discrimination, Education, Gambling, Recession, Wealth, and Welfare.

what do you have against
DISCRIMINATION?

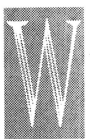

When a person ambles through the economy, hunger is, of course, an avoidable malady. At the present, I'm easily tempted by a hamburger, fries, and large cola—a pedestrian meal if there ever was one. As luck would have it, we've found ourselves at the door of Big Ott's Boiled Burger Buffet. Luck, though, is not totally on our side. Big Ott's has a large sign prominently posted at the entry to his establishment. It screams in no uncertain terms: No Pedestrians Allowed. As a well-known, card-carrying pedestrian, I am, to say the least, taken aback. Why on earth would Big Ott's Boiled Burger Buffet refuse service to pedestrians? A quick quiz of an employee reveals that Big Ott once swerved off the sidewalk to avoid striking a pedestrian, causing extensive damage to his sleek, new OmniMotors XL GT 9000 convertible sport coupe. His anger has since been extended to all who travel by foot.

Discriminating tastes

Big Ott's view is that he'll sell his boiled burgers to whomever he damn well pleases. And nobody, and that means nobody, will make him sell burgers to any foot-crazed pedestrian. While Big Ott isn't all that good at preparing burgers, he seems to have become quite proficient at *discrimination*.

So what is this discrimination and when do you know it's happening? Let's first think about the simplest, most general meaning of the word "discrimination." It's the process of distinguishing between things that are different. As such, if you decide that you like *Brace Brickhead, Medical Detective,* a hard-hitting dramatic television series, but aren't real crazy about *The Egotistical Comedian's Show,* a whimsical half-hour situation comedy, then you're discriminating.

These shows are different and you're astute enough to discern those differences.

That, however, is not the sort of discrimination that Big Ott likes to practice. He has decided to treat every member of a group (pedestrians) the same regardless of individual characteristics, personalities, or actions. Why he made this choice is a matter that we'll take up in a few paragraphs.

For the present, though, we need to note the abundantly obvious: All kinds of people discriminate (in the second sense of the word) against others in all kinds of ways. A few well-known and some lesser examples are in order:

- A black youth is refused a job because, well, black teenagers are basically no-good, gun-totting, drug-selling juvenile delinquents.

- A female junior executive is passed over for promotion to midlevel management in favor of a male, because men are the family providers and she'll probably just get pregnant and quit anyway.
- Everyone past the age of 65 should retire from the workforce to make way for more productive younger people.
- If you want good doctors, lawyers, or comedians, make sure they're Jewish.
- The four black basketball players never pass the ball to their sole white teammate because blacks have more athletic ability than whites.

These sorts of all-encompassing statements, criteria, and choices are the heart and soul of discrimination. For all we know, the black teenager is an honor student; the male is living with his parents, while the female is raising a family of six; the old guy is a Nobel Prize–winning scientist; the Jewish doctor, lawyer, and comedian are incompetent, crooked, and not really very funny; and the white basketball player is a five-time all-star and future member of the Hall of Fame.

Paying for prejudice

The bottom line on discrimination is the bottom line, at least for profit-seeking businesses. When a business like Big Ott's Boiled Burger Buffet refuses service to a class of potential customers, then profit suffers. Bit Ott has lost some sales that he would have had.

Discrimination against potential employees also hits a business's bottom line. When a company promotes an incompetent male jerk over a better-qualified female, then output suffers, and so does profit.

What is true for one business holds for our economy. Societywide discrimination against whole groups of people—be they black, Hispanic, women, elderly, or from a different planet—retards production, *efficiency,* and economic growth.

Why? Why? Why?

If discrimination is such a big problem, why do we do it? And make no mistake that we all do it, whether we know it or not. Discrimination is not something practiced only by "good old boys" in a backwoods southern state. As you'll see, some people are just a heck of a lot better at discrimination than others.

I'll give you my three favorite reasons for discrimination. Feel free to add your own.

1. *Genetic.* Over the past million or so years, our ancestors survived to reproduce because they had the genetic inclination to "fight or flight." We have, built into our physiological makeup, the ability to detect all sorts of threats to our well-being. The early members of our species who didn't have this ability didn't live long enough to reproduce and pass along this deficiency. So as we muddle through our daily lives we carry with us this genetic warning system that alerts us to anything new or different, such as someone with different skin tones. That means whites feel safer when they're around other whites, and blacks are similarly inclined with other blacks. The result is a white boss hires a white guy over an equally qualified black guy, often without the boss's even knowing *why* he feels more comfortable with the white guy.

2. *Information.* As we've seen in many places, information is scarce and costly to acquire. Information about groups of people, statistical averages, and the like are usually more readily available than detailed information about individuals. While groupwide statistical averages can provide useful information, they can also be exceedingly misleading. Let's take the all-too-familiar case of Natural Ned's Nursery and Garden Center. Over the years, Ned saw fit to hire 10 graduates of the Buford Busman Landscaping School for the Criminally Stupid. And every one of those ten graduates turned out to be lazy, worthless, incompetent, and prone toward stealing creeping junipers. Because of Ned's past experiences, he

has discarded, without a second thought, each and every application for employment from graduates of Buford Busman Landscaping School. Unfortunately for Ned, one application he discarded was that of Gerald Johanson, who went to work for the Green Thumb Plant-A-Rama. Because of Gerald's landscaping acumen, Green Thumb Plant-A-Rama eventually drove Natural Ned's Nursery and Garden Center out of business. Oh, the irony!

3. *Control.* Income, wealth, resources, and all of the stuff that make up our economic pie is unequally divided among members of society. That's an economic fact of life we will always have. The question, though, is what we do with our slices. For the most part we're inclined to protect it and perhaps try to enlarge it. Some groups are better able to pursue these goals because they control really, *really* large slices. While the goals could be achieved in different ways, one that often surfaces is discrimination. The one group that stands out in the good old U.S.A. is white males, especially those with a European ancestry. As a group they own a significantly large slice of the pie, which they tend to use to impose discriminatory restrictions on anyone who isn't a white male of European ancestry. In other words, the white male president of Omni Conglomerate, Inc., uses his position to promote other white males (who by chance happened to belong to the same college fraternity) to executive positions, while overlooking females, blacks, Hispanics, Asians, and pretty much everyone else. This perpetuates control by the "white, male club" over a large segment of the pie. (You might want to check into the entry on Political Views for more on this sort of thing.)

TIPS FOR THE DISCRIMINATING PEDESTRIAN

- Everyone has prejudices. It's altogether natural for each of us to feel threatened by those who are different. We are inclined to make first-impression judgments about people from very limited information. The big question, though, is whether or not we let those prejudices affect our decisions. Another huge question is whether or not the prejudices are justified.
- The only way to overcome the first point is through more information. If you're not a first-class bigot and really *want* to give everyone an equal opportunity, then you need to forego group stereotypes in favor of person-specific information.
- Now let's turn the tables a bit. In our modern days of political sensitivities to discrimination, some charges of discrimination may be unjustified. On occasion a white male actually *is* the best choice for promotion. You need to ask whether someone who cries discrimination is truly a victim or just a no-good, lazy bum, who's looking to place blame on others for his or her own deficiencies.

See also: Crime, Education, Unions, Worker Safety, and Working Women.

ECONOMIC
FORECASTING

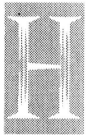

How often has this happened to you? You've packed a tasty picnic lunch, donned your spiffy-looking swimwear, loaded up the beach blanket and umbrella, then headed for the artificial waves of the local Happy-Time Gala-World Fun-Land Water Park expecting bright sunshine and warm temperatures. However, on reaching Happy-Time Water Park, you find that the economy has fallen into a deep recession, with high unemployment rates and sluggish production, and the owners of the Happy-Time Water Park have been forced to turn off the artificial wave machine, dismantle the water slides, and drain the pool. (It's also raining and 50 degrees. We will, however, ignore those problems because this book isn't "Meterological Literacy.")

If only you had known

A big problem for most of us, as we saw with Fact #6, Our Unknown Economy, is that the future is, well, unknown. If only you had known that the price of OmniTech stock was going to triple, that a pickup truck was going to run that stoplight as you passed through the intersection, or that your high school prom date was going to develop an allergic reaction to pine tar and pickled herring (no time for details, but it wasn't a pretty sight), then your life would be a whole lot better.

While it's pretty tough to predict allergies and drivers' actions, serious efforts have been made in the realm of forecasting economic events. For example, stockbrokers, speculators, and assorted investors spend a lot of time trying to predict stock prices for reasons that should be pretty obvious. (If

it's not obvious, check out Stock Markets.)

Less obvious may be the efforts of pointy-headed economists, statisticians, and others, lovingly referred to as "number crunchers," who try to forecast all sorts of economic stuff, such as inflation, unemployment, production, income, and interest rates. Unlike the local weather guys, you seldom hear their names, but their forecasts often surface in newspapers, magazines, and the nightly news. More importantly, their efforts are used behind the scenes to help government and business leaders of the first two estates make decisions that involve gadzillions of dollars.

Although decisions affected by future economic events that are made by members of the third estate don't climb into the gadzillion-dollar category, they can be pretty darn important. As such, it might be useful

... opens the wrong door

to know a little bit about this economic forecasting business.

Connecting the dots

Let's say that you've been given four numbers—2, 4, 6, 8—and you need to make a guess about the fifth. You don't need a room filled with high-speed, mega-capacity computers to come up with the number 10. All you have to do is "extrapolate the trend." Sometimes this is a pretty good way of making a forecast. If Master Sprocket's convenience store has two customers on Monday, four on Tuesday, six on Wednesday, and eight on Thursday, then there's a good chance that ten customers will show up on Friday.

It can also, however, be dangerous if you don't know *why* the numbers went from 2 to 4 to 6 to 8. Did the number of customers increase on each subsequent day because Master Sprocket's kept lowering the price on its quick-frozen seminutritious deli sandwich? Or perhaps Captain Car-Hop, a close competitor, was running out of an essential product like, let's say, gasoline, increasingly forcing its customers to seek out alternatives.

You gotta have a theory

- Did the inflation rate go up? Why? The money supply? Government spending?
- Did the economy's production pie

grow last year? Why? Technology? Labor? Capital?

• Did the interest rate decline? Why? The federal deficit? Consumer borrowing?

If forecasters can figure out why the economy went this way or that way *last year,* then they have a much better chance of guessing where it will go *next year.*

If the customer count at Master Sprocket's went from 2 to 4 to 6 to 8 because the price of quick-frozen seminutritious deli sandwiches went from $2.00 to $1.80 to $1.60 to $1.40, then we can make a pretty good guess about the number of customers on Friday, *if* we know the price of quick-frozen seminutritious deli sandwiches. A ten-customer forecast would be out of line if the price of quick-frozen seminutritious deli sandwiches jumps back to $2.

Life's a gamble

Economists and economic forecasters have developed some very elaborate theories over the past 200 years to improve their forecasts. They look at hundreds, even thousands, of different parts of the economy to see how everything fits together. But (and here's another one of those important *buts*), forecasters are only able to come up with educated guesses. They can never know *for certain* what will happen *before* the fact.

To illustrate why, let's say that you're flipping a two-headed coin. It should have a 100-percent chance of coming up heads, right? Not necessarily. It could come to rest on it's edge, fall through a crack in the floor, or be swallowed by a very, *very* large cockroach. If you predict that the coin will land heads up, then you have a pretty good chance of being right—but, *not* a 100-percent chance.

Unfortunately for those who make a living doing this forecasting thing, the economy is fraught with a great deal more uncertainty than a two-headed coin. If forecasters can get within 90 to 95 percent of being right, then they're pretty darned pleased with themselves.

Here are three reasons why you should con-

sider economic forecasts as educated guesses:

1. All sorts of unpredictable things like natural disasters, wars, and irrational government policies can screw up even the best economic forecasts.

2. Sometimes forecasters use bad theories. Politicians, in particular, tend to dredge up forecasters who use bad economic theories. Incumbent politicians, hoping to remain incumbent, try to get the most optimistic forecasts possible—whether or not they have any validity. Aspiring, nonincumbent politicians tend to uncover bad theories that give the most pessimistic forecasts, hoping that they can convince voters to see deficiencies, real or not, with the incumbent.

3. Errors, no matter how small, tend to multiply. Even if you're 99-percent certain that you can separately forecast ten different things like the interest rate, inflation, and unemployment, you can only be 90-percent certain of accurately forecasting all *ten* of them at once. In that the economy is complex and highly interactive, if forecasters miss on one tiny little item, then everything they forecast can be off the mark.

CAUTIONARY TIPS ON ECONOMIC FORECASTS

• Just because some government official or business leader with an impressive-sounding job title reports that production or interest rates are *expected* to go up or down doesn't make it so. All forecasts are guesses; some are just better than others.

• Forecasts are like any consumer good; shop around to find the best. This doesn't mean that you should run to the library every time a nightly newscaster reports on a recently released economic forecast. However, if you're considering a big decision, like changing careers, buying a house, or investing in the stock market, then look for several forecasts—your public library should have some. If you make a major decision based on a bad forecast, then you stand to lose your shirt or ruin your life.

- Along the same line, it wouldn't hurt to question the source of any publicized forecast. Of course, politicians are prone to play up forecasts that are most likely to help them achieve their political aspirations. Others can be just as guilty. If you're considering an investment in stocks, bonds, gold, silver, or any other financial market, be wary of forecasts supplied by brokers who earn a living from the transactions. They say the price is headed up, but they get their fee *when you invest* whether the price goes up or down.

See also: Economic Growth, Federal Deficit, Financial Markets, Gambling, Insurance, Interest Rates, Investment, Political Views, and Recession.

pumping up the
ECONOMIC GROWTH

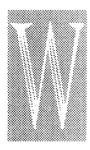

We need to pay another visit to Scarcity Stan's Ye Olde Bakery Shoppe and Confectionery Palace. But this is not a social visit, nor is it intended for some delectable pastries that will add a few extra pounds to our waistlines. We're here on official economic business. Stan's at wits' end. He doesn't know what to do. There's been so much demand for his economic pie, what with society's unlimited wants and needs, that he needs to make it bigger. Our job is to figure out how. While we're doing that, we'll also see how to put our economy on the path to economic growth.

The answer is Q and Q

As we saw with Fact #1, Our Limited Pie, the only way to increase the size of our pie is to increase the quantity or quality of our *resources*. The more resources we have, or the more productive are those resources, then the larger is our economic pie. The growth of our economy—"economic growth" for those of you making note of the official terms—thus depends on how much or how rapidly we increase the quantity and/or quality of our resources.

Okay, that's the simple answer for Scarcity Stan and our economic pie. Let's now get into some details, the old nitty-gritty of economic growth, for each of our basic resources: natural resources, labor, and capital.

- *Natural resources.* In that natural resources are by definition natural, there's not a whole lot we can do to improve the *quality* of natural resources. Increasing

the *quantity* of our natural resources, however, is a pretty straightforward road to take. We find more resources through exploration. Yet, because we've already populated six of the planet's seven continents, we're beginning to run out of places to explore. Of course, there's the ocean, and perhaps we'll eventually begin using the resources of the moon and other planets. But for now, most quantity increases in natural resources are centered on the *technology* used to find and extract the stuff. We use more sophisticated detection equipment and dig deeper with bigger shovels.

- *Labor.* The *quantity* side of labor is also pretty simple: Get more people working. The size of the population, and ultimately the number of workers, can be increased through births or *immigration* from other countries (see Immigration). For obvious reasons the birth route takes a little more time, but both work in the long run. We can also increase the fraction of the population that's selling the labor services. The *quality* side of labor is probably more important for our economy than the quantity. Labor quality is enhanced through *human capital,* especially *education,* training, and experience.

- *Capital.* We can increase the *quantity* of capital by, well, getting more capital. This, however, means that the resources used to make capital can't be used to make other goods that provide immediate consumer satisfaction. Of course, this is our old friend *investment.* The *quality* of capital is increased through *technology* improvements that let capital produce more output using fewer resources. Research, scientific advances, and engineering breakthroughs are all methods of improving technology and the quality of capital.

You might have detected two common threads running through these three resource categories. One is *investment.* The other is *technology.* The best way to increase the quantity or quality of our resources is through some form of investment, either in the actual number of resources or in the technology behind those resources. That is, we give up some consumer-satisfying goods today in order to increase the quantity or quality of our resources in the future and thus the ability of producing even more consumer-satisfying goods tomorrow.

While assorted types of investment can be important, perhaps the most important is technology. Technology—our knowledge of how best to transform natural resources into consumer-satisfying goods—is a valuable use of investment efforts. Whether we're talking about getting a college education, teaching a new employee how to run a cash register, doing scientific research on farm pest control, or developing a high-speed forklift, these investments divert resources away from other production. A bunch of economists have concluded that most of the growth of the U.S.A. over the past 200 years has been from technological advances that have improved the quality of our resources. Therein lies future growth as well.

Growth is good, right?

Expanding our economy's ability to produce consumer-satisfying stuff does a lot of good. When we think about that ever-present problem of *scarcity,* growth gives us more stuff that satisfies more wants and needs. This is good. This is an important purpose of our lives. This is the whole reason for our economy's existence. How can growth be bad?

Well . . .

Like most things, especially in the economy, there is good and there is bad. Increasing the quantity and quality of our resources and expanding the size of the economic pie are not without cost. We've already noted that expanding the pie requires investment and giving up current consumption. There are other costs, other problems, that we should also note:

- *Resource depletion.* The blue-green planet we call Earth came with a limited amount of natural resources, the materials used to satisfy our needs. The more we produce and the more our economy grows, then the less we have left for the future. While we're still doing okay at the moment, eventually we'll either have to find more resources (the moon?) or kick our nasty habit of satisfying wants and needs.
- *Pollution.* Not only do we use natural resources to satisfy our needs, when we're through with them, we send it *all* back to the environment as *pollution.* In fact, every ounce, every gram, every molecule of material we take out of the environment will eventually go back, often as pollution. The more we produce and grow, the more pollution we'll have. (For details on this, see Pollution.)
- *Job displacement.* Technology, the guid-

ing light of economic growth, also causes a restructuring of the economy. Workers employed at one job for 20 years may find that job eliminated by new and improved technology. What do we do with a 50-year-old who's too young to retire, but too old to retrain?

- *Cultural change.* Along with changes in the workplace, economic growth causes changes throughout society. The old ways, the old customs, the old culture, may become seriously outdated with new technologically advanced ways of doing things. This causes a loss of satisfaction for those who grew up enjoying the old ways.

Okay, so what is best to consider in terms of this economic growth stuff?

ECONOMIC GROWTH TIPS FOR THE WISE AND WARY

- Don't be left behind by economic growth. When the economy grows, it usually does so unevenly. Some cities, regions, and industries grow more than others. Keep an eye out for those industries and locations that are doing best.
- Do your part to stay on the growth bandwagon. Invest in *your* personal economic growth by expanding the quantity and quality of *your* resources. In addition to helping the economy's pie expand, it will also increase your bank account.
- Be wary of short-run government policies that adversely affect long-run growth. Sure, there are a lot of bad things that happen in recessions, but let's not cut off our leg to avoid the hurt of a stubbed toe.
- While short-run sacrifices are needed for long-run growth, we don't want too much sacrifice. All work and no play, all capital and no consumption, isn't good for the economy. If you invest every penny of your paycheck in the stock market, then you'll die of starvation after a paycheck or two.

See also: Economic Forecasting, Education, Federal Deficit, Inflation, Investment, Political Views, Recession, Stock Market, and Wealth.

learning all about
EDUCATION

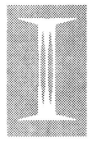

It's a bright spring morning, the sort of day that makes poets and pedestrians pontificate profusely about our wondrous world. But, wait. . . It's a test day! You're late for an exam! You hurriedly roam the school halls, opening door after endless door along an infinite hallway, in search of your exam. All you discover, though, is Maurice Finklestein who smirks knowingly while ridiculing your tardiness. Why do we do it? Why do we put ourselves through 12 to 20 years of oppression in the halls of academia, learning stuff of questionable value? Why? Why? WHY?

An unquenchable thirst?

For some, education is a means of seeking answers to the great questions of life, such as those that deal with our existence, the creation of the universe, and what happens to socks lost in the dryer. This view of education places it in the same category as eating, drinking, and sleeping, all of which fulfill a few of our unlimited wants and needs.

There's something to be said about this view. Most of us have a "need to know" that motivates us to buy newspapers, watch the news, read books, dismantle a perfectly good clock, or ask about the latest gossip on family and friends. When education aligns itself with this need to know, we can best think of it as a consumption good. As you might buy a sardine pizza, a pair of bikini underwear, or a spiffy OmniMotors XL GT 9000 sports coupe just for the satisfaction, so too you might spend 4 months

in a college course learning about insects indigenous to the mountains of Northwest Queoldiola. Ahh, the pleasure of it all!

But, of course, there's more to education. With the exception of a few bespectacled scholars, most people voluntarily pursue an education because it improves their job prospects and ultimately their incomes. "To get a good job, get a good education." This falls under the favorite topic of many economists—human capital.

The steel and bricks of human capital

Human capital includes the skills and knowledge that make labor more productive. We've used the term "capital" in many places throughout this guide when concerned with factories, buildings, equipment, machinery and the like. The really nifty thing about capital is that it makes labor more productive. While a carpenter *might* be able to build a house with nothing but a pair of

A PEDESTRIAN ...

. . . goes to school

Aa Bb Ee F

MAY I BE EXCUSED MRS. GOOBERMANN? I'M LATE FOR WORK!

$\begin{array}{r} 1 \\ +1 \\ \hline 2 \end{array}$

Welcome to Mrs. Goobermann's First Grade Class

THE SHOE GUY

O M Amos

bare—albeit really strong—hands, it's a heck of a lot easier with a hammer, table saw, electric drill, and a truck or two to deliver materials. Likewise, a carpenter's job is a heck of a lot easier if the carpenter *knows* how to build a house.

As *regular* capital makes workers more productive, so too does *human* capital. While there are a bunch of different ways that you and I can get the knowledge and skills of human capital, there are three that really stand out:

1. *Experience.* Just doing stuff on your own as you learn by trial and error, repetition, and practice is a pretty good way to increase your stockpile of human capital. For example, a good

carpenter might know that nailing a 2-by-4 in a certain way works best because walls, roofs, ceilings, and floors keep falling apart if done differently. Experience is a good teacher.

2. *Training.* On some occasions it helps to be guided through the maze of learning by someone who's already been through it. Training is when someone who knows the ropes shows you the best ways to do stuff, like a wise and woolly master carpenter who instructs an eager young apprentice how best to nail together two pieces of walnut.

3. *Education.* The last of these three can best be thought of as a formal, classroom education, including elementary school,

high school, and college. The key here is that you usually learn more than just the "how to" of something. There's also a lot of the "why" and "so what."

The big payoff

The reason for human capital—especially for those who have been subjected to 12 years of public school and extra years of college—is extra work productivity. And (here's a really important "and"); with extra productivity comes extra income. We seek human capital for the same reason that businesses invest in physical capital: the return, the big bucks, the burgeoning bank accounts.

Here are a few numbers to ponder. A high school diploma will give you $6,000 to $7,000 more than an eighth-grade education. Salaries for college graduates are an average of $3,000 to $5,000 more a year than with a high school degree. The icing on the cake is that advanced degrees (masters and doctorates) tend to give you $10,000 to $15,000 more than a bachelor's degree.

These numbers, of course, are only averages. Actual differences depend on the sort of human capital acquired with the differing education levels. Your bachelor's degree in a high-paid occupation like accounting might give you more income than someone with a doctorate in medieval philosophy. Likewise, a skilled *entrepreneur* who dropped out of school in the third grade, like Waldo Millbottom (of the noted Waldo's TexMex Taco World), may earn more than an entire roomful of MBAs.

Overall, though, the evidence is pretty darn compelling. Workers with more education earn more income. The exceptions are few.

Just another investment

Here's another point to ponder. The money spent on a college education is about the best *investment* that you can make. If you have, let's say, $100,000 primed and ready to invest, you might consider the stock mar-

ket, mutual funds, starting your own business, or plopping it down on an assortment of government securities, corporate bonds, or other such investments. The best return, however, is likely to be a college education. (Check out Financial Markets, Investment, Mutual Funds, and Stock Market for more on the multitude of these investment alternatives.)

Make no mistake, education and what it does for human capital is an investment. It has all of the features we look for in an investment.

1. You give up some current consumption. If we're talking about college, there are the obvious out-of-pocket expenses for tuition and books that you can't use to spend on other stuff, but there's also a mess of other nonmonetary costs like giving up work, leisure, and the better part of your life for 4 years.

2. Like other investments, you expect a return for your efforts. That's where the extra income and productivity comes in. Like a business that expects profits to rise when a new factory is finished, a college graduate expects more income.

3. There's a significant risk when investing in education. Okay, so you thought there would be a big demand for doctorates in medieval philosophy when you started college. Maybe there was—when you started. Maybe you were just misinformed. But you took a chance, and it didn't pay off. Then again, Waldo Millbottom seldom admits that he was also the entrepreneur behind the failed Waldo's Fancy French Pedicure Shop and Sock Warehouse.

Let's not be selfish

As good as education and human capital are for you on a personal level, they're even better for the economy. They're a really big part of *economic growth*. Two reasons stand out:

1. Human capital is a key part of the quality dimension of labor. In fact, human capital *is* the quality dimension of labor. When we talk about improving the quality of labor, we're talking about human capital.

2. Education is also a direct route to improving technology. The more people know, the more they're likely to come up with better ways of doing stuff—and that's what *technology* is all about.

Over the years (as noted in the entry Economic Growth), a significant part of economic growth in the U.S.A. can be traced directly to improvements in technology and human capital. It's a good investment for our country.

There are, however, other benefits from education. In particular, education has a big *public good* dimension. You might recall that a public good is something the government produces, like national defense, because you can't keep people away (no *excludability*) and there's really no reason to keep them away (no *rival consumption*).

Here are some "public" goods that we all enjoy because of education:

- *Less crime.* While education doesn't prevent crime, as a general rule the more educated we are, the fewer crimes we commit. (For more on the logic behind this, check out the entry on Crime.)

- *Better citizens.* Education also tends to make us better citizens. In addition to obeying the laws, we tend to be better informed voters and elect better leaders if we're more educated.

- *Better products.* Education and human capital also improve the quality of output produced, over and above all of the stuff we talked about with economic growth. For example, a carpenter who is better educated in the fine art of construction will build a better house.

Enter the first estate

Economic growth alone would probably justify a lot of what the government does to promote, fund, and subsidize education. But when you throw in the public goods dimension, you have a clear-cut need for the first estate. Keep this in mind when you hear some of the wealthy members of the second estate, who educate their offspring at the finest private schools in the world, criticize government-funded education for the common folk. Perhaps they would like to keep the third estate groveling in ignorant peasant bliss.

TIPPING THE SCALES ON EDUCATION

- It's hard to say too many good things about education. It has been a source of an extended increase in our standard of living for two centuries.

- As any government-sponsored good, education attracts really bad policies. Many of these are caused by special-interest groups that have their fingers in the government's education pie. While it would be nice to think that every dollar spent on education provides benefits, such is not the case. Some dollars are siphoned off into inefficient and unproductive uses. Whose pockets are being lined in your city? Keep informed to see if your education tax dollars are invested wisely.

- On a personal level, you should see that your own education dollars are invested wisely. If you get a lot of satisfaction from studying medieval philosophy (and want little income), then by all means go for it. However, other human-capital investments will likely add more to your bank account.

See also: Advertising, Athlete Salaries, Crime, Discrimination, Health Care, Immigration, Political Views, Wealth, and Working Women.

trading some ideas on
EXCHANGE RATES

*ne potential problem with any far and wide ambling tour of the economy is ambling too far or too wide. Such is the case as we find ourselves in the quaint and courteous Republic of Northwest Queoldiola. While we're here, let's take the opportunity to explore the quaint and courteous economy of the Northwest Queoldiola. Our impromptu economic expedition is faced with an immediate roadblock. I have a pocket filled with good old U.S. dollar bills, but the quaint and courteous people of Northwest Queoldiola don't trade their wares for good old U.S. dollar bills. They prefer the quaint and courteous Northwest Queoldiolan currency, the queold. All we need to do is trade my U.S. dollar bills for queolds.*

The foreign-exchange market to the rescue

The place to do any exchanging of one currency for another is the *foreign-exchange market*. While this isn't quite the same as heading down to the Mr. Market Super Food Discount Store for a chunk of cheddar cheese, many banks can accommodate your desire to trade one currency for another. Our luck places us before the doors of the First National Bank of Northwest Queoldiola.

While we now know *how* to trade dollars for queolds, it would help if we knew *how much*. If we take one good old U.S. dollar into the First National Bank of Northwest Queoldiola, how many quaint and courteous queolds can we expect to get back? This question is answered by the *exchange rate*—the price of one currency in terms of another. You might occa-

sionally hear one of the network news guys report, with a wry smile, that the exchange rates between U.S. dollars and yen, marks, or pounds have gone up, down, or stayed the same. If you're not into wry-smiling network news guys, most major newspapers regularly print currency exchange rates.

For our little excursion, let's note that the exchange rate between dollars and queolds is 29.2 million queolds per dollar. In that I have $137.65 in my pocket, I can trade my U.S. currency for 4,019,380,000 queolds.

Let's consider who else might be interested in trading one currency for another.

Travelers and coin collectors

Northwest Queoldiola is certainly a quaint and courteous country, and a tourist mecca for all travelers seeking quaint and courteous countries. Those travelers would clearly need to exchange dollars for queolds. But if you're not into quaint and courteous and don't intend to travel beyond the boundaries of the good old U.S. of A., is there any good reason to have an interest in the foreign-exchange market or the exchange rate?

We can quickly dispense with the obvious interest of coin collectors, and jump right into the importance of the exchange rate to the average, overworked, underappreciated members of the third estate. The exchange rate has a direct effect on the trade that occurs between nations (see Foreign Trade for more). To see why, it's best to think about the exchange rate as the price of a currency. The "price" of a dollar in our example is 29.2 million queolds. The price of currency is important because it affects the relative prices of the goods that countries buy and sell.

- If the price of a nation's currency goes up (for example, a dollar increases to 30 million queolds), then that nation is likely to *export* fewer goods and *import* more. In terms of queolds, U.S. products are now more expensive, so U.S. exports to Northwest Queoldiola drop. However, in terms of dollars, Northwest Queoldiolan stuff is cheaper, and their imports into the United States rise.
- If the price of a nation's currency goes down, then you can reverse everything: Exports go up and imports go down.

All of this importing and exporting comes home to the average, overworked, underappreciated members of the third estate.

- *Exports create jobs.* When the United States exports more stuff to other countries, then more people have jobs. Therefore, a higher exchange rate can eliminate jobs, while a lower exchange rate can create jobs.
- *Imports give consumers satisfaction.* When the United States imports more goods, more cheaply, because of the higher exchange rate, it has more satisfied consumers. If those imported goods are eliminated, then consumers aren't as happy.

A higher exchange rate would increase your satisfaction from consuming imports, but you could lose your job in the process. A lower exchange rate tends to reduce your satisfaction, but expand your job opportunities. Like a lot of stuff in the economy, there aren't any obvious, clear-cut, once-and-for-all, ideal options for the exchange rate.

EXCHANGE-RATE TIPS

- If you're not in an exporting industry (like cars or farm products), but you consume a lot of imported goods (like chocolate and Japanese electronics), then a higher exchange rate is best for you.
- If, however, your livelihood depends on consumption by people in other countries, and you buy only American products, then a lower exchange rate is your ticket to happiness.

If you're the sort of person who keeps track of who's winning the global race for number 1 on the economic front, then exchange rates can help. In general, a country that is healthy, growing, and prosperous, with low rates of *inflation,* tends to have a strong currency that's in great demand. This translates into a rising exchange rate. In contrast, no one is likely to demand the currency of an also-ran country that's ailing and stagnant. Its exchange rate will tend to fall.

If the United States is growing faster than the Republic of Northwest Queoldiola, then the price of dollars in terms of queolds will tend to rise. One dollar will get you more queolds, and a billion queolds will get you fewer dollars.

Who's in charge here?

Exchange rates are market prices, and like other prices they bounce around from competitive force—or the lack thereof. In particular, it's worth noting major participants in the foreign-exchange market. They are: (1) everybody else and (2) governments. If the "everybody elses" buy and sell currencies, then the foreign-exchange markets tend to be *competitive markets* because there are a lot of "everybody elses" out there. Governments of the world, however, are never too far away from activities in the foreign-exchange market. That's because (1) they're in charge of their currencies—they print the money that's being traded—and (2) the exchange rates have a big impact on exports and imports, which affect the health and stability of an economy and consequently the likelihood that government leaders stay in power.

As such, governments tend to let the everybody elses of the world do their buying and selling, except when the exchange rates go up or down too much. What's too much? It depends. If the exchange rate goes up in a country that's importing a lot and exporting very little, then their government is likely to jump into the foreign-exchange market and start buying or selling currencies. The same rise in the exchange rate would probably pass with no action if the country is doing very little importing and a lot of exporting.

If this government control of the exchange rate is somewhat intriguing, check out the definition of "managed float" in Section 3.

See also: Financial Markets, Foreign Investment, and Immigration.

getting your share of
FARM SUBSIDIES

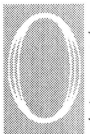

Our pedestrian excursion through the economy has helped me work up a ferocious appetite. I vote for a quick stop at the Mr. Market Super Food Discount Store where we can purchase a loaf of bread, assorted meats, and some cheese, all for a luncheon tribute to the Earl of Sandwich. While a self-made tribute to the Earl is less expensive than any purchased from Manny Mustard's House of Sandwich, the ingredients from Mr. Market Super Food Discount Store still carry a hefty price tag. If you're hungry and have limited cash on hand, you might wonder whether food prices are higher than they need to be.

A view from the market

Whenever the question of prices arises in a conversation, we need to think in terms of the *market*. As we saw in Fact #2, Our Subjective Values, and Fact #4, Our Monopolized Markets, prices result from buyers and sellers doing their buying and selling. Such is the case for food prices.

A view from the market tells us that food prices might be high because:

• The sellers are doing very little selling.
• The buyers are doing a lot of buying.

For example, if Godzilla left Tokyo and decided to devour southern Florida, then the reduction in citrus production would likely increase the prices of oranges, grapefruit, and the ever-popular tangerines. More realistically, a similar result would be expected if the land of sunshine and tourist attractions had a hurricane, spring freeze, drought, or some other devastating natural disaster that reduced the supply of delectable citrus products.

Higher citrus prices would also be observed at the Mr. Market Super Food Discount Store if nutrition researchers uncovered a link between citrus products and mental telepathy. A veritable throng of mind-expanding buyers would push up prices as they purchased unusually large amounts of vitamin C–laden fruits.

Price gyrations caused by these sorts of changes in supply and demand are quite common in markets for food products—as well as for a lot of other stuff. There is, however, something else that can assist food prices to higher ground: our good old friend, government.

Our necessary evil lends a hand

The good thing about being a card-carrying member of the first estate (which most of us aren't) is that virtually anything you do carries the force of law. Whether you're democratically elected or rise to power through the extensive use of large military

A PEDESTRIAN ...

... gets subsidized

HERE'S $10,000! DON'T PLANT THAT!

HE GAVE ME $500 NOT TO LAY EGGS!

ME, TOO!

O M Amos

tanks, what you say goes until the next election or Supreme Court decision, or if you encounter larger tanks.

Food prices are the recipients of extensive use of this government power. In fact, it's very, *very* difficult to find any farm product that's not subject to a myriad of government laws and regulations affecting its price. If the government says that a price is $5 a bushel, $10 a ton, or $15 a gallon, then that's what it is.

This power can be used for good or bad. Because good and bad are relative concepts, I'll (try to) let you form your own opinion on government's influence of farm prices. From an economist's standpoint, however, it's not good. For most members

of the third estate who have developed a nasty habit of eating, it's not particularly good, either. But don't let me bias your opinion before you know the details, the first of which is why the government screws around with food prices.

It's the right thing to do

Recall if you will, the plight of Hapless Herb, a wheat farmer from western Kansas whom we met in Fact #3, Our Unfair Lives. Herb's grandson, Harv (Hopeless Harv) continues to operate the family wheat farm under the watchful eyes of the western Kansas skies. Hopeless Harv, however, is as helpless as Hapless Herb when it comes to extracting a successful living from the Kansas plains.

We can note a couple of reasons for Hopeless Harv's horrendously poor plight.

- *The unpredictable weather.* Farming, as an industry, is world famous for relying on the natural generosity of the weather. Harvests can be plentiful if farmers like Hopeless Harv get the proper mix of sunshine, rain, temperature, and other assorted meteorological events in the right amounts at the right times. Nature, however, very seldom gets everything right during the same growing season, meaning Hopeless Harv and the others are typically warding off one near financial disaster after other.

- *A whole bunch of competition.* Farming is also one of the more competitive industries—at least on the supplying side—that we have in the economy. There are gadzillions of farmers ready, willing, and able to supply every farm product imaginable. As a general rule it's very, very difficult to monopolize the production of farm stuff. And as we saw in Fact #4, Our Monopolized Markets, competition on the supply side of the market tends to keep prices very close to production costs. Unlike cable television, there's not a lot of extra profit to be had in farming.

- *Competition and weather don't mix.* Because of competition among farmers, *bad* weather can be *good* and *good* weather can be *bad.* Hopeless Harv will be quite happy if he has good weather while other wheat farmers have bad weather. The bad weather for the others will limit the wheat supply and drive the price up. Harv's good weather will lead to a bountiful wheat harvest, sold at high prices, which gives the Hopeless Harv homestead a high income. Of course, if Harv succumbs to bad weather, while other wheat farmers have good weather, then wheat prices will be down and Harv will be doubly hopeless with very little harvest and low prices.

For these reasons farm prices and the farmers' incomes tend to be highly unstable. The good times are seldom good enough to compensate for the bad. At best, farmers are usually just getting by.

What do all red-blooded Americans do when faced with dire circumstances that threaten their livelihoods? Call in the government. Farmers would have nice steady incomes, if only those darn prices didn't jump around with every little change in the markets.

Subsidies to the rescue

The answer, for more decades than most of us have been around, has been an assortment of farm subsidies that offset low incomes when prices drop. In fact, over half of a typical farmer's income, like Hopeless Harv's, comes from one form of government subsidy or another.

While the variety of farm subsidies reflects a century of government types thinking up different ways to subsidize farmers, we can lump most of them into one of three categories:

1. *Price supports—keeping prices high.* Government works very hard to keep prices high enough to ensure a good living for farmers. If $5 for a bushel of wheat is what Hopeless Harv needs to stay in business, then, by the force of law, government can mandate that all wheat will only be sold for $5 a bushel. If there aren't enough buyers at the mandated price, which is usually the case—then government buys the *surplus.* Consumers not only have the "good fortune" of paying higher prices at the grocery store, our taxes are used to buy the surplus as well. The surplus is then stored away in a grain silo, storage shed, or warehouse until it rots.

2. *Crop reduction—keeping supply low.* Government tries to get around the rotting-surplus problem by making sure that stuff is never produced. The most common method is to pay farmers *not* to grow stuff. If Hopeless Harv and

other wheat farmers remove part of their land from wheat production, then the supply of wheat drops and the price rises. The higher price, together with government payments for *not* growing stuff, should give farmers a decent living. While consumers still get to pay high prices, the tax bill for *not* growing is usually less than that for buying the surplus.

3. *Direct payments—keeping incomes up.* Often government decides to stop beating around the bush, and just give farmers extra income. In this case, the market is left to work out a price. If prices are below what government thinks farmers need to maintain their livelihood, then it pays them the difference. If Hopeless Harv needs $5 a bushel, but can only get $3 from the market, then the government makes up the $2 difference. While this keeps consumers' food prices low, it keeps the tax dollars moving swiftly between consumers and farmers.

The good and the bad of farm subsidies

In that most of us can find a veritable throng of farmers among our ancestors a generation or two past (some even less), it's difficult to argue with the intended benefits of farm subsidies. Without subsidies many farmers would have to park the tractor, sell the land to a nefarious suburban developer, and move into the city with their kids, forever destroying an American family-farming tradition. As taxpayers and consumers of this country, however, we pay a high price to maintain cultural icons of the 1800s. Prices are high, tax dollars are spent, and perhaps most importantly, we have lost some *efficiency.*

When we subsidize farmers who could not remain in business otherwise, we are forcing the economy to use more resources for farm production than consumers want. If we *really* wanted as much stuff as the farmers could produce, then prices would

be high enough to keep them in business. The more we subsidize farmers, the more they produce, the more their incomes fall, and the more they need subsidies. This is a loop that never ends.

The problem with farming really stems from our longer-run *economic growth.* Note these two points of interest:

1. *People don't eat as they used to.* Today, consumers like you and me eat just about the same amount of food as our ancestors did 200 years ago. However, we're a whole bunch richer and we spend a smaller fraction of our income on food. In addition, when our economy grows a little, and our incomes go up, then farmers (unlike doctors, politicians, factory workers, and shoe clerks) get almost none of it. In fact, farming is what we call a "shrinking industry." Over the years it has become much smaller compared to the overall size of our economic pie.

2. *Technology doesn't quite come to the rescue.* In fact, technological improvements in the way farmers do their farming has helped shrink the farming slice of the economic pie. Because farmers can produce 10 times as much food now as 100 years ago, we need one-tenths as many farmers to do their farming. Problems, however, crop up when we still have two-tenths of the farmers *trying* to do their farming thing.

The only sure way to improve the plight of farmers is to get a bunch of them out of farming and into something else. Doing so, however, runs counter to numerous special-interest groups who claim to be protecting the interest of farmers. The U.S. Department of Agriculture is at the top of this list, followed closely by scores of producer groups, like the American Dairy Association.

TIPS ON THIS WHOLE FARM SUBSIDY BUSINESS

- We first need to ask if farm subsidies are worth the cost. Is keeping a bunch of farmers in business worth higher food prices, higher taxes, and the inefficient use of our resources?

- If your answer is No, then you need to face the political realities. Farm subsidies have been a way of life for 100 years. It's very difficult to convince farmers that taking away 50 percent of their income will be good for them in the long run. In the short run, of course, they still need to pay their bills.

- It's also an uphill battle because of the scores of powerful special-interest groups that are looking out for the "interests" of farmers. A few spirited politicians and consumers have waged the war against these groups, but most have come away bloodied and defeated.

See also: Business, Economic Growth, Foreign Trade, Profit, Regulation, Taxes, and Welfare.

taming our beastly
FEDERAL DEFICIT

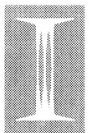 *It's almost impossible to take a leisurely stroll around the economy without crashing headlong into the federal deficit. It doesn't take a microscope to see it bulging from the windows and doors of the Sylvester J. Peabody Federal Office Building as we pass by. It's a monstrous beast that seems to be growing by the minute. But is the federal deficit really as ghoulish and gruesome as drawn by political cartoonists? Should we make a detour of our pedestrian trek to avoid the beast? Considering its size, is avoidance even possible? To answer these questions, let's consider the pluses and minuses of our federal deficit.*

The joys of deficit spending

Most of us hate to pay taxes, but we enjoy the public goods made possible by federal government spending. For this reason we can be quite thankful that the federal government tends to spend a lot without finding it necessary to extract as many taxes from our pockets. We garnish the myriad benefits of government spending, without paying the taxes. What more could we want from our government?

Because we don't pay for all of our federal government goods through taxes, we must borrow the rest. The borrowing used to finance this government benevolence is the oft-discussed *federal deficit*.

Would you know the deficit if you met it in a dark alley?

What is this beastly deficit that politicians and economists have debated for years? Should you be on the lookout for the evil

politician who feeds this fiend with fewer taxes and more spending, or hope against hope for a public-spirited white knight who will slay the deficit with higher taxes and less spending?

Technically, the federal budget deficit is the difference between the federal government's tax collections and its spending. The difference is made up by borrowing through the issuance of *government securities*. (For background on this sort of thing check out Financial Markets.)

A few points to note about this definition:
- It includes only what the *federal* government is doing. *State* and *local* governments, which often spend *less* than their tax revenues and thus run *budget surpluses,* are not included in everyday discussions of the *budget deficit.*
- Some federal government spending items are "off budget," which means they are not to be included in the budget deficit calculations. It's a simple correc-

tion, however, to put "off-budget" items back on the budget, if you know what to include.

What's so bad about the deficit?

There's nothing intrinsically wrong with borrowing to finance expenditures; businesses and consumers do it all of the time. Few factories would be constructed, and even fewer houses would be built, if they were financed *without* borrowing. Borrowing can, however, create problems.

- *Excessive borrowing.* Like consumers, if government borrows too much, it can place a strain on the ability to repay. In the early 1990s the total *public debt*—the accumulation of all previous deficits remaining unpaid—was approaching 70 percent of our *gross domestic product* pie. This is large, but not unprecedented, compared to the years of World War II, when the public debt was over 100 percent.
- *Borrowing for the wrong reasons.* Generating a deficit to finance wild parties or current consumption is not a very good idea. Few businesses could stay out of *bankruptcy* court if they borrowed merely for current consumption. If the deficit is used to finance investment, this is good. If it's used to finance current consumption, this is bad.
- *Limiting options.* A large deficit reduces the government's ability to take actions that stimulate the economy during bad times. The 1990-91 recession offers an example. The economy remained sluggish because government could not stimulate our economy by spending more and taxing less in light of a $300-billion deficit.

Can the deficit be good?

The usually maligned federal deficit is not without a few good points. For example:

- During slow economic periods, one of the best things for the government to do is run up the deficit. This increases spending, which as seen in Fact #7, Our Circular World, helps stimulate the economy. The *worst* thing to do during a recession is to cut the deficit or run up a budget surplus.
- Because the government, believe it or not, is extremely trustworthy, the federal deficit and the corresponding public debt offers a very secure, low-risk investment to the financial markets. Banks and others who value safety and security hold onto these safe and secure government securities.

One way to reduce the deficit

The deficit can be reduced in a simple straightforward manner: Cut spending and/or increase taxes. Nothing could be easier in principle but harder in practice. One reason this simple approach is nearly impossible is the way our oft-envied system of government works.

Political candidates who promise high taxes and few government services are seldom elected to office (unless the other candidate promises higher taxes and fewer services, or is a real jerk). Elected officials have every incentive in the world to tax less and spend more—an alternative, which if practiced enough, generates a deficit. It should come as no surprise, then, that the federal government has only operated with a budget surplus in 6 of the last 50 years.

One method of reducing the deficit is to grow out of it. As the economy's pie grows, more tax dollars come into the U.S. Treasury. In fact, many of those 6 years of budget surpluses occurred because the economy grew, and the tax dollars rolled in, faster than Congress and the President could spend them.

This leads to one inescapable conclusion:

A FEDERAL-DEFICIT TIP

- If the federal government borrows, it best borrow for things that can make the economy grow. This was a lesson learned long ago by businesses, but a lesson often less obvious in government. A business pays back borrowed funds, hopefully, through returns generated by investment in something productive, like a factory. The government can do the same by investing in growth-promoting public goods.

What about a balanced-budget amendment?

A balanced-budget amendment would be an amendment to the U.S. Constitution forcing Congress and the President to spend *only* the tax dollars collected each year. If the federal government collected 5-gadzillion tax dollars this year, then it could spend only 5-gadzillion dollars this year—*no more.* This sort of spending constraint already exists for many state governments and a bunch of city governments, too. Why not the federal government?

Here's the good and bad of this balanced-budget amendment.

Controlling our necessary evil

One desired effect that's often championed by proponents of a balanced-budget amendment is limiting the power of the federal government. It probably isn't surprising that balanced-budget advocates have tended to be political *conservatives* who generally follow the doctrine that the "best government is the least government." (More can be found on this topic under Political Views.) Here are a couple of consequences that tend to make conservatives happy:

- *Small is beautiful.* If the federal government can't borrow, then it can only spend more by raising taxes. Because voters, as a rule, don't look kindly on higher taxes, government would tend to be smaller, spend less, and keep its inefficient meddling out of the economy. This would also prevent reelection-minded politicians from throwing *borrowed* pork-barrel money at constituents. Politicians would be forced to consider (some say at long last) the interests of angry taxpaying voters.

- *No more recessions.* Part of the meddling prevented by a balanced-budget amendment would be stabilization policies There are those who feel that the federal government, through the inappropriate use of its spending and taxing abilities, causes the booms and busts of the *business cycle.* As such, the booms and busts would be eliminated by removing any sort of discretionary control over spending and taxes. The tax dollars come in, then the federal government spends them. Congress and the President wouldn't be able to monkey around with taxes or spending in useless attempts to stabilize the economy.

Making a bad situation worse

Like any controversy, controversy surrounds the balanced-budget amendment only because there are two opposing views. You shouldn't be too surprised to discover that political liberals tend to feel differently about a balanced-budget amendment. Here are the liberal counterpoints to those offered by conservatives:

- *Government is our friend.* The federal government is the last resort and only hope for fixing many problems. Some things, like wars and natural disasters, not only require immediate responses but need funds over and above available tax dollars. Other public goods, like bridges and highways, are investments best financed with borrowed funds. A balanced-budget amendment that restricts spending to current tax dollars would keep the government from doing what it needs to do. (There are those who claim that the big federal deficits run up in the 1980s under conservative Republican Presidents were really intended to do just that.)

- *No recessions, but big depressions.* One problem the government tries to fix is the business cycle. It's called a "business cycle" because businesses play a big part in the instability. The federal government can step in, through timely spending and taxing policies, to alleviate the business cycle problems of *unemployment* and *inflation*. If the federal government has its hands tied by a balanced-budget constraint, then business cycle problems might even worsen. In a *recession*, when everyone spends less and pays fewer taxes, a balanced-budget constraint would force the government to spend less, as well. Every recession likely would be worsened, and some could be transformed into 1930s-like *depressions*. In fact, in the early years of the 1930s Great Depression, the federal government did the "prudent" thing by keeping its budget balanced. The Great Depression didn't really end until the onset of the wartime budget deficit of the early 1940s.

A BALANCED-BUDGET TIP

• Part of the problem with the federal government is the tendency for voters to elect politicians who promise lower taxes and more spending. We could all name dozens of programs that the government should eliminate that benefit others: Don't cut my benefits. Just cut my taxes! If you think that the federal deficit is a problem, then let your elected representatives in Washington, D.C., know that you're willing to pay higher taxes and get fewer government benefits. If not, then get your TV remote, a bag of chips, some bean dip, a soft drink, and don't worry about it.

See also: Economic Forecasting, Economic Growth, Farm Subsidies, Financial Markets, Interest Rates, Investment, Recessions, and Taxes.

borrowing through the
FINANCIAL MARKETS

We never know whom we might encounter on our leisurely stroll through the economy. Passing by the marble columns of Interstate OmniBank— the beacon of safety and security—we have the good fortune of crossing paths with our Ivy League–educated pillar of the financial community, Winston Smythe Kennsington III. Although he seems to be a touch condescending, he's kind enough to show us a freshly signed check for $37 gadzillion, which is but a small part of a multigadzillion-dollar loan from the Interstate OmniBank. To what constructive purpose Winnie will put these funds remains unclear. How this loan will be repaid, he never says. But Winnie proudly reminds us several times that this loan once again proves his unchallenged standing as the majordomo of the financial markets.

The tools of the trade

Before we get into the ins and the outs, the nuts and the bolts, the nitty and the gritty of *financial market* exchanges, it's worth a moment or two pondering the basic stuff exchanged through financial markets. To do this let's divide our economy into two piles:
1. *Real stuff.* This pile includes our physical goods and resources: labor, capital, natural resources, and the output that they produce—in other words, our economic pie.
2. *Financial stuff.* This pile includes the legal claims on the physical goods and resources, such as corporate stocks, bonds, and money—that is, the pieces of paper that show who owns our economic pie.

The first pile of stuff is real because, well, it's real: You can hold it, touch it, taste it, see it, and smell it. It's also what satisfies our wants and needs. Its value depends

directly on consumer satisfaction. The second pile, representing legal claims on the economic pie, especially ownership of it, is what we trade in financial markets. The value of any of the financial stuff ultimately depends on how well the real stuff satisfies consumers' wants and needs. For example, the value of one share of Omni Conglomerate, Inc., corporate stock *isn't* worth the paper it's printed on. It i*s*, however, worth the productive capability of Omni Conglomerate, Inc.

Bringing buyers and sellers together

The purpose of financial markets, the very reason for their existence, is to bring buyers and sellers together. This, of course, isn't an Earth-shaking revelation. The purpose of any market is to bring the buyers who want stuff together with the sellers who

A PEDESTRIAN . . .

. . . doesn't get a loan

OMNI

I DON'T NEED IT! BUT, IT'S NICE TO KNOW I CAN GET IT!

WILL WORK FOR WALKING SHOES

THEY'RE PRACTICALLY GIVING THIS STUFF AWAY

O M Amos

have the stuff. Rather than tacos, lawn-mowers, or ice cream scoops, the stuff of financial markets are the legal claims on our economic pie.

So who does the buying and selling in financial markets?

- *Buyers are lenders.* A straightforward view of financial markets would tell us that the demand side includes those who want to gain possession of these legal claims, much like the demand side of the taco market includes those who want possession of tacos. But there's a little more to the exchange. When you buy a legal claim you're also *lending money* to the financial market. For example, buying a gov-

ernment security is really making a loan to the government. Any spare change that I deposit into a savings account also means that I'm buying a legal claim from the bank, their promise to return my money.

- *Sellers are borrowers.* If buyers provide the funds, then sellers in financial markets must be getting them. Those who sell legal claims, like banks with their consumer savings accounts, or government and the securities it uses to finance the *federal deficit,* do so as a way to borrow money.

Here's where we get to the very reason for financial markets: gaining access to money. The buying and selling of legal claims is really a secondary part of financial-market transactions. Those who sell financial claims don't want to sell financial claims so much as they want money. While you might argue that money is just another lump in the pile of financial stuff, it stands alone as something that can be used easily and quickly to buy any of the real stuff that makes up our pie. You can't say that for other legal claims. (More on this intriguing point can be found under the definition of *money* in the glossary, Section 3.)

For example, suppose Interstate Omni-Bank is willing to give me the cold, hard cash that I need to buy a brand new car. All I have to do is sign a piece of paper promising to repay them at some time in the future. I sell this legal claim, Interstate OmniBank buys it, I get the money, and I buy a new car. Pretty nifty, eh?

Big piles from little piles

Many financial markets not only move money from lenders to borrowers, they also help to accumulate the money into big piles. As we'll see in a few paragraphs, those who borrow money usually need a lot, and I mean a whole lot. Any given borrower might need a gadzillion dollars to build a factory, finance the federal deficit, or something similar. Most people, however, don't have a gadzillion dollars to lend. The hardworking, taxpaying members of the third estate who do most of the lending are lucky to come up with thousands to lend, let alone gadzillions. Financial markets, therefore, help to accumulate the funds from a bunch of people, each with a little bit of money, before making large sums available to those who borrow.

That, in fact, is the primary function of banks. While you might think that the most important goal of financial beacons like the Interstate OmniBank is to keep your deposits safe and secure, it's not. Their primary goal is to get a little bit of money from a lot of people which they can loan out in the gadzillion-dollar category to the likes of Winston Smythe Kennsington III. Safety and security is simply part of the price banks pay to get your money.

Why borrow? Why lend? Why not?

Okay, let's consider a few specifics on why borrowers borrow and lenders lend:

- *Suppliers of funds.* Those who supply money to the financial markets do so for two reasons. (1) They want to "store money" they can spend on something at a later time, such as on a college education or a factory. (2) They are enticed by an interest payment, *dividend,* or expected increase in the value of the legal claim. (See Interest Rates for more on this.)

- *Demanders of funds.* Those who borrow money do so because of some intended use. We already noted that the federal government wants (I should say needs) money for the federal deficit. Likewise, consumers often want to buy stuff like houses or cars but don't have enough money readily available. Businesses also borrow for investing in capital goods and do so because they expect this to generate profit.

This last part about *investment* is among the more important for our economy. Investment in capital goods helps our economy by expanding the size of our pie, producing more stuff, and doing all sorts of other good things that you can read about under Economic Growth. If financial markets didn't make it so easy for businesses to accumulate the funds needed to invest in capital, we would have a much, *much* smaller economic pie.

A financial market smorgasbord

While we're all very familiar with the face of Winston Smythe Kennsington III from the society pages of the newspaper, *he* is most comfortable among the financial pages. Like most newspapers, the financial pages of Winnie's paper report on the transactions and prices that are the lifeblood of any financial aficionado.

By far the most prominent financial market commonly covered by newspapers is the *stock market*. There are, however, also financial markets for corporate bonds, government securities, municipal bonds, mortgages, foreign exchange, and legal claims on such things as gold, silver, petroleum, and assorted farm products. While it's easy to short-circuit your brain over the array of financial markets in our economy, a few classification points can reduce the confusion:

- *Equity and credit.* Some financial markets deal in equity, while others deal in credit. Equity is the actual ownership of something, the most common example being corporate stock traded over stock markets like the New York Stock Exchange. *Credit,* in contrast, stems from a loan, which is simply the promise to repay borrowed funds. The most common credit markets trade government securities, corporate bonds, or municipal bonds.
- *Spot, futures, and options. Spot* markets are those that exchange an actual "something" between buyers and sellers. The stock market is not only an equity market, it's also a spot market—a spot, equity market. *Futures* markets, in contrast, exchange the right to buy or sell "something" at a specified price and at a specified time in the future. Although you might not think of spot markets for farm products and petroleum as financial markets, the futures markets for these sorts of goods are. Options markets are much like futures markets, but instead of setting up an actual exchange at some later date, you only set up an "option" to buy or sell stuff. You don't have to go through with the buying or selling if you don't want to.
- *Money and capital.* We can also divide up the credit part of financial markets into short-term and long-term. Short-term loans that are paid off in less than a year are part of the *money market* and include such things as treasury bills and commercial paper. Long-term loans that are paid off in more than a year, often up to 30 years, are traded in *capital markets,* and include Treasury bonds, Treasury notes, municipal bonds, and corporate bonds.

More than the financial pages

A whole bunch of the financial stuff in our economy never makes it to the newspaper pages. Because the financial pages are news oriented, they report on those markets that either are open to a lot of buyers and sellers or are some key indicator of what's going on in the economy.

A few examples of unnewsworthy financial stuff is also in order:

- *Banking.* You deposit some spare change into your savings account, make your monthly mortgage payment, or use your credit card to purchase a few essential items from Mega-Mart Discount Warehouse Super Center. All of these activities place you four-square into the middle of financial markets.
- *Insurance.* You expand your life insurance coverage or get sick and make a claim on your medical insurance. Once more, the financial markets and legal claims come into play.
- *Money.* You remove a crisp, new dollar bill from your pocket, and after admiring the portrait of George Washington spend it on a Waldo's Super Deluxe TexMex Gargantuan Taco (with sour cream and peppers). Guess what? That dollar bill is also part of a financial market.

The Winston Smythe Kennsington IIIs of our economy aren't the only ones who spend a lot of their time in the financial markets. Sure, he may be able to add gadzillions of dollars to his wealth each day through the financial markets, but these markets are equally important to consumers of the third estate. We would all find it very, *very* difficult to function as consumers, workers, and (unfortunately) taxpayers without financial markets.

See also: Credit Cards, Exchange Rate, Federal Deficit, Foreign Investment, Gambling, Insurance, Mutual Funds, Profit, Stock

a translation of

FOREIGN INVESTMENT

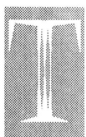*This Means War!! Batten down the hatches! Circle the wagons! Sound the alarm! Head for the fallout shelter! Those seemingly quaint and courteous folk from the Republic of Northwest Queoldiola have upset the delicate balance of world peace. Perhaps I should explain. A group of investors from Northwest Queoldiola have been snooping around Shady Valley with the evil intentions of buying Shady Valley's very own Sonny Sullivan Sundials Extraordinaire manufacturing plant. How dare they! This is the good old U.S. of A. We don't want any foreigners buying up good old U.S. property, do we? Before nuking Northwest Queoldiola we should consider this potentially messy topic of foreign investment.*

The fine art of investing

In that "F" comes before "I," you might not yet have wandered across the entry on Investment. If you haven't, this would be a good time to do so, because foreign investment is just a special sort of investment. A lot of the basics found under Investment are also useful here.

Let me hit some of the high points:

- "Investment" means giving up current consumption goods to produce some sort of *capital* goods that will (hopefully) enhance future production. You sacrifice something now for more later.
- This "more that you get later" is the return on the investment. Most businesses measure return in terms of extra profit. The trick to investing is selecting the capital with the greatest return.

- The return on capital is weighed against the return that could be had from the financial markets. A business could use that extra gadzillion dollars it has laying around for capital or an array of corporate stocks, bonds, government securities, or whatever. The capital route is better if it has the highest return.
- Following a similar thought pattern, it's also wise to borrow the money needed to invest in capital if the capital return is greater than the *interest rate* on the loan.

As a general rule—and the one that's most important here—investment monies search out those opportunities with the *highest return*. It could be the stock market, government securities, renovating an office building, building a new factory, or buying an existing one. And (here's one of those important "ands") investors are more interested in the "how much" than in the "where." However, the "where" often puts us into the realm of foreign investment.

Buying up another country

Foreign investment is as much a part of U.S. history as Christopher Columbus, westward expansion, and every "war to end all wars" that we've ever fought. Our original 13 colonies were begun as foreign investment by European countries. Although we've been independent for a couple of centuries, we still have significant foreign ownership of U.S. property. Britain, France, Canada, and others have long found U.S. capital to be extremely worthy of their investment dollars. The news guys tend to be most interested in the topic, however, when one of our primary competitors in the global economy goes on a U.S. property–buying binge. In the recent past we've had concerns about Saudi Arabian and Japanese ownership. How dare they? Now Shady Valley is faced with investments from those supposedly quaint and courteous thugs from Northwest Queoldiola. Let's get to the bottom of this.

A great place to invest

Put yourself in the position of investors from Northwest Queoldiola who are searching for a good investment. Their search has led them to Sonny Sullivan's Sundials Extraordinaire factory. Of all potential investments in factories, buildings, equipment, stocks, bonds, government securities, or whatever around the globe, they've selected the Sonny Sullivan's Sundials Extraordinaire factory right here in Shady Valley. I wonder why?

The most likely reason is that they think Sonny Sullivan's factory is the most profitable use of their investment money. That speaks volumes of good about the Sonny Sullivan factory and its workers. It also says a lot about foreign investment in general. A country with a great deal of foreign investment must be a relatively productive nation,

profitably producing the stuff that people want to buy.

To illustrate, let's say that our Northwest Queoldiolan visitors have $1 million to invest. They could buy or build a sundial factory in their home country of Northwest Queoldiola. Calculations show that this investment will net $100,000 each year in extra profit—working out to a 10-percent return on their $1 million investment. A quick look at Sonny Sullivan's books, though, reveals that it generates $200,000 in profit a year. This would give our Queoldiolan investors a 20-percent return on $1 million dollars. What would you do in their shoes? I'd probably buy the Sonny Sullivan factory. What makes Shady Valley's favorite sundial factory more profitable than the Northwest Queoldiola alternative? Here are a few possibilities:

- *Lower cost.* Shady Valley's factory might produce sundials more cheaply because wages, material prices, taxes, or any number of other items are less costly. An important cost item is transportation. If the Shady Valley is located closer to the market than Northwest Queoldiola, then the cost of shipping sundials is lower.
- *Greater revenue.* It's also possible that revenue is greater for sundials produced in the Shady Valley factory. The Sonny Sullivan's Sundials Extraordinaire name could command a higher price because it's widely recognized for quality.

Money, money everywhere

Something else could be behind the Northwest Queoldiolan's interest in our Shady Valley factory: *foreign exchange.* Here's the catch: The Shady Valley factory investment is made in U.S. dollars, while any similar investment made in Northwest Queoldiolan is with its own currency, queolds. The Queoldiolans might be interested in buying up Sonny Sullivan's Sundial factory because they have a bunch of U.S. dollars that they're looking to spend on something in the United States. Where did they get these U.S. dollars?

Here are two possibilities:

1. They could have sold the United States some goods produced in Northwest Queoldiola, perhaps some imports that came right here to the citizens of Shady Valley.

2. Some U.S. companies could have made capital investments of their own in Northwest Queoldiola. (According to Winston Smythe Kennsington III, Omni Conglomerate, Inc., recently completed an OmniMotors XL GT 9000 sports coupe assembly plant in Northwest Queoldiola.)

In both cases, U.S. citizens spend U.S. dollars on stuff of Northwest Queoldiolan origin. When the Queoldiolans get these dollars, they return the favor by buying stuff of U.S. origin—in this case Sonny Sullivan's factory.

The best price around

The Northwest Queoldiolans might also be interested in buying Sonny Sullivan's factory, whether or not they have any extra U.S. dollars, because of the *exchange rate* between dollars and queolds. While you might want to run through our little pedestrian look at this topic under the heading of Exchange Rate, such is not crucial. The important thing to note about the exchange rate is that different countries use different currencies, and they're frequently traded for one another. The price of one currency in terms of another is the exchange rate, which like other prices rises and falls from changes in demand and supply. Exchange-rate (price) changes can then affect foreign investment:

- *Cheap dollars.* If the price of dollars, in terms of queolds, is low, then Northwest Queoldiolan investors can buy a lot of dollars with relatively few queolds. Their money goes further in the United States than in Northwest Queoldiola. This gives them the opportunity and incentive to buy American—especially Sonny Sullivan's Sundials Extraordinaire factory.

- *Expensive dollars.* On the flip side, if the price of dollars in terms of queolds is pretty high, then it takes a bunch more queolds to buy U.S. dollars. Their money goes further in Northwest Queoldiola than in The United States. This discourages foreign investors from seeking opportunities in places like Shady Valley.

A number of countries, the United States included, keep a close eye on exchange rates, and even try to get them up or down as a means of encouraging or discouraging foreign investment. The reasons for this should become clear with a look at the good and bad of foreign investment.

Who owns what? And so what?

Here are two of the most publicized concerns of foreign investment:

1. *Control.* When another nation owns part of "our" property, it takes away some of our control. Foreign owners, being foreign, may not do things that are necessarily "good" for the country. Their number-1 concern is a financial return. Forget the civic responsibility stuff; just take the profit and run.

2. *Income.* The profit and income from foreign-owned capital goes back to the foreign owners, income they're likely to spend on consumption in their own country. This can be a drain on the domestic economy, which then suffers all sorts of consequences for the multiplicative, cumulatively reinforcing (whew!) circular flow: fewer jobs, less income, unemployment, recessions.

Now for the good part of foreign investment:

1. *Prosperity.* Foreign investment is usually a sign of a productive, expanding economy. If foreign countries are willing to spend their investment bucks here, then they must be expecting good things from the country.

2. *Growth.* You must never, ever, never forget that capital investment is a key

to the economic growth that expands the size of our economic pie. When you add foreign investment to domestic investment, our pie expands just that much faster, with all of the good things that result. We get more jobs, income, production, consumption, goods, and a lot of other stuff. (If you've forgotten any of this, see Economic Growth.)

Unless foreign investment is (1) excessive and most of the country is owned by foreign types, or (2) in strategic, national-defense–sensitive capital, it's not all that bad. After all, most hardworking, taxpaying consumers are employed by second-estate owners from another part of the country. Does it matter if your paycheck is signed by someone who lives in Northwest Queoldiola, Japan, New York, or California? The most important thing is to have a *signed* paycheck.

As the Northwest Queoldiolan investors finalize their purchase of the Sonny Sullivan's Sundials Extraordinaire factory, let's wrap up this entry with a few foreign-investment tips:

INVESTMENT TIPS, FOREIGN STYLE

- Keep in mind that foreign investment is a symptom or indication of what's going on in the economy. A really dumb knee-jerk reaction is to prevent foreign investment just for the sake of preventing foreign investment. Foreign investment is a sign of good times and often helps the goods times continue.

- If you have some spare investment cash of your own laying around, you should consider this foreign-investment option as well. There are a number of mutual funds that specialize in investments in other countries. They're risky, but they can be rewarding to your bank account.

- We probably should draw the line on foreign ownership of some sorts of capital, such as military installations, that would put us in a vulnerable defense position, or historical landmarks, that might not be fully appreciated by those with a different culture and heritage.

See also: Financial Markets, Foreign Trade, Interest Rates, Immigration, Recession, and Stock Market.

the wide, wide world of
FOREIGN TRADE

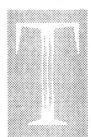 *Two blocks directly south of the Mega-Mart Discount Warehouse Super Center, we'll find that Natural Ned's Nursery and Garden Center is having a grand-opening celebration. I'd like to saunter over to check out their sundials, a valuable and long-sought-after acquisition for my backyard garden. In fact, Natural Ned's Nursery and Garden Center has a new shipment of sundials imported from the sundial capital of the world, the Republic of Northwest Queoldiola. If I'm going to get a sundial, I should get the best. Right? Northwest Queoldiola produces the finest, least-expensive, and most technologically advanced sundials in the world. However, Mega-Mart Discount Warehouse Super Center has an ample supply of good old American-made sundials. They're a little more expensive and not quite as good, but they're made in the U.S. of A. by good old Americans. What a dilemma!*

Trade is the name of the game

Before making this all-important sundial purchase, let's consider some basics:

- In our modern, complex economy, few people, if any, come close to what we might call "self-sufficient"— i.e., producing everything consumed.
- This means, as a general rule, that each of us specializes in producing some stuff, then *exchanging* that stuff for other stuff.

Why do we do this? Why do we forego self-sufficiency in favor of specialization? *Because we want to!* Specialization makes us a lot better off than self-sufficiency.

As we saw in Fact #3, Our Unfair Lives, specialization lets us become really, *really* good at one thing rather than being sort of good or even mediocre at a lot of different things. Becky the carpenter makes a nice china cabinet for Phil the gardener. Phil the

gardener grows some zucchini for Becky the carpenter. Both end up with more stuff than they could have produced individually. When everyone in the economy specializes, we have a larger economic pie that (depending on how it's divided) can make everyone better off.

This little specialization and exchange fact of economic life helps explain why we humans are willing to associate with each other in a civilized society. We need others to buy what we produce, and others to produce what we want to buy.

Foreign trade—same game, different countries

If Phil the gardener and Becky the carpenter are better off by specializing and trading, does it make a difference where they live? No! Becky and Phil are no better off if they both live in the same town of Shady Valley, U.S.A. We get the same benefit from trade if Becky plies her trade in Norway and Phil grows his vegetables in Mexico. The benefits of specialization and exchange have no regard for country of residence. The only real difference is that we don't just call this "trade"; we call it "foreign trade."

In that foreign trade is foreign trade only because it crosses national boundaries, let's pause momentarily to ponder this concept of nation. A nation is best thought of as a group of people who have a common *central government* and common *currency* or *money*. Many nations also share common *heritage* and *culture*, but that's not particularly critical. Common money *is* pretty important to foreign trade, however, because that's what we use for buying and selling. When we buy stuff from another nation, we also have to trade one currency for another. (More can be found on this topic under the heading Exchange Rates.) Common government is also critical, because it can, and often does, control what comes into a nation *(imports)* and what goes out (exports). As we'll see in a few paragraphs, governments seldom pass up the opportunity to use their powers of control, and most nations take an active role in restricting foreign trade. Before we get to the *how* of government meddling in foreign trade, let's consider the *why*.

Some win, some lose

There's one thing that almost all economists have agreed on since the dawn of economic time: the overwhelming benefits of foreign trade. *Everyone* is better off with foreign trade. Well, not quite everyone. The benefits of foreign trade are not equally dispersed among the peoples of a nation. Let's think about buying those sundials from Northwest Queoldiola to see why.

- *Imports are good for consumers.* When the United States imports sundials from the Republic of Northwest Queoldiola, U.S. consumers are better off because they have a greater sundial selection. Because U.S. sundial manufacturers have *competition* from Northwest Queoldiola, the price of sundials tends to be lower, a definite plus for sundial consumers.
- *Imports are bad for producers.* However, what's good for consumers is usually bad for producers. Faced with greater competition, U.S. sundial producers get lower prices. Some of the U.S. producers that are barely able to eke out a profit with no foreign competition are very likely to close up shop with it. This will send U.S. sundial workers into the ranks of the unemployed. U.S. sundial producers and their employees would rather not see any imported sundials from Northwest Queoldiola.

Now let's look at those imported sundials from a different perspective, the Republic of Northwest Queoldiola.

- *Exports are good for producers.* When Northwest Queoldiola begins shipping sundials to the United States, Northwest Queoldiolan producers have a larger market and more potential buyers. Greater business means higher prices and more profits for the Northwest Queoldiolan producers.
- *Exports are bad for consumers.* When producers gain, consumers lose. The higher prices and larger market for sundials is a definite minus for sundial consumers in Northwest Queoldiolan.

If so many are hurt by foreign trade, how can economists smugly say that it's good? It's good because more people benefit— and benefit a lot—than are harmed. The good that comes to consumers from imports is more than the harm that hits the producers. The good that comes to producers from exports outweighs the harm that befalls consumers.

How can I be so sure? In large part because the bad stuff is short termed and more apparent than real. A closed factory or a lost job is clearly bad for those involved. It is, however, also an opportunity to reallocate resources into something that is more productive. If jobs are lost in the U.S. sundial industry, then the workers have the opportunity to seek employment in another industry. They end up making stuff that consumers would rather have and thus value more. As such, they also get more income.

Foreign trade is much like a trip to the dentist. Sure, it may hurt a little bit now, but it can prevent a whole lot of suffering— like a root canal—later on. Unfortunately, those who suffer the most in the short term from foreign trade (producers) also tend to have the most political power. That means, our economy seldom visits the dentist even though cavities have eaten away our teeth and we've grown delirious from infection.

Keeping those un-American imports *out*

As we've seen, business leaders of the second estate tend to have more income, wealth, and political power than consumers of the third estate. The second estate also tends to be hardest hit by imports. Now, if you were the president of Omni Conglomerate, Inc., the leading U.S. producer of sundials, and you faced competition from Northwest Queoldiola, what would you do?

Two options are:
1. Make better, less expensive, and more technologically advanced sundials.
2. Eliminate the foreign competition.

The second option is usually the action of choice. The president of Omni Conglomerate, Inc., is likely to take up this topic with a duly elected government leader. The Omni CEO is also likely to mention how much money was donated to the leader's reelection campaign and how many voters' jobs are at the sundial factory in the politician's district. The politician, doing what politicians do, is then likely to have government restrict those un-American, job-destroying imports. Unfortunately, very little attention is paid to the interests of the sundial consumers of the third estate, most of whom aren't in the politician's district.

While the variety of import restrictions is almost as great as there are politicians with constituents who face foreign competition,

the two most common are:
1. *Import quotas.* These simply restrict the amount of stuff that can be imported from a country. For example, Omni Conglomerate, Inc.'s favorite politician might be able to get a law passed saying that Northwest Queoldiola can ship no more than 27 sundials to the United States each year.
2. *Tariffs.* These are *taxes* on imported goods intended to raise prices and reduce sales. Even though Northwest Queoldiola can produce better sundials at a lower cost than Omni Conglomerate, Inc., a 2,000-percent tariff might convince me to buy the lower-quality U.S.-made sundial at Mega-Mart.

A country also discourages imports with devious restrictions on production, such as mandating the use of ingredients, parts, or inputs that can be found *only* in the home country. European countries have set the standard for these sorts of standards. For example, France mandates that wines sold in the country must use grapes grown in France. Germany does similar things with sausages.

Are these sorts of restrictions justified? In some cases, yes. While health, safety, or other such benefits may be had by placing rigid standards on imports, the motive is usually to keep imports out and eliminate competition.

Making the world safe for exports

Exports are as good for second-estate producers as imports are bad. When exports rise, so do second-estate profits. Omni Conglomerate's favorite politician is not only likely to support import restrictions on sundials but also to devise some method of promoting or subsidizing sundial exports. The quaint and courteous Republic of Northwest Queoldiola might be threatened with all sorts of diplomatic sanctions (and perhaps nuclear annihilation) if they don't make a concerted effort to buy more U.S. sundials. After all, we buy theirs; they should buy ours.

You might notice a problem that's likely

to arise when every nation in the world tries to export more and import less. If everyone exports, who imports? Those nations with the most global political power often "force" others to do the importing. Would it be a surprise to learn that the politically powerful nations tend to export to the not-so-powerful ones? I didn't think so.

Yet this "politicizing" of foreign trade usually does little more than add to our world's existing conflicts. In fact, most wars and conflicts throughout history had a significant foreign-trade component. The American Revolution was as much about foreign trade with Europe as it was about political independence from England. The Civil War also emerged as much from trade between the North, South, and Europe as from the question of slavery.

Where does this foreign-trade business leave us as consumers, workers, and taxpayers? Here are a few tips:

FOREIGN-TRADE TIPS FOR CONSUMERS, WORKERS, AND TAX-PAYERS

- As a consumer, you're better off with a wider variety of lower-priced stuff. Imports are your ticket to happiness. The more imports coming into the country, the better.
- If you work in an export industry, that's great. Let's just hope, though, that your company exports stuff because it's a better producer than other nations, and not because government has blessed it with favorable, but inefficient, policies.
- If you work for a company that's heavily besieged by better-quality, lower-priced imports, then keep your career options open. Sure, your industry might get government to restrict imports, but our economy is better off if you get a job in another industry that doesn't need government help to stay afloat.
- As a voter and taxpayer, your interests are best served by unrestricted foreign trade. Your tax dollars shouldn't be wasted on government policies that promote an export here or restrict an import there.

See also: Business, Economic Growth, Exchange Rate, Federal Deficit, Foreign Investment, Immigration, and Unions.

the odds on
GAMBLING

I'm sure there's a great philosopher somewhere who once uttered the words, "Life's a contradiction and we're all a bunch of hypocrites." Take me for example. Just this morning I walked by Smilin' Ted's All-Comers Insurance Agency to drop off my annual shoe insurance premium (for protection against blowouts), then made a pit stop at Master Sprocket's convenience store where I plopped down $5 on five (count 'em, five) Super Luck-O Multi-State Lottery tickets. Within a space of two blocks and 20 minutes, I bought $37.56 worth of shoe insurance to avoid risk and then spent another $5 to take on some risk. Am I a walking contradiction, or what?

Life's a gamble

As we saw in our journey through information with Fact #6, Our Unknown Economy, the world is filled to the brim with uncertainty. We're never quite sure what the future will bring to our pedestrian lives. That's where insurance and gambling come in. You can find out a heck of a lot more about insurance elsewhere in this guide (hint: look under the issue entitled Insurance), but a quick comparison between insurance and gambling is well worth the effort.

Insurance is what you do to protect yourself against the risk of a loss. This includes, of course, the various kinds of car, life, home, and shoe insurance sold by Smilin' Ted. You pay a little bit now to avoid the risk of paying a lot more later.

Gambling is a lot like insurance, but in reverse. With gambling you pay something

for the chance of getting even more. We have traditional gambling like the games of chance in Las Vegas casinos, church-run bingo, state lotteries, and assorted legal and illegal betting on sports. Less-obvious activities are also forms of gambling, including starting a business, playing the stock market, searching for a job, and getting an education. Many of the less-obvious ones are all also forms of Investment: You pay something now in hopes of getting more later—that is, investment is also a gamble.

So the question remains: Are gambling and insurance a contradiction? Can you do both?

Are scaredy cats gamblers?

We also noted in Fact #6 that people have different inclinations toward risk. *Risk-averse* scaredy cats prefer certainty over uncertainty

A PEDESTRIAN...

... goes scuba diving

I THINK I'D RATHER BE RISK AVERSE AFTER ALL!

HEY! LIFE'S A GAMBLE!

O M Amos

and are willing to pay for it. *Risk-loving* gamblers, however, enjoy risky situations over certainty. And *risk-neutral* in-betweeners have no preference one way or the other. Insurance would appear tailor-made for the risk averse, with gambling the elixir of life for risk lovers. That's more or less, but not totally, the case. Let's throw a bunch of numbers together to see why.

Suppose that you have a 5-percent chance of losing $1,000 from a car accident on a cross-country vacation. The expected loss of this predicament is $50, meaning that if you take 100 cross-country vacations, 5 will lead to $1,000 accidents. The $5,000 car repair bill total, when averaged over 100 trips, is $50 per trip.

If you're risk neutral, then on any given trip you don't care if you pay $50 to Smilin' Ted for insurance or are stuck with the 5-percent chance of a $1,000 loss. Risk-averse types, however, are willing to pay *more* than $50, and risk lovers are willing to pay *less*. As discussed elsewhere (hint: see Insurance), insurance is typically sold to the risk averse because insurance companies need to charge more than $50 for this sort of coverage.

Gambling works much like insurance, but in the opposite direction. Suppose that you have a 5-percent chance of winning, rather than losing, $1,000 on something like a charity raffle. What price would you be willing to pay for such a chance? The expected gain for the raffle is $50, meaning that doing this raffle thing 100 times would lead to 5 wins of $1,000 each. Your $5,000 total winnings would then average out to $50 for the 100 raffles.

Much like insurance, a risk-neutral in-betweener sort of person would feel the same about paying $50 for the 5-percent chance of winning $1,000 or keeping the $50 and saying to heck with the raffle. A risk-averse person, however, would be willing to pay *less* than $50 for this chance of winning. A scaredy cat, remember, prefers to have certainty (a sure $50) over uncertainty (the chance of winning $1,000). And a risk lover would be quite eager to pay *more* than $50, because gamblers enjoy the thrill of a risky situation.

The crux of the matter is that all sorts of people, risk neutral, risk averse, and risk loving, are willing to take a gamble, *if the price is right*. As a risk-averse person, there's no contradiction if I willingly pay $60 to avoid the 5-percent chance of losing $1,000, and at the same time pay $40 for a 5-percent chance of winning $1,000. I can pay my shoe insurance premium and buy lottery tickets without fear of contradiction.

The house always wins

Although I'm buying, who's selling? Who in their right mind would be willing to give me a 5-percent chance of winning $1,000 for the low, minuscule price of $40.

Let's ponder this from the bookies', er, sellers' side of gambling. Suppose, your charitable organization intends to raffle off a year's supply of Hot Mamma Fudge Bananarama Ice Cream sundaes, valued at $1,000. If you sell 20 raffle tickets for $50 a pop, then you'll raise the $1,000 needed to buy $1,000 worth of Bananarama Ice Cream sundae coupons from Hot Mamma Fudge. Moreover, each of the 20 raffle tickets has

an equal 5-percent shot at this most-valued prize. Those 20 tickets will be snapped up by risk-loving types, with perhaps a few purchased by some risk-neutral people, but no risk-averse person will take part. Remember, the risk-averse are willing to pay *less* than $50 for a 5-percent chance of $1,000. If you want to entice any risk-averse person into your charity give-away, then you've got to lower the ticket price.

That's easy to do. If you sell 100 tickets, then you can raise the needed $1,000 for the Bananarama Ice Cream sundae coupons by charging a mere $10 per ticket. This should entice the risk averse, right? The problem is that each ticket now carries a lower 1-percent chance of winning. If the potential ticket buyers are risk averse and they recognize these shrinking odds, then they're willing to pay not just less than $50 for the chance but now less than $10. If, however, they *still* think they have a 5-percent chance of winning, then they too will snap up those tickets.

You're probably way ahead of me on seeing some sources of big profit in the gambling arena:

- Your revenue as a seller depends directly on the number of people who pay for the opportunity to gamble and how much they bet (the price they're willing to pay for the privilege of gambling).
- *More* people are *more* inclined to bet *more* if they think their chances of winning are greater. The trick is to make people think that their chance of winning is greater than it actually is. This would even sucker, er, entice the risk averse into gambling.

Most common forms of gambling—casinos, state lotteries, bingo, contest give-aways, and sports betting—are profitable because bettors are seldom aware of their actual chances of winning. (By the way, what are the odds of winning the state lottery?) You can bet your last lottery ticket that casino owners, state lottery commissions, and bingo parlors know the odds of winning. And (here's one of those important "ands") they'll charge enough to cover the prize, plus a little extra for their efforts. Whether *you* win or not, they'll be certain to make a profit. The house *always* wins!

Even when bettors know their actual chances of winning, it often means very little. What does it *really* mean if the chance of winning is one in a million or one in ten million? When the odds are this slim, unfounded optimism usually takes over. "Hey, someone's going to win, why not me?"

It's just for fun

Of course, a lot of gamblers don't expect to win anything, but partake in the activity merely for recreation. Is there any real difference between spending five bucks on the Super Luck-O Multi-State Lottery versus the latest Brace Brickhead action adventure movie at the Shady Valley Shopping Mall cinemaplex? Both give you a bit of entertainment. On the one hand, your pulse can race as you vicariously watch Brace Brickhead burst through plateglass windows. On the other, your pulse can race when you discover you have guessed correctly the first two lottery numbers and anxiously await the remaining four. Does it matter that you leave the movie theater physically unscathed or that you rip your lottery ticket to shreds having once more guessed only two of the six correct numbers? Both give you a few moments of excitement.

Gambling, thus, falls into the entertainment category that includes movies, tourism, theater, television, novels, and a score of similar pleasures. It gives many who gamble (especially risk lovers) a degree of excitement and satisfaction that they could not achieve otherwise. This is good. This is what our economy does: satisfy unmet desires.

But there's a shady side to gambling as well. A shady side that doesn't, contrary to what you might be thinking, have anything to do with criminals and other nefarious types. By shady I mean an unproductive waste of resources.

Robbing Peter to pay Paul

When we exclude the entertainment value of gambling, we're left with nothing more than a transfer of wealth and income. When some win, others lose. The Las Vegas winners hit the big-time jackpots only because other people have lost their nickels and dimes. The multigadzillion winners in the Super Luck-O Multi-State Lottery are basking in the misfortune of gadzillions of people who have wagered a few bucks here or there. Many of the megafortunes acquired in the Stock Market by buying low and selling high are at the expense of others buying high and selling low.

The transfer of wealth and income from gambling wouldn't be such a bad thing, except that society wastes resources in the process. The casino pit boss could be making something productive, like Hot Mamma Fudge Bananarama Ice Cream Sundaes. Or the company that prints lottery tickets could be manufacturing air filters for the Omni-Chopper 3000 lawnmower.

There is, of course, one big exception to the wastefulness of gambling. That is when gambling involves investment. In this case, the payoff for the winner, a new factory or innovative product, also generates a big payoff for the economy (see Economic Growth). We have a creation of income and wealth, rather than a transfer.

Although I can't help you pick the winning horse at the racetrack, here are a few gambling tips:

THE WINNING TIPS ON GAMBLING

- Try to determine if you're more inclined to be risk averse, risk neutral, or risk loving. If you're risk loving, then feel free to satisfy your desire for risk through the thrill of gambling. However, you might want to decide if you enjoy gambling more than other things—like a house, car, stable family life, and bank account.

- Before considering any sort of gambling, you need to discern the odds of winning as best you can. Keep in mind that those who sell gambling services, like casinos and state lottery commissions, will do their best to convince you that the odds of winning are very good. Be wary of their claims.
- From a public-policy view, keep in mind that a lot of the gambling, except for the investment variety, involves a considerable amount of income and wealth transfer. You need to ask whether society can put those gambling resources to a more useful purpose.

See also: Advertising, Crime, Education, Foreign Investment, Mutual Funds, Product Safety, and Wealth.

the sick state of
HEALTH CARE

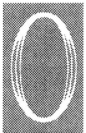

Our pedestrian's guide to the economy would be remiss if we failed to stroll past the Shady Valley Memorial Hospital and my very own physician's place of business, the Dr. Dowrimple T. Bedside Family Clinic, to examine the considerable controversy over health care. A debate has raged for years over health care in the United States, including, but not limited to, the quality of services, their cost, their slice of the economic pie, who pays, who doesn't, and who should.

One big chunk of pie

The good old U.S. of A. has been devoting an increasing slice of economic pie to health care over the past several decades. As recently as 1960, about 5 percent of our pie (measured in terms of *gross domestic product*) was for health care. In 1994, this number was closer to 14 percent. By the time you read this, the percentage will be even greater.

The health care slice has grown, in part, from rising health care prices and, in part, because we're using more resources for health care. We're not yet a nation of wealthy pediatricians, neurosurgeons, and orthodontists who do nothing but examine, diagnose, and operate on each other, but we're getting there.

Yet, we are *the* United States and should expect to have *the* most advanced (and expensive) health care in the world, right? Unfortunately, we spend 14 percent of our

pie on health, while other countries like Japan, Germany, Britain, Canada, and Sweden spend a mere 6 to 9 percent of their pies, and their populations are as healthy or healthier than ours. They spend less, but get more.

The question is: Do we want the hungry health care monster to consume an increasingly larger share of our pie? If the answer is No, we need to get to the source of the problem. Let's start with doctors.

Those overpaid doctors

A frequent target for blame in the health care debate is the medical profession—even my own friendly family practitioner, Dr. Dowrimple T. Bedside. Here is the physicians' contribution to our health care mess:

- *Market control.* Health care professionals are a very select group who require extensive training (Dr. Bedside trained for over a decade), certification, and licensing. This keeps quacks, charlatans, and assorted con artists from performing brain surgery on unsuspecting patients. However, limited admission prevents otherwise-qualified people from joining the health care ranks and gives physicians a fair amount of market control. With the suppliers' *market control* comes higher prices.

- *Information control.* Prices, though, are not the only thing under the thumb of Dr. Bedside. Not only does Dr. Dowrimple T. Bedside and his colleagues control the supply of health care, they also have a great deal to say about demand. They diagnosis your ailment, then recommend the cure that *they* provide. Because their incomes are based on both diagnosis and cure, they have a pretty good incentive to recommend more treatment than needed. (This is an example of the *principal/agent problem* that you can find defined in Section 3.)

A prescription for market control

Let's consider this market control side of higher prices. Physicians and the health care industry maintain a degree of market control in two ways.

1. *Medical school accreditation.* Physicians, through the American Medical Association (AMA), control accreditation of the nation's medical schools. Nonaccredited medical schools are considered, at best, second rate. By controlling accreditation, however, the AMA also controls the number of physicians trained and the total number operating in the profession.
2. *Certification and licensing.* The AMA's market control doesn't stop with training. Once trained, health care practitioners need to be certified or licensed by state medical boards, which, as you might suspect, are comprised of professionals in the industry. This ensures quality control, *but* it also reduces competition.

The bottom line is that Dr. Bedside and

his cohorts have very little competition and a fair amount of market control, and can charge higher prices.

Trust me! You need the operation

Now some details on information control. With the ability to recommend their own services, physicians and other health care types have a powerful inclination toward excessive treatment. Two common forms are:

1. *Unneeded operations.* Hysterectomies, caesarean sections, and gall bladder removals are three common—and lucrative—operations that are often cited as unnecessary. Other examples abound, way too many to list.
2. *Unneeded tests.* Simple laboratory tests, X rays, and CAT scans are just a few of the tests that may be unnecessarily recommended to reach a diagnosis. Two tests may be just as good as one, but they're twice as expensive. Because doctors do the tests and get paid for them, this adds to their incomes and health care costs.

In defense of my good friend Dr. Bedside and other physicians, health care is an inexact science—each patient's illness is unique. Physicians seek as much information as they can get before making a diagnosis and recommending therapy. Because doctors aren't generally inclined to kill their patients or get sued for malpractice, they tend to recommend a few extra tests that might be unneeded, but could improve their diagnosis.

Insurance picks up the tab

The best thing about rising prices, extra tests, marginally justified operations, and higher health care costs for most of us is that we pay only part. Our insurance companies (mine is Smilin' Ted's Allcomers Insurance Agency) pay the rest. Or if you happen to be poor, retired, or disabled, the government pays a bunch of it through Medicare and Medicaid. Is this a great system, or what? Yes and no. Unfortunately, this system of *third-party payments* by private and government insurance helps keep the cost high. Here's why.

You tend to buy more of a good when the price is lower. This holds for coffee, Hondas, movie tickets, *and* health care. If you pay only 20 percent of your health care bill, then you're prone to buy more than if you paid it all. Okay, maybe you won't have elective open-heart surgery, but you might be more inclined to visit your doctor, get a few extra tests—*just in case*—and have some elective plastic surgery.

Who, though, really pays this other 80 percent? In the case of private insurance, the other policyholders pay. In the case of government insurance, like Medicare and Medicaid, taxpayers foot the bill. While you might not pay the physician directly, you end up paying indirectly through higher insurance premiums and taxes. (Check out Insurance for more on this insurance stuff.)

Cutting a smaller slice of health care

Market control of the industry by the likes of Dr. Bedside encourages extra treatment *and greater cost*. Third-party payments through government programs and private companies like Smilin' Ted's insurance agency encourage greater demand *at higher prices*. It's difficult to keep health care prices and cost down with both sides working against us.

The real cost, though, is not so much what we pay as what we give up. Given our first and most fundamental fact of economic life—a limited economic pie—when we use more resources for health care, we give up other stuff.

There are, however, a few things that you can do to control your health care expenses.

CONSUMER HEALTH CARE TIPS

- Make sure that your doctor has a very good reason for any recommended tests. If you think your doctor is conducting too many tests, then make your feelings

known. If you don't get a satisfactory answer, find another doctor.
- Make sure that an operation is truly the best cure for your ailment, and don't be afraid to get a second opinion on any sort of nonemergency, elective surgery.
- If you have any questions about health care expenses and treatments, contact your insurance company. As it tries to hold down *its* payments for health care, it can help you get the best service for the buck.
- It also wouldn't hurt to stay healthy. High health care prices don't hurt if you don't buy.

Unfortunately a single person alone can't prevent the meteoric rise in health cost. This leaves it up to the actions of government. Here are a few policies that might help keep the cost down.

HEALTH CARE TIPS FOR THE VOTING BOOTH

- *More competition in the health care profession.* Quality standards can be maintained without overly restricting the supply of professionals. Movement between occupations, such as physicians and nurses, would help. Nurses, paramedics, and physicians' assistants can establish their own practices to provide health care without the specialized training of physicians.
- *National health insurance.* As a general rule, private insurance let's you pay a small amount to avoid paying a larger amount for an illness, accident, or disaster. A national health insurance, whether run by government or a government-authorized private agency, could provide a similar service. While this won't prevent people from demanding more health care, it can help balance the market control of providers.
- *Fee schedules.* Government Medicare and Medicaid, as well as many private insurance companies, have begun adopting

standardized fee schedules for health care services. For example, they might reimburse surgeons, *at most,* $2,000 for a standard appendectomy. This would prevent providers from raising some prices. Unfortunately, the providers tend to tack the extra fees onto patients who aren't constrained by fee schedules.

- *Preventive health care.* Health care costs can be controlled if no one gets sick. A number of health problems, many of which require some of the most expensive health care, are preventable. These include, but certainly are not limited to, heart disease, cancer, and car accidents. Preventative health care can begin with regular doctor visits, but would also include healthier lifestyles, eating properly, reducing smoking and drinking, and improving automobile safety.

See also: Social Security, Taxes, Welfare, and Worker Safety.

in the neighborhood of
IMMIGRATION

 *Few pedestrians would argue that the Republic of Northwest Queoldiola is anything but a quaint and courteous country. The Northwest Queoldiolans have a cute habit of wearing those little hats with the squirrel tail hanging from the back. They also manufacture the best sundials that money can buy. As a tourist mecca, there's nothing quainter or more courteous than the Republic of Northwest Queoldiola. But, as you may have noticed during our pedestrian trek, several Queoldiolans have decided to pursue permanent residence, and presumably U.S. citizenship, right here in Shady Valley. They have undertaken the age-old process of immigration. But why Shady Valley? These Queoldiolans have some pretty darn peculiar habits. While we're all fond of sundials, they've raised fondness to a religious fervor. Their clothing is, to put it mildly, pretty darn peculiar. The worst part of it: They're willing to work cheap!*

To the ends of the earth

Before we let Winston Smythe Kennsington III assault some of the newly arrived Queoldiolans with a verbal tongue lashing, we had better get to the bottom of immigration.

Our point of departure for immigration is a close conceptual relative: migration. Here are two summary points on migration:

1. When we move from one place to another, we do so in search of higher wages, better jobs, and improved living conditions.

2. A barrier to migration is distance and the associated cost of moving. This has become less important in the United States in recent decades because of better transportation, but it remains pretty significant worldwide.

How does immigration relate to migration? Immigration is simply migration that occurs between countries; that is, people cross national boundaries when they move. More specifically, we talk about "immigration" as migration *into* a country, while a related term "emigration" is migration *out* of a country. These, of course, are merely two sides of the same action. Immigration into one country is nothing more than emigration out of another. In that immigration tends to get the most publicity, especially from vote-seeking politicians, that's the term we'll use here.

Here is the key for immigration: Immigrants tend to move from poorer, lesser-developed countries to wealthier, more-developed ones. Those immigrants

... takes a shower

from Northwest Queoldiola are attracted to Shady Valley because we have higher-paying jobs, a better standard of living, goods of unmatched quality, superior public services, and all sorts of things that make our lives more enjoyable. Shady Valley is like a porch light attracting Queoldiolan moths.

Similar immigration occurs in most of the wealthier nations in the world. Immigrants come into the United States from many lesser-developed nations, especially our close southern neighbor, Mexico. The European nations of Germany, France, and Britain get theirs from poorer African, Middle Eastern, and East European countries. In fact, any country that's doing better than its neighbors is likely to see immigrants knocking on the door asking for a slice of economic pie.

A natural nation of immigrants

While I haven't seen the scientific documentation from those biology types who carve up our chromosomes in search of what makes us tick, I wouldn't be surprised if they didn't eventually identify some kind of "wanderlust" gene. As a species, we've certainly shown the inclination to move around.

That fact is most evident right here in the U.S.A. While some people, like Winston Smythe Kennsington III, have been American born and bred for several centuries, you'll find that their ancestors were born and bred elsewhere, if you go back far enough. That also applies to Native American Indians who did their wandering thousands of years earlier. In this nation, we're clearly a bunch of immigrants.

Our wanderlust inclination is not the only natural inclination that plays a role in immigration. We're also naturally suspicious of strangers. In that our evolutionary survival over the eons was made possible by quickly identifying and reacting to potential threats, we tend to be wary of anything that's new and different (like Northwest Queoldiolans). When we've staked out our territory in a given country, we don't look too fondly on strangers who move in. (There's more on this natural knee-jerk reaction to be found under Discrimination.)

Now that we've had our genetic, biological overview of immigration, let's consider the economics of this issue.

The new kids in town

The most important question we need to ask is: What's the big deal if some Queoldiolans move into Shady Valley? Or as some economic types would ask: What is the cost and benefit of immigration?

Let's list a few of the more well-known concerns expressed by "natives" when immigrants hit town:

- One of the biggest concerns is that immigrants will take away jobs from the natives and cause wages to drop. The extra competition alone is likely to push wages down. However, a big reason for immigration is the dismal state of life and employment opportunities in the home country. Many immigrants are willing to do more for less.
- Another big concern is that immigrants, being poor people from poor countries, are likely to need more public services such as Health Care and Welfare than the natives. This costs the taxpayers and probably keeps some deserving natives from being helped.
- An often unstated concern that's probably shared by most natives is cultural infringement. When immigrants move into a country, they bring with them their own culture, beliefs, and social values. This isn't a problem if the immigrants take up the native culture. If, however, they hang onto their own values or try to impose their beliefs on the natives, then resentment fills the air like a Los Angeles smog alert.

These problems accompany any immigrants from a poorer, culturally different country who seek a better life in a more prosperous land. Immigrants, though, bring some good stuff as well.

- *Labor* is, of course, an important resource for our economy and a key source of economic growth. A significant amount of growth in the U.S. economy during the 1800s can be traced directly to the millions of immigrants who came from assorted European and Asian countries.
- Being from poor countries, most immigrants are not only willing to work for lower wages, they're also willing to do stuff that natives won't. Immigrants often perform the grungy work that comes with being a housekeeper, migrant farm worker, or gardener. Many of the jobs are too disgusting for the natives and might go wanting without immigrants.
- Continuing this line of thought, because immigrants are willing to work for lower wages, the cost of producing goods is also lower. This is, of course, a windfall for the profit-seeking members of the second estate. However, it's also good for consumers who pay lower prices.

Like a lot of other stuff in our economy, immigration doesn't just have good and bad points; it's good for some people and bad for others. If you're working in a grungy, low-paying job, in an area that tends to attract new immigrants, then you stand to suffer. Immigrants will compete for your job and inflict their culture on your neighborhood. If you're a middle-class suburban consumer, then your taxes might go up for the public services used by immigrants, but you also stand to get lower prices on what you buy.

Keeping in mind that we all have a different stake in this immigration issue, here are a few tips to consider:

IMMIGRATION TIPS

- Try to avoid being a knee jerk when it comes to immigrants. Our natural inclination is to be suspicious of foreigners, but people are okay once you get to know them. Don't forget that we're all from a long line of immigrants.
- Of course, it's not easy being compassionate when an immigrant has taken your job. If you're in this position, the best long-run solution is to remove yourself from the grungy-job competition by getting a better education or more training.
- An often-overlooked solution to immigration "problems" is to improve conditions in other countries. Immigrants come here in search of a better life. Why not give them a better life back home? While it's unlikely that all countries will achieve equal wealth, improvements among the poorer ones will reduce the inclination to search out our bright porch lights.
- We should keep in mind that immigration is not *all* bad. It's a source of growth and prosperity. Like all types of migration, it moves labor resources to places where they're more efficiently used to produce stuff. With that, we all benefit.

See also: Education, Exchange Rate, Foreign Investment, Foreign Trade, and Unions.

keeping the lid on
INFLATION

It's Thursday! It's 2:30 in the afternoon! It's pretzel time!! We must make a brief stop at one of Shady Valley's most acclaimed business establishments: Max Mulroney's Pretzel Haven. My favorite, of course, is pretzel-on-a-stick. An ample supply of barbecue sauce is standard fair. I'm taken aback! Max has raised his pretzel prices once again—for the third Thursday in a row. What sort of chicanery is at work here? Is Max trying to gouge the pretzel lovers of Shady Valley? Max says, quite emphatically, No! His pretzel-producing cost has risen. It seems, he explains, to be a pervasive problem throughout Shady Valley. He's not alone in pumping up prices. A quick price-checking, window-shopping expedition through the Shady Valley Central Town Sprawling Hills Shopping Mall, Mega-Mart Discount Warehouse Super Center, Manny Mustard's House of Sandwiches, and even Dr. Nova Cain's dental office reveals truth to Max's claim. Prices all over Shady Valley are rising. I suspect that there's only one way to unravel the intricacies of this mystery; we need to examine the topic of inflation.

On the rise

Inflation is one of those on-again, off-again topics that sometimes catches politicians' and the public's fancy, then falls by the wayside in favor of another. Inflation stirred much public interest in the 1970s but was barely heard from in the 1980s. It comes, it goes. Before we can figure out why the beast is so erratic, we need to figure out what it is.

Here's a straightforward definition of inflation (one of the few straightforward definitions you'll get outside of Section 3): Inflation is a rise in the economy's average price level. Well, that seems to be a simple, straightforward definition, yet it raises an additional question. What is *"the economy's average price level"*?

Measuring our elusive price level

The price level is, quite simply, an average of the prices of goods and services in the economy. In other words, it is the "price" at which our economy's *gross domestic product* (GDP) is sold. It's typically measured with an index, such as the consumer price index (CPI) and the GDP price deflator. Each measures the average of thousands of different prices. During most periods, some prices are rising and some are falling. Inflation occurs when most, but not necessarily all, prices are rising.

A PEDESTRIAN...

The two most common price indexes are:

1. *Consumer price index.* This is the average of prices of the sorts of goods purchased by consumers. As such, it includes the prices of stuff like VCRs, cars, toothpaste, appendectomies, granola bars, Colorado ski vacations, and Hot Mamma Fudge Bananarama Ice Cream sundaes.

2. *GDP price deflator.* The good pointy-headed people of the Department of Commerce give us a more comprehensive index of prices than the CPI: the GDP price deflator. When these folks measure gross domestic product, they measure it in both in *nominal dollars* and *real dollars*. The ratio of *nom-*
inal GDP to *real* GDP gives us our price index.

While there are some differences between the CPI and the GDP price deflator that can be found in Section 3 definitions, they're pretty consistent most of the time.

Crunching some inflation rate numbers

So how is inflation measured from either of these indicators of the average price level? Whether we use the CPI or the GDP price deflator, the procedure is the same. For the sake of argument and illustration, let's say that the CPI for one year (call it year 1) is 100 and for a second year (call it year 2) is 105. (Note that indexes are set up such that a so-called "base year"—our year 1—gets a number of 100.) To find the rate of inflation from year 1 to year 2, we simply calculate the percentage change from 100 to 105. Our example is a pretty easy one, giving us 5-percent inflation. If we wanted the inflation rate from year 2 to year 3 (with a number of 107), then the computation isn't quite so simple. The rate in this case is (107 minus 105)/105, or 1.9 percent.

This method is used for an *annual* price index. However, the CPI and the GDP price deflator numbers come out monthly or quarterly. For example, when the news guys get the monthly CPI numbers, the inflation rate that's calculated is annual rate. In other words, if we calculate the percentage change using this procedure, we would have an inflation rate for one month *only*. The monthly rate needs to be multiplied by 12 to give us an annual inflation rate—sort of the rate that would exist if the rest of the year were exactly like this one month. Annualized rates make it easy to compare periods of differing lengths, such as this month with last year or 6-month period two years ago.

Here's an example: Let's say the CPI is 125.6 in March and 126.2 in April. The percentage change for one month is then (126.2 minus 125.6)/125.6, or 0.47 percent. However, the annualized inflation rate is 12 times as great, or 5.7 percent. When you hear news guys talk about a 5.7 percent inflation rate last month, it doesn't mean prices went up by 5.7 ppercent last month; they increased actually by only 0.47 percent. The 5.7 percent is the annualized inflation rate.

Keeping an eye out for inflation

Throughout the 200-plus-year history of the good old U.S.A., we've had very few years with no inflation. On occasion we see prices holding steady for a few months, or even a few years. We might even see a decline in prices, what the economists term "deflation." Rising prices, though, tend to be the norm.

Yet, there are some periods when we can expect prices to rise more rapidly than others. As we noted in Fact #7, our economy is prone to experience *business cycles*. Our pie expands for a few years, then it contracts for a year or two. Then it begins to expand once more. When the economy contracts, *unemployment* rises; when the economy expands, unemployment falls. (See Recession for more on this.)

Inflation is also inclined to rise and fall over the course of business cycles—moving, though, in the opposite direction of unemployment. When the economy contracts, the inflation rate tends to drop (and occasionally give us some of that *deflation*). When the economy expands, the inflation rate tends to increase. While you might not care to wager your entire life savings on this relationship, you might want to keep track of the business cycle if your plans over the next few years depend on the inflation rate.

The why of inflation

Inflation is out there, usually lurking near the expansion of a business cycle. The question is: Why? What causes inflation? The simple answer is *money*. Our average price level tends to rise when we have too much money.

Here's the story. Money is used to buy stuff. (Without money, we would need a *barter* system—trading one good for another.) Prices of the stuff you buy and sell depend directly on the total amount of money in the economy. For example, let's consider the situation in the quaint and courteous Republic of Northwest Queoldiola. Their currency of choice is the queold. Suppose that the Northwest Queoldiolan government has issued a total of 10 billion queolds. Given this number of queolds in circulation, you can purchase a sundial (a product that has made Northwest Queoldiola famous worldwide) for 50 queolds. What would happen, though, if the Northwest Queoldiolan government decided to bump the number of queolds in circulation to 20 billion?

Although Queoldiolians would have twice as much money, there would be no increase in the production of sundials. The going price for sundials would therefore jump up to 100 queolds. Inflation, as such, is nothing more than too much money chasing after too little stuff.

Throughout the history of our planet, inflation has followed lockstep with increases in money. More money means higher prices. Over the course of business cycles, money tightens up during a contraction, so inflation declines; then money becomes more plentiful during expansions, thus inflation rises. Part of this is by the design of the first-estate leaders, but part is just a natural part of business cycles.

Your worst nightmare?

The records clearly show that inflation is considered by many to be one of the most serious problems facing our economy. Why?

- *Trade a lot, produce a little.* With high inflation rates, people devote more effort to buying, selling, and exchanging, and less to producing. For example, if prices are expected to double by the end of the day (an inflation rate that is actually pretty mild compared to some historical examples), then you will want to spend your money as fast as you can. If you don't spend it in the morning, then it's worth half as much by nightfall. You end up using more time buying and selling stuff *every day,* with less time left for actual working. High inflation rates (10 percent or more per year) usually trigger a fall-off in production.

This production drop, however, is not the biggest problem of inflation. That honor is bestowed on the distribution of wealth and income.

- *Haphazardly transferring wealth around.* Income and wealth are redistributed when prices rise at different rates. Suppose, for example, that our economy has two goods, health care and food, with

each constituting an equal share of our economic pie. If health care prices rise by 10 percent and food prices don't change, then the *average* inflation rate is 5 percent. However, consumers with resources employed in health care get 10 percent more income, while those resources in food production get no additional income. The result is that health care resources get 55 percent of the income, and wealth and food production resources end up with 45 percent. We have a redistribution of income and wealth to health care resources.

Let's wrap up this inflation excursion, giving me a chance to enjoy my pretzel-on-a-stick, with a few tips:

INFLATION TIPS

- Inflation tends to be most deadly to those who are caught unaware. While no one can predict the future with any certainty, you can keep an eye out for assorted forecasts of the economy's conditions for coming years. One of the main things to watch is the money supply. When it starts rising a bunch, then brace yourself for higher inflation rates.

- The redistribution of wealth caused by inflation is usually a bigger problem for the second estate (who have the wealth) than it is for the third estate. As such, the business leaders of the second estate think inflation is a greater problem than unemployment. However, in that underappreciated consumers and workers are the ones most likely to be unemployed, inflation tends to be the lesser of these two evils for the third estate. This difference should be considered when politicians champion their favorite antiinflation or antiemployment policy. Which estate are they most interested in helping?

See also: Economic Forecasting, Economic Growth, Federal Deficit, Financial Markets, Health Care, Interest Rates, Political Views, Taxes, and Wealth.

The risky business of
INSURANCE

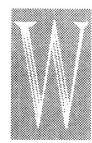

We've avoided the clutches of Smilin' Ted, the insurance guy, during our saunter through the economy, but our luck has run out. Here he comes, ready to offer you, me, and everyone else within earshot the chance to buy auto, health, life, and property insurance. If you really, Really care to ask, I'm sure that Smilin' Ted has other insurance possibilities as well. But I'm not going to ask. If you want to know, then you have to ask.

A world filled with scaredy cats

Avoiding Smilin' Ted's sales pitch is one thing; avoiding insurance is something else. We're all likely to buy some insurance during our pedestrian trek through life. Maybe we won't buy it from Smilin' Ted, but we're likely to buy from someone, somewhere, at sometime. Why? Because it fulfills an important need: to lessen our innermost fears of risk and an uncertain future.

As we saw in Fact #6, Our Unknown Economy, most of us tend to be scaredy cats (or *risk averse*). We tend to prefer a safe, known, and sure income more than an equal amount of income that involves some degree of risk. Another way of looking at this is that we would be just as happy with a lesser amount of known income than a greater amount of risky income, and we're willing to give up part of our hard-earned income to avoid this uncertainty.

That's exactly what insurance does. We pay premiums to an insurance company,

thus leaving us less income to spend on other stuff, but avoiding the adverse financial consequences of illness, accident, fire, theft, or natural catastrophe.

Let's say that you have a 5-percent chance of contracting an illness that would send you to the hospital for a few days and run up a $10,000 bill. The *expected* cost of this event is $500, or 5 percent of $10,000. In other words, if you live 100 different lifetimes, you have the illness leading to a $10,000 hospital bill in 5 of those lifetimes. The average is then $500.

If you're an in-betweener (*risk neutral*), you would be just as happy living an uninsured life and risking the $10,000 hospital bill or paying $500 to an insurance company that agreed to pay your bill in the event of an illness. A gambling, *risk lover* sort of person would be willing to pay something *less* than $500 for the insurance. If you're risk averse, like many people, then you would be willing to pay *more* than $500 to avoid the risk. How much more you

A PEDESTRIAN...

... flies a kite

WOULD SOMEONE CALL MY INSURANCE AGENT?

WHEW! THAT WAS CLOSE

I'M COVERED ONLY FOR LOW FLYING JETS

scREEECH

O M Ames

would be willing to pay depends on your degree of risk aversion. If the price is right, all of us—scaredy cats, gamblers, and in-betweeners—would pay to avoid risk.

Insurance agents to the rescue

We buy, but who sells? Fortunately insurance agents in every mini-mall in every city, town, and community across the nation are willing to sell us insurance. But *why* are they willing to sell? What do they get out of this deal anyway?

One thing they get is access to large sums of money. Insurance companies, like banks and stock brokers, participate in our economy's financial markets. They accumulate

premiums from their clients which they invest in assorted capital, or loan out to others, until such time as they need to pay the claims.

But this is not *the* reason for the seemingly omnipresent likes of insurance guys like Smilin' Ted. Insurance itself is a valuable service that insurance companies are happy to provide, given suitable compensation. They provide this service through the magic of *risk pooling*.

Risk pooling occurs when individuals are lumped into large groups, such that the uncertainty for one becomes a calculated risk for the whole group. For example, let's reconsider your 5-percent chance of hospitalization. In fact, let's throw you into a group of 100,000 people, all with the same 5-percent chance of contracting this horrendous $10,000 illness. (In light of rising health care costs, this might be little more than a sprained ankle. More on this controversy can be found under Health Care.)

We can expect that 5,000 people or 5 percent of 100,000 will get sick. We don't know which 5,000 people, but we're pretty sure that the number will be 5,000. How can we be so darn certain that 5,000 people will get sick? Insurance companies spend a lot of their time keeping records on gadzillions of people to determine what percentage experiences different losses, like our $10,000 illness. (Of course, any miscalculation on their part could be a multigadzillion-dollar error.)

If 5,000 people do, in fact, contract this $10,000 illness, the total hospital expense is $50 million. Would Smilin' Ted be willing to insure this group of 100,000 people against this debilitating illness? Yes, if the price is right.

By charging each of the 100,000 people $500, Smilin' Ted would generate the $50 million needed to pay the hospital expense. This is, however, the absolute minimum charge. Smilin' Ted would need to tack on a little extra, say $50 per person, for administrative expenses and the profit that makes it worth his while.

Insurance for everyone?

A few paragraphs back I noted that scaredy cats, gamblers, and in-betweeners would all be willing to buy insurance, if the price is right! The question is whether Smilin' Ted's $550 charge is the right price for everyone.

Risk lovers aren't viable candidates, because they're willing to pay something *less* than $500 for insurance against a 5-percent chance of loss. They enjoy risky situations and trying to beat the odds. The risk-neutral types, who are willing to pay *exactly* $500 for Smilin' Ted's insurance,

also fall short of the $550 insurance premium. That leaves us with the risk averse, the scaredy cats. They are the only ones who are willing to pay *more* than $500 for insurance protection against a 5-percent chance of losing $10,000. They are the ones who benefit from insurance and are the ones who buy. Because most of us tend to be risk averse, Smilin' Ted has a large group of potential customers.

Subsidies for the unlucky

Perhaps you've noticed a feature of Smilin' Ted's insurance coverage: 95 percent of our group (95,000) pay their $550 premiums, *but get no benefits.* More importantly, these 95,000 healthy people are the ones who ultimately pay the hospital bills of the 5,000 sickly ones. The insurance company is really just a go-between. Feel free to point this out the next time those you know who smoke heavily, drink a lot, drive fast, eat fatty foods, ride motorcycles without helmets, or hang glide tell you it's *their* life to live as they please. When they crash and burn, the rest of us foot the bill.

Why then would those 95,000 who don't get sick be willing to subsidize those 5,000 who do? The answer, of course, lies with uncertainty. As far as we know, any of our 100,000 could get sick. It might be you. It might be me. We just don't know who it will be. This is the essence of insurance: protection against uncertainty. In fact, you might want to think of an insurance premium as the price you pay for being lucky.

But is everyone equally lucky, with an equal chance of getting ill, being in a car wreck, or having their house burn to the ground?

Some make their own luck

Risk can be divided into a part that's purely random—it could happen to anyone at anytime—and part that is controllable. Anyone could have a heart attack, but overweight smokers have a higher risk. Anyone could get into a car wreck, but drunk drivers stand a better chance. As such:

- Given a preference, insurance companies would only insure healthy, excellent drivers, who don't drink or smoke, exercise regularly, eat well-balanced meals, and have weekly home safety inspections. In short, they would insure only people with a low risk of suffering a loss and filing an insurance claim.
- However, if consumers are given a choice, the healthy, excellent drivers—who don't drink or smoke, exercise regularly, eat well-balanced meals, but who do have weekly home safety inspections—wouldn't buy any insurance at the going rate if they knew their minuscule risk of loss. The only ones who would buy are those most likely to suffer a loss.

Mandatory insurance?

We're getting into a real sticky problem here. If insurance companies are left to their own devices, they will cover only low-risk people. If people are given a choice, however, only those with a high risk will be willing to pay the premiums. That's one reason why many types of insurance are mandatory. In most states, car insurance is mandatory. Many businesses require all employees to participate in company health care insurance. And when you think about it, we're all covered by several sorts of mandatory government insurance programs like welfare, unemployment compensation, and social security. The working folk in the country pay into these systems, in part, just in case they're needed in the future. In fact, a lot of what the government does is sort of insurance. We pay our taxes, often begrudgingly, just in case we need the government to "fix" some unexpected problem that arises.

Let's throw this valuable insurance knowledge into three tips:

INSURANCE TIPS FOR THE HEALTHY, WEALTHY, AND WISE

- For nonmandatory insurance, like life insurance or dental plans, try to evaluate your own personal risk. Are you a prudent driver who lives a healthy lifestyle? Then you might not need a lot of insurance.
- With this in mind, be wary of slick-talking insurance agents. Remember, insurance companies make the most profit by selling insurance to people who need it least. The more they try to sell, the less you probably need.
- If you must have insurance, large group plans tend to be best, because administrative expenses and claims are spread out over more people. It's probably not a real good idea to join a group health care plan with only two other people if one has cancer and the other has a chronic heart condition.

See also: Farm Subsidies, Gambling, Lottery, Mutual Funds, Product Safety, Social Security, Welfare, and Worker Safety.

some prime stuff on
INTEREST RATES

*One unexpected benefit from our foot-paced view of the economy is loose change. Keeping our eyes to the ground has uncovered a nickel here, a quarter there, and an occasional dollar bill. My total is up to $137.65, an amount that I'm reluctant to keep on my person. Fortunately Interstate OmniBank has a branch very close the Dr. Nova Cain's dental office. I can deposit my booty in a safe, secure savings account under the watchful eyes of Interstate OmniBank employees, to be withdrawn if needed at a later date. Not only will Interstate OmniBank keep my $137.65 safe and secure, they'll also pay me an interest. That's I deal I just can't pass up.*

An interest rate buffet

The amount that Interstate OmniBank pays me for keeping my money safe and secure depends on an interest rate. While the rate changes from time to time, Interstate OmniBank is currently paying a 5-percent interest rate. That means, for each $100 I let them keep safe and secure for a year, they add $5 to my account. For my $137.65, they add $6.88. (Actually the total amount of interest depends on their compounding method—that is, the number of times during the year that they add interest to my account. To see more on this, check out "compound interest" in Section 3.)

The interest rate that Interstate OmniBank pays to keep my money is only one of several interest rates in the economy—about a gadzillion at last count. You've probably had personal experience with some, no more than a nodding acquaintance with others, and are a veritable stranger to many

more. While anything resembling a complete listing would take more time than we have and, quite frankly, would be as exciting as reading the phone book, a few of the more common ones are: prime rate, rate on Treasury bills, home mortgage rate, discount rate, commercial-paper rate, yield on corporate bonds, savings rate, and credit-card rate.

The one compelling, overwhelming observation that we can make from noting this myriad of interest rates is that they range far and wide. The Treasury-bill interest rate, for example, might be a paltry 3 percent, while the interest rate on your Interstate OmniBank Platinum Diamond Express credit card tops out near 20 percent.

This compelling, overwhelming observation opens up our theme for the next few pages: Why does the *federal government* pay 3 percent when *it* borrows to finance the federal deficit, but *you* pay 20 percent when *you* borrow using your Interstate OmniBank Platinum Diamond Express credit card? Why do I get 5 percent on my savings account, but pay 10 percent on a home mortgage loan? Why are some interest rates higher than others?

Another quick jog through the financial markets

Let's ponder the purpose of interest rates to answer these overwhelming and compelling questions. In so doing, we'll also need to trip lightly through the Financial Markets.

Financial markets trade legal claims on goods or resources in exchange for money. Examples include the stock market, bond market, market for government securities, insurance, and assorted bank accounts. Some people have money they're willing to trade for legal claims, and others have legal claims they're willing to trade for money. Interest rates are the prices that match up the buyers and the sellers—lenders and borrowers—in many of these financial markets.

For example, when my $137.65 of loose change is deposited in the Interstate OmniBank, I become a lender. When you use your Interstate OmniBank Platinum Diamond Express credit card, you become a borrower. In fact, if you charged $137.65 on you credit card, it wouldn't be too far off to say that you borrowed it from me—with a little assistance from the bank.

The question we need to ask now is: Why am I willing to part with $137.65 and why are you willing to pay for the privilege of charging $137.65 on your credit card?

Those sacrificing consumers

An answer to this question comes from a close scrutiny of our preferences for time. Some prefer the present over the future, and thus need a high interest to coax them into lending, or are willing to pay a high interest for borrowing. Others are a little more inclined toward the future and need a lower interest rate for borrowing and lending.

- The bottom line on lending is sacrifice, giving up current consumption. The $137.65 of loose change that I deposit in my Interstate OmniBank savings account could be used for buying stuff that would add to my satisfaction right now. For me to postpone that satisfaction, I need compensation. If I'm willing to lend the Interstate OmniBank $137.65 for 1 year at a 5-percent interest rate, then I'm willing to forego $137.65 worth of satisfaction this year in order to get an extra $6.88 of satisfaction next year. If I need more than $6.88 worth of extra satisfaction to give up my $137.65 for one year, then I won't lend it to the bank. Lending my loose change to Interstate OmniBank is just like supplying my labor. I'll work for $10 an hour, if I'm willing to give up my leisure for that wage. If I need more than $10 to compensate for my lost leisure, then I won't work.

- On the other side of the financial markets, borrowers are willing to pay for the privilege of a little extra consumption today. Suppose the $137.65 charge on your Interstate OmniBank Platinum Diamond Express credit card (with its 20-percent interest rate) is for an evening of fine food with four friends at Gary's Authentic French Cuisine and Truck Stop. You willingly give up $27.53 worth of consumption next year (the interest charge) for the privilege of eating $137.65 worth of authentic French cuisine today. Why would you do this? Perhaps you expect to have more income next year than this year, and thus the interest charge will be more easily paid. Or maybe you're just downright hungry today. Maybe you're so hungry today—to the point of malnourishment—that $27.53 a year from now means very little to you. You're willing to sacrifice future consumption to get the food you need to let you live long enough to have a future.

Don't forget about investment

Consumers, however, don't do all of the lending and borrowing. In fact, one of the more important reasons for borrowing is business investment in capital goods. The interest rate businesses are willing to pay for investment borrowing depends on how much return they receive (or expect to receive) from their capital.

For example, suppose that Gary's Authentic French Cuisine and Truck Stop decides to double its seating, so that twice as many fine-food fanciers can fancy fine food, with an investment price tag of $100,000. Gary, the owner of this fine establishment, would be willing to pay an interest rate up to 10 percent if the extra capacity brings in an additional $10,000 per year in profit (which is 10 percent of $100,000).

Slicing the interest rate three ways (plus cost)

We're now to the point where we can answer the question: Why do I get 5 percent on my savings account, but you pay 20 percent on your credit card?

Every interest rate—whether it's for credit cards, T-bills, or corporate bonds—includes at least three parts (and most have a fourth that we'll note momentarily).

- *Real return.* The first and foremost base for every interest rate stems from the consumer time preferences or business investment stuff we just noted. In an ideal world (one that doesn't have risk or inflation) the real return compensates consumers for current sacrifices and/or results from the productivity of capital investment.
- *Risk premium.* Unfortunately we don't live in an ideal world—in part because the future is uncertain. A lender never knows for certain that a borrower will pay off a loan. A lender, therefore, tacks a few extra percentage points—a *risk pre-*

mium—onto the interest rate to compensate for this risk.

For example, suppose Interstate Omni-Bank needs a real return of 10 percent on $1,000 loans to each of 100 borrowers. That is, after 1 year Interstate OmniBank needs to collect $10,000 in interest on $100,000 in loans. But what if one of those 100 borrowers defaults on the loan, failing to pay off both the original $1,000 loan and the interest? That means Interstate Omni needs to collect a grand total of $11,000 in interest from the remaining 99 borrowers. This is accomplished by charging each borrower 11.11-percent interest rather than a mere 10 percent. The extra 1.11-percent interest is the *risk premium.* When that one low-life, slime-ball fails to pay up, the bank still gets the needed $110,000 from the other 99.

- *Inflation premium.* Another deviation from an ideal world is *inflation.* The problem with inflation is that a dollar today isn't worth the same as a dollar next year. In fact, the higher the inflation rate, the less value a dollar has next year. As such, if a lender needs a particular *real* return on a loan, the interest rate will need to be bumped up to adjust for the rate of inflation. (See Inflation for more.)

To see why, let's go back to Interstate OmniBank's 10-percent real return needed on $100,000 worth of loans. The bottom line is that Interstate OmniBank needs to get back $110,000 in 1 year. Or better yet, Interstate OmniBank needs to have $110,000 in *purchasing power* in 1 year. But what if the inflation rate is 5 percent? What if you need $105 next year to buy the same stuff that you can buy this year for only $100? In this case, $110,000 isn't going to be enough. In fact, what you as a lender need to have next year is about $115,500 to compensate you for the 5-percent inflation. As such, you need to charge a 15-percent interest rate, a 10-percent real return and a 5-percent *inflation premium.*

• *Administrative costs.* The fourth factor that we don't want to overlook is administrative costs. One big difference between the interest rate banks pay for savings and what they charge for loans is administrative expenses. To stay in the business of helping lenders and borrowers get together in the financial markets, they hire employees, pay the electric bill, and generate a bit of a profit. Of course, we must not overlook that fact that lenders with more market control can also extract extra profit by charging higher interest rates.

Now that we've divided up interest rates into their basic parts, let's consider what sort of tips this offers us for any excursion into the financial markets:

INTEREST RATE TIPS

• Riskier loans carry higher interest rates. If you're a good credit risk and aren't likely to default on a loan, then you should be able to get a low interest rate with a small risk premium. Don't subsidize some low-life who can't pay off a loan.

• Be wary of inflation. No one knows for sure what the inflation rate will be next year, but borrowers and lenders make their guess and add them to interest rates. If the actual inflation rate is greater than what everyone thought it would be, then lenders lose and borrowers win. If the actual rate is less than expectations, then lenders win and borrowers lose.

• Information is a key commodity in the financial markets. Some lenders and borrowers know a lot and others don't. Banks, governments, and business leaders, card-carrying members of the first two estates, tend to have more information than consumers of the third estate. They also tend to have more market control. As such, they're likely to overstate risk and inflation premiums as lenders and understate them as borrowers.

See also: Business, Credit Cards, Foreign Investment, Insurance, Investment, Mutual Funds, Profit, Recession, Stock Market, and Wealth.

the business about
INVESTMENT

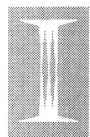

I had fun that last time we wandered into Shady Valley's very own Happy-Time Gala-World Fun-Land Amusement Park. Didn't you? Let's stroll through it again, just to see what adventures we might find. Okay, I admit to an ulterior motive. The Happy-Time Gala-World Fun-Land Amusement Park recently added a new ride: the Cap'n Space Fright Whirl. If you thought the Monster Loop Death Plunge roller coaster was exciting, then you're in for a real treat with this one. My interest in the Cap'n Space Fright Whirl, however, is not from the standpoint of risking a recently eaten meal. On the contrary, I'm going to don my pointy-headed economist disguise and check out this mass of twisted metal and high-flying cages as a prime example of capital. In the process we might be able to gain some insight into the whys and wherefores of the thing we call "investment."

Give a little to get a little—or a lot

We've come across this *investment* idea a number of times on our pedestrian amble through the economy. That's because investment is pretty darned important to topics like Education, Economic Growth, and Wealth. It also pops up in the Federal Deficit, Foreign Investment, and Stock Market. Let's spend the next few pages getting to the bottom of investment.

It's best to begin with what we already know. In Fact #1, Our Limited Pie, we saw that investment occurs when our resources produce more capital goods and fewer consumer goods. We sacrifice some well-being today for capital that will (hopefully) give us more satisfaction tomorrow. While investment takes place in a number of day-to-day consumer areas—like education, job train-

ing, personal planning, and the like—our focus here is business investment on capital goods, such as factories, machinery, and equipment.

All sorts of capital

Here are some of the specific categories of capital bought as investment:
- *Business structures.* These are the buildings that house our economy's business operations, including factories, office buildings, warehouses, shopping centers, hospitals, and, well, any building that keeps the wind and rain from our nation's production. Economists refer to business structures as "fixed plant," meaning the buildings aren't easily moved.
- *Durable equipment.* This is the machinery and tools used by businesses to pro-

A PEDESTRIAN ...

... buys a house

IT SEEMED LIKE A GOOD INVESTMENT

ROVER

I'M NOT LEAVING!!!

I WALK THEREFORE I AM

O M Amos

duce output. Although we could try for an exhaustive list of equipment—starting with abacuses, aircraft, anchors, awls, and axes—by the time we made our way to yokes and zeppelins I would be out of space and you would be pretty darn bored. Durable equipment and business structures are what we usually think of when the term "capital" arises.

- *Residential structures.* A third category might not fall into preconceived ideas of capital. It includes the houses, apartment buildings, duplexes, fourplexes, and every other building designed to accommodate a bed, a refrigerator, and a television set for our pleasure. As business structures give businesses a place to produce output, residential structures give consumers a place to produce homemade, but quite valuable, satisfaction.

- *Inventories.* These are the additions to, or subtractions from, the stockpiles of unsold products or raw materials awaiting processing that businesses keep on hand. It's best to think of inventories as sort of *working capital*—the fuel that's needed to prime the pump of production. For example, if Mega-Mart Discount Warehouse Super Center built a new store, it would need to invest in the building, equipment, and inventory. All three must be in place before Mega-Mart opens its doors.

- *Infrastructure.* Our last category includes streets, bridges, highways, railroads, airports, telephone systems, electric lines, and a bunch of other stuff that moves people, materials, goods, information, and energy. While some infrastructure investment is undertaken by businesses, most is done directly by government, or at least subsidized by taxes.

Saving some pie

Economists use the term "saving" for the part of our economic pie *not* consumed and set aside for investment. Each of our three estates saves in its own way.

- *Consumers saving.* The hardworking, underappreciated, taxpaying consumers of the third estate do find a way to save a few bucks each year. This includes savings stashed in a bank account, like the $137.65 that I found on our pedestrian journey and deposited in the Interstate OmniBank. However, it also includes such things as income you put into a private pension plan and the mortgage payments you make on your domicile. In fact, any portion of your income that is not spent but diverted into the multitude of financial markets, would be considered savings.
- *Business savings.* While consumers save billions of dollars of their hard-earned income each year to help finance capital investment, businesses contribute two to three times that amount. Our second estate diverts a lot of income into investment long before it makes its way to the third estate. This diversion is accomplished in two basic ways: depreciation expenses and retained earnings. Depreciation expenses are part of business revenues set aside to replace worn-out capital. Retained earnings are profit that a business decides to use for capital investment rather than paying out as *dividends* to the stockholders.
- *Government savings.* You're probably thinking: government savings? Does our government save? Our first estate, in prin-

ciple at least, saves if tax collections are greater than spending. At the federal level, a *budget surplus* of taxes over spending is a rare event indeed. The norm for the federal types is a *budget deficit*, with spending greater than taxes. However, many state and local governments do run budget surpluses. And their budget surpluses, when combined, cancel out some if not all of the federal deficit and occasionally generate a little extra for business investment. Moreover, part of the federal deficit is used by the first estate for a bunch of the infrastructure investment. As such, when government builds a highway, our tax dollars are actually saved and invested in capital at the same time.

We could end our discussion of savings with these three estates. However, in so doing, we would leave out a source that's becoming increasingly important in light of our interdependent global economy. That is, our economy also gets investment funds from other countries. During the 1980s and early 1990s, foreign sources financed almost as much capital investment as did consumer savings. It's big, it's important, and it's not likely to disappear any time soon. (See Foreign Investment.)

The investment choice

Let's take a stroll behind the scenes to examine the whys and wherefores of business investment. Our story picks up with Hortense McClintock, the owner and proprietor of the Happy-Time Gala-World Fun-Land Amusement Park. The setting is her office, the time is 1 year ago, the topic of discussion is Cap'n Space Fright Whirl. Should Hortense add this new ride to her assortment of thrill-instilling adventures at the Happy-Time Gala-World Fun-Land Amusement Park, or should she decline?

What does Hortense need to know before making her decision?

1. *The investment cost.* Construction, from start to finish, of the Cap'n Space Fright Whirl is $500,000, and it will take

approximately 1 year to complete. That means our economy must forego $500,000 worth of consumption goods for a year while construction is underway.

2. *Source of funds.* From our savings list, we can identify two ways Hortense can get the $500,000 needed for the Cap'n Space Fright Whirl: existing amusement park profits or the financial markets. She either uses her own money or borrows it. How the borrowed money gets into the financial markets—from households, governments, or foreigners—is unimportant to her situation.

3. *The interest rate.* What is important, however, whether she borrows the money or uses her own, is the interest rate. If Hortense borrows the $500,000 from a bank, raises it by selling shares of stock in the amusement park, or issues some sort of corporate bond, then she needs to consider the payment for those funds, a cost that depends on the interest rate. If Hortense uses amusement park profits, then she must consider the *opportunity cost* of any interest that she *could* have received.

4. *Return on the capital.* Last, but not least, Hortense needs to consider the expected profit to be had from operating the Cap'n Space Fright Whirl. This, of course, is the whole reason for doing the investment. Hortense expects that her patrons will be willing to pay for the Cap'n Space experience. The creation of extra satisfaction with this capital is one example of our whole "expansion of our economic pie" thing.

Let's throw some numbers together and see what sort of investment choice Hortense should make. We already know that the investment cost is $500,000. Let's say that the interest rate Hortense would pay to borrow the needed money is 8 percent. She also has $500,000 of retained earnings receiving a 6-percent interest rate in the financial markets. And finally, Hortense calculates that enough additional patrons will be attracted to the amusement park by the Cap'n Space Fright Whirl to add about $50,000 a year in profits.

Do the prospects for investing in the Cap'n Space Fright Whirl look promising or not?

- Let's take that $500,000 in retained earnings that's getting 6 percent. If left in the financial markets, Hortense collects $30,000 per year. If that money is used to finance the Cap'n Space Fright Whirl, she would get $50,000 per year—an extra $20,000. This alone tells us that the Cap'n Space Fright Whirl is a sound investment. But can she do better by borrowing?
- If she borrows the needed $500,000, then her interest cost at 8 percent is $40,000. The $50,000 generated by the Cap'n Space Fright Whirl would more than cover this expense, leaving her with a cool $10,000. While this option would be good choice, it's not as good as using her retained earnings.

Let's sum this up. When a business ponders an investment, it needs to consider the vast array of potential interest rates and returns to be had, or to be paid, in the financial markets. If a business has the money in hand, then it merely searches out the highest return. This could be the capital investment or in the financial markets. If a business borrows the money, then it needs to compare the interest cost with the anticipated return on the investment capital.

The world is a risky place

The tricky thing about investment, though, is that the expected returns are only that—*expected*. You're never quite sure if the return you expect is what you'll actually get. Hortense would be most disappointed if the Cap'n Space Fright Whirl failed to generate $50,000 in profit. If the return ends up in the $10,000 range, then hindsight tells us that she made a bad investment. But this *risk,* my friends, is the heart and soul of investment. Many businesses have passed up capital investments that ended up far exceeding their expected returns when picked up by others. Others have dumped gadzillions into the toilet by making capital investments that fell far short of expectations.

Most of the big-time investment falls in the domain of the second estate. That, however, doesn't mean it should be ignored by the third. Here are a few tips to consider:

INVESTMENT TIPS FOR THE THIRD ESTATE

- Begin by thinking about the "investments" that you make on a daily basis. Anytime you give up current satisfaction in hopes of getting more future satisfaction, then you're investing. Buying a house, car, or other *durable goods* is an investment. Changing jobs, getting an education, or moving to another state are also investments. Even things like exercising, dieting, or visiting a dentist fall into this investment category.

- Once you identify a potential investment, the next step is to compare expected returns with the cost. If you borrow $10,000 for a car, will it provide you with enough satisfaction each year to compensate for the interest expense? If you use your own savings to buy the car, does the satisfaction compensate you for the lost interest?

- You should also keep these investment rules in mind when you get the chance to dabble in the financial markets. For example, you might want to think twice about borrowing at 15 percent (as with a credit card) while you're lending at 3 percent (as with a savings account).

See also: Business, Financial Markets, Gambling, Health Care, Insurance, Interest Rates, Profits, Recession, Taxes, and Working Women.

a tycoon of the
MUTUAL FUNDS

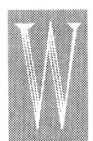

Winston Smythe Kennsington III, our second-estate financial maestro, has given me a hot, and I mean really hot, investment tip. Waldo Industries, the parent company of Waldo's TexMex Taco World, is making plans to expand its franchises. Marketing studies show that people are ripe and ready for Waldo's Super Deluxe TexMex Gargantuan Tacos beyond the confines of Shady Valley. For a minimal investment, I can grab a share of this money-making opportunity. A minimal investment to our Ivy League friend Winnie is $500,000. Unfortunately my bank account, including recent deposits of loose change found on our pedestrian trek, is a few zeros short. Is this another surefire financial opportunity that will pass me by?

Money begets money

It seems as though the only way to *make* a gadzillion dollars by investing in financial markets, including the likes of the stock market, is to *start* with a gadzillion. (See Financial Markets and Stock Market.) Card-carrying members of the third estate, with limited financial assets, find it difficult to play the game like Winston Smythe Kennsington III and his second-estate gadzillion-aire cohorts.

It's an unfortunate fact of life that Winnie and his second-estate cohorts *can* make their gadzillions grow like mold on month-old bread. Most members of the third estate, without gadzillions, don't quite have the same chance. Here are a few notable reasons why:

- *Information.* Risk and uncertainty are the hallmarks of the financial markets. But, as we saw in Fact #6, Our Unknown

Economy, the information needed to reduce risk and uncertainty is costly to get. The greater your wealth, the more information you can have at your disposal. The second estate employs many financial advisors who spend their entire lives searching for the best ways to turn $1 gadzillion into $2 gadzillion.

- *Transactions costs.* Moving your investments through the maze of financial markets, buying here and selling there, rings up brokerage fees, telephone expenses, and assorted costs. Those costs, however, are much smaller relative to a $10-gadzillion investment than a $137.65 investment. Relatively less is eaten up by transactions costs if gadzillions are invested.

- *Diversify.* Risk and uncertainty also make diversification a wise investment technique. It's much easier to diversify into dozens of different investments with $10 gadzillion than it is with $137.65. Some investments, like Winnie's tip on Waldo Industries, need a minimum "entry fee," so to speak. You can't diversify if you have enough for only one investment.

Enter mutual funds

While the second estate might dominate in terms of total dollars in the financial markets of our economy, the third estate actively participates. The primary function of financial markets is to match up lenders with borrowers. In many cases, the lenders are members of the third estate with a few bucks, and the borrowers are the businesses of the second estate aiming toward investment.

Banks and insurance companies play a big part in accumulating funds from the third estate and making them available to the second estate. However, they're somewhat limited in how they use the third estate's accumulated funds. For example, banks don't fiddle around in the stock market.

Wouldn't it be great if the members of the third estate, even though we might not have gadzillions to invest, could gain direct access to some of the highest-return financial markets? Wouldn't it be nice if I could somehow get in on Winnie's hot tip on Waldo Industries even though I don't have a big initial investment? Here's a thought: If I teamed up with a couple of hundred other pedestrians, then together we might have enough for Winnie's money-making investment. This is, in essence, the objective of mutual funds. They give investors with small bank accounts the opportunity to participant in various financial markets that would be out of reach otherwise.

A mutual fund works like this: A mutual fund company administers the combined investment dollars accumulated from thousands of consumers. Because the mutual fund has gadzillions to invest, rather than mere thousands, it operates just like any really wealthy member of the second estate: better information, lower transactions costs, and a great deal of diversifi-cation. In that a mutual fund provides fewer services than banks, it also has fewer expenses. The end result is that investors get higher returns.

All sorts of mutual funds

As most daily newspapers show, there are hundreds of mutual funds offered by a multitude of different mutual fund companies. What the newspaper doesn't show is that different mutual funds usually pursue different objectives. If you're contemplating the mutual fund route with any of your spare change, you need to get a good handle on these objectives. A few of the common ones are:

- *Liquidity.* Several sorts of mutual funds put their funds into so-called "money markets," which deal in short-term Treasury bills, commercial paper, and the like. These act much like savings accounts (but pay a higher interest rate) with the goal of keeping funds liquid or easily transferred into other funds.

- *Bonds.* A popular investment of mutual funds is the wide assortment of long-term corporate bonds, Treasury bonds, and municipal bonds. Some of these funds, especially those for municipal bonds, can provide tax-free interest. However, be sure to read all of the fine print to see if you qualify.

- *Growth.* These search out stocks that are most likely to experience a rapid price increase. The basic philosophy here is to buy low and sell high. Of course, this tends to be very risky because it seeks out the short-run ups and downs of the financial markets. Be careful with these.

- *Income.* These funds rely primarily on quarterly or annual dividends or returns paid on stocks and/or bonds. The goal here is more long-term, secure investments that prosper along with the long-term growth of the economy.

- *Growth and income.* These funds seek to balance the risk of high-growth stocks with the returns from more secure, long-term growth of stocks and bonds. They're not a bad sort of general mutual fund investment.

- *Commodities*. Some mutual funds invest exclusively in gold, silver, farm products, or other commodities. As such, they perform right along with these commodities, which means you can stand to gain or lose *a lot*.

- *International*. A number of mutual funds buy nothing but stocks and/or bonds from another country or group of countries. These funds gain or lose with the growth or decline of the country or countries. The *exchange rate* is also important for these funds (see Exchange Rate).

- *Selected industries*. Many mutual funds invest exclusively in the stock of a particular industry, such as health care or telecommunications. A fund's performance is tied directly to the profitability of the underlying industry.

TIPS FOR THE MUTUAL FUND TYCOON

- Some mutual funds are better than others. In addition to differences in what the funds try to do, there are differences in how well they do it. Some pay high returns and have low administrative costs, and others don't.

- Several consumer and business publications provide annual mutual fund evaluations. Check them out before jumping into the mutual fund ball game. It's worth the effort to do a little research before investing.

- Every mutual fund, by law, provides a *prospectus* to potential investors that outlines, in some detail, the goals, structure, fees, and types of investments of the fund. This is something that you want to read carefully before investing.

- Overall, mutual funds are a viable investment and saving option for anyone without a lot of extra money. Many funds require no more than a few hundred dollars to open.

See also: Credit Cards, Foreign Investment, Gambling, Insurance, Interest Rates, Investment, Profit, and Wealth.

conserving our

NATURAL RESOURCES

Mona Mallard Duct Tape Industries, the world's leading producer of duct tape (that all-purpose, omnipresent, shiny gray tape), is located right here in Shady Valley. Perhaps you've heard that they recently developed a new-fangled form of duct tape that's certain to revolutionize duct tape as we know it. This revolutionary development has, however, created a "situation" that we, pedestrian explorers of the economy, should consider. Mona Mallard's new duct tape uses "quagliminium," a relatively limited mineral found only in the quaint and courteous Republic of Northwest Queoldiola. Prior to this duct tape development, quagliminium had only one use, as a lubricant for OmniStraight shoestring straighteners. The Northwest Queoldiolan supplies were sufficient to lubricate shoestring straighteners well into the year 3000. As a duct tape input, though, quagliminium deposits will be exhausted in a scant 50 years. Should we, could we, allow Mona Mallard to exhaust the supply of quagliminium? If they do, how will future generations lubricate their shoestring straighteners? Should we call for a moratorium on quagliminium use?

We eat to live

Before we get too deeply into the question of conserving quagliminium and other natural resources, we must face an unwavering fact of human existence. To perpetuate our lives, we *must* (let me reiterate *must*) make use of our planet's natural resources. We *must* cut down trees, bust the sod with tractors, suck oil from the ground, bulldoze an occasional mountain, slaughter some cows, and, yes, use quagliminium. Our natural environment cannot remain in its pristine, natural state as long as we're on the planet.

The *quality* side of our natural environment is discussed in more detail under the heading of Pollution. The next few pages are devoted to the question of *quantity*.

A shrinking pie

My favorite planet—the third one from the sun—is blessed with bountiful natural resources. It provides us with an abundance of raw materials that we have used over the millennia to satisfy our myriad wants and needs. But—as we noted all the way back in Fact #1, Our Limited Pie—these natural resources are limited. Our planet came with only so much stuff. Certainly the quantities are large, but they are limited. This, of course, is our age-old problem of *scarcity*.

The situation facing quagliminium is representative of that for most natural resources on our planet. Our supplies of fossil fuels (coal, oil, and natural gas), minerals, clean air and water, fertile soil, wilderness areas, and, well, most every natural feature on the planet, seem to be on a rapid road to exhaustion. The reason for this is two fold:

1. We have a great many people roaming around the planet, more so than at any time since the beginning of time. At last count, there were 5 1/2 *billion* sets of wants and needs seeking satisfaction.

2. We're rapidly increasing the *standard of living*—that is, the quantity and quality of stuff consumed—of these 5 1/2 billion people. Providing food, clothing, and video games for 5 1/2 billion people requires increasing amounts of natural resources.

Let's reiterate that we, right now at this very moment, are hitting the pinnacle of humanity's use of natural resources. We are mining, extracting, and transforming our natural resources at a rate unmatched in the history of our planet. Pretty awesome thought, eh? Let's dig a little deeper.

All resources are not created equal

While our resources are fixed, some are more fixed than others. Economists, and others who lose their hair worrying about the supplies of natural resources, like to note three sorts:

- *Perpetual.* These are resources, like rainfall and sunshine, that persist regardless of anything we do. The sun keeps shining and the rain continues to fall. The amount available today is certainly fixed, but like magic, their supplies are automatically replenished tomorrow.

- *Renewable.* These are resources, like plants and animals, that naturally perpetuate themselves without any actions on our part. Their supplies are also fixed

at any given time, but they can be expanded. In fact, unlike perpetual resources, we *can* affect the supplies of renewable ones. We can help their growth—a process that is exemplified by farming, forestry, and fisheries. Or we can exhaust their supplies if we're not careful. We haven't the space to list the plant and animal species that have achieved the distinction of extinction in the last 100 years through the, often unknowing, efforts of human beings.

- *Nonrenewable.* These are other resources, like fossil fuels and minerals that have absolutely, totally, completely fixed amounts for all time. Some of these resources (minerals) were bestowed on our planet by the forces creating the universe billions of years ago. Others (fossil fuels) were provided by the benevolence of the geological forces shaping our planet a scant hundred million years ago. The forces creating them are unlikely to return in the foreseeable future. Once these resources are used up, they are gone, nada, no more.

Making the most of what we have

On the one hand, we have natural resources that are limited in different ways. On the other hand, we have 5 1/2 billion people demanding goods and other stuff produced from these resources. Our mission is to determine the best—that is, most efficient—way of using these resources.

It is not, however, just those 5 1/2 billion people that enter into our efficiency question. Billions of people, yet unborn, will be greatly affected by our use of natural resources today. Any resources we use now cannot be used by future generations. Let's see what we need to consider for each of the three sorts of resources noted above.

- *Let the sun shine in.* We don't need to concern ourselves over the use of perpetual resources. It matters not how much we use today, because more will be waiting tomorrow. In fact, from an efficiency view, we should make the most use of any and all available perpetual resources. When we don't use perpetual resources, we're missing out on a valuable opportunity that has absolutely no cost. Let me reiterate that point: Using perpetual resources—*especially the sun's energy*—imposes no opportunity cost on future generations. This is as close as we can get to a *free* good.

• *Use, but don't abuse.* Renewable resources can be used like perpetual resources, to a point. Renewable resources have what we can call a "rate of regeneration," that is, the natural rate of growth. So long as the rate we use renewable resources is less than this rate of regeneration, we're in good shape. We'll never exhaust the supply or cause extinction. For example, if 10,000 trout in a stream have a natural 5-percent growth rate, then we can catch 500 each year without reducing the total below 10,000. Moreover, if a new seedling is planted each time a mature tree is chopped down, then our forests will continue into perpetuity. Problems, of course, result when our use outpaces regeneration.

• *Use a little, save a little.* The question regarding nonrenewable resources is: How much do we use today to satisfy our wants and needs, and how much do we save for future wants and needs? Each drop of oil, every cubic inch of natural gas, and any molecule of iron used today imposes an opportunity cost on humans of the future. We get it and they don't. For efficiency's sake, we need to make sure that the value we get from today's use is equal to the opportunity cost on the future—the value future generations give up. We need to spend more time on this question. Read on.

An unknown value

There's a big problem in efficiently using nonrenewable resources, because we don't know the opportunity cost imposed on the future. In that the people are yet to be born, we don't know what value they'll place on

resources and the goods they produce. Will our descendants 100 years from now think a gallon of gasoline is worth $1? Will they think it's worth 10 cents? $10? Who knows? We certainly don't. Not now. Not today.

If we don't know the future value, then how can we decide how much to use today and how much to save for tomorrow? If, for example, we conserve a gallon of gasoline, giving up $1 worth of satisfaction in the process, but our descendants give it a 10-cent value, then we made a big mistake. We've traded $1 dollar of satisfaction today, for 10 cents of satisfaction tomorrow. Alternatively, if we use a $1 gallon of gasoline now that would have been worth $10 for future humans, then we've screwed up once again. We've lost $10 of future satisfaction for $1 of current gain.

Thoughts on future value

While we may not know what the future will bring, we can make some educated guesses. Let's ponder some of the things that are likely to affect the future value of a nonrenewable natural resource. In that value is affected by both supply and demand, let's consider each.

• *On the supply side,* the most obvious source of value is the quantity of nonrenewable resources available. All things considered, if the supply is less, the value is likely to be higher. We naturally tend to value stuff more when we have less of it. This alone would make future, diminished supplies of nonrenewable resources more valuable.

• *On the demand side,* the value of nonrenewable resources springs from two related items. First, resources are more valuable when they produce more valuable (consumer-satisfying) goods. Oil is valuable today because it's used to power our beloved and highly valued cars. Future supplies of oil would be less valuable if future people didn't value cars as greatly. Second, resources are more or less valuable depending on the availability of alternatives used to produce valuable goods. A tankful of oil is much less valuable if we have another source of car fuel.

Taken together, these two items suggest that our future generations will tend to place a greater value on our (their) shrinking supplies of nonrenewable resources, unless and until alternative resources are found.

A whimper, not a bang

When we use nonrenewable resources today, their prices (that is, values) will tend to rise into the future. With smaller supplies, future generations will value what's left more dearly. As such, they (the future folk) are naturally going to conserve. They're going to direct what's left to their own highest-valued uses. They'll also seek out alternatives to their limited supplies.

Contrary to occasional projections of gloom and doom, we're not likely to suddenly "run out" of our finite natural resources. Over the years, our resources will dwindle and we'll be forced to develop, discover, or invent new ones. We may eventually run out of some resources, but it won't be an event reported with blaring headlines in the morning newspaper. It'll probably be little more than a sentence or two buried in a book (or on computer disk) somewhere deep in a dusty library: "Historians estimate that ___ (fill in your favorite nonrenewable resource) was no longer used during the first/last (pick one) half of the ___ century."

Some options

The question, though, is: What can we, or should we, do at the present? Should we conserve the limited resources we have, to reduce the opportunity cost on future generations? Should we let the future worry about its own resources?

- *Conserve.* If we pursue the option of intense conservation, saving as much as we can today, then future generations will certainly have more resources available.

Is this, however, a wise choice? Historically, each generation has been better off (higher living standard) than the previous one. Technological advances are largely responsible for this. As such, by conserving we're probably sacrificing needlessly. We may conserve gasoline for cars that will never be built, replaced instead with something far superior.

- *Invest.* The probable prosperity of posterity, however, should not be taken for granted. Exhausting our resources today, doesn't mean they should be used unwisely. Technological advances and a rising standard of living are the result of investment. We have a high living standard today because our ancestors had the foresight to invest in productive resources. We could use our nonrenewable resources for current gratification. If we, however, used those resources for investment in technology, education, research, and capital, then future generations will be better able to deal with exhausted supplies.

This all means that we shouldn't be overly concerned with future supplies of quagliminium. If society wants and needs the newfangled duct tape developed by Mona Mallard Duct Tape Industries, then we don't want to haphazardly prevent it's production. As the supply of quagliminium runs out, then OmniStraight will have the impetus to seek out new lubricants for its shoestring straighteners. In fact, they might find or develop an even better lubricant. That's how it has worked before. Conserving just for conservation's sake usually creates unnecessary hardships.

With this in mind, here are a few tips:

NATURAL RESOURCE CONSERVATION TIPS

- Care should be taken *not* to overuse renewable resources, like plant and animal life. If used properly, they can last into perpetuity.
- Perpetual resources need to be used as much as possible. Each day that sunshine

goes unused is a wasted day. This is an area of public (government) investment that is sorely lacking. A great deal of solar energy technology is on the horizon, but it needs the big-time investment bucks that only government can provide. If you ever considered writing an elected official about anything, this is a good choice.

• We're probably more concerned with exhausting our nonrenewable resources than we need to be. They *will* be exhausted—eventually. Our concern is best directed toward *how* they're used before exhaustion. The more we use these resources for investments in technology, education, and productive capital, the fewer problems our descendants will face.

• Another way to alleviate some problems of resource exhaustion, one that's growing in importance, is recycling. Every ton of materials reused today is a ton of stuff that's not extracted from the ground. Recycling is a double-bonus coupon for our society. Not only does it limit the use of resources, it also reduces pollution.

See also: Economic Forecasting, Economic Growth, Education, Federal Deficit, Financial Markets, Foreign Investment, Investment, Social Security, and Wealth.

the economics of dueling
POLITICAL VIEWS

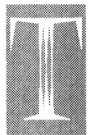 *There seems to be a disturbance on the steps of the Shady Valley City Hall. Why, it's the twins, Donna and Rhonda, engaged in yet another of their long-running, and overly heated, political arguments. Donna, you see, is a devoted Democrat, and Rhonda is a rigid Republican. They haven't found much to agree on since, well—come to think of it, they've never agreed on anything. In their current debate, Donna is making a strident case for stricter regulation of the banking industry, and Rhonda is championing the virtues of free enterprise. I had better hitch up my jogging pants and intervene before their argument comes to blows—again. While I do, let's ponder the source of differing political views.*

What's the difference?

If you're like most card-carrying members of the third estate, you probably wonder if there are any real differences between politicians who espouse liberal Democraticese and those who profess conservative Republicanism. Aren't they all just a bunch of slick-talking, vote-seeking, pocket-lining, power-hungry egomaniacs bent on deceiving the public and getting elected? Well, sure, but they also tend to have some basic philosophical differences guiding their slick-talking, vote-seeking, pocket-lining, power-hungry pursuit of office.

Let's see if we can discern a few of the fundamental political, social, and economic differences among conservative Republicans and liberal Democrats.

- *Conservative Republicans.* Like Rhonda, conservatives tend to champion free enterprise, or limited government control of the economy. They make the argu-

ment that people should be rewarded for their hard work and shouldn't expect government handouts through the welfare system. They are also heavily into national defense, law enforcement, and promotion of the fundamental values of family, God, and country on which this great nation of ours was founded. (Makes you want to sing the "Star Spangled Banner," doesn't it?)

- *Liberal Democrats.* As Donna is prone to note, liberals take a more paternalistic view of the government. It is the last and only hope for many members of society who have suffered at the unscrupulous or uncaring hands of others. They contend that business would run amuck, exploiting workers and consumers in every market exchange, if not for government oversight. They also tend to be more concerned that everyone in society has equal access to a fair share of the eco-

A PEDESTRIAN...

... gets a raise

CONGRATULATIONS, SON! YOU'RE NOW RICH ENOUGH TO VOTE REPUBLICAN!

BUT, IT'S ONLY TWO DOLLARS

FOOT SOLDIER

© M Amos

nomic pie, regardless of race, creed, sex, religion, shoe size, bank account, eye color, or planet of birth. (Their hearts bleed for all.)

These differences often (not always, but often) place conservatives and liberals, Republicans and Democrats, on different sides of issues such as school prayer, environmental quality, worker safety, abortion, the death penalty, welfare reform, business regulation, sexual harassment, and, well, just about every other newsworthy topic over the past 10 gadzillion years.

But, you say, "Wait one moment! I'm a registered Democrat, but I support school prayer and think taxes are excessive—two conservative favorites." Or you might contend, "I'm a lifelong Republican, but I want a cleaner environment and support a woman's right to abortion—both of which are usually in the domain of the liberals." Does this make you schizophrenic, hypocritical, or both? Not necessarily, as we'll see in a few paragraphs. In fact, there are few *truly* liberal Democrats or *absolutely* conservative Republicans who support, without question, the "straight" party line. Many members of the third estate have a combination of liberal and conservative views.

A first stab at the second and third estates

A good jumping-off point on political views is the difference between the second and third estates. As we've already noted a few times, your own personal membership in the second or third estate is based largely on your ownership and control of resources and your resulting wealth and income. Members of the second estate tend to have extensive ownership and control over resources, especially highly valued capital and natural resources. The third estate, in comparison, includes a lot of consumers, workers, and taxpayers who control little more than their own labor resources.

My job here would be a heck of a lot easier if the dividing line between the second and third estates was crisp and clear. Unfortunately (for me), there are some people like Winston Smythe Kennsington III who are charter members of the second estate, with vast wealth and the ownership of several Fortune 500 companies, and others who personify the third estate by toiling away for nothing more than a weekly paycheck that's quickly eaten up by taxes, food, rent, and gasoline. But there are a whole bunch of people who fall into an enormous gray area separating the second and third estates. If you do a lot of working, consuming, and taxpaying but also have an impressive investment portfolio, are you in the second or third estate?

This question is important because Republican and Democratic views originate with the second and third estates. Republicans tend to be from the second estate and Democrats are populated with the ranks of the third. The reason is that political ideology is often guided by economic interests. If I'm a wealthy second-estate Republican, then I would like to see policies that increase and protect my wealth. This would make me really, *really* big on law enforcement and national defense. If, however, I'm a hardworking, consuming, taxpaying Democrat from the third estate, I'd like to see a close government eye kept on the exploitative tendencies of business. I want the government to give me a chance to increase my own wealth. *Different economic interests give us different political views.*

Our economic mountain

In Fact #1, Our Limited Pie, we talked about the economy as an economic pie. A slightly different metaphor is more suited to this trek through political views—a mountain. The more resources, production, income, and wealth you have, then the higher you are on the economic mountain. Some of us toil near the base, and others exert control from the top.

Our economic mountain tends to have three pretty distinct terraces: top, middle, and bottom. The top of the mountain is reserved for the fortunate wealthy few who are members of the first and second estates. The majority of the population who make up the third estate occupy the middle and bottom terraces, with the middle class conveniently on the middle terrace and the poor huddled at the bottom.

More than rocks

Our mountain, though, is more than just economic wealth; it's really the combined political, cultural, social and economic institutions, ideals, and values of society. Think of it as *cultural* wealth. In the good old U.S.A., our cultural wealth includes such things as the English language, a European heritage, the ideals of family and marriage, a Judeo-Christian religious inclination, private property, individual liberties, the U.S. Constitution, and assorted beliefs that we probably take for granted most of the time.

This means that your position on the mountain depends not only on your economic wealth but also on the degree to which you possess these common political, cultural, social, and economic institutions ideals; and values. A poor, black, Satan-worshipping, Portuguese-speaking, female immigrant from Haiti, who practices polygamy, is likely to be on the bottom terrace. However, our good friend, Winston Smythe Kennsington III, who is a white, Anglo-Saxon, Protestant male, with ownership of several Fortune 500 companies, and direct ancestral lines to the Founding Fathers, is right there at the top.

Looking up and down

Those at the pinnacle of the mountain and those at the bottom have some pretty straightforward, although opposite, goals in life. If you're in the second estate, then you want to stay at the top and are most concerned about protecting yourself from the lower terraces and from those from another mountain—that is, foreign country—who want to invade your turf. Thus, you favor a strong police and military to protect your property, an educational system that instills your cultural wealth in your kids, and a legal system that lets you do whatever you damn well please with *your* mountain. Conservative Republicans tend to reside at the top.

If you're on the bottom terrace, in contrast, you have nowhere to go but up. When you try to climb to the middle or upper terraces, you're confronted with barbed wire, avalanches, and other barriers imposed from above. The second estate, in particular, seems to enjoy throwing rocks at you from their exalted perch. Your only chance of rising to a higher elevation may be to flatten the entire mountain with a bulldozer—which scares the hell out of the second estate. You support policies that equalize income, tax the wealthy, regulate the business practices of the second estate, and change the cultural wealth of the mountain to include your own personal beliefs. This is the domain of liberal Democrats.

The middle-class occupants on the middle terrace are right there in the middle of this battle between the top and bottom. The big question then is: Are you more concerned with the rocks hurled at you from the top or with the thundering hoards and their bulldozers at the bottom? Or alternatively: Who is your biggest threat, the top or the bottom?

Your Democratic or Republican political leaning depends on your answer to these questions. Democrats tend to feel more threatened from the top, and Republicans are more wary of those at the bottom. But it doesn't have to be all one or the other. Because our economic mountain is complex and diverse, you might tend towards the Democratic view on some topics and the Republican view on others.

Enter the first estate

Although political leaders of the first estate reside at the top of the mountain, they can do so only with the support of the second and third estates. In that the first-estate Democratic leaders tend to have the numbers on their side (most people are in the third estate) as they champion the interests of the huddled masses at the bottom, they would seem to have an easy time staying in power. However, the first-estate Republican leaders with the backing of the small, but incredibly wealthy, second estate, are formidable political adversaries.

The trick, of course, is to get the middle class siding with the top against the bottom, if you're a Republican leader, or the bottom against the top, if you're a Democratic politician. Unfortunately for the middle class, the political ploys between Republicans and Democrats best help those at the very top or very bottom, with only minimal benefits for the middle. Such is life!

With that in mind, consider a few tips on political views:

TIPS ON OUR IDEOLOGICAL ECONOMIC MOUNTAIN

- All of us, whether we realize it or not, have a political view shaped by our location on the economic mountain. In fact, in many cases, our view is shaped by our parents' location on the mountain when we were young.

• Support or opposition for government policies is invariably shaped by ideology. Be wary about those who favor or criticize something until you know their underlying view.

• Don't be used as a pawn for those on the top or bottom of the mountain. Be wary of sacrificing your body just to protect the wealthy from the encroaching hoards at the bottom. Also, don't let the bottom use you as a stepping-stone to greater heights.

• Perhaps most importantly, keep an open mind. It's a big mountain.

See also: Discrimination, Foreign Trade, Stock Market, Regulation, Wealth, and Welfare.

scraping up the
POLLUTION

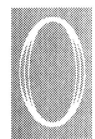 One of Shady Valley's featured factories is Mona Mallard's Duct Tape Industries. It's the world's leading producer of duct tape—that shiny, seemingly omnipresent, clothlike tape that's used for everything except ventilation ducts. Mona Mallard's Duct Tape Industries also employs thousands of voting, taxpaying Shady Valley residents. The amount of campaign money, legal and otherwise, contributed by Mona Mallard herself to Shady Valley politicians is, well, incalculable. All of this means that our little pedestrian exploration through the backlot dumping ground of Mona Mallard's Duct Tape Industries main production plant puts us on very, very sensitive turf. The reason, of course, is that the duct tape plant has been discarding sticky, toxic, gooey junk onto the ground. This is a potentially hazardous situation, not only because this sticky, toxic, gooey junk appears to be leaking into the Shady Valley River but also because a Mona Mallard's Duct Tape Industries security guard is headed in our direction. Rather than confront this guard, I suggest we spend our time exploring the problems of pollution. Run!

Is it pollution, or isn't it?

If put to a vote, I suspect that a majority of us would agree that the sticky, gooey junk dumped behind the Mona Mallard's Duct Industries plant is pollution. After all, it's a waste product that's fouling up what would be an otherwise clean environment. You shouldn't be too hasty, however, in casting your vote for or against. Let's see why.

Pollution is some sort of waste material spewed into the environment. The sticky, gooey junk from the duct tape plant is certainly a good candidate. Noxious gases coming out of car mufflers is another. Being a waste material and being spewed into the environment, though, only sets the stage for pollution. To be more specific, pollution occurs if we have damage or harm

caused by waste material that's spewed into the environment. If there's no harm, damage, or what balding, bespectacled economists would note as *opportunity cost*, then there's no pollution.

Here's an example to illustrate the point. One of our biggest sources of water pollution in the good old U.S.A. is municipal sewage. This sewage contains organic material with the *potential* to foul up a body of water. It can lead to dead fish, obnoxious odors, sick people, and all sorts of other damages. This sewage is not necessarily harmful under all circumstances. If, for example, you dump just a tiny bit of sewage, like that created by one house in one day, into a really big body of water, like Lake Michigan, then it's likely to cause little or

. . . catches a few rays

I WONDER IF THERE'S ANYTHING TO THIS GLOBAL WARMING STUFF?

© M Ames

no harm. The reason is both simple and quite important. Our natural environment has the ability to assimilate, breakdown, and eliminate some waste materials. The plants, animals, bacteria, and other natural components of Lake Michigan will break up a small amount of sewage without creating problems for humans or other living things.

The problems from municipal sewage, however, surface when there's more than the environment can handle. For example, if you dump a year's worth of municipal sewage from New York City into a small fishing pond, the pond's ability to break down the stuff is overwhelmed. Then the bad things happen.

Some is worse than others

The damages caused by waste depend on the sort of waste it is. Here are three alternatives:

1. *Degradable.* Organic waste, like municipal sewage and the waste from food-processing plants, is considered degradable because it can be naturally broken down by the environment. Degradable materials need not be a pollution problem so long as there's not too much.
2. *Nondegradable.* At the opposite end of the spectrum lies waste materials that *cannot* be broken down by the environment. Examples include certain met-

als like lead, mercury, and chromium, or compounds containing these metals. While these occur naturally in the environment, they pose serious health problems when they're concentrated. This is particularly troublesome in that much of our economy's production does just that—increases the concentration of stuff.

3. *Persistent.* Between degradable and nondegradable, we have waste materials that can and do break down, but the process takes time. Persistent stuff usually includes complex synthetic materials, like pesticides and plastics. Many of the pollution problems of persistent materials result because (1) they're synthetic and our natural environment doesn't know what do with them, and (2) they remain in their synthetic state for years, decades, or even centuries, doing whatever damage they do for a long time.

Time is pretty crucial when we're concerned about pollution damages. A degradable, organic residual might cause a little bit of damage for a short period of time. A nondegradable metal like lead, however, can do its dirty deed for a long, *long* period. Even though it causes a tiny bit of damage this year, it continues causing that tiny bit of damage every year we're on this planet.

A big question, as we sludge through Mona Mallard's toxic backlot, is: How significant is our pollution problem? Has it been blown out of proportion by alarmist, environmental nuts? Or will it cause the end of civilization as we know it? Read on.

What comes out, goes back

Pollution is a fundamental part of life. We depend on our natural environment. We need the air to breath, the water to drink, and the land to grow our food. The natural environment, or what we've referred to as "natural resources," provides us with all of the "stuff" we use to satisfy our wants and needs.

But here's the important part. According to the basic laws of nature, none of the stuff, the "matter," we use to satisfy our wants and needs is destroyed. We might change it around, make it look different, combine it with other things, but it never disappears. If we take a ton of something from the ground, then we have a ton of stuff. It doesn't magically shrink to a half a ton.

What happens to this stuff when we're through with it? After it has done it's needs-satisfying job, where does it go? The answer of course is: back to the environment—to the air, water, or land. Some of it goes back almost immediately, and some stays around for years, decades, even centuries. Eventually, though, every ton, every pound, every ounce, every single atom and molecule returns to the natural environment as unneeded, unwanted waste. Some may return during production, some during consumption, and the rest after consumption, but it will return. Therein lies the potential for pollution.

So how do we keep these omnipresent waste materials from doing their damaging deed?

When markets fail

Balding, bespectacled economists like to talk about *efficiency*, efficient markets that efficiently allocate our scarce resources in the most efficient manner possible. If a market has a lot of buyers and sellers, such that none has any *market control,* then we usually think of it as efficient.

A market might also be inefficient, if (here is a notable exception, one that's pretty darn important to this topic) some of the opportunity costs don't enter into the seller's price. The market has failed to use our economy's resources efficiently. In particular, with the extra cost floating around in the economy, paid by someone who's not connected with the market, our society then uses too many resources to produce too much of the stuff.

Let's see how that works for duct tape. When Mona Mallard's Duct Tape Industries dumps its gooey stuff on the land behind the plant, two things happen.

1. Mona Mallard's Duct Tape Industries doesn't pay to dispose of this pollution. That saves cost—for them. This is good for the duct tape business, but potentially bad for everyone else.

2. If this gooey stuff is in fact toxic, then its existence in the environment poses a health hazard to people, plants, animals, and other living things. In other words, someone is hurt, harmed, or damaged by this gooey stuff. Those who are hurt, harmed, or damaged pay the cost. It might be medical bills or the psychic harm of an ugly-looking river. But Mona Mallard's Duct Industries doesn't pay.

The cost of producing duct tape is thus less than it would be with *all* opportunity cost included. The price of duct tape is also less than it would be with all opportunity cost included. And buyers buy more duct tape than they would if all opportunity cost is included. This gives us one solution to pollution problems. Make polluters pay the opportunity cost.

Make 'em pay

Many pollution problems could be solved if polluters simply paid the cost of their pollution. If Mona Mallard's Duct Industries, for example, paid for the damages caused by that gooey, sticky, toxic stuff, then they would charge a higher price. Buyers, who pay the higher price, would tend to buy less duct tape, which would mean a cut in duct tape production, and we would end up with less of the toxic, sticky, gooey stuff dumped.

How do you make polluters like Mona Mallard's Duct Tape Industries pay this extra cost? The simplest way is with a tax. While taxes are generally thought of as a "bad" thing, here they can actually do a lot of good. If government slaps a tax on duct tape production, equal to any pollution damage cost, then Mona Mallard's Duct Tape Industries and their duct tape buyers will act as if they're the ones suffering. And

they are, with the tax.

As such, Mona Mallard's Duct Tape Industries has a big incentive to reduce pollution, because with less pollution, they pay less tax. In fact, Mona's factory will reduce pollution (and thus the tax) until it's more expensive to clean up the toxic, sticky, gooey stuff than it is to pay the tax. Without getting into any complicated mathematical equations, suffice it to say that this would give us that magical state of *efficiency*. The opportunity cost of cleaning up the mess would be equal to the opportunity cost of damages caused by the mess.

A regulation alternative

Taxes, however, may not be the best way to correct all pollution problems. For some waste materials, pollution damage problems and cost are unknown. We have no way of knowing what sorts of damages result from the whole range of persistent and non-degradable materials returned to the environment each year. Even now, we're only beginning to find out some of the pollution damages from waste products returned to the environment decades ago.

The health problems from asbestos, lead, and mercury are a few that have popped up in recent years. We're still debating the possibilities and potential problems of global warming caused by carbon dioxide and of the destruction of the atmosphere's ozone layer caused by fluorocarbons. The pollution cost of newly developed synthetic materials may not be known for decades to come.

It's difficult to use a tax without knowing the damages. That's why some potential pollution problems fall under the general heading of government *regulation*. In some cases, perhaps even many cases, the government is better off just saying "Thou shalt not pollute."

A final word on pollution politics

Pollution is an area of our economy that screams out for some sort of government action. The private dealings between third-estate consumers and second-estate businesses just won't solve the problems. Once again, however, the question of who the first estate represents becomes important. Our little excursion behind Mona Mallard's Duct Tape Industries has a number of real world implications. If the first estate has, in fact, obtained sizable campaign donations from the likes of Mona Mallard, then they're less inclined to force an extra tax on the second estate.

In contrast, third-estate control of the first (which does happen from time to time) can cause excessive improvement in environmental quality. "What?" you ask. "How can the environment be too clean?"

We can use too many resources to clean the environment too much. While we might have a pristine environment, everyone dies of starvation.

The answer is a balance. The best public servant is one who seeks a balance between the interests of the polluter and the pollutee—one who seeks the middle road. While this advice on moderation is important in most areas of public policy, none is more critical than pollution.

See also: Business, Health Care, Investment, Natural Resources, Political Views, Product Safety, Regulation, Taxes, and Worker Safety.

a somewhat defective look
at
PRODUCT SAFETY

Wait! Stop! My shoe's untied! And my blasted shoestring is tangled! Fortunately I have my handy OmniStraight shoestring straightener, a product developed by a team of former NASA scientists which is designed to straighten and untangle even the most convoluted shoestrings. Oops! You might want to continue your pedestrian journey without me. It seems as though my handy OmniStraight shoestring straightener has inadvertently dissected my shoestring, mangled the upper half of my jogging shoe, and introduced several gashes to the top of my foot. As I faint face-first onto the sidewalk from the loss of blood, you can consider some of the ins and outs of my predicament.

Limping through some options

What do I do in a situation like this? A product that I bought in good faith has not performed as promised. I've read and followed all instructions. I've cared for my OmniStraight shoestring straightener like it was a prized Stradivarius violin. However, a defective cog or malfunctioning lever or discombobulated spring has led to some injurious consequences. What to do? What to do?

I could return the OmniStraight shoestring straightener to Mega-Mart Discount Warehouse Super Center, the place of purchase, and request a refund. I'm sure they'll be accommodating. But even with a purchase price refund, I'm left with a dissected shoestring, a mangled jogging shoe, and several gashes in my foot.

Maybe OmniStraight will compensate me for the cost of my shoe and medical expenses. Or maybe they won't. What if

they don't? I suspect I'm looking at an extended battle of legal wits with Omni-Straight, their parent company Omni Conglomerate, Inc., and a veritable army of lawyer-types. Who knows how many other defective OmniStraight shoestring straighteners have been used by unsuspecting consumers. Does this sound like one of those David and Goliath sagas? Read on!

The customer's always right?

Let's crunch our rather complex economy down into a simple, uncomplex nutshell. If I'm dissatisfied with my OmniStraight shoestring straightener, then I'm *not* about to buy another. Makes sense. In fact, with a bloodied foot I'm really, *really,* Really likely to tell other potential customers about my problem. If OmniStraight has enough defective products and thus dissatisfied customers who extend their horror stories to a number of potential shoestring straight-

A PEDESTRIAN ...

... has a birthday

I DON'T THINK CANDLES ARE SUPPOSE TO DO **THAT!**

KA BOOM!!

Happy Birthday

CANDLES

O M Ames

ener customers, then OmniStraight's business will suffer.

This devastating possibility gives Omni-Straight a big incentive to turn out defective-free shoestring straighteners. If I'm the head, president-type, of OmniStraight, with a careful eye on my bottom-line profit, then I want to make sure that I have high-quality, defective-free shoestring straighteners. No complaints. No problems. A bunch of profit. Right?

Unfortunately it doesn't always work this way. My goal as president-type of Omni - Straight is *not* to keep every customer happy with high-quality, defective-free shoestring straighteners—in spite of what my commercials say. No, my goal is to make a profit. This can be accomplished in two ways:

1. I can charge high prices to customers who are exceedingly satisfied with high-quality, defective-free shoestring straighteners. Of course, while the production of high-quality, defective-free shoestring straighteners is costly, profits remain high as long as the exceedingly satisfied customers are exceedingly willing to pay exceedingly high prices for defective-free quality.

2. I can also make a bunch of profit by using inferior materials, eliminating quality control, and cutting whatever production corners are there to be cut—anything and everything that can keep my cost down. Aha! This is obviously where defective products enter the

Product Safety   171

But isn't it best, profitwise, to take the high road of high-quality, defective-free products? Won't I lose my customers if I crank out inferior shoestring straighteners? Where's profit without sales? Here are a couple of reasons why it might be more profitable to take the low road and let some defective products escape the half-closed eyes of quality control inspectors:

1. Making sure that every shoestring straightener is defective-free is costly. Okay, so a few customers lose a toe or two, then they sue, and I end up with hefty legal costs and pay out tons of money for damages. It might be more profitable for me to go this law suit route, if my legal cost are less than my quality control cost.

2. The low road can be profitable if I maintain demand. My biggest incentive to take the high-quality road is that word of defective products and disgruntled customers will decrease demand. If I can keep demand and price up while taking the low road of inferior, defective products, then my profit will be well into the lucrative range.

I have just two things to say about the profitability of taking the low road: information and *market control.*

What you see isn't what you get

Here's a shocking observation: *We live in a very complex world.* It's difficult, and growing more so all of the time, to get all the information you need about all of the products you buy and use. Going back to Fact #6, Our Unknown Economy, we know that information is a scarce and costly good. It's this cost that keeps us from knowing everything that we, as consumers, would like to know about the quality of cars, VCRs, toilet paper, and, yes, even shoestring straighteners.

We could spend the time and effort needed to collect product information by reading through consumer publications, watching television to catch a random con-

sumer feature on the nightly news, or digging through volumes of scientific reports buried in the deepest recesses of the library. But, hey, who's got the time?

The cost of information, however, is much less for producers and sellers because they own the good. They've designed it and produced it. It's easy, and relatively inexpensive, for them to know all about *their* good. You, the unsuspecting buyer, however, tend to know very little about it.

In fact, most, if not all, of the information we get about the stuff we buy comes from the sellers themselves, usually through advertising. This, of course, is the same advertising that's created by the sellers who want nothing better than to sell you, the consumer, more of their product. You can probably already see some *big* potential problems with this situation. Here are two of my personal favorites:

1. Sellers tell only the good, not the bad. Their objective with advertising is to sell products. They won't sell many products if potential buyers hear all sorts of bad things. Sellers have every incentive in the world to go out and discover anything *good* about their product—even if it's not totally true. OmniStraight, for example, will do its best to find out and inform you if shoestring straighteners *could* be conceivably be used to fasten your bow tie.

2. Not only won't sellers tell you about any *known* deficiencies in their products, they'll also do their best *not* to discover them. And if they've discovered them, they'll do their best to keep this knowledge from you.

This unequal access to product information is in itself not totally devastating. News travels fast, and bad information travels really fast—that is, when it can.

A battle between the second and third estates

It's a harsh reality, as we saw in Fact #3, Our Unfair Lives, that ownership and control of our economic pie is not divided equally. Moreover, the mega-behemoth producers of the second estate tend to have a great deal more control over resources, production, and markets than consumers of the third estate. This, of course, includes product information.

Let's reexamine my nearly decapitated foot. OmniStraight has a defective product. In its defense, it may be unaware of its defects because it has little incentive to find out. But if it does know, it will also do everything in its exceptionally abundant power to make sure that this information is not widely available. To what legal or illegal extremes it will go is difficult to say. I suppose murder is out of the question—unless it's the most cost-effective route.

In most cases, however, the route is probably a matter of spending some big bucks on positive advertising, employing an army of security guards to protect information, intimidating disgruntled customers in court and forcing them to pay enormous legal fees, and, of course, using bribery and blackmail where appropriate.

Under the circumstances, I might be better off quietly buying a new pair of jogging shoes and paying my own medical costs. We need not bother OmniStraight about something as trivial as a defective shoestring straightener, right?

Another job for the first estate

One of the big reasons we put up with government is that it protects the less powerful third estate against the sometimes malicious actions of the second. When the second estate becomes too powerful, the job of the first estate is to balance out the scale. A whole bunch of government Regulation, especially by the Consumer Product Safety Commission and Federal Trade Commission, is intended to do just that. Laws that deal with product safety are but one part of this whole regulation spectrum.

Here's how the first estate goes about protecting the third against the second:

- *Information.* In that a lot of product safety problems rest with the lack of information, a key role for government is to provide information to the consuming public. That's why several government agencies perform safety tests or require sellers to supply relevant information to consumers. Some of the most noted examples are ingredient labels on food products, mileage estimates on new cars, and drug testing that uncovers harmful side effects. Most consumers can make sound buying decisions when they know about potential risks or defects.
- *Safety standards.* Some defects are just so potentially destructive that mere knowledge is insufficient. The government also imposes numerous safety standards on products. This includes health standards for food and drugs, construction inspections on new buildings, and assorted pollution emission standards on cars and factories. (This would be a good place to direct your attention to the entry on Pollution.)
- *Product recalls.* The government is also inclined to force producers to fix defective stuff or otherwise remove them from store shelves. Cars, food, drugs, and children's toys are some of the goods that are most prone to recall because defects are discovered after they're produced.

We shouldn't leave the first estate and its role in protecting consumers against defective products, without noting a few problems.

1. Overzealous government types, prompted by overzealous consumer groups, can *overprotect* consumers from time to time. Consumer protection needs to balance the risk from defective products against the satisfaction the products provide. Nothing in life is perfectly safe. Our world is an inherently risky place to live. If a product with a 1- in 10-million chance of harming someone is removed from the market, then 9,999,999 satisfied consumers suffer for the protection of one.

2. The first estate, in its role of protecting the third estate, frequently works on behalf of the second. When this happens, product safety actions can be used to protect sellers rather than buyers. One of the most common ways is to use safety standards, under the guise of protecting consumers, to restrict the entry of potential competing suppliers into a market. We want stringent standards for doctors and other health care workers, but we have to ask whether the standards do little more than keep competition out and prices high.

TIPS FOR THE SAFETY-CONSCIOUS CONSUMER

- Our economy is inherently designed to send defective products into the hands of the consuming public. *It will happen!* Information can protect you from defects, but of course you can't find out everything. For example, the high price of a house probably warrants spending some bucks on an inspection. The same can be said about getting information before a potential car purchase. However, it's probably *not* worth the trouble to discover which brand of writing pencil is most reliable.

- In spite of my somewhat cynical view of the second estate, it should be said that many businesses do try to keep customers happy. If you get a defective product, let them know. This is your first recourse, and in many cases the business will do what it can to keep you satisfied. If not, this action will give you useful documentation to pursue other options.

- One of the other options is to get the government on your side. Many cities, most states, and a number of federal agencies have people who deal with product safety. Usually a call to the office of your state's attorney general or your local district attorney will set you on the right track. Local Better Business Bureaus are also a good place to turn.

See also: Gambling, Health Care, Insurance, Political Views, Profit, and Worker Safety.

A perfect picture of
PROFIT

Good news! Manny Mustard, my longtime friend and proprietor of Manny Mustard's House of Sandwiches, is having a special on his Deluxe Club Sandwich. Let's drop in for a brief respite—and lunch. More good news! Manny is bubbling profusely about the vitality of his business. Last month he turned a profit. Yes, that much-cherished profit, the goal of business firms, be they large or small. On closer inspection Manny's profit calculation might be suffering from an oversight or two. It seems as though Manny neglected to pay himself a wage. Nor did he bother to include any interest expense on the savings he invested in his House of Sandwiches venture. But what the heck, he earned a profit—didn't he?

The many faces of Manny's profit

I'm afraid that Manny's jubilation will turn a bit sour once his profit calculations are refined. That's because the number on the bottom of his profit-loss statement isn't really profit. Oh, it might be profit as far as some accountants are concerned, but it won't satisfy pointy-headed economists. It's not that Manny or you should spend your lives satisfying the whims and eccentricities of economists (heaven help us if we did that!). But there are a few interesting things about profit that the economists can tell us, like a different perspective on so-called "profits."

As if our world isn't complicated enough, there are different ways to define and calculate profit (three at last count). Each has its own meaning and interpretation. Keep an eye out for the one favored by the economists. Here they are:

- *Accounting profit.* This is simple enough. It's the revenue a business takes in minus the expenses it pays out, and it's aptly termed "accounting profit" because it's what you'll get from a roomful of accountants punching numbers into their calculators. I don't mean to speak badly about accountants—what would we do without them?—but there are a few problems with accounting profit. In particular, when accountants follow standard accounting practices, tax codes, and the like, they're inclined to include some expenses that aren't really "cost" and ignore other "cost" altogether. The result is that accounting profit may or may not bear any relationship to actual profit.

Before we continue, perhaps we should think about what we really mean by "profit." The simplest definition is probably the best: "revenue less cost." In other words, profit is the excess of revenue over cost. The revenue in most profit calculations is pretty straightforward; however, the cost is not. For economists the term

A PEDESTRIAN...

. . . isn't invited to a board meeting

GENTLEMEN, I'VE DECIDED TO GIVE US A 300 PERCENT RAISE

ANY OBJECTIONS?

DO WE GET STOCK OPTIONS AGAIN THIS YEAR?

O M Amos

"cost" means *opportunity cost;* it means what you give up to get something. Many of the business expenses that accountants punch into their calculators are honest-to-goodness opportunity cost. A business pays out some bucks to get labor, materials, or whatever. There's no problem there. Under some circumstances, however, a business doesn't pay out accounting bucks when opportunity cost is incurred. Under other circumstances, a business pays out more than opportunity cost.

We'll pursue these thoughts further in a few paragraphs. However, at the moment, we have enough information for our second kind of profit.

- *Economic profit.* This is the most important profit for our economy, our society, and our efforts to use our limited resources efficiently. Specifically, economic profit is revenue minus *all* opportunity cost—most that are explicit accounting expenses and others that are implicit cost with no cash changing hands. In other words, economic profit is the difference between the revenue buyers are willing to pay for stuff (which depends on the satisfaction received) and the opportunity cost of producing the stuff (which is the satisfaction that consumers *don't* get from stuff that's *not* produced). Here's the importance of economic profit:

Our economy efficiently uses our limited resources, *only* when there's no, *and I mean absolutely no,* economic profit. If a business, any business, has an economic profit, then the value of the good it produces is worth more to us, consumers of the third estate, than the value of the stuff we're giving up. In other words, we want more of it than we're getting, and we're willing to give up other stuff to get it.

Sometimes you pay, sometimes you don't

Before we get to our third kind of profit, let's look into some opportunity cost that is likely to differ from accounting expenses.

- *Pollution.* This is a good example of an opportunity cost that doesn't show up as an accounting expense, unless the government forces it on a business through taxes or regulations. The trick is that pollution tends to inflict opportunity cost on people who have nothing to do with the production, sale, or consumption of a good. A business doesn't compensate these people with a cash payment, and may not even know an opportunity cost exists. (For more on this topic, see Pollution.) However, this unaccounted opportunity cost means that accounting profit *overstates* economic profit.

- *Economic rent.* Of course, you're probably familiar with the term "rent." That's what you pay the landlord each month for your leased apartment. However, economists have a slightly different, although not totally unrelated, meaning for the term "rent." *Economic rent* is the payment a resource owner receives over and above the opportunity cost of the resource. In other words, if you're willing to do your job for $10 an hour, but you get paid $15, then you're getting $5 an hour in economic rent. You can probably see how this might affect the calculation of profit. If resources are getting more than their opportunity cost, accounting expenses are greater than opportunity cost. The

inescapable result is that accounting profit *understates* economic profit.

Let's not pass by this point too quickly. *Market control,* as we see with Fact #4, depends on the degree of *competition* on each side of the *market.* If a resource supplier has little or no competition, and thus a lot of market control, then there's a real, *real,* Real good chance that the price will be greater than the opportunity cost. The supplier gets economic rent. It further means that some of the economic profit that would have gone into the pocket of an owner goes instead into the pocket of the resource supplier. This idea of sharing-the-profit is a main objective of unionized labor. If company profit is up, then unions are out to get their share. (See the entry on Unions for more on this.)

- *Proprietor resources.* A third difference between accounting expenses and opportunity cost is what transformed Manny Mustard's jubilance into despair. A proprietor, as the owner and operator of a business, is inclined to use a number of personal resources in a business with no payment and thus no accounting expenses. The reason is pretty obvious. The proprietor, like Manny, gets to keep all revenue remaining after out-of-pocket expenses are paid. That's proprietor's income. Someone like Manny doesn't care *why* he gets the income, he's only concerned with *how much.* While he called it "profit," it's really part profit (perhaps) and part payment for some of his resources. For example, as his number-1 employee, he uses a lot of his own unpaid labor to operate Manny Mustard's House of Sandwiches. He also, as I alluded to at the beginning, invested some of his savings in the restaurant, without paying any explicit interest. Manny might also have overlooked payments for some natural resources that he owned, like the land where his House of Sandwiches is located. These are all cost, they're all important, and they all need to be deducted to calculate economic profit.

The last of the profits

We've now come to our third kind of profit. This last profit isn't really a profit so much as it's a cost—an opportunity cost. Let me explain this potentially perplexing statement.

- *Normal profit.* All resources have an opportunity cost. If they're not doing one thing, they could be doing something else. This includes those risk-taking folks in our economy who organize resources into production: entrepreneurs. Manny aptly fits the description of entrepreneur. He's taken a big risk by starting Manny Mustard's House of Sandwiches. He rented some space in the mini-mall; purchased some tables, chairs, and kitchen equipment; hired a few workers; bought the necessary sandwich-making ingredients; then started selling sandwiches. Here's the key, he could have applied these entrepreneurial efforts to another business. He could have started an ice cream parlor, convenience store, garden center, pet store, or anything else. The economic profit that he's giving up from those other alternatives is an opportunity cost—a normal profit. In fact, it's as much an opportunity cost as the six-figure salary he gave up when he quit his job as a video game tester to "hire" himself as a sandwich maker. That six-figure wage was a payment for his labor resources; the normal profit he could have earned by organizing another business is a cost of his entrepreneurial resource.

Any business that wants to compute its true, totally accurate, economic profit, needs to subtract a normal profit.

The best ways to get some economic profit

Economic profit (as opposed to accounting profit or normal profit) is the excess of revenue over opportunity cost. When it exists, our economy is inefficient. That doesn't mean it's all bad. In some cases economic profit is good. To see why, we need to see why economic profit emerges.

- *Market control.* The truly bad, *bad,* Bad economic profit arises from market control. For example, if a monopoly supplier (like Merciless Monolithic Media Masters cable television) raises the market price, then economic profit usually results. In the process, resources are inefficiently used. After years and years of long, hard study, economists have found nothing good to say about this source of economic profit.

- *Innovations.* A very, *very,* Very good way to get some economic profit is to introduce an innovative product or idea. If the public likes what you're doing, then you stand to accrue a small fortune, by way of economic profit. While such profit is inefficient, the innovation helps our economy expand and prosper. The short-term inefficiency of economic profit is a small price to pay for the new products that improve our long-term standard of living. (More on the economy's growth can be found under Economic Growth.)

A word on the two estates

Our look at profit would be incomplete without considering the second and third estates. While there is good that comes from economic profit, there's also bad.

Profit is the number one way the second estate gets a larger slice of our economy's pie. When the economic profit rolls in, the second estate becomes wealthier. When the second estate becomes wealthier, they seize more market control (and political power) and get even more economic profit. If left unchecked it could lead to (and in past societies has led to) servitude or slavery for the third estate. We're pretty fortunate in the good old U.S.A. because we have all sorts of checks and balances that (usually) prevent this. Our democratic principles give the third estate enough political clout to keep the accumulation of wealth from tipping too far in the direction of the second estate.

This is a delicate balance in light of the good that economic profit does for our economy. How much inefficient economic profit and inequitable wealth accumulation will give us the desired economic growth and prosperity? Without profit, there's no growth. With too much profit, there's servitude.

See also: Athlete Salaries, Business, Farm Prices, Interest Rates, Mutual Funds, Regulation, Stock Market, Taxes, and Wealth.

on the lookout for a
RECESSION

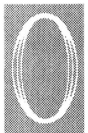 *One pitfall facing any pedestrian who explores the intricate details of the economy is large potholes lurking along the path. Look Out! You can probably expect a few bumps and bruises from abruptly introducing your face to the pavement. But after the cast hardens and the gashes have been stitched, you can be on your way—a little more experienced, no doubt, but forging ahead in spite of it all. Our economy also steps into an occasional pothole en route to an expanding economic pie.*
"Recession" is the nifty term we use for this sort of economic pothole, and it will be are our topic for the next few pages. Oh no! Look Out!

Making acquaintance with recessionary potholes

As our economy moves along the unrepaired highway of life, we encounter a great deal of unevenness, much of which is inconsequential. We shake, we rattle, but we usually keep rolling. On occasion, however, we hit one doozy of a pothole. Our economy is thrown into a tailspin that lasts for a year or two. The first question we need to address is: How do we separate the economy's inconsequential shaking and rattling from an actual, bonafied, real-life recession? Or alternatively: What is a *recession* and how do we know when we're in one?

In principle, a recession is a general decline in economic activity—a shrinking of our economic pie—that lasts 6 months or more. There's nothing really magical about the 6-month time period other than it keeps the government types from worrying too much about incidental shaking and rattling. Instead, they're able spend their

time (and our tax dollars) dealing with leg-breaking, teeth-jarring potholes.

We usually know when we're in a recession by looking at *real gross domestic product,* the best measure of our economic pie that we have. When our pie shrinks, real gross domestic product goes down. Other measurements, however, can also tell us that we're in a recession. Some of the more common indicators are:

- *Unemployment rate.* This is the percentage of people who would like to work, but who aren't working. When a recession hits, the unemployment rate goes up. When a recession is over, the unemployment rate goes down.
- *National or personal income.* This is the amount of income earned from producing our economic pie. With less pie produced, and fewer workers working, there's less income.
- *Retail sales.* As the name suggests, this is the amount of stuff that consumers buy

A PEDESTRIAN ...

... gets a job

IT'S BEEN A REALLY TOUGH RECESSION

I APPLIED BUT THEY SAID I WAS OVERQUALIFIED

O M Amos

from stores. During a recession, we aren't working and producing as much, and we have less income; thus we buy less stuff from stores.

- *Government taxes.* A recession also tends to see a decline in government tax receipts because we're getting less taxable income and buying fewer taxable goods.

I could continue this list, but you probably have a good idea that a lot of stuff in the economy shrinks in a recession. That's the idea behind the "general decline in economic activity." Like tripping over a pothole, our economy falls down during a recession, suffering a few bruises or breaking a minor bone, but we're usually able to get up and keep going.

The short and the long of it

While recessions get the headlines and publicity from the news media, they're only part of the ongoing economic process we term "business cycles." Let's put it all in context by pondering the short run and long run of the economy.

- In the *long run*, the size of the economic pie tends to expand with increases in the quantity and quality of the resources. You can find out more about this under the heading of Economic Growth. However, what we need to note here is that the ability of the economy to produce and supply consumer-satisfying stuff in the long run increases with economic growth.

- In the *short run,* however, we may or may not buy all of the stuff that our economy is *able* to produce. This is where recessions enter the picture. If we, the buyers, don't buy everything our expansive economy can produce, then we have a recession. If, however, we try to buy *too* much—more than our economy can produce—then we end up with inflation (see Inflation for more).

As such, here's the picture: Our economy has a certain production ability based on the quantity and quality of our resources. We're always trying to make full use of that ability—no more and no less. This is not an easy task. At some times, for reasons to be explored in a few paragraphs, we fall short of this ability, and a recession results. At other times, we overshoot our abilities, and we get higher rates of inflation. Up and down we go, always trying to match our production abilities, but frequently missing it in one way or another.

So what?

Newsguys, leaders of the first and second estates, and pointy-headed economists, all tend to be quite worried about recessions. Either they're fretting that one is about to begin, wringing their hands about when (or if) the current one will end, or blaming each other for one that just ended. Okay, what's so bad about recessions?

- *Unemployment.* The first and biggest problem of a recession (especially for taxpaying, hard-working consumers of the third estate) is unemployment. When the economy takes a downturn, fewer resources—especially *labor*—are hired to produce stuff. A lot of people are thrown out of work for periods ranging from a few months to a year or more. A typical recession gives us 2 to 3 million unemployed workers, who have less income and thus either consume less or use up a lot of their savings. It's not a pretty picture.
- *A shrinking pie.* Even if you're among the fortunate 90-plus percent of the labor force who escape the problems of unemployment, it doesn't mean you escape a recession entirely. When our economic pie shrinks, there's less stuff for everyone. It also means that more of your tax dollars go toward helping the less fortunate through unemployment compensation, welfare, and even social security.

Although recessions have undeniable problems, there's some good to be found from lying face down on the pavement. Three sorts of good can come from a recession:

1. If our economy has been expanding rapidly for several years, a recession lets it pause to catch its breath. Recessions let workers and businesses take an involuntary, but often much needed, "vacation."
2. Recessions tend to weed the inefficient resources from an industry. The first workers to be laid off and the first businesses to close their doors are the least productive ones. Bad for them in the short run, but good for the economy in the long run.
3. In that most of us are basically creatures of habit, once we get into a job we're prone to remain there unless something extraordinary happens. Recessions and the resulting unemployment gives many workers that extraordinary something needed to find a better job.

Are recessionary potholes inevitable?

While recessions, like potholes, seem to pop up every so often, are they avoidable? Is their any chance that we (that is, *we* as in *government*) could eliminate them through what are termed "stabilization policies"? To answer these questions, and many more, we need to get a firm grasp on why recessions occur.

Most of the scholars who look into this sort of thing have come up with three possible explanations. We're not quite sure which one is *the* answer, but more than likely they're all somewhat important.

- *National mood.* If you buy into the idea that the economy needs to rest every so often, then it makes sense to think that everyone in the economy collectively grows tired from the pressures of an expanding economy. That is, businesses, consumers, and even the government say that we've done a lot of growing, let's stop for a rest. This is seen when consumers who have bought a lot—furniture, houses, cars—decide that they just don't need anything else. Or businesses that have done a great deal of investment decide that they don't need any more capital. When we all stop buying, we produce less, and we get a recession.

- *Politics.* The government has a lot of power over the economy. Those in control of the government can use this power for the wrong reasons: to get reelected. A number of economists say that the expanding and recessing economy is caused by politicians who spend heavily in one period—before an election—then cut back during another—after the election. Spending a bunch here, then cutting back there, can trigger an expanding economy for a while, then a recession later on.

- *Extracurricular events.* It's also possible that a recession is the result of things that happen outside the confines of our economy—things over which we have no control. For example, a natural disaster might decimate a large part of the economy and trigger a recession. Then as the economy rebuilds, it begins to recover from the recession. Wars, political revolutions, and global trading conflicts are but a few of the extracurricular events that could cause our economy to rise and fall.

Looking out for the potholes

We've now come to the most important part of this recessionary business. How can you tell when a recession is on the horizon? The honest answer is that you can't. However, this hasn't stopped economists and others from trying. There are a few

warning signs of an imminent recession that can be gathered from the newspapers and nightly newscasts. Keep in mind, though, that the signals they give are occasionally wrong.

- *Economic forecasts.* As noted in the entry on Economic Forecasting, many pointyheads spend their working lives developing sophisticated mathematical models that allow them to forecast oncoming recessions. In general, these tend to be about as reliable as weather forecasts—without the colorful maps. They aren't perfect, but they are better than flipping a coin.

- *Leading economic indicators.* A valuable set of government published data is referred to as "leading economic indicators." These are things like stock market prices and housing construction permits that tend to rise or fall a few months before the rest of the economy rises or falls. Unfortunately these aren't perfect either, as suggested by one economist who noted that they have predicted ten of the last seven recessions. (Think about that for a moment.)

Recessions are good for some of us and bad for others. While the government spends a lot of effort trying to control recessions and keep our economy on a straight and narrow path of growth, they seldom reach perfection. While you can't spend your entire economic life looking over your shoulder for the inevitable onset of a recession, there are a few things that you can do to survive.

RECESSIONARY TIPS FOR THE NIMBLE-FOOTED PEDESTRIAN

- Don't panic. Even during the worst recessions of the last 50 years, 90 percent of the workforce and population has survived with little hardship.
- Avoid recession-prone industries. The construction, automobile, furniture, and appliance industries all tend to be hardest hit during recessions. If you seem to

get laid off when a recession hits every few years, then you might want to consider a new industry or career. Health care is one industry that tends to be "recession-proof." Others abound.

- There are areas that even expand during recessions. Education tends to be hot in recessions because laid-off workers return to school. Bankruptcy lawyers are also in big demand during recessions, for obvious reasons. It might be worth the effort to search out those industries that do well during recessions.

- As recessions hit industries unevenly, they also hit some parts of the country harder than others. In fact, it's not uncommon for some states to boom during a national recession. If you're tired of frequent recessionary layoffs, then check out some states that tend to do well during the nationally bad times.

- And last, it doesn't hurt to have a financial cushion, especially if you're stuck in a recession-prone state or industry. Because states and industries that do the most declining during a recession also tend to do the most growing at other times, you might want to save a little extra during the good times to prepare for the inevitable recession.

See also: Federal Deficit, Investment, Political Views, Stock Market, and Taxes.

laying the ground rules on
REGULATION

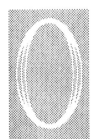 *Our journey has brought us to the "R's," which means, among other things, that my feet are a bit sore. Fortunately, we've also found ourselves at the front door of the Good Time Pharmacy. (Isn't coincidence wonderful?) My quick shopping trip for a pair of cushioned insoles, analgesic rub, and an ankle wrap is lengthened, however, by crossing paths with the normally quiet Stella von Steincamp. Stella, the pharmacist and proprietor of the Good Time Pharmacy, has taken the opportunity of our meeting to voice a rather vehement complaint over a new Shady Valley city government pharmaceutical regulation mandating the use of disposable rubber gloves when preparing and dispensing medicine. She is livid! Her primary complaint (among several) is that the cost of this regulation will send her pharmacy onto a short path into bankruptcy. In the interest of maintaining pharmaceutical services for the residents of Shady Valley, I think we should explore this topic of government regulation.*

The regulatory ground rules

One of the best reasons to keep our evil first estate around is to provide stability in what could be a rather haphazard existence. Government does this by imposing all manner of laws, rules, and restrictions on our lives. Some of these rules—like the one about not killing each other—make sense, while others are annoying or even downright ludicrous. Although we can nitpick about this one or that one, without the rules governing civilized behavior we wouldn't have, well, civilized behavior. We would be a pack of barbarians for whom anarchy is the rule of the day—everyday. Without rules of civilized behavior, as we saw with Fact #2, we would have little success producing and exchanging the stuff that satisfies our wants and needs.

This is the screen upon which government regulation of our economy is projected. When pointy-headed economists, business leaders, and government leaders (our favorite) talk about regulation, they're referring to the rules, laws, and restrictions that have a direct bearing on second-estate production, third-estate consumption, and exchanges between the two estates.

We can put most of the regulations we have into one of two categories:

1. *Industry.* These are regulations that control production, pricing, and an

assortment of other practices, in an *entire industry.* Some of the better-known industries subject to this regulation are the telephone, banking, and electric utilities. There is logic behind industry regulation. Production technology is such that a small number of companies, often only one, tend to acquire excessive *market control.* To prevent the unavoidable tendency to play monopoly and abuse its control, government becomes an active partner in the process, dictating what business can and cannot do. At one time we had a lot more industry regulation in the good old U.S.A., but much of it was given "walking papers" in the 1980s under a wave of deregulation. We'll see why in a few pages.

2. *Social.* A more popular form of regulation in recent decades has been aimed at correcting the social ills that any complex economy is likely to create. Examples of these include, but are not limited to, pollution, the lack of information, and a myriad of costs or benefits that tend to be outside the normal demand and supply decisions of our markets. As such, social regulations usually extend beyond the confines of a single industry. (Check out Advertising, Pollution, and Product Safety for more on some social ills.)

Industry and social regulations are really no different from other laws governing civilized behavior. We have a law that says it's wrong to kill another person with a gun, presumably because we want to protect the rights of the victim. We also have laws that prevent businesses from dumping death-inflicting, toxic chemicals into our streams for presumably similar reasons. There seems little room for debate.

However, when a business, for example, has been polluting a stream for a generation or two, it thinks of it as its "right" to do so. If you, I, or the government tries to take that "right" away, then we're in for a big battle. In that you have made it all of the way to the "R's," you're probably aware that the second estate has the wealth and power needed to put up a good fight when it comes to something like regulations.

Some regulatory tools of the trade

Let's ponder some of the more popular methods that government uses to regulate our economy:

- *Laws and restrictions.* The most straight-forward way to regulate anything is to pass a law or impose some form of rule or restriction. It can be declared illegal—subject to punishment—to buy this, sell that, produce a good, possess a good, or whatever. Our government has used this for things like plutonium, certain pesticides (DDT), narcotics (cocaine), and other stuff that we probably don't even know about because they've been banned from our economy.

- *Standards.* Another favorite regulatory tool is to set a standard or rigid guideline. For example, automobiles have to meet pollution emission standards and physicians have to pass certain proficiency exams for licenses to practice their trade.

- *Taxes.* The favorite regulatory tool of most economists is taxes, especially for things like pollution. This works best when there's a cost that's beyond the *market.* A tax forces the market, especially the producers, to make any supply decisions as if they were paying those extra costs, because they are—as taxes.

- *Information.* One of the simplest and more effective tools for regulating the economy is to ensure that people have necessary information. At this point in our pedestrian journey you're probably well aware that information plays a big role in a lot of stuff. Part of the harm inflicted on some (third estate) by others (second estate) is often the result of inadequate information. Making better information available can clean up a number of problems. (More specifics can be found under Product Safety.)

The politics of regulation

When we get into any sort of government policy, we can't avoid the diverging interests of the second and third estates. Nowhere is this more true than regulation. As we've seen a number of times, the second estate tends to have more wealth and power than the third. A main reason for government is to protect the hardworking consumers and taxpayers of the third estate against the nefarious doings of the second estate. However (there always seems to be a "however"), while the first-estate government leaders might side with the third estate at times, they're also inclined to walk arm and arm with the second estate. In this latter case, some very good regulations can be turned on their head, creating worse problems than they sought to solve. The best example lies with industry regulation.

When the inmates take over

Let's visit our good monopoly friends at Merciless Monolithic Media Masters Cable Television. As we saw with Fact #4, if left unrestricted, they have a strong, very strong, inclination to charge high prices and provide bad service. You, I, and every other pedestrian consumer of Shady Valley have little recourse. We either buy their services or we don't. There's no competition—a situation that is (hopefully) corrected by government action.

Let's say that the responsive government of Shady Valley sets up a regulatory board to oversee the pricing and production decisions of the 4M people. If the cable company wants to charge higher prices, the board has to give its approval. Likewise, the board can impose rules on the timeliness of service calls, provision of services to all potential customers, and the quality of the signal. The board is also likely to guarantee that the cable company receives some profit for its efforts. The profit won't be as high as the unregulated profit, but enough to keep it operating. This seems

like a fair way to handle things.

Here's where the politics of wealth and power enter the picture. The 4M company has a lot to gain from favorable decisions by the Shady Valley regulatory board: Gadzillions is an amount that comes to mind. The cable company will do its best to gain control of the Shady Valley regulatory board, in legal or illegal ways. You can imagine some of the illegal stuff, but a common legal method pops up when former (and likely future) employees of the company serve on the regulatory board. After all, who knows more about regulating a cable company than someone who once worked for a cable company? This all-too-common practice, by the way, is usually referred to as the "rotating door" of regulatory agencies.

The result is a regulatory board that serves as an extension of the company it's regulating. The members of the regulatory board don't protect the customer's interests as much as they protect the company—and their own future careers. This has been, and probably will continue to be, a common practice for industry regulation. In the 1980s, it also prompted deregulation of a number of industries, like airlines, trucking, and railroads.

Going to extremes

First-estate control, however, can go both ways. Excessive influence by the second estate not only can affect industry regulation, it can also sway the government against consumer-protecting social regulation. Excessive influence by the third estate on the government can also create problems. How is this possible?

The overworked, underappreciated members of the third estate can be over-protected as well. Regulation can cause too many of our economy's resources to be spent cleaning the environment or making defective-free products. It's nice to have a clean environment, but at what price? Would we be willing to give up our jobs, incomes, and material possessions for a pollution-free world? Probably not.

The trick is to strike a balance between the benefit of regulation and its cost. Some regulations are extremely beneficial and cost very little. Others tip the scales in the opposite direction. It would be convenient if we could clearly determine which is which, but we can't. One reason is that the cost of a given regulation is often obvious, and well documented by shrieking business leaders who pay them. The benefit from a regulation, however, tends to be pretty nebulous. What is the benefit of eliminating roadside trash?

Because the cost of regulation is usually known and the benefit isn't, doesn't necessarily mean benefit outweighs cost. It may or may not. We usually don't know which way it goes. Our only real hope is that people tend to scream loudly when the cost and benefit get too far out of balance.

A REGULATORY TIP

- Whenever the topic of regulation is broached, you have to consider the source of alternative viewpoints. Consumers tend to favor regulations and businesses oppose them. Carefully weigh the eloquent rhetoric that you're likely to hear from both sides. Keep in mind that the second estate tends to have wealth, power, and information control on their side. As such, I'm usually inclined to favor the arguments given on behalf of the underappreciated and often less powerful members of the third estate. But that's my personal bias.

See also: Business, Farm Subsidies, Health Care, Political Views, Taxes, and Worker Safety.

planning on
SOCIAL SECURITY

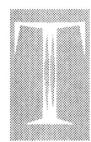 *This may be the greatest day of my life. The musical group to top all musical groups—The Strollers—has just released its latest CD with a song that's certain to be a foot-tapping classic. Of course, you know the song of which I speak—"Sidewalking." Let's stop into the Musical Sound CD Emporium in the Shady Valley Central Town Sprawling Hills Shopping Mall and fulfill my dreams. Everyone in Shady Valley, however, does not share my joy. As the 17-year-old emporium clerk, Alicia Hyfield, completes my transaction, she confesses more than a bit of disgruntlement over her just-issued paycheck. A little investigation reveals some displeasure with the size of the FICA deduction. Her disgruntlement isn't lessened by her knowing that this is for the government's social security program that's supposed to provide a source of income in her golden years. She seems more than a bit skeptical of ever seeing any returns. Maybe we can alleviate her concerns (and mine) with a quick run through social security.*

A safety net

Our social security system was established, along with several other social programs, during the Great Depression of the 1930s. This was a time of exceptionally high unemployment and suffering by millions of people with little or no income. In a rare move of siding with the workers and consumers of the third estate, government instituted a number of programs to protect the citizenry against economic hardships. Our current social security system that provides a source of income for the elderly, disabled, and their dependents is one. Another program for the poor (which you can read about under Welfare) was also started in the 1930s. Here's how our social security system works:

- *Collecting the bucks.* The social security system gets its money from taxes collected on wage and salary income. This

is somewhat important, because unlike the income tax system, which taxes income, only wage and salary income is taxed for social security. Income not taxed includes interest, rent, and profit. Employees pay about 7 percent of any wages up to a given amount (currently over $50,000) into the social security program (this is the FICA paycheck deduction). Employers pay an equal amount. I'm being a little fuzzy on these numbers, because they're subject to change—that is, increase. Anyone who pays into the system for several years is then eligible for benefits.

- *Paying out the bucks.* You get a check from the social security system if you're elderly and retired, disabled, or a dependent on someone who is disabled. In that the social security system was designed

Social Security 189

as a safety net for people who couldn't work, recipients get fewer benefits if they are able to work and earn extra income. However (and this is an important "however"), social security benefits are unaffected by any *nonworking income,* like retirement income from private pension plans, dividends from Fortune 500 companies, or rent on oil-rich farmland.

A net with big holes

You might have noticed a few second-estate versus third-estate problems.

1. While the system was intended as a safety net to help poor disadvantaged workers, you don't need to be poor to get it. There's nothing to prevent that bastion of the second estate, Winston Smythe Kennsington I (our friend Winnie's grandfather), from collecting a monthly social security check. Winnie I is officially retired, but has gobs and gobs of income from stock dividends. The irony in this situation is that someone like Lewis Langley, a retired shoe store clerk from right here in Shady Valley, will have difficulty paying his monthly bills with his meager social security check. While he can work part-time at the shoe store for a little extra income, if he earns too much, he'll lose his social security benefits. Not so for Winnie I. There's no limit to nonwage income.

2. Because the FICA tax is collected only on wages up to about $50,000, but excludes everything else, it hits workers of the third estate hardest. Most card-carrying members of the third estate have little or no rent, interest, or profit income. The second estate, however, gets a bunch of income from rent, interest, and profit. Moreover, the darn tax is paid only on the first $50,000 of wage income (depending on the current limit set by Congress). Someone who earns $10,000,000 in wages each year pays exactly the same

FICA tax as someone who earns $60,000. In our entry on Taxes, this is what we call a *regressive tax.*

Is this any way to run a retirement system?

Let's take this opportunity to dispel a myth: The social security system is *not* a retirement program. The social security system collects taxes from people who are currently employed and gives that money to people who are currently retired or disabled. Unlike most private pension plans, there are no dollars set aside with your name on it. The amount you will eventually collect has *no* relationship to the amount you pay.

With many private retirement programs, if you pay in bunches of money, then you stand to pull out bunches of money. The dollars paid in are typically invested in stocks, bonds, or other similar assets. On retirement you can cash in those suckers and start spending the money.

Under the social security system, the amount of your retirement benefits depends on the length of time you paid into the system, but not on the amount paid in. Most importantly, it depends on the *amount* of taxes workers are currently paying into the system. You collect big bucks when you retire if our economy has a bunch of young, healthy, productive workers who earn a lot and pay a lot of FICA taxes. If you don't have that pool of productive workers, then you don't get the bucks.

Enter the "baby boomers"

The current and future of the social security system depends heavily on a group of people who have achieved the distinctive title "Baby Boomers." This generation, born between 1946 and 1960 (in no small part because of the love-hungry soldiers returning from the War), is extremely large, well educated, and productive. There were many more babies born in the Baby Boomer years from 1946 to 1960 than directly before (1931 to 1945) or after (1961 to 1975). This is good and bad.

1. *The good.* Because there are a lot of Baby Boomers who began entering the labor force in the 1970s and are real close to their peak of productive lives, they're contributing tons of money into the social security system. This has been a gold mine for those who retired in the 1980s and earlier. Many current social security recipients have been able to get back several times what they paid in. (However, lest we seem too critical of these elderly, retired folk for living off of the hard work of the Baby Boomers, keep in mind that investments in 1950s and 1960s by these elderly, retired folk made it possible for the Baby Boomers to be well educated and productive.)

2. *The bad.* In the year 2011, the first of the Baby Boomers will hit their 65th birthday, with aspirations of many golden retirement years ahead. By the year 2025 most of the Baby Boomers will be in retirement. If this large, productive group is no longer working, who's going to pay into the social security system and supply the big, *big,* Big bucks needed to pay for the Baby Boomers' golden retirement years? Remember, we didn't have very many babies born between 1961 and 1975 (often termed "Generation X"). Each member of this smaller group will have to pay a lot more into the social security system to keep Baby Boomers up to their accustomed lifestyles.

Let's consider a few of the options when those Baby Boomers reach retirement age:

• *Don't retire.* One way to reduce the payments to retired Baby Boomers is to keep them from retiring. By the year 2011 the retirement age for full social security benefits will probably be 70 rather than 65. It's already on its way up to 67. People weren't expected to live much past 65 when the social security system was estab-lished in the 1930s. Now that life expectancy is approaching 80, later retirement makes a lot of sense whether we have a bunch of Baby Boomers or not.

• *Boomers get less.* A second option is that Baby Boomers will be forced to divide up their retirement pie among a larger number, with each Boomer getting a smaller share. A word of warning. The Baby Boomers represent a large group, *as in voters.* Throughout their lives the Boomers have gotten what they've wanted in terms of politics, culture, etc. And noting that older people tend to be more politically active and vote more, it's hard to imagine a politician doing too much that would upset these elderly Boomers.

• *Others pay more.* That leaves us with the third option: Those in Generation X and the rest will be forced to pay more into the social security system. The big question is whether they can afford to pay more. If the Boomers demand more, but the economic pie isn't big enough to accommodate them, we're going to be in a heap of trouble. The solution, of course, is a bigger pie. All of those Generation X workers need to be very, *very* well educated; very, *very* productive; and earn gobs and gobs of income.

Getting the most from the X generation

The path to a larger economic pie has been noted in the entries on Economic Growth and Investment. If Generation X is going to be part of an expanded pie, then our economy needs to improve the quantity and quality of their resources *before* the Boomers retire. That means foregoing current consumption for investments in *capital, education, and technology,* to name the three most important ones.

Now for the bad news. We don't seem to be making these needed investments. If we don't make them now, it will be too late. Let's have a roll call of bad decisions made over the last few decades that could spell a pretty dreary retirement for the Boomers.

- *Government consumption.* Our government, that well-meaning group in Washington D.C., and the assorted state capitals throughout the land, has tended to spend more tax dollars on consumption goods and fewer on public investments. Examples of government consumption include national defense, fire protection, law enactment and enforcement, bureaucratic paper shuffling, and encouraged or subsidized private consumption. I'm not saying this stuff is totally unneeded, it just won't help future growth.

- *Government investment.* In recent decades, there hasn't been an overwhelming move by government to invest in assorted public goods, like transportation systems, education, and scientific research. Sure, we had that NASA moon shot back in the 1960s, but other than the interstate highways system of the 1950s and 1960s, the government hasn't gotten really fired up about public investment. An occasional billion will be thrown at this project or that, but nothing to rival expenditures on defense or other consumption programs.

- *Business investment.* The 1980s stand out as a decade of intense business investment, but not in newly produced, economic-growth-enhancing, capital. It was "investment" in mergers, buying out this company or that company. A lot of our nation's resources were used to trade assets rather than create new ones. Bad move for the Boomers.

- *Household consumption and saving.* Over the years you, I, the Boomers, and everyone else have gotten heavily involved in consuming stuff. That's fine in that it satisfies our wants and needs. However, in the process, the share of income we save has dropped. It is this saved income, we should note, that's used by business for investment. With less saved, it becomes more difficult for businesses to produce new capital. We can top off this problem by noting the big run-up in the federal deficit in the 1980s absconding with an increasingly larger share of our dwindling pool of saving.

With these tidbits of information in mind, the prospects of a big increase in the economic pie in the near future don't seem bright. In spite of the likely political power to be had by the retired Boomers, I don't think they should count on a golden retirement from the social security system.

So, what can we do about social security? Here are a few tips:

SOCIAL SECURITY TIPS

- First, don't count on much of anything from the social security system. If you're a Boomer, then you had better get yourself into private retirement programs. Even those programs may face similar problems if the economic pie doesn't grow enough. Remember, whatever the source of your income, it all comes from the same economic pie.

- It's not too late to get the government off its short-sighted fanny and pursue the pie-augmenting investments we need. But it will be late for the Boomers when the year 2020 rolls around.

- If you're currently working, you had better plan on continuing until your 70s. The 65-year-old retirement age will probably be locked away in the same museum as the pony express and black-and-white televisions.

- If you're currently retired, enjoy it while you can. You also might want to be a little careful about squeezing too many benefits from the current system. If the Boomers reach a point where they decide to flex their collective political muscles, it's bad news for you.

See also: Athlete Salaries, Health Care,

playing the

STOCK MARKET

*The hazards of being a pedestrian are many. Of course we have a good chance of crossing paths with a rabid Bengal tiger that has highjacked a street cleaner and intends to whitewash every pair of jogging shoes encountered. Or a throng of overzealous religious fanatics might try to slip fresh flowers into our hands and literature into our pockets. And especially when we amble through the financial district, we might be crushed by falling stock market investors who have mistakenly bought high and sold low. While the actions of the Bengal tiger and overzealous religious fanatics might be understandable, what's so almighty important about the stock market that would make investors place the well-being of innocent pedestrians in jeopardy?*

A source of instant wealth?

For many, the words "stock market" bring to mind images of high-powered wheeling and dealing by the likes of such high-powered wheeler-dealers as our good Ivy League friend Winston Smythe Kennsington III. The stock market has a reputation not unlike that of casino gambling in Las Vegas. The dream is that almost any low-life with a few thousand dollars to invest *might* be able buy the "right" stock just before its price shoots through the roof. Because of the notion of an uncertain future, as we saw with Fact #6, Our Unknown Economy, the risks of investing in the stock market can and do reward some with a big-time payoff. However, it can and does eliminate the bank accounts of others.

I'll have more to say about this idea of instant wealth in Wealth and Gambling. For the moment, however, let's put aside instant wealth, without totally dashing it against the rocks. Instead, let's ponder the essence of the stock market, the king of financial markets. (If you haven't read the entry on FInancial Markets, now would be a good time.)

Buying a corporation

A stock market really has a very simple purpose in life: to buy and sell ownership shares in corporations, *corporate stock*. The ownership shares are the "stock" part of the stock market. For example, suppose that over the years Omni Conglomerate, Inc., has issued 100 million shares of stock. If you are the proud owner of one of those 100 million shares, then you own one-hundred millionth of Omni Conglomerate, Inc. You have a legal right to one-hundred millionth of the profit Omni Conglomerate, Inc., makes each year. If they make $100 million in profit this year, then your share is $1.

To see why this is such a big deal, let's consider a few alternatives on the business side of our economy:

A PEDESTRIAN ...

... buys some stock

I THOUGHT IT WOULD GO UP

THIRD ONE TODAY

- *Proprietorships.* This is a business owned and operated by one person, a proprietor. A proprietor makes all decisions, takes all risks, and gets all rewards. In particular, a proprietor has *unlimited liability,* meaning there's no legal difference between the business and the person running the business.
- *Partnerships.* A partnership is like a proprietorship with more than one owner, each sharing the decisions, risks, and rewards. The partners also share *unlimited liability,* meaning a great deal of trust is needed among partners. If one screws up, everyone pays.

The main problem with proprietorships and partnerships, recognized early on in the industrial revolution, is that neither can be very large. A proprietorship is limited by the wealth one person can accumulate. Partnerships can be somewhat bigger, but the problems of unlimited liability and trust keep them from growing too big.

- *Corporations.* Our third form of business, the corporation, doesn't have this unlimited liability problem, because government considers them and their owners separate legal entities. The owners thus have what is legally termed "limited liability"; they can lose their investment, but no more. Unlike a partnership, you don't need unwavering trust in each and every single investor when you're part owner of a corporation. This makes it possible to form corporations with thousands, even millions, of owners.

With this corporate-form of business, ownership shares (corporate stocks) can be sold right and left. The means of trading the shares (drum roll, please) is the stock market. Or maybe I should say the stock markets, because there are several different markets that trade these ownership shares around. Let's highlight a few.

Big daddy and the kids

The stock market of stock markets in this country and worldwide is the New York Stock Exchange. If you want to get your company's stock into the *big time* of stock markets, then you want to be listed on the Big Board of the New York Stock Exchange, which is literally located on the famous Wall Street in New York City. This is the stock market that gets most of the publicity when Dan Rather, Tom Brokaw, Peter Jennings, and the other news guys report financial statistics on the nightly news. The Dow-Jones average is an index of prices of stocks traded on the New York Stock Exchange. The Standard & Poor's 500 is another stock price index from the Big Board.

The American Stock Exchange, with its progress measured by the AMEX index, is number 2 on our economy's hit parade of stock markets. We also have the Pacific Stock Exchange that operates on the West Coast and the so-called "over-the-counter" stock transactions through the National Association of Securities Dealers, which you probably hear about in terms of the NASDAQ index. Unlike the other stock markets, where the trading takes place in one location, the over-the-counter trading is through dealers, and their computers, all over the country.

For stock investors with an international flair, virtually all major industrialized nations and a growing number of minor ones have stock markets. The most widely known, in large part because of their importance to the world economy, are the stock markets in Tokyo and London. Even the likes of Communist China and the formerly Communist Russia have made headway into the stock market arena.

Dividing up the assets

It's time to get into the nitty-gritty of how stock markets work and what they mean for pedestrians strolling around the economy.

First, let's dispel a myth. While stock market indexes, like the Dow-Jones average, are often used as indicators of what's happening in the economy, they are *not* the economy. A rise or fall in the stock market does *not* mean our economy—the economic pie of our production, income, and employment—is rising and falling.

What, then, do the various stock market price indexes actually mean? The indexes are nothing more than the average price of the stocks traded on their respective stock market. As with any market, stock market prices come about through mutual agreement between buyers and sellers. What, though, are they mutually agreeing on? The simple answer is: the value of corporate assets.

Let's take an example. Suppose that Omni Conglomerate, Inc., has $10 billion in assets and has issued 100 million shares of corporate stock. Each share represents one-hundred millionth of $10 billion in assets. In general, then, buyers and sellers should be willing to trade one share of Omni Conglomerate, Inc., for $100, or $10 billion divided by 100 million.

Now, here's where things get a little tricky. What if you, as a potential buyer, expect that Omni Conglomerate is going to do "something extraordinary" in the coming months, such that its asset value will increase by 10 percent. In this case, you would be willing to pay up to $110 a share. In fact, if you could buy the stock at $105, then you could resell it for $110 when this "extraordinary something" happens, making $5 per share. If you bought

10 gadzillion shares, then you make $50 gadzillion on the deal.

However, if you're not alone in your expectations, then other buyers, perhaps *every* other buyer, is willing to do the same thing. The result: The price goes up to $110 per share before anything "extraordinary" actually happens. If the "extraordinary" never happens, then the stock price will likely drop like a rock and "crash" below $100. (If you want to find out more on this, check out "speculation" in Section 3).

Long-run health

While there are many short-run ups and downs in stock prices, the bottom line on stock prices is literally the bottom line. Stock market investors buy and sell based on how productive and profitable they think companies are at the present and, equally important, will be in the future. Of course, individual stock prices depend on what an individual company is doing or planning to do. Good, productive, profitable companies have rising stock prices. Poorly run, unprofitable ones see stock prices fall.

For the entire stock market, however, prices usually (not always, but usually) reflect the health and productivity of our entire economy. Rising stock market indexes, like the Dow-Jones average, indicate that businesses are profitable and that the economy is healthy. Falling indexes suggest the opposite.

TIPS ON THE STOCK MARKET

- I can't resist the temptation to go for the easiest tip: Buy low and sell high. (Whew! I'm glad I got that out of my system.)

- Information is the fuel that stokes the stock market furnace. If you want to be a serious player in the stock market, then you must be willing to invest the time and energy needed to accumulate and stay abreast of all relevant information. The big boys who make a living in the stock market have this information, and they'll eat your lunch, breakfast, and midnight snacks if your information isn't as good.

- If you don't have the information for short-term buying low and selling high, long-run investing is a sound alternative. In that the stock market reflects the long-run prosperity of the economy, you usually can't go wrong by buying stocks and holding them for several years or even decades. That makes the stock market a pretty good place to invest retirement funds.

- Moreover, in that many companies enter and exit the economic scene over the years, the best approach is to diversify—that is, buy a lot of different stocks. The easiest way to do this is through stock mutual funds.

See also: Business, Economic Forecasting, Economic Growth, Foreign Investment, Insurance, Interest Rate, Investment, Profit, and Recessions.

paying
TAXES

The time has come to take a firm stand! The Shady Valley Gazette Tribune-Journal has published an inflammatory editorial calling for a "pedestrian" tax on anyone who ambles around the economy. This tax, as every pedestrian would surely agree, is misguided and short sighted. It's also unfair and probably unconstitutional. How dare the editors of the Shady Valley Gazette Tribune-Journal call for a "pedestrian" tax. Sure, they argue that ambling pedestrians should help pay for the sidewalks, traffic signals, and other assorted public goods. But, it's certainly not in my best interest as a pedestrian to pay this misguided, short-sighted, unfair, and probably unconstitutional tax.

A taxing life

Whether we like it or not, taxes are an inherent, unavoidable, absolutely necessary feature of our economy. As we saw with Fact #5, Our Necessary Evil, government provides us with highly valued stuff that can't be produced without tax dollars. As such, we *voluntarily* let governments (federal, state, and local) *force* us to pay taxes. And governments are very good at this task. That's why we have a bunch of different taxes—some of which might not be even recognized as taxes. Here's a list:

- *Income.* The most popular on any top-40 list of taxes is, of course, the income tax. This is the primary source of revenue for the federal government (which we can affectionately call "the Feds"), collected by our good friends with the Internal Revenue Service. Many states also take a slice of income taxes from our personal economic pies, and a few city governments

have sharpened their knives as well.
- *Sales.* Probably the second most popular—sales tax—is that levied on retail sales, a major source of revenue for state and local governments. The Feds impose a few of their own selected sales taxes, usually termed "excise taxes," on such things as cigarettes, alcohol, gasoline, and automobile tires.
- *Wages.* In addition to the ever-popular income tax, the Feds have a tax on workers' wages for the Social Security system—the FICA deduction on your paycheck. (More on this can be found under Social Security.)
- *Property.* Local governments—cities, counties, and the like—are prone to collect a lot of revenue with property taxes. These are taxes on property within a government's political jurisdiction.
- *Corporate profits.* An always controversial tax is that levied on the profits of our mighty (and not so mighty) corporations

A PEDESTRIAN ...

of the second estate. This is a significant source of revenue for the Feds, but a few state and local governments also do a bit of corporate profits taxing.

- *Inheritance.* The Feds collect a tax on a portion of the wealth that is passed on from one generation to the next, an inheritance tax.
- *Fees and user charges.* All levels of government have fees and charges for stuff. While these are often thought of as prices, they're also taxes. They include, but by no means are limited to, drivers license fees, turnpike fees, parking and speeding tickets, public golf course greens fees, public park entrance fees, college tuition, and grazing fees on pub-

lic rangeland. While a government service or good typically comes with the fee, unlike other prices, the fee seldom is related to production cost.

If you think it's tough to do anything in our economy without running across some sort of government tax, you're right. Then again, it's also difficult to go anywhere or do anything without benefiting from government-produced goods.

We all pay, some just more than others

When pointy-headed economists compare different taxes, like those listed here, they do so as a percentage of income. Even though property taxes, user chargers, sales taxes, and many others are based on assorted activities, each ultimately eats away part of your income. The big question in this sort of comparison is: Do taxes as a share of income increase, decrease, or stay the same for rich versus poor. Here are the three possibilities:

1. *Proportional.* Everyone, regardless of income, pays the same percentage in taxes. For example, we have a proportional tax if you pay $1,000 on $10,000 of income and your neighbor pays $2,000 on a $20,000 income. Both of you pay 10 percent.

2. *Progressive.* A tax in which people with more income pay a larger percentage. A progressive tax occurs if you pay $1,000 on a $10,000 income, while your neighbor pays $4,000 on a higher $20,000. While you pay 10 percent, your neighbor pays 20 percent.

3. *Regressive.* Those with more income pay a lower percentage. With a regressive tax you and your neighbor both pay a $2,000 income tax, even though your $10,000 income is less than your neighbor's $20,000 amount. Your 20-percent tax rate is higher than your neighbor's 10 percent.

As you might suspect, there's a constant, long-running battle between the second and third estate over progressive and regressive taxes. The relatively wealthier members of the second estate prefer regressive taxes, while the third estate thinks progressive taxes are more justified. As is often the case, the government leaders of the first estate waffle in their support of both sides. That's one reason why we seem to have such a variety of taxes. When the first estate follows the wishes of the wary consumers, unappreciated workers, and disgruntled taxpayers, then we tend to see more progressive taxes, such as those on inheritance, profit, property, and income (if designed properly). However, when the second estate gets the government in its clutches, we see more regressive taxes, like sales, social security, and a revamped income tax system.

If you take a level-headed, balanced approach to taxes, you might think that proportional is the best alternative. Hey, make everyone pay the same percentage and be done with it! There are, however, some good reasons to go with either regressive or progressive taxes.

• A progressive tax would seem to be more "fair" in that wealthier people don't spend as much of their income on basic necessities (food, shelter, clothing, and energy) but use a larger share of income for luxury stuff (jewelry, vacations, country club memberships). They can share a larger burden of the expense for government-provided necessities (police and fire protection, education, transportation, and national defense) with relatively less suffering.

• A regressive tax, however, would leave more income in the hands of the wealthy that could be used for investment in capital. Because poorer people spend most of their income on basic necessities, they don't have much left over for investment. The wealthier you are, the more you invest. Our economy gets all sorts of benefits from capital investment that makes life better for both the second and third estates. (More on these benefits can be found under Economic Growth and Investment.)

The best taxes money can buy

Few people (if any) like to pay taxes. But taxes have to be collected to do what the government does. The trick, then, is to collect taxes in a manner that is as painless as possible. By painless here, we're not concerned with physical pain as much as a disruption of the economy—in other words, *efficiency.* We want the economy to be as efficient in the allocation of scarce resources as possible after the government collects taxes. In fact, taxes can actually make our economy *more* efficient as well as *less* efficient.

Let's do the *less* efficient first. Suppose our government imposes a sales tax on some sort of good like "dirt" that, as we saw in Fact #4, is exchanged via a very *competitive market*. The price buyers are willing to pay is equal to the cost of producing this commodity, and the market exchange is efficient. If you put a sales tax on dirt, then the price buyers pay (with the tax) will be greater than the cost of production (after taxes are deducted), and the market becomes inefficient. This tax, though, isn't a big problem if buyers and sellers continue to buy and sell the same quantity after the tax as before. Inefficiency arises if the buyers' price goes up so much that buyers decide to buy something else, or if the sellers' price goes down so much that sellers decide to produce something else.

Governments, bless their tax-collecting hearts, do recognize this fact. That's why you see a lot of taxes on stuff that we keep on buying and selling in spite of the taxes. Examples include sales taxes on cigarettes, alcohol, gasoline, food; income taxes on income; social security taxes on wages; and taxes on inheritances. As a society we're pretty addicted to smoking, drinking, driving, working, and dying, and we're not likely to change too much because of some little government tax.

Now for a look at the *more* efficient side of taxes. Some markets do *not* do an efficient job of producing and trading stuff. The best examples of markets that need a little help to get the price equal to production costs are those that have some pollution. While you can find out more about this under Pollution, suffice it here to say that pollution is a cost that goes beyond the normal workings of a market. In other words, it's a production cost that's not part of the buyers' price. A tax on a market with pollution can improve efficiency.

Make 'em pay, make 'em pay!

As a licensed, certified member of the third estate, you probably prefer taxes on businesses. Hey, they have the money, let them pay. There is, however, a problem in this. As producers and suppliers, businesses pass along the taxes they pay to consumers—if they can.

As a general rule—with a bunch of exceptions—buyers and sellers both tend to share in the ultimate payment of a tax. For example, let's say that Frosted Honey-Coated Super Sugar Junks cereal sells for $2 a box without a tax. That means it costs the suppliers $2 a box to produce, and buyers are willing to pay the same $2 amount to consume this most-satisfying product. All is happy in cereal land.

This changes, though, if a 10-cent tax is attached to each box sold. Buyers now get their morning sugar fix by paying $2.10 per box. If buyers are reluctant to pay this higher price, and switch to something else, like a wholesome pound of bacon, then less cereal is sold. As consumers buy less and producers sell less, production costs are likely to fall because producers can get rid of some high-priced, and unneeded, resources. If their costs go down to $1.95 per box, then the buyers' price, with the tax, is only $2.05. As such, buyers pay 5 cents of the 10-cent tax and sellers pay the other 5 cents.

The tax, however, is seldom divided equally among buyers and sellers. Which side pays more depends on market control. If buyers have the control, then they can effectively say "We won't pay the tax," and sellers will be forced to pay most or all of it. The alternative, of course, is that sellers use their market control to force buyers to pay the bulk of the tax.

Recalling that the second estate tends to have the most market control, either as sellers in the product markets, or as buyers in the resource markets, you can probably guess who ends up paying most of the taxes—the wary consumers, unappreciated workers, and disgruntled taxpayers of the third estate.

A FEW TAX TIPS

- In that taxes hit some people harder than others, consider the source when anyone advocates more or fewer taxes. Keep an eye on the progressivity or regressivity of all taxes. Who stands to benefit and who's likely to be hurt by any tax changes?
- Some taxes can be good for our economy if they correct some sort of inefficiency like pollution. Keep in mind that whoever is responsible for the inefficiency is likely to cry murder if forced to pay the tax.
- Some politicians and second-estate leaders try to make it seem as though businesses pay taxes that are really passed along to consumers. Businesses with significant market control tend to pay a small share of a tax.

See also: Federal Deficit, Political Views, Regulation, and Welfare.

An altogether look at
UNIONS

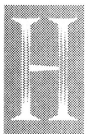 *Hey, look! Is that who I think it is? Yes, of course, that's Dan Dreiling the drywall guy. You might recall that Dan repaired a hole in my living room wall back in Fact #7. He's coming out of the Mona Mallard Duct Tape Industries plant with all of the duct tape factory workers. And he seems most distressed. Let's get to the bottom of this. Here's his story. The drywall business sort of dried up, and Dan has taken up employment in the exciting field of duct tape fabrication. The duct tape workers, though, are talking union. Dan's indecisive about this move toward unionization. Perhaps we can help him out. Let's stroll around the often controversial topic of labor unions.*

Solidarity

Unions are organizations of workers—in the same industry, working for the same company, or in the same occupation—that negotiate with their employers over things like wages, fringe benefits, working conditions, hiring and firing procedures, and most other job-related stuff. The formal negotiation, where the union and the company (or "management") seek to work out a contractual agreement on these various issues, is termed "collective bargaining,"

In recent years, most of these collective bargaining agreements have been pretty straightforward. Unions demand a few things, companies return with their "best" offer, then they haggle back and forth until they ultimately reach a compromise. If this sounds a lot like buying a car or house, it is. It's the same sort of one-on-one negotiation that takes place in many markets. Occasionally, however, negotiations don't reach a compromise that's satisfactory to both sides. In that case, there are a few alternatives.

- *Mediation.* This pertains to an outsider (a mediator) like a judge or high-ranking government official who is acceptable to both sides and tries to work out differences between unions and management. The mediator usually offers a solution that will finalize the collective bargaining agreement. However, neither side is legally compelled to accept the solution.
- *Arbitration.* This is a lot like mediation; however, the solution proposed by the arbitrator is legally binding. This is much the same as taking the collective bargaining agreement to a court where a judge makes the final decision. We should also note that arbitration is most often used to interpret an existing agreement rather than to forge a new one.
- *Strike.* This is a well-known alternative where everyone in the union decides to stop working, hoping that the loss of production will hurt management more than the loss of wages will hurt the workers. This was effectively used by unions in

the past. It also got pretty bloody. More on this in a few paragraphs.

- *Lockout.* A company's own version of the strike in which it keeps workers from entering the plant. This is typically used to counteract a planned strike by the union. The company hopes to get a jump on the union before it's ready to strike.

These are a few of the more popular options. Other union stuff includes work slowdowns (don't strike, just don't work very hard) or even occasional product sabotage. Management has been known to speed up production before a strike or hire nonunion workers (so-called "scabs") during a strike.

A classic confrontation

While the sorts of things that unions and management do to each other might appear childish, they have a serious and violent history. Their confrontations are as fundamental as the differences between the second and third estates. We can find the seeds of their conflicts growing out of our economy's transition from the simple fabrication methods of blacksmiths, carpenters, and other medieval craftsman to the large factories that marked the onset of the industrial revolution.

In the early years of the Industrial Revolution, with hundreds or even thousands of workers in a single factory, the balance of *market control* was tipped to the side of the second estate. The handful of employers were pretty much able to dictate wages and working conditions. Workers were inputs—not people, just inputs. They had about the same status as felled trees, molten steel, or railroad cars filled with slaughterhouse-bound cattle. If the wheels of industry happened to grind an occasional worker into a bloody mass, well, replacements could be found. As such, wages were extremely low and working conditions were, at best, downright deadly. That's when unions came onto the scene.

The concept of unions had been around since the craft guilds of the Middle Ages,

but it really began to take off for common laborers in the mid-1800s. Workers found that they could risk life and limb in the factory or risk life and limb battling management for higher wages and safer working conditions. The secret to any success, though, was speaking with a single voice— a "one for all and all for one" sort of strategy. Their goal, whether or not it was fully recognized, was to balance the market control of their second-estate employers. Rather than a one-sided slaughter, companies now found a competitive adversary that could battle them on an increasingly equal footing.

The battles often turned bloody. Companies didn't hesitate to use force—armed security guards and government soldiers— on the rabble-rousing unions. The unions fought back with an assortment of their own guerrilla tactics. Most of this violence ended with laws and court cases in the 1930s that forged a set of collective bargaining rules.

We've now reached a point where both sides tend to negotiate peacefully. Of course, even though life is more peaceful, businesses think that unions have become too powerful, demand excessive wages, eat away company profits, and are a pain in the butt. Unions, however, are always suspicious that the companies are out to destroy them and return to the good old days of low pay and abused workers. Both sides are probably right—to a degree. Each is in for trouble if the other gets the upper hand in their ongoing game of market control.

A balance of power

Let's consider this balancing act. Have unions achieved their goal of protecting workers or have they actually gone too far?

Let's first put things into perspective. From a peak of about 25 percent of the labor force in the 1950s, only about 15 percent of workers in the good old U.S. of A. belong to unions today. That's a shrinking fraction, but it still includes around 16 to 17 million people. Here are a few notable consequences of unions:

- *Unions raise wages and improve working conditions.* Few would argue with this. However workers' wages are companies' costs. Some critics argue that unions have appropriated too much pay for too little work. This often means that consumers pay higher prices, and U.S. companies can't compete with other nations around the world.
- *Higher union wages mean lower nonunion wages.* Unions usually keep wages high by restricting the number of workers. This creates a surplus of workers who are driven to find employment in some nonunionized company. With more nonunionized workers, nonunion wages drop.
- *Unions protect the well-being of both union and nonunion workers.* Unions have fought for shorter workweeks, safer working conditions, more holidays (such as Labor Day), and improved health care benefits and retirement programs that have benefited all workers in the economy.
- *Rigid rules create inefficiencies.* Unions tend to create rules that prevent the flexible use of resources. They might specify, for example, that a simple task must be done by only one type of worker, even though anyone could do the job.

The bottom line

So the question remains. Do we advise Dan Dreiling, the former drywall guy, to join the duct tape union or not?

Unions play a valuable role in our economy. Without them, businesses of the second estate would most likely slip back into their abusive ways. Good for business, bad for workers. Unions provide a needed labor market balance.

Yet, some unions have excessive market control. The best way to strike fear into any small business owner, and perhaps send the company into bankruptcy, is for workers to join a large, national union. Like many long-standing institutions, unions are often inclined to expand into areas where they are unneeded.

Unfortunately, there's no way to know which direction Dan's prospective unionization actions will take the economy. Will it tip the balance of power toward unions? Is it a needed move to counteract some abusive problems by Mona Mallard Duct Tape Industries? We can't answer these questions without a great deal more information than we can gather from this trek around the economy. We can, however, propose two question-based tips for Dan and other prospective union members to consider:

TWO UNIONIZING TIPS

1. What are the costs of joining a union, especially dues and the hardships created by a potential strike? What are the chances that unionization will force your employer into bankruptcy and you into the unemployment lines?
2. What are the benefits of being a union member? Will you be getting higher wages and better working conditions? Do they have neat parties every Friday night at the union hall?

See also: Athlete Salaries, Business, Education, Foreign Trade, Health Care, Immigration, Recession, Social Security, Worker Safety, and Working Women.

creating

WEALTH

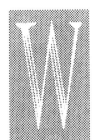

Wealth: What is it and how do you get it? Perhaps one of those home business franchises that sells cleaning products, housewares, or perfume can be your source of financial independence. And, as evidenced by those late-night infomercials, the always-lucrative area of real estate investment is almost certain to turn you into a gadzillionaire by next Thursday. Or perhaps tinkering in the financial markets with penny stocks, gold futures, or silver options is more your cup of tea. (My personal favorite is the Darling Donna's Chimney Sweep outfit that gives you the opportunity for a meaningful career in the high-profile field of chimney maintenance products.) The question for today is: Are any of these get-rich-quick schemes better than buying a lottery ticket?

What it means to be rich

Before we can get a handle on the best ways to acquire wealth, we had better decide what it is we're trying to acquire. As a first stab at defining wealth, think of it as your material possessions, like a house, car, clothing, and other assorted stuff. In other words, it's the things that you own.

There's two things to note about ownership and wealth:

1. Owning a *lot* of stuff doesn't necessarily make you wealthy. What you need to own is a lot of *valuable* stuff. For example, owning 349 distributor caps from 1949 Fords is *not* likely to place you high on the list of wealthy Americans. However, owning 349 precious jewels, passenger airplanes, or Fortune 500 companies is a different story. The ownership translates into greater wealth if society places a high value on the stuff. As we saw in Fact #3, Our Unfair

Lives, J. D. Goodluck became very, very wealthy because society placed a great value on the petroleum resources under his farmland.

This further means that wealth arises not just from *owning* valuable stuff but also from having the ability to *produce* valuable stuff. In other words, part of your wealth includes not just ownership of valuable wants-satisfying goods but also ownership of productive resources: labor, capital, and natural resources. We'll ponder this difference between goods and productive resources in a few paragraphs.

2. It's not just what you own that makes you wealthy, it's the difference between what you *own* and what you *owe*. For example, if you borrow $100,000 to buy a $100,000 house, then you're not really any wealthier. Sure, you own a $100,000 house, but that's canceled out by the $100,000 that you owe to the

A PEDESTRIAN . . .

. . . creates wealth?

AFTER I'M THROUGH WITH THESE TENS I'M GOING TO DO SOME TWENTIES

bank. As such, wealth is best thought of as the difference between *assets*— what we own—and *liabilities*—what we owe. If you want to be truly wealthy, then you have to own a great deal more than you owe.

A little side note: Assets, like houses, cars, and such, are typically more apparent to outside observers than liabilities, like mortgages and car loans. That means, many people have the appearance of wealth because they give lavish parties in expensive mansions and tool around town in sporty cars. This wealth, however, may be totally superficial because of unseen liabilities. A word to the wise: If you're trying to keep up with the Joneses, make sure that you're aware

of both sides of the Jones's wealth: assets and liabilities. Now that we know what we're after, let's turn to a few get-rich-quick schemes and their promises of wealth.

A license to steal?

First, let's point out right from the beginning that almost every get-rich scheme involving real estate, financial investments, home product sales, or many others *can* make you wealthy. They can expand your assets well above your liabilities such that you not only have the appearance of wealth, *you actually are wealthy.* The same can also be said for a state lottery or a rich, but dearly departed, relative. There is, however, an important feature that must be noted: These deal with the *transfer* of wealth, not the *creation* of wealth.

Let's consider the prospects of becoming a gadzillionaire in the stock market. The task is simple: Buy some stock at a low price, then sell it for a higher price. Sounds simple. It is simple, if you can find someone else who is willing to buy the stock for more than you paid. With one exception (that I'll note in the next paragraph), the extra wealth that you get is given up by the sucker, er, investor who buys the stock from you. A lot of the wealth acquired from the stock market and other assorted financial markets is really acquired from others. If you're good (or lucky), you win and they lose.

The exception is wealth that results from the long-run growth of the economy. As we noted in our survey of the stock market, a long-term rise in the stock market occurs from the long-term growth of our economy. An increase in wealth resulting from this long-term growth does *not* come from anyone else. It is truly created.

The stock market aside, other short-term, get-rich-quick schemes usually work in this madcap, wealth-transferring way. Many fortunes were made during the 1970s by buying land, then reselling a short time later for a big profit. However, while some made out like bandits, others lost their shirts. No wealth was created, only transferred.

Let's hear it for pyramid power

Here's a particularly appealing wealth "creation" scheme: home-marketing systems. A good example is offered by Darling Donna's Chimney Sweep products. A Darling Donna's Chimney Sweep distributor has a twofold mission in life: (1) to sell valuable Darling Donna's Chimney Sweep products to those in need of clean chimneys and (2) to entice others to become Darling Donna's Chimney Sweep *distributors*. While providing chimney products to consumers is a noble service worthy of reward, this usually isn't the

hook that attracts wealth seekers to the Darling Donna's Chimney Sweep products family. The big bucks lie in the prospect of becoming a Darling Donna's Chimney Sweep distributor and getting others to do the selling for you.

However, this "chaining" of Darling Donna's Chimney Sweep distributorship is a little on the suspect side. Here's how a wealth creation system like this tends to work. Joe, our number-1 Darling Donna's Chimney Sweep distributor, entices five other people to become Darling Donna's Chimney Sweep distributors by holding rooftop chimney sweep "parties." Joe then supplies these five new distributors with Darling Donna's Chimney Sweep distributor starter kits. Joe makes a tidy sales commission on the starter kits, and the Darling Donna's Chimney Sweep company makes a profit for producing the kits.

Now, if each of these five distributors entices five more rooftop party-goers to become Darling Donna's Chimney Sweep distributors, Joe, the first five distributors, and the Darling Donna's Chimney Sweep company can sell 25 additional starter kits with all of the sales commissions and profits that go with them. Joe and the Darling Donna's Chimney Sweep company can really get into some big bucks if each of those 25 distributors gets five new distributors, who then get five new distributors, who then get five new distributors, in an ever-growing pyramid.

In the fifth level of this pyramid, there are 3,125 people trying to sell Darling Donna's Chimney Sweep products. In the tenth level there are close to 10 million distributors, giving Joe tons of commission on 10 million Darling Donna's Chimney Sweep starter kits. The Darling Donna's Chimney Sweep also made piles of profit on these kits.

Moreover, Joe can be used as an example of the wealth to be had by participating in the Darling Donna's Chimney Sweep distributor program. His participation has "created" incalculable wealth—for him—

including expensive sports cars (an Omni-Motors XL GT 9000), housing, and other highly valued assets. Your own path to riches is a Darling Donna's Chimney Sweep distributorship. Right? There are some problems with this:

- All of Joe's wealth was "created" without the need to clean a single chimney. Joe didn't make his wealth from cleaning chimneys, nor from selling chimney-cleaning products to people who cleaned chimneys. His wealth came from selling chimney-cleaning distributor starter kits. Not a single productive, consumer-satisfying thing was accomplished for Joe's wealth.
- Ten million Darling Donna's Chimney Sweep distributors are likely to have chimney-cleaning starter kits stored in their basements. Each prospective distributor spent a few bucks on a starter kit hoping to accrue the mind-boggling wealth displayed by Joe. If the dream didn't materialize, then, well, it was only a few bucks. No big deal.

Here's the bottom line on Darling Donna's Chimney Sweep system. Wealth is transferred from the bottom of the pyramid up to the top. Those at the top, by getting a few bucks from a bunch of people, accrue massive fortunes. Those at the bottom, however, get nothing. The secret to wealth in this sort of pyramid is to make sure that you're very close to the top, with a whole bunch of other people beneath you.

Most get-rich-quick schemes do little more than transfer wealth from one person to another. If a Darling Donna's Chimney Sweep distributor grows wealthy without any chimneys cleaned, then someone else grows poorer. If an astute financial investor buys low then sells high, some other not-so-astute financial investor is selling low and buying high. If there's no production, then the wealth accumulated by one must be lost by someone else.

The road to productive wealth

The only true key to wealth lies in production. While you can increase your own wealth at the expense of others, we all become wealthier when productive resources are increased. Greater wealth for our economy lies in increasing the quantity or quality of productive resources: labor, capital, and natural resources. As discussed more thoroughly in Economic Growth and Investment, this is done by investing in education, capital goods, research and development, and technology.

What works for our economy can also work for each of us. You can acquire wealth by education, buying productive capital goods, inventing a new product, and assorted other improvements in productive resources.

WEALTH-CREATION TIPS

- Many get-rich-quick wealth creation schemes do nothing more than transfer wealth. On a personal level, that may be okay if you're the recipient of the transferred wealth. In general, however, there tend to be more people on the losing end of the transfer than on the winning end.
- A lot of people get their wealth by selling dreams. Financial brokers get their commission on transactions. If they can convince you that untold wealth is to be had by taking the plunge, and you take the plunge (plus paying their commission), then their wealth is ensured, whether or not you get yours.
- Productive resources are the ultimate source of wealth for our economy—everything else just transfers it around. If you want to be truly involved in creating wealth, then invest in productive resources.

See also: Credit Cards, Education, Financial Markets, Foreign Investment, Gambling, Insurance, Investment, Mutual Funds, Profit, and Welfare.

collecting

WELFARE

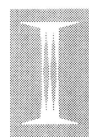 *I know word travels quickly among pedestrians of Shady Valley, but perhaps you haven't heard the latest. Pollyana Pumpernickel, the proprietor of Pollyana's Pet Palace, is no longer a pet proprietor. She's fallen on hard times, and fallen quite hard. Her husband of 12 years, Paul Pumpernickel, has dumped her and their three young children to pursue insurance alternatives with Tricia Comer—Smilin' Ted's sister and business partner in the All Comers Insurance Agency. Pollyana is distraught, to say the least. Paul Pumpernickel had been the dutiful househusband and caring father in his marriage partnership with Pollyana, but those duties fell onto the heavily burdened shoulders of Pollyana. The burden was too much. Pollyana's Pet Palace plundered into oblivion, leaving Pollyana penniless and jobless. Her only alternative was our government's public assistance program—what you and I know as "welfare." She's not pleased with her current social status, and neither, apparently, is Winston Smythe Kennsington III, who ridicules poor Pollyana at every opportunity.*

Catching your fall

Welfare, or public assistance, is part of the federal government's safety net of benefits for those who, like Pollyana, have fallen onto hard times. Along with social security and other New Deal programs, it sprung from the 1930s Great Depression. The 1930s was a period in which many people plummeted to the hard-packed, drought-parched ground. Bunches of consumers lost their income as the unemployment rate ran well into double digits. Bunches also lost their savings as thousands of banks closed their doors. These people fell, and fell hard, with nothing to keep them from crashing onto the jagged rocks.

As one part of the safety net system, welfare was designed to catch women (origi-nally widows) and their dependent children who were knocked down by the economy's turbulence. While single mothers and their children are the primary group of welfare recipients today, the program has been expanded over the years to assist others who are poor. Unlike social security, which is based on age and disability status, the criteria for welfare is poverty.

A myth or two makes for good campaign speeches

Before we get into the nuts and bolts of the welfare system, it's a good idea to dispel a few myths often propagated by vote-seeking politicians.

- *All (or most) welfare recipients are black.* The overwhelming majority of those who receive welfare benefits are white. What is true, however, is that blacks are more likely to be on welfare than you would expect from their share of the general population. While blacks make up about 13 percent of the population, they constitute about 25 percent of those on welfare. While blacks tend to be poorer than whites, poverty hits all races.

- *All (or most) blacks are welfare recipients.* In general about 10 percent of whites and 30 percent of blacks are officially poor. While blacks might have a greater likelihood of being poorer and less likelihood of being wealthier than whites, they're not all poor.
- *All (or most) welfare is paid to people who don't really need it.* The welfare system, like Congress, has its share of fraud and corruption. There are a number of people who collect welfare even though they hold down jobs. The few who accomplish this, however, get far more publicity, because of office-seeking politicians, than the millions who play by the rules.
- *All (or most) welfare recipients are out for a free ride at the taxpayers' expense.* Our economy is filled with lazy, shiftless people. Some are poor, others work in factories, and still others are in positions of wealth and power. But the overwhelming majority of welfare recipients would rather have a job than collect welfare.

The welfare mess

Almost anyone you ask tends to agree that our current poverty-fighting welfare system is a big mess. It has an overbloated bureaucracy, wastes a lot of tax dollars, and doesn't seem to help the poor. Let's see why.

- While welfare is mandated by the federal government, each state is responsible for operating its own system. As such, we really have 50 different welfare programs, some better than others.
- In particular, each state provides part of the funding on top of any federal tax dollars, and it sets up its own qualification

guidelines. Some states tend to be very generous, with loose guidelines, and others have extremely rigid qualifications with minimal payments. As you might expect, the "easy" states tend to have poor people move in to collect benefits.
- The "welfare system" is actually composed of several different programs. Let's see if we have enough space to list a few. At the top of the list is the Aid to Families with Dependent Children, which is what we normally think of in terms of welfare. There's also Supplemental Social Insurance, which is part of the social security system but provides benefits based on need rather than age or disability. We also have food stamps, school lunch programs, assorted veteran's benefits, Medicare, Medicaid, housing assistance, low-rent public housing, earned income tax credits, low-income energy assistance, job-training programs, and the list goes on. A big problem is that separate federal, state, and local government agencies deal with these different programs. Because there's little coordination, some people are boggled by the paperwork and don't get needed benefits, while others play the system like a concert violin and get undeserved checks.

How well does it work?

A common theme of this guide is that perfection is seldom found in our economy. The big question when we trek through something like the welfare system is whether or not the minuses cancel out the pluses.

- First, the pluses. Over the decades, our welfare system has provided valuable assistance to millions of poor people. In so doing, it has helped many remove their names from the poverty roster of our economy. It's also helped compensate, to some degree, for the unequal distribution of resources, income, and wealth that's caused by luck and happenstance.
- Now, the minuses. A lot of tax dollars are eaten up by the bureaucratic sys-

tem that administers welfare. While any government program in a complex economy is besieged with waste, the welfare system abuses that privilege. Because single mothers who aren't working are the ones targeted for benefits, the system has tended to encourage large families, unwed mothers, divorces, and unemployment.

Does it get any better than this?

Suggested alternatives for improving welfare are as numerous as there are politicians, administrators, welfare recipients, and taxpayers. While almost everyone has a thought on the matter, let's ponder a few of the more popular.

- *Tie it to concrete blocks and dump it into the ocean.* The suggestion has been made more than once (usually by deeply entrenched members of the second estate) that we should rid ourselves of the entire system. People would thus need to fend for themselves and undertake the personal investments needed to improve their lives. Truly needy people would be helped by private charities. (Of course, without welfare, people would be willing to work for lower wages, and thus the labor cost for businesses would decline.)

- *Simplify, streamline, and consolidate.* The whole system could be more effective if it were coordinated. Rather than hundreds of agencies, forms, and qualification guidelines, the poor, the taxpayers, and all parties concerned would benefit by getting rid of the layers upon layers of bureaucracy. The big obstacle, however, is that the bureaucratic

layers have created lifelong careers, political power, and assorted special-interest groups. One person's waste is another's income. None of these is easy to eliminate.

- *A stepping stone.* The original objective of our safety net programs, especially welfare, was to catch people who fell. These recipients would then bounce back. However, over the years, many people have hit the safety nets without bouncing. The welfare system could be better if used to help people invest in productive skills or otherwise improve themselves, rather than providing just consumption. Suggested reforms include education, job training, work incentives, and drug rehabilitation. However, if not implemented right, the system could do little more than provide some businesses or governments with a source of cheap labor.

While improvements are possible in our welfare system, it's nice to know that someone like Pollyana Pumpernickel is protected from excessive hardship when her life crumbles. With a little bit of luck and some hard work, her stay on the safety net will be temporary. Had it not been there, however, her problems and those of society might have been far worse. Homelessness, drug abuse, drug dealing, prostitution, thievery, suicide, or any number of other socially despicable problems could have been in Pollyana's future. Millions of other hardworking, taxpaying consumers are only a natural disaster, closed factory, or major illness away from following Pollyana's path.

See also: Crime, Discrimination, Education, Health Care, Insurance, Political Views, Recession, Taxes, and Working Women.

a careful view of
WORKER SAFETY

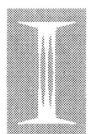*It was the most-exciting baseball game in the long rivalry between the Shady Valley Primadonnas and the Oak Town Sludge Puppies. Two out, two on, the bottom of the ninth, the hometeam down by a run, and Harold "Hair Doo" Dueterman—the Primadonnas' star center fielder—up to bat. What excitement! What drama! Unfortunately, Hair Doo hit the ball directly at the Primadonnas' runner on first. A line shot to the head. The runner was out. He was also unconscious. Game over. That was not the end to the excitement, though. Chucky Calhoun, the peanut vendor, was inadvertently decked by an enthusiastic fan and suffered a number of injuries as he tumbled down some concrete steps. Chucky, who has made repeated complaints to the Primadonnas owner (D. J. Goodluck) about unsafe working conditions, has filed a workers' compensation claim. What a mess! Too bad Hair Doo just didn't strike out as he usually does.*

Life is risky; then you die

What's the big deal about workers' compensation and workplace safety? Does Chucky Calhoun, the peanut vendor, have a valid claim? Let's pursue the subject.

First, we need to clearly note that life is a risk. Nowhere in the manual of life are we promised any guarantees about safety. After all, childbirth itself is a pretty dangerous event. Then there's a chance that a deranged kindergarten classmate will bring pointed scissors, rather than the rounded ones, to class. The dangers of life aren't limited to school either. We daily face the risks imposed by stray dogs, plummeting stockbrokers (who invested unwisely), potholes in the sidewalks, and physicians who graduated at the bottom of their medical school class.

With that said, we also need to note that most of us are better off reducing risk. This goes back to our little discussion of *risk averse, risk loving,* and *risk neutral* in Fact #6, Our Unknown Economy. Those who are risk averse prefer certainty over risk and are willing to pay for it. While there are risk-lover types who are inclined to gamble or seek danger in risky occupations—like mercenary soldier, shark trainer, and door-to-door solicitor—most of us don't want to put our lives on the line every day.

Now what does that mean for the millions of workers who expect to return home each night with the same number of appendages and vital organs that they left with in the morning? It means that they want to pursue a job and earn an income without a high risk of death or injury. It

A PEDESTRIAN...

... goes to work–carefully

IS THIS WHAT THEY MEAN BY "UNSAFE WORKPLACE?"

O M Ames

means that they would just as soon have a safe place to work. But can they?

The power of the second estate

We've often noted in our pedestrian journey that the second estate tends to have more market control than the third estate. This is particularly evident for labor. The history of the good old U.S.A. is etched with labor markets dominated and controlled by businesses of the second estate. Those markets saw very low wages and extremely hazardous working conditions. When one company employed everyone in a given town, either in the company mine, company factory, or company store, the work-

ers had very little to say about the wages and workplace safety. They either worked for *the* company or they didn't work at all.

Second-estate dominance of employment was pretty much the norm in the 1800s when the Industrial Revolution changed our economy from self-sufficient farmers to over-worked, underpaid, and frequently crippled factory workers. During this period, labor was treated by the second estate (as well as by the first estate) with the same amount of compassion as a lump of coal. Labor was just another input into the great profit-making engine of the U.S. economy. With second-estate dominance of the labor markets, a dismembered or deceased worker could be readily replaced by another.

Meanwhile, back to the present

Workplace conditions have changed significantly since the early days of the Industrial Revolution. Labor unions and assorted protective government laws have improved worker safety enormously. Oh sure, you'll find an occasional "sweatshop" where the workers (usually illegal immigrants) are overworked and underpaid in a very dangerous work environment, but unions and government have made big strides to prevent this. Let's see where we currently stand on this worker safety thing:

- Workers, and their array of champions in unions and government, continue to eliminate workplace risks. The primary government advocate of worker safety is the Occupational Safety and Health Administration (or OSHA). OSHA is often criticized (by businesses) for pushing this safety topic too far, the same sort of malady that inflicts many government agencies. OSHA has a job to do, and they're going to damn well do it regardless of the consequences.

- Businesses, of course, have their eyes on the bottom line. All of those blasted safety rules and regulations forced on them by OSHA and the unions increase cost and reduce profit. And if a business fails to comply with some blasted nitpicky little rule, then it has to pay a fine.

Like a number of other things we've seen on our journey, these two sides of the worker safety debate are both partly right and partly wrong. That, however, is the beauty of our system: a balance between the interests of the second and third estates. Our real problems emerge if one side gets too much control over the situation. If OSHA stopped harassing businesses over worker safety, then we would probably find fingers, toes, and other appendages in the products we buy. However, if OSHA eliminated *all* risk in every job, then the stuff our economy produces would be so incredibly expensive that no one could afford it.

Workers' compensation

What does this all mean for Chucky Calhoun, the peanut vendor? To answer this, we need to evaluate the risk Chucky faced in the workplace. Were the aisles too narrow for passage? Were the steps covered with grease before each game? Were razorblades attached to the handrails?

Maybe Chucky's injury was his own fault. Maybe it was the result of negligence and irresponsibility on the part of D. J. Goodluck, the Primadonnas owner. Or maybe, just maybe, it was simply an unavoidable accident.

That brings up the topic of workers' compensation. For the most part, anyone injured on the job, doing job-related stuff, can collect benefits provided by this government-run insurance program. The benefits include reimbursement for medical expenses and payment of lost wages. The funds used to pay these benefits come from insurance premiums paid by businesses. As with other forms of insurance, these premiums depend on risk. Businesses that tend to be riskier for workers, as documented by past injuries, pay higher premiums.

Let's consider a few of the stickier points of controversy over workers' compensation:

- Small businesses can be bludgeoned into bankruptcy by excessively high insurance premiums. If a small company is unlucky enough to have several workers seriously injured, then premiums skyrocket through the roof, profit drops through the floor, and the owners file for bankruptcy.

- Perhaps, more so than other forms of insurance, workers' compensation is besieged with false claims. Some doctors, lawyers, and workers have made comfortable livings from this system, *without* the pain and suffering that comes from actual injuries.

- Workers' compensation is mandated at the federal level but run by state governments. This leads to a great deal of variation in premiums and benefits from state to state. In fact, lower employer premiums and worker benefits are often used to attract new businesses into a state. Good for business, bad for workers.

The hidden injuries

Another pretty important problem with worker safety is the number of unseen, long-term health problems caused by employment. Our economy is becoming so technologically complex that a growing number of work-related injuries are not of the "chopped-off-toe" variety. People may unknowingly have worked around hazardous chemicals and cancer-causing substances or performed repetitive tasks that led to injuries and health problems years or even decades later. The inability to know for sure which chemical caused your cancer or which repetitive task crippled your hand throws a kink into the workers' compensation system. Some who shouldn't collect benefits do, and others who should don't.

While a number of risks have been eliminated from the workplace over the past century, the complexity of our economy means that working today may be as hazardous as ever. What can you do about worker safety?

SOME TIPS ON WORKPLACE SAFETY

- You need to recognize that risk and the potential for injury are an inherent part of life. You can reduce it, but you can't eliminate it.

- As such, you need to be alert for any sorts of "accidents waiting to happen" around the job. If your employer greases the steps leading up to the building every morning, then you probably have a good cause for concern.

- If you have safety concerns, the first action is to inform your employer. Most employers of today aren't bloodthirsty, sadistic swine; they do recognize that healthy workers are productive workers. If not, OSHA is ready to remind them of this fact.

- Perhaps most importantly, with the growing complexity of our economy, be alert to potential long-term hazards. Do you occasionally get the whiff of some strange chemical through the ventilation system? Is this a health hazard? You might want to find out.

See also: Athlete Salaries, Business, Discrimination, Education, Health Care, Insurance, Product Safety, Pollution, Regulation, Unions, Welfare, and Working Women.

<h1>getting the most out of</h1>

WORKING WOMEN

No pedestrian excursion around the economy could be even remotely considered complete without a stop at the Shady Valley Museum of Traditional Family Life. Just beyond the freshly painted white picket fence and the newly mown lawn resides a full-scale, lifelike, fully functional model of the traditional family. The two-car garage houses Mom's good old reliable family station wagon right next to Dad's sensible four-door sedan. Inside the humble, but well-kept, abode, we can find young Billy, who aspires to a career as a highly paid doctor, and his sister, little Debbie, who hopes to marry a highly paid doctor. The faithful family dog, Spot, is resting comfortably at the feet of our traditional husband, provider, and father, who has just returned from a long, hard day at the office. He has worked long and hard on this day to provide for his traditional family. Purring at the feet of our traditional wife, mother, and homemaker is Fluffy, the family cat. Our traditional wife is busily preparing the night's traditional family fare of pot roast, potatoes, and green beans. After the meal, she will gaily clean the evening's dishes, a fine ending to her day that has been filled with shopping, baking, and cleaning. How quaint!

Reality check! Reality check!

Meanwhile, back in the real world, we find very few (if any) families that fit this traditional model. Of course, many families have two cars, two children, two pets, and a mown lawn. But a great number of families in our economy have only one parent, quite often the mother, who does the cleaning, cooking, shopping, and *providing*. And many more families send both parents into the workforce each morning in desperate search of family provisions. It's becoming increasingly difficult for any family to follow this quaint, traditional pattern of working husband and stay-at-home housewife.

Let's throw a few numbers out to illustrate this point. Roughly 45 percent of the labor force in the U.S.A. are women. Moreover, while 76 percent of working-age men in the economy are working, 58 percent of the working-age women are also putting their share of bread onto the family table. So much for women staying home and baking pies.

Yet, while traditional families are few and far between, many strings of traditionality still dangle, tugging and pulling on both men and women as they struggle through the daily routines of a working life. For example:

- Many women are viewed, usually by men but also by other women, as unwanted party crashers into our economy's workforce. In spite of the realities of our complex economy, women are supposed to stay home and do womanly things around the house.

- Women who venture into the labor force are typically paid less than men in comparable positions. The number two-thirds sticks in my mind for comparing the average wage for women with that for men.
- Part of the problem for this two-thirds number is that women usually wind up in lower-paid, less-productive positions, such as secretary and nurse, rather than executive and doctor.
- Women who try to push the limits of the labor force often find themselves bouncing against the top of what is termed a "glass ceiling." Women advance up the ranks of the corporate hierarchy much slower and attain much less loftier heights than men of equal training and ability.

Secure your jogging shoelaces and firmly tie the drawstring on your running suit, because our mission over the next few pages is to run through this somewhat annoying and downright frustrating predicament facing millions of working women in our economy. (Let me also direct your attention to the entry on Discrimination, which has a few more things to say on this topic.) On to the plight of the working woman.

The choice

To work or not to work? that is the question (with all due respect to William Shakespeare). Stemming from changes in those old traditional roles of husband-provider and wife-homemaker, women are more frequently facing the choice of (a) seeking income-earning employment beyond the confines of their white picket fences or (b) doing nothing but the homemaker deeds that need doing at home.

Here's the choice: Are the efforts of gainful employment more rewarding than tending to family rearing, toilet scrubbing, and meal cooking? Let's consider the benefit and cost on both sides of this choice.

- *To work.* The most obvious benefit of working for any woman pondering the possibility of employment is a wage, salary, or other income. This includes the myriad of fringe benefits that come with a job, such as retirement, health insurance, free parking, or whatever. There are also nonmonetary "psychic income" benefits (that is, where money doesn't change hands) that include having a career, being with (adult) friends and colleagues, and doing something useful. Of course, some or all of these nonmonetary "benefits" might actually be "costs." For example, you might not like the people at work or you just might hate your job.
- *Not to work.* On the other side of the ledger sheet we have numerous nonmonetary benefits and a few costs from not working. The top of the list for most people is probably leisure, the time spent watching television, piddling around the house, or just doing stuff that's fun. There's also a category of things we can term "household production," an area that tends to be pretty significant for working women and includes cleaning, family rearing, cooking, shopping, and sundry other activities needed to run a household. The psychic income stuff is also a big part of not working, and can be a plus or minus as well. For example, you like staying at home and raising a family (a plus), or alternatively you're bored down to your toenails from sitting around the house watching soap operas (a definite minus). There are also some actual monetary benefits from not working, such as welfare payments, unemployment compensation, or even social security.

Thus, the choice for *potentially* working women is this: Are the benefits of staying home more or less than the benefits from gainful employment? Other ways of posing this question are: Can a woman afford to work? Or can a woman afford not to work? Is the wage and associated benefits so low that a woman can't be enticed to enter the labor force? Or are the benefits of working so great that a woman can't afford to stay home?

A choice for all

Although we're asking this question about working women, the same decision is faced by virtually everyone in the economy. Women get our scrutiny here because, other than the title of this entry, their choice gives us a clear picture of both sides of the balance sheet. The scales of the balance sheet for many men, most all children, a great number of retirees, and a lot of the disabled clearly tip in one direction or the other. The benefits of working usually far outweigh those of not working for adult males. The choice usually (not always, but usually) goes in the other direction for kids, elderly, and the handicapped. The situation for women, however, is not as clear cut. Many women could go in either direction. The reasons behind this are worth a look.

The whys and wherefores of working women

Let's take another tour through the Shady Valley Museum of Traditional Family Life. The traditional roles of husband-provider and wife-homemaker come from a deeply embedded cultural norm that itself has resulted from obvious physical differences between men and women. Men, with greater physical strength, on average, have historically played the part of hunter and protector. Women, with childbirth capabilities, have always assumed the responsibilities of tending to the flock of offspring.

Although we've left the caves and moved into a modern, complex, industrialized economy—with two cars, two pets, two kids, and a mown lawn—men have continued their role as provider, and women have maintained their position as homemaker. Men are "supposed" to work, and women are "not supposed" to work. In the traditional past, this cultural and genetic stuff made women more valuable and men less valuable around the home—in the eyes of many people. In terms of working, this enhanced the relative benefits of men and reduced those for women.

This, however, is exactly what is changing. Well, the genetic stuff about childbirth hasn't changed, but the cultural norms have. Income, wages, and other benefits of working are rising for women. Because providing the family meal seldom requires killing a mastodon, women have found that they're just as capable as men. They, too, can make executive decisions while lounging around the water cooler, in spite of their deficiencies in physical strength. Modern technology has also reduced the amount of effort required for family rearing, toilet scrubbing, and meal cooking. Long gone are the days when homemaking was a full-time sun-up-to-sun-down job that required hours each day just for butter churning. Even men (gasp!) can microwave a three-course TV dinner or order a pizza.

As the benefit of working rises and that of not working falls, we have seen a larger fraction of women in the workforce. Traditions, however, change slowly. That's why women tend to have less lofty positions than men, and the two-thirds number for male/female wages pops into my head again. We will, however, leave further discussion of the assorted male-dominant barriers that keep women "in their place" for the entry on Discrimination. For the time being, though, let's consider a tip on this basic work decision:

TIPPING THE BALANCE ON WORK

- Everyone, regardless of race, age, sex, or planet of origin, needs to evaluate this work/not-work choice. For many, there is no choice: You have to feed your family. If, however, you have a working spouse who makes a ton of money, then you might be able to go either way. Whatever your own situation, consider the options.

See also: Athlete Salaries, Business, Education, Immigration, Political Views, Social Security, Unions, and Welfare.

SECTION

3

A WHOLE BUNCH OF
ECONOMIC TERMS AND
DEFINITIONS

ECONOMIC TERMS

A

absolute advantage The general ability to produce more goods using fewer resources. This idea of absolute advantage is important for trading that occurs between both people and nations. A nation can get an absolute advantage from an advanced level of technology or higher-quality resources. For a person, an absolute advantage can result from natural abilities or the acquisition of human capital (education, training, or experience). Trade is possible, and even expected, if two people or nations have absolute advantages in two different goods. For example, Saudi Arabia, with an absolute advantage in oil production (through the luck of prehistoric conditions), and Japan, with an absolute advantage in car production (resulting from investment in technology and capital goods), would find trade worthwhile. Along similar lines, someone skilled at math and another talented in public speaking could specialize in accounting and game show hosting, respectively. Compare "comparative advantage." See "foreign trade."

accounting profit The difference between a business's revenue and its accounting expenses. This is the profit that's listed on a company's balance sheet, appears periodically in the financial sector of the newspaper, and is reported to the Internal Revenue Service for tax purposes. It frequently has little relationship to a company's economic profit because of the difference between accounting expense and the opportunity cost of production. Some accounting expense is not an opportunity cost (see "economic rent") and some opportunity cost does not show up as an accounting expenses (see "externality," "normal profit").

ad valorem tax A tax that is specified as a percentage of value. Sales, income, and property taxes are three of the more popular ad valorem taxes devised by government. The total ad valorem tax paid increases with the value of what's being taxed. Compare "per unit tax."

Aid to Families with Dependent Children (AFDC) See "welfare."

American Stock Exchange One of three national stock markets in the United States (see "National Association of Securities Dealers" and "New York Stock Exchange") that trade ownership shares in corporations. In terms of daily stock transactions and the number of stocks listed, the American Stock Exchange is the smallest of these three. However, its composite index of stock prices—the AMEX—is considered important enough to be flashed briefly on the nightly news. See "Dow Jones averages," "Securities and Exchange Commission."

amortization The process of paying off a debt (liability) and accrued interest through a series of equal, periodic payments. Car loans and mortgages are two debts commonly paid off through amortization. Your monthly car payment, for example, partially pays for interest accrued on the outstanding balance and partly reduces that balance. Because one payment reduces the outstanding balance, each subsequent payment has a smaller portion for interest. If the proper amortization schedule has been calculated, your loan will be paid off with the last payment. Compare "annuity," "present value."

annuity The receipt of payments at regular intervals from an established fund. Annuities are commonly used for insurance and retirement programs. It works in this way: A fund, which can be established either through a one-time sum of money or a series of payments, is exhausted over time with fixed, periodic payments. The amount of each payment depends on the interest accrued on the outstanding balance in the fund and the length of time scheduled to exhaust the fund. For example, if your pension plan is based on an annuity that begins payments at age 65, then the size of the payments depends on whether you expect to live 5, 10, 15, etc., more years and set up payments accordingly. It's very similar to "amortization," but in the reverse direction.

antitrust laws A series of laws passed by the U.S. government that tries to maintain competition and prevent businesses from getting a monopoly or otherwise obtaining and exerting market control. The first of these, the Sherman Antitrust Act, was passed in 1890. Two others, the Clayton Act and the Federal Trade Commission Act, were enacted in 1914. These laws impose all sorts of restrictions on business ownership, control, mergers, pricing, and how businesses go about competing (or cooperating) with each other. If one "big business" alone or a small number together begin to act too much like they have monopolized a market, then the Justice Department or the Federal Trade Commission (the ones responsible for enforcing these laws) have the legal authority to spring into action. However, the ferocity with which government springs depends on whether the first estate is more sympathetic to the plight of third-estate consumers or is more inclined to protect the interests of the second-estate businesses. All in all, antitrust laws have effectively punished companies that had fulfilled their dreams of monopoly. Perhaps more importantly, these laws have instilled the fear of lengthy, costly court cases and have prevented other businesses from pursuing monopolistic aspirations. See "natural monopoly," "price fixing."

appreciation A more- or less-permanent increase in value or price. "More or less permanent" doesn't include temporary, short-term jumps in price that are common in many markets. Appreciation is only those price increases that reflect greater consumer satisfaction and thus value. While all sorts of stuff can appreciate in value, some of the more common ones are real estate, works of art, corporate stock, and money. In particular, the appreciation of a nation's money is seen by an increase in the exchange rate caused by a growing, expanding, and healthy economy. Compare "depreciation." See "revaluation."

arbitrage Buying something in one market, then immediately (or as soon as possible) selling it in another market for (hopefully) a higher price. Arbitrage is a common practice in financial markets. For example, an aspiring financial tycoon might buy a million dollars worth of Japanese yen in the Tokyo foreign-exchange market, then resell it immediately in the New York foreign-exchange market for *more* than a million dollars. Arbitrage of this sort does two things. First, it often makes arbitragers wealthy. Second, it reduces or eliminates price differences that exist between two markets for the same good. See "hedging," "speculation."

arbitration Intervention of an impartial third party to settle disputes between two others. The decisions of this third party— the arbitrator—are legally binding, much like the ruling of a judge in a court of law. Arbitration is commonly used to interpret a collective bargaining agreement between unions and their employers. Much like a judge (in some cases it is a judge), an arbitrator determines how some given union and employer conflict stacks up against the terms of an existing agreement. Note that an arbitrator doesn't try to decide what's "best, "fair," or mutually agreeable to both sides—as would be the case with mediation—but only what's in line with the existing agreement. Compare "mediation."

asset Something that you own. For a person, assets can be financial—like money, stocks, bonds, bank accounts, and government securities—or they can be physical stuff—like cars, boats, houses, clothes, food, and land. The important assets for our economy are the output we have produced and the resources—labor, capital, and natural resources—used to produce that output. Compare "liability."

automatic stabilizer A feature of the federal government's budget that tends to reduce the ups and downs of the business cycle without the need for any special legislative action. Automatic stabilizers should be contrasted with fiscal policy, which is special legislative action, like tax cuts or spending increases designed to stabilize the business cycle. The two key automatic stabilizers are income taxes and transfer payments. When our economy drops into a recession, unemployment rises, production declines, and people have less income. But with less income, they pay less income tax, and thus there's less of a drain on consumption than there might have been. Likewise, many who are unemployed get transfer payments in the form of unemployment compensation, welfare, or social security. This lets them consume more than they would have otherwise. During an expansion, both of these go in the other direction. As a result, a recession sees more spending and fewer taxes, while an expansion has less spending

and more taxes, all occurring quite automatically. See "business cycle."

B

baby boomers Those citizens of the good old U. S. of A. who were born between the period 1946 to 1960. They represent a relatively large segment of the population and outnumber any other group, such as those born from 1931 to 1945 or from 1961 to 1975. Over the years, they've tended to set the standard for consumption, production, and politics. They have had and will continue to have a big impact on the social security system. As workers, they've provided an ample pool of tax funds and thus sizable benefits to social security recipients during the 1980s and 1990s. When these Boomers retire in the 2020s and beyond, however, they will leave a big gap in the labor force and also demand a great deal from the social security system.

balance of payments A record of the transactions that one nation has with all other nations. The balance of payments has two parts: "current account"—showing the value of exports and imports—and "capital account"—showing investments in physical and financial assets. The intriguing thing about the balance of payments is that it always *balances.* In other words, if the current account is running a deficit (exports are less than imports) then the capital account must be running a surplus of an equal amount. A capital account surplus means that foreign investment in domestic assets is greater than domestic investment in foreign assets. For example, if the U.S.A. imports a lot of stuff from Japan (current account deficit), then Japan will take those U.S. dollars and return them to the U.S.A. and buy up some good old U.S. assets (capital account surplus).

balance of trade The difference between a nation's merchandise exports and imports. A "trade surplus," or favorable balance of trade, occurs when exports are greater than imports. A "trade deficit," or unfavorable balance of trade, is what occurs when exports are less than imports. In general, a nation would like to export more than it imports. However, it should be pretty obvious that all nations of the world can't have a "favorable" balance of trade at the same time. When one nation exports, another must import. It is quite common, though, to run a trade deficit with one foreign country and a trade surplus with another. This balance of trade comprises a large portion of what's termed the "current account" in the "balance of payments." See "comparative advantage."

balanced budget An equality between the revenues and expenditures that constitute a budget. The notion of a budget is most important for governments, where revenues are taxes and expenditures are assorted public goods, administrative expenses, etc. While the federal government is notorious for its failure to have a balanced budget, many state and local governments are very good at this sort of thing. Compare "budget deficit," "budget surplus," "federal deficit."

bank panic Economywide concern over the stability of the banking system prompted by the failure of a few banks, which then contributes to the failure of many more. These failures occur because extremely worried people try to withdraw—in a very, very short period—more money from banks than the banks have on hand. When one bank can't pay out, it closes its doors, and is frequently forced into bankruptcy. The depositors of that bank lose their life savings, get mad, and tell their friends, who then seek withdrawals from other banks. This process snowballs, creating bank failures right and left and, of notable importance, reducing the amount of money people have to spend. This causes a contraction in the economy (see "recession" and "depression"). Bank panics were all too common

through much of the 1800s and into the Great Depression of the 1930s. However, the Federal Reserve System and the Federal Deposit Insurance Corporation—which were created in part to alleviate these problems—have generally made bank panics a thing of the past. See "money," "fractional-reserve banking."

bank reserves The "money" a bank uses to conduct day-to-day transactions and withdrawals of its customers, including "cashing" checks or otherwise processing checks written on other banks. The "money" in question includes any actual currency kept in the bank (vault cash) and deposits the bank has with the Federal Reserve System. Specifically, vault cash includes any paper money or coins that a bank keeps on hand to pay to customers. The accounts banks have with the Federal Reserve System are used to process the millions of checks written each day in a systematic, centralized fashion. Using these deposits, the Fed acts as a central clearing house for checks, being able simultaneously to debit the account of one bank and credit the account of another. More on the importance of bank reserves can be found under "fractional-reserve banking."

bankruptcy A legal declaration that the liabilities of a proprietor (individual), partnership, or corporation are greater than assets. In other words, a consumer or business unable to pay the bills can go to court and be formally declared bankrupt. The impetus for entering a court can come *voluntarily* from the deadbeat who has acquired more liabilities than assets, or involuntarily from the creditors who haven't been able to collect from the deadbeat. The procedure for declaring bankruptcy is governed by a series of federal laws, with the most popular coming under three "Chapters." Either individual or corporate deadbeats can file for Chapter 7, which involves *liquidating,* or selling off, assets and dividing the proceeds among creditors in some orderly fashion.

Unlike a corporation, an individual who files for Chapter 7 is able to keep some personal property (toothbrush, undershorts, or whatever). Chapter 11 is used by corporations that want to *reorganize* debts. During this reorganization, which could take years, the corporation continues to operate, but its debts are frozen until an acceptable plan of paying off debts, forgiving debts, merging with another company, selling off some assets, or another ingenious alternative is worked out. I might note that Chapter 11 is occasionally abused by businesses to renege on their liabilities: Run up some debts, file for Chapter 11, then don't pay the debts. Chapter 13 is a similar reorganization option for individuals, in which outside help—a trustee—is brought in to help the deadbeat, er, debtor determine the best way to pay off debts with future income.

barter A method of trading goods, commodities, services, or other stuff that takes place in the absence of "money." In a barter exchange one good is traded directly for another. This sort of exchange is easiest with what is termed a "double coincidence of wants," meaning that you have the good I want and I have the good that you want. Without a double coincidence of wants, so much time is spent trying to trade stuff that very little time is left for any production. In fact, inefficient barter trading was most likely the reason that the concept of money sprang from the creative minds of our ancestors. With money, more time can be spent producing and less time is needed for trading. See "market."

bear market A condition of the stock market in which stock prices are generally declining and most of the participants expect this decline to continue. In other words, the stock market is into an extended period of "hibernation" that could last for months or even years. This isn't the same as a "crash" of falling stock prices over a short time (like one day). A bear market usually occurs because

investors see a sluggish, stagnant economy with few signs of robust growth. Compare "bull market." See "speculation."

benefit-cost ratio The benefit of some activity per dollar of cost. Benefit-cost ratios (or, alternatively, cost-benefit ratios) are frequently estimated for many forms of government spending, as well as a growing number of business investments. This technique was originally developed to determine if public investment projects, like dams, public parks, highways, etc., were worth doing. The logic is simple: If benefit is greater than cost, then the project is worthwhile; if it's less, then it isn't. This procedure is both necessary and difficult to implement for government spending because benefit is usually quite hard to measure. For example, while the cost of renovating a public park is pretty straightforward, the benefit isn't. What's the value of an afternoon spent twiddling your toes in the tulips? This little fact of life tends to be a double-edged sword. Opponents of a project can underestimate the benefit, while proponents are inclined to overestimate it. As such, some worthwhile projects go undone, while wasteful ones blight the landscape.

big business A small number of the largest businesses (usually corporations) in our economy that (1) produce a substantial share of total output, (2) control a bunch of our economy's resources, and (3) have a great deal of "market control" in their respective industries. A listing of the Fortune 500 companies would give you a good feel for those businesses that have achieved the status of "big." The second estate obtains most its members from the presidents, shareholders, boards of directors, and high-level managers of big business. Compare "small business."

bilateral An action, often used in terms of an international trade agreement, that mutually affects two parties. As such, a bilateral trade agreement is one negotiated by two countries. For example, the

United States might enter into a bilateral agreement with Germany over car sales, such that each agrees to restrict the number of imports from the other. Compare "multilateral," "unilateral."

black market An illegal market in which the price of some stuff sold is above a legally set maximum price. A black market invariable results whenever the government imposes a "price ceiling" on a good. A common example of a price ceiling includes that imposed on rental apartments in large cities. Although landlords cannot legally rent apartments for more than the specified maximum, they often do so illegally by charging "finders fees" and "tenant association dues." In so doing they have entered into the realm of black markets.

blue chip The corporate stock of a relatively large, U.S.A. company that tends to be consistently profitable, pays out consistently high dividends, and is a consistently stable force in the economy. The blue chip stocks are often considered synonymous with those included in "Dow Jones averages." See "big business."

bond The general term for a long-term loan in which a borrower agrees to pay a lender an "interest rate" (usually fixed) over the length of the loan and then repay the principal at the date of maturity. Bond maturities are usually 10 years or more, with 30 years quite common. Bonds are used by corporations and federal, state, and local governments to raise funds. Most bonds are negotiable, or can be readily traded prior to their maturity date. The price at which a bond sells depends on the original amount borrowed, the interest rate the bond pays, and comparable interest rates and returns on other investments in the economy. For example, a $100,000 bond with a fixed 10-percent interest rate will sell for $100,000 if comparable interest rates are 10 percent. If, however comparable interest rates are less than 10 percent, the bond will sell for a "premium," more than $100,000.

The bond would sell at a "discount" if comparable interest rates are more than 10 percent. One of the more important things to note here, as you scrutinize financial reports on the news, is that bond prices move in the opposite direction of interest rates. When bond prices are up, interest rates are down. See "government security," "corporate bond."

boycott An organized effort to reduce the sales of a particular good that's intended to punish the producer. Boycotts are promoted by labor unions to inflict harm on companies and (hopefully) encourage employers to settle labor distributes (see "collective bargaining," "strike"). "Special-interest groups" also use boycotts to achieve assorted political goals. Some groups, for example, have called for boycotts of products advertised on "undesirable" television shows, while others have boycotted companies that do business in politically "undesirable" countries.

broker Anyone who is paid to bring together buyers and sellers to complete a market transaction. Common examples of brokers are real estate agents, stockbrokers, and insurance agents. The thing to note about brokers is that they don't buy or sell anything, but merely bring buyers and sellers together. This little function is different from that of a *dealer*. A dealer is one who is always ready to help a transaction by selling to those who are buying, or buying from those who are selling. As such, while stockbrokers are in fact brokers, matching up buyers and sellers, many are also dealers, ready to buy or sell if no one else does. See "stock market."

budget deficit An excess of budgetary expenditures over revenues. The federal government is well known for its inclination to operate with a budget deficit. But it is not alone. Consumers also find themselves in this position on many occasions. When a budget deficit occurs, the excess spending is financed through borrowing. For the federal government, this involves issuing "government securities." For households it typically involves some sort of bank loan, credit-card purchase, use of savings (borrowing from thyself), or hitting a friend up for a few bucks. See "balanced budget," "budget surplus," "federal deficit."

budget surplus An excess of budgetary revenues over expenditures. This seemingly rare event is in fact commonly practiced by many state and local governments—albeit because of constitutional mandates. The federal government has even accomplished this feat once or twice. Consumers operate a budget surplus whenever they're able to put a little bit of their income into saving. See "balanced budget," "budget deficit."

building cycle The recurring periods of first active and then stagnant home sales and housing construction. A complete cycle usually lasts from 10 to 20 years. The source of these ups and downs rests with the competitive nature of the home construction business, the length of time it takes to build a house, and, perhaps most importantly, the length of time before a house "depreciates." Here's a typical building cycle scenario: If there's a shortage in the market for housing in a given locale, dozens or even hundreds of home builders are likely to step forward to do their part to satisfy the excess demand. However, because it takes a year or more to buy the land, prepare the plans, and get government permits, none of the builders is likely to be aware of the many others also trying to fill the shortage. And there's usually too many. The result is too many houses. This overbuilding sends the housing market into a slump of declining prices and inactivity. A period of time (5 to 10 years) passes before population growth and the deterioration of existing houses eliminate the excess and then create another shortage that starts the process once more. The time to buy is when the market has a big surplus, and prices are down. The time to sell, if you own a home, is during the shortage and the subsequent high prices. Compare "business cycle." See "investment."

bull market A condition of the stock market in which stock prices are generally rising and most of the participants expect this to continue. In other words, the stock market is into an extended period of "charging ahead" like a mad bull. A bull market usually occurs because investors see a healthy, vibrant, profitable economy on the horizon. Compare "bear market." See "speculation."

business cycle The recurring "expansions" and "contractions" of the national economy (usually measured by "real gross domestic product"). A complete cycle lasts from 3 to 5 years. Here's the situation: Our economy's ability to supply "full employment output" grows through increases in the quantity and quality of resources, but the demand for this output is occasionally too much or too little. When demand is too little, the economy drops into a contraction, or recession, causing an increase in "unemployment." A recession usually lasts from 6 months to 2 years, at which point a recovery begins. This then moves into a full-blown expansion, with steady growth and less unemployment, that lasts from 2 to 3 years. However, if the economy tries to expand more rapidly than the growth of full employment output, then "inflation" results. To avoid the inflation and unemployment problems of business cycles, the federal government frequently undertakes various "fiscal" and "monetary policies." See "circular flow."

buyers' market A condition in a competitive market when there's a surplus, such that buyers are able to force the price down. Note that a buyers' market is not the same as a market in which buyers have market control caused by the lack of competition. A buyers' market simply has a temporary imbalance between the amount buyers are buying and the amount sellers are selling. Compare "sellers' market."

A Whole Bunch of Economic Terms and Definitions   227

C

capacity utilization rate The ratio of actual production by the businesses of our economy to their potential production. This rate indicates if our economy's factories and other capital are being used as effectively and as fully as possible. Like the "unemployment rate," the capacity utilization rate measures how close our economy is to full employment. And like unemployment, this rate moves up and down over the course of a "business cycle." During expansions, the rate is near 85 percent (considered full employment), and during contractions, it's in the 70-percent range. In addition to an overall rate, there are also separate rates for manufacturing, mining, and utility industries.

capital One of the three general categories of resources, or factors of production (see "labor" and "natural resources").It includes the manufactured, or previously produced, resources that are used to manufacture or produce other things. Common examples of capital are the factories, buildings, trucks, tools, machinery, and equipment used by businesses to make their products. Capital's primary role in the economy is to assist labor in the transformation of natural resources into goods that people want. We should note that the term "capital" is also used in business circles to mean pools of financial funds. There is logic to this dual use. In many cases, "financial" capital represents ownership of "physical" capital. For example, corporate stocks, a well-known financial capital, are the ownership shares of a corporation's factories, buildings, and equipment. Other sorts of "financial" capital, like a big bank account, are often funds used to purchase "physical" capital. See "financial market," "investment."

capital account One of two parts of a nation's balance of payments (see "current account"). It is a record of all purchases of physical and financial assets between a nation and the rest of the world in a given period, usually 1 year.

On one side of the balance of payments ledger account are all of the foreign assets purchased by our domestic economy. On the other side of the ledger are all of our domestic assets purchased by foreign countries. The capital account is said to have a surplus if a nation's investments abroad are greater than foreign investments at home. In other words, if the U.S.A. is buying up more assets in Mexico, Brazil, and Hungary than Japanese, German, and Canadian investors are buying up U.S. assets, then we have a surplus. A deficit is the reverse.

capital gains tax A tax on the difference between the sales price of a "capital" asset and its original purchase price. The capital assets subject to this tax include such things as real estate, stocks, and bonds. This tax is frequently a source of controversy between the second and third estates. In that the second estate owns and sells a lot of this sort of capital, they don't like to pay taxes on capital gains. However, because the third estate doesn't have much capital, it seems like a pretty good thing to tax. Those who oppose the capital gains tax argue that it takes away funds that would be used for further capital investment, which thus inhibits economic growth. Those who favor it argue that it helps equalize unfairly unequal income and wealth distributions. See "corporate income tax," "progressive tax."

capital market A financial market that trades bonds, stocks, or any other long-term financial instruments used by businesses to raise funds. The term "capital" comes from the notion that businesses commonly get their funds to finance investment in capital from these markets. Compare "money market."

capitalism A type of economy based on: (1) private ownership of most resources, goods, and other stuff; (2) freedom to generally use the privately owned resources, goods, and other stuff to get the most wages, rent, interest, and profit possible; and (3) a system of relatively competitive markets. While government establishes the legal "rules of the game" for capitalism and provides assorted public goods—like national defense, education, and infrastructure—most production, consumption, and resource allocation decisions are left up to individual businesses and consumers. The term "capitalism" is derived from the notion that capital goods are under private, rather than government, ownership (compare "communism" and "socialism"). Capitalism contains numerous incentives that promote efficiency, but it is not without problems. The primary problem stems from the fact that resource ownership, especially capital, tends to be unequally distributed, and because of the unequal opportunities created, inequality is perpetuated by capitalism. As might be expected, the biggest proponents of capitalism are those who own the most capital, members of the second estate, and thus have the most to gain from their unrestricted use. See "free enterprise."

cartel A formal agreement between businesses in the same industry, usually on an international scale, to get "market control," raise the market price, and otherwise act like a "monopoly." The most famous international cartel is the Organization of Petroleum Exporting Countries (you probably know it as OPEC), which often seeks control over the world oil market. Other cartels have existed, or still exist, in the global markets for uranium, diamonds, long-distance telephone services, and airlines. A cartel tends to be unstable because the artificially high prices it sets give each member of the cartel an incentive to "cheat" with a slightly lower price. When only one member of the cartel lowers the price, it can make oodles of profit by taking customers away from the other members. If they all cheat, the cartel falls apart. While cartels damage efficiency, they're power is often short-lived because of this cheating. Like "collusion" and other techniques of market control, cartels are illegal in the United States.

caveat emptor A handy little Latin term meaning to "let the buyer beware." It's a warning to buyers that sellers will try to extract a high price for low-quality stuff, and a heed that every hardworking consumer of the third estate should take. If you find you've been "taken," note that government has established consumer protection guidelines that businesses are legally compelled to follow. As such, you can seek action through the Federal Trade Commission, Consumer Product Safety Commission, your state attorney general, and in all likelihood your local police department. Compare "caveat venditor."

caveat venditor This is a Latin term meaning "let the seller beware." It was developed as a counter to the buyer's warning, caveat emptor, and suggests that sellers too can be "taken to the cleaners" in a market transaction. While it's less important than caveat emptor to underappreciated consumers, I've included it here for the sake of objective, unbiased completeness.

central bank The banking authority of a nation that's in charge of ensuring a sound money supply and conducting the country's monetary policy. It's usually authorized by, and works closely with, the government to achieve full employment, low inflation rates, economic growth, and all of the other stuff that makes people happy, healthy, and wise. Unlike many other nations that have a *central* bank, the U.S.A. actually has a *decentral* bank (see "Federal Reserve System" for an explanation).

circular flow The continuous movement of production, income, and resources between producers and consumers. This flow moves through product markets as the gross domestic product of our economy and is then the revenue received by businesses in payment for this production. This stream of revenue then flows through resource markets as payments by businesses for the resources employed in production. The payments received by resource owners, however, are nothing more than their income. Resources owners use this income to purchase goods and services through the product markets, coming full circle to where we began. This flow is diverted in a number of different ways, especially by government. Taxes are sliced from income, wages, profit, etc., but are then used for expenditures by government on other things bought through the product markets. Consumers also divert a portion of their income into saving, which is then used to finance the federal deficit or business investment. The primary lesson of the circular flow is that there's only so much moving through the pipes. If there's more going through one pipe, then there's less going through another. See "financial market."

closed economy An economy with little or no foreign trade. A country with an open economy can usually tend to it's problems without worrying about other countries. During the 1950s and 1960s, the U.S.A. had relatively little foreign trade and was very nearly a closed economy. But that was a unique period in the United States, unmatched before or since. In fact, it's very difficult to find a real-life closed economy anywhere in the world today. Because of this, you should take a close look at the entry "open economy."

coincident economic indicator One of four economic statistics that tend to move up and down with the expansions and contractions of the business cycle. You can get a pretty good idea of what our economy's doing *right now* by looking at these. The four coincident indicators are: non-farm employment, industrial production, real personal income (after subtracting transfer payments), and real manufacturing and trade sales. These indicators, and their siblings—"leading economic indicators" and "lagging economic indicators"— are compiled by their parents, those pointy-headed economists at the National Bureau of Economic Research.

collective bargaining The negotiation process between a "union" and the company that employs the union's members, usually going by the moniker of management. The purpose of collective bargaining is to find mutual agreement on wages, fringe benefits, workhours, promotion criteria, grievance procedures, and everything else that has to do with employment. The end result of this process is a collective bargaining agreement, which is a formal contract between management and the union. A negotiation process that breaks down without reaching an agreement might lead to a "strike," "lockout," or "mediation." See "arbitration."

collusion A usually secret agreement among businesses in an industry to control the market, raise the market price, and otherwise act like a "monopoly." The reason for the secrecy is that such behavior is illegal in the United States under antitrust law. See "cartel," "market control," "merger," "unfair competition."

commercial paper Short-term negotiable financial instruments, or promissory notes, sold by corporations to raise working capital. The maturity length of commercial paper is less than a year, often 30, 60, or 90 days. The corporations that issue commercial paper are usually the largest, most stable, and most profitable businesses in the country (see "blue chip," "big business"). Their credit worthiness, together with the fact they cut out the middleman, means that they're able to pay lower interest rates than if they borrowed from a bank. Unlike "corporate bonds," issued to finance investment in capital, commercial paper is used either for working capital (sort of money a business needs to cover expenses until payday) or to finance consumer purchases. All of the big car companies, for example, have finance branches that make car loans to their customers. See "financial market."

commodity exchange A financial market that trades the ownership of various commodities, such as wheat, corn, cotton, sugar, crude oil, natural gas, gold, silver, and aluminum. The two biggest commodity exchanges in the U.S.A. are the Chicago Board of Trade and the Chicago Mercantile Exchange. Unlike, let's say, a grocery store in which commodities physically trade hands, commodity exchanges trade only legal ownership. This is much like a stock market, which trades the ownership of a corporation but leaves the factory at home. Commodity markets offer two basic sorts of trading: "spot" (immediate delivery of a commodity) and "futures" (delivery of a commodity at a future date). These markets provide for stable prices and a continuous supply of the commodities traded, most of which are the raw materials used to produce consumer goods. See "hedging."

common market An agreement among two or more nations to eliminate trade restrictions with each other, to adopt a common trade policy with other nations, and to allow free movement of resources among their countries. There is, however, no effort to adopt common monetary or fiscal policies. This is considered the third of four levels of integration among nations. See "customs union," "economic union," "free-trade area" for the other three levels. See also "trading bloc."

common stock See "corporate stock."

common-property good A good that's difficult to keep nonpayers from consuming (see "excludability"), but use of the good by one person prevents use by others (see "rival consumption"). Examples include oceans, the atmosphere, many lakes and streams, and large tracts of wilderness area or public parks. The term "common property" aptly describes the situation here: It's commonly owned and thus everyone has access to it, but it can be easily used up or destroyed. Many of our pollution problems occur because common property becomes a convenient place to dump waste materials. For "efficiency," government needs to take charge of common-property goods; private exchange through markets can't do the job. See "near-public good," "private good," "public good."

communism In theory, an economy based on: (1) a classless society, where everyone does their best to contribute to the common good, (2) a common, rather than individual, ownership of all resources, (3) the complete disappearance of government, and (4) income allocated based entirely on need rather than on resource ownership or contribution to production. Theoretical communism was considered by its inventor, Karl Marx, as the final stage of human progress, following feudalism, "capitalism," and "socialism." It was the notion that communism was the future of all capitalistic economies that scared the hell out of capital owners in the U.S.A. during the better part of the 1900s. In contrast to this idealistic notion, in practice communism is a type of economy based on: (1) government ownership and control of most resources, goods, and other stuff and (2) excruciatingly detailed economic planning by government. This was the system employed by the Soviet Union and other countries for several decades during the twentieth century but crumbled in the late 1980s and early 1990s, in large part because it was an incredibly inefficient way to allocate resources.

comparable worth The notion that different jobs requiring comparable, but not identical, skills should be paid the same wage. The logic behind comparable worth is that centuries (perhaps even millennia) of discrimination by men against women have relegated women to second-class, poorly paid jobs, with little or no chance for advancement. Men, in contrast, with the same education, skills, and abilities are able to get the better, higher-paying jobs. Comparable worth would be a program in which different jobs are evaluated and scored, based on the skills, responsibilities, and education needed. Jobs with the same scores would then be required to have the same pay. While there is little doubt that a long history of discrimination has forced many women into lower-paying jobs, and kept them there, comparable worth ignores the fact that the jobs themselves are probably not very productive. That is, we don't place a great deal of value on the stuff produced in these jobs. Rather than overpaying for goods we don't want, a better solution is to get women to produce goods that we value more.

comparative advantage The ability to produce one good at a relatively lower opportunity cost than other goods. While economists developed this idea for nations, it's extremely important for people. A comparative advantage means that no matter how good (or bad) you are at producing stuff, there's always something that you're best (or least worst) at doing. Moreover, because you can produce this one thing by giving up less than what others give up, you can sell it or trade it to them. This idea of comparative advantage means that people and nations can benefit by specialization and trade. You do what you do best, then trade to someone else for what they do best. Both sides in this trade get more and are thus better off than before. Compare "absolute advantage." See "foreign trade."

competition In general, the actions of two or more rivals in pursuit of the same objective. In the context of markets, the specific objective is either selling stuff to buyers or alternatively buying stuff from sellers. Competition tends to come in two varieties: (1) the sort that occurs when a market has so many buyers or sellers that none is able to influence the market, or (2) a market with only a small number of buyers or sellers such that each has some degree of "market control." Competition of the first variety means that the market participants are

forced to accept the going market price on a take-it or leave-it basis, with little or no concern over what other participants are doing. Competition of the second variety leads to intense rivalry, where each participant achieves the objective only by beating the others. A "small business," or any card-carrying consumer of the "third estate," generally competes in markets in the first variety. A "big business," or a member of the "second estate," in contrast, engages in the second variety of market competition. See "demand," "supply."

competitive market A market with a large number of buyers and a large number of sellers, such that no single buyer or seller is able to influence the price or any other aspect of the market: No one has any "market control." A competitive market achieves "efficiency" in the use of our scarce resources, if there are no market failures present.

compound interest Interest that's added to a principal at regular intervals such that each subsequent interest calculation is based on the original principal and the added interest. For example, suppose you have a $100 savings account that pays 5-percent interest. Without compound interest, such that your 5-percent interest is paid only at the end of a year, you will have exactly $105 in one year. However, if your interest is compounded each month, you end up with $105.12 after a year. The extra 12 cents comes from interest on the interest paid the first month, interest on the interest paid the second month, interest on the interest paid the third month . . . well, I could go on. If you want to calculate your own compound interest, here's a handy little formula: $b = a(1 + i)n$, where b is the balance you'll end up with at the end, a is the principal at the beginning, i is the interest rate, and n is the number of periods. You might make a note that the interest rate and number of periods need to be consistent. If your periods are years, then the interest is an annual rate. However, if your period is months, then the interest rate needs to be a monthly one.

confidence index A measure of consumers' confidence in the economy. The two most noted measures of consumer confidence are put out by the University of Michigan and the Conference Board. Each is based on a survey that asks consumers an assortment of questions about their confidence in the economy. The question are something like: Are you better off now than a year ago? Do you plan to buy a new car? Do you think the economy is in good shape? The respondents can answer these questions in one of five ways: strongly disagreeing, disagreeing, neutral, agreeing, strongly agreeing. The fraction of total respondents who agree or strongly agree on selected questions are then compiled into the confidence index. Unlike other statistics, confidence indexes are short and sweet. They take relatively little time to prepare, and they don't require a lot of data. Compare "coincident economic indicator," "lagging economic indicator," "leading economic indicator."

conglomerate merger See "merger."

conservative A political view that favors: (1) limited government, (2) extensive reliance on markets, (3) strong national defense, (4) protection and promotion of existing cultural ideals and beliefs, and (5) economic rewards predominately based on productive efforts. Conservatives tend to come from the ranks of the "second estate" (or second-estate wannabes), with extensive ownership of and control over resources. As such, they support policies and "first-estate" leaders who protect their interests. Compare "liberal."

consumer price index (CPI) An index of prices of goods and services typically purchased by urban consumers. This index, compiled and published monthly by the Department of Labor, gives us a pretty good idea of the average prices in the economy and is thus used to estimate the "inflation rate." One of it's main failings is that it only measures goods that consumers buy, and then only those bought by urban consumers. Ignored in the numbers are things that might be bought only by rural folk and a lot of stuff purchased by government and business, such as capital goods. The index is based on a so-called "market basket" of goods and services that are determined in a survey of urban consumers. The quantities bought, the prices paid for the goods and services, and the total expenditures for this market basket are identified and fed into a computer. Then every month, the number crunchers at the Department of Labor pretend that they're buying that same market basket again. They compare total expenditures this month with total expenditures on the original basket, molding the ratio of the two into an index with 100 for the original base year. Anything over 100 means that prices have risen. The percentage change from month to month, or year to year, is our most common measure of the inflation rate. The number crunchers also like to break this number down into subcategories—like food, energy, health care, and the like—to see where inflation is most pronounced. More on this thought can be found under "core inflation rate." Compare "GDP price deflator."

Consumer Product Safety Commission (CPSC) A regulatory agency formed by the Consumer Product Safety Act (1972) that's charged by Congress with: (1) protecting the public against unreasonable risk, (2) developing uniform safety standards for consumer products, (3) helping consumers evaluate the safety of products, and (4) promoting research that will improve product safety. It's run by a five-member commission that has the authority to remove unsafe products from the stores. See "Federal Trade Commission."

consumer sovereignty The notion that consumers are "king" of the economy because they're the ones who will ultimately determine what goods are produced and how our limited resources are used. Like most notions, this one has a fair amount of validity, but also a notable exception. On the validity side, businesses can produce whatever goods they damn well please, but consumers won't buy them if they don't want them. If consumers don't buy, then businesses close their doors, and resources are diverted (ultimately) to the production of goods that consumers do want. On the exception side, consumers may not know what sorts of goods they actually want and may be easily swayed into buying something they don't want. Advertising plays an important, and hotly debated, role in this swaying process.

consumers' surplus The satisfaction that consumers obtain from a good over and above the price paid. This is the difference between the maximum "demand price" you would be willing to pay and the price you actually pay. For most consumers, under most circumstances, the demand price is greater than the price paid. Even competitive markets overflowing with efficiency generate an ample amount of consumers' surplus. However, a common goal of second-estate businesses is to obtain as much of this consumers' surplus as they can. "Price discrimination" is one notable method.

consumption The use of natural resources, goods, or services to satisfy wants and needs. While we often think of consumption as "using something up," in this process of satisfaction, this really doesn't happen. At best, consumption involves little more than the transformation of stuff from something that can satisfy needs to something that probably can't. Compare "production." See "pollution," "materials balance."

consumption tax A tax on consumer's spending for goods, services, and the other stuff they buy. One sort of consumption tax is the sales tax. Some politi-

cians and balding, bespectacled economists argue that the current income tax system should be replaced with a consumption tax. This means any income that's saved wouldn't be taxed. The idea behind a consumption tax is to encourage saving, which is then used for "investment," which then promotes "economic growth." Such a tax would be easily implemented (you get a deduction for saving on the current income tax form), but it would tend to be a regressive tax hitting the poor harder than the wealthy.

contraction One phase of the "business cycle." A general period of declining economic activity. During a contraction, real gross domestic product declines by 10 percent or so, and the unemployment rate rises from its full employment 5-percent level up to the 6- to 10-percent range. Inflation tends to be low or nonexistent during a contraction. Contractions last anywhere from 6 to 18 months, with 1 year being common. Compare "expansion." See "depression," "recession."

core inflation rate The underlying inflation rate of the economy after volatile energy and food prices are removed. This core inflation rate is a good measure of the inflation rate consumers, business, and others expect over the next few years.

corporate bond A bond issued by a corporation to raise the funds used for capital investment. A corporate bond usually has a maturity date of 5 years or more, with 30 years common. Most corporate bonds are negotiable and traded through financial markets after issue. Compare "commercial paper," "government security."

corporate income tax A tax on the accounting profits of corporations. This tax is only levied on corporations, and excludes businesses that are proprietorships or partnerships. This tax is often criticized (usually by members of the second estate) because corporate dividends are taxed twice—once as corporate profits, then a second time as income with the personal income tax.

corporate stock The ownership shares in a corporation that have legal claim to the corporation's assets. Stock is usually divided into two types, *common stock* and *preferred stock*. Preferred stock has first claim to the corporation's net assets, and common stock comes in second. However, if a corporation has no preferred stock, the common stock has exclusive claim. Most stocks are negotiable and are traded on a stock market.

corporation One of the three basic forms of business organization (see "proprietorship" and "partnership"). It's considered a legal entity, with a perpetual life, that's separate and distinct from it's owners. As such, the owners have what the lawyer-types term "limited liability," which means that the owners cannot be held personally responsible for the corporation's debts. The owners can lose only the amount that they have invested, but no more. Corporations achieve this status of limited liability through the sale of ownership shares, or corporate stock.

cost See "opportunity cost."

cost of living The amount of money needed for a given standard of living. The cost of living varies from place to place, which can have a big effect on anyone who decides on the age-old ritual of migration. It also changes from year to year because of inflation. This latter bit of information is important for cost-of-living adjustments (COLA for acronym lovers) that are included in many labor union contracts and are a part of social security payments. See "purchasing power."

Council of Economic Advisors A three-member board that advises the President of the United States on economic policy and helps prepare an annual economic report. These three men are economists (they're usually, but not always, men and usually, but not always, economists) who keep the President up-to-date on current economic statistics and do most of the dirty work in terms of formulating the details of economic policies. The Chair-

man of the Council of Economic Advisors has one of the two most important non-elected voices on economic policy in the nation, with the other being the Chairman of the Board of Governors of the Federal Reserve System. See "fiscal policy."

credit The promise of future payment in exchange for money, goods, services, or anything else of value. Car loans, mortgages, credit cards, corporate bonds, commercial paper, and government securities are all forms of credit. In fact, credit is an extremely widespread and critical part of our economy. About one-third of the stuff consumers buy and nine-tenths of business expenditures are on credit. Most business capital and consumer car and home purchases would be impossible without credit. Moreover, given the time lapse between paying for resources and selling output, few businesses could produce much without credit.

credit crunch An economywide reduction in the ability of banks to make loans or otherwise issue credit. A credit crunch is usually caused by contractionary "monetary policy" of the Federal Reserve System. Compare "easy money." See "tight money."

creditor nation A nation that owes less to foreign governments, businesses, and consumers than foreigners owe to domestic governments, businesses, and consumers. The United States was a creditor nation for many decades, being one of the chief sources of lending to other nations in the world. It has now achieved the status of "debtor nation." See "balance of payments," "capital account," "current account."

crowding out A decline in investment caused by expansionary fiscal policy. When government counteracts a recession with an increase in spending or a reduction in taxes (both resulting in an increase in the federal deficit), interest rates tend to increase. Higher interest rates then inhibit business investment in capital goods. Some economists argue that investment crowding out completely offsets any intended expansionary policy, but the jury's still out on this one. To the extent that crowding out occurs, economic growth is reduced if (and this is an important "if") government has not seen fit to offset the loss in business investment with public investment in infrastructure, education, or other growth-promoting expenditures.

current account One of two parts of a nation's balance of payments (see "capital account"). It is a record of all trade, exports and imports between a nation and the rest of the world. The current account is separated into merchandise, services, and what's called "unilateral" transfers. The merchandise part is nothing other than the well-known "balance of trade." There's also a lesser-known balance of services: the difference between services imported and exported. For example, if you travel to Sweden for a sex-change operation, then you're *importing* health care services into the United States. Likewise, a German citizen who buys a ticket to see the Sacramento Kings play basketball is having a U.S. service *exported.* Unilateral transfers are simply money that's exchanged between countries without any goods or services coming in the other direction. A big component of this is foreign aid by the federal government to other countries. If the money coming into a nation for exports and transfers is greater than the money going out, then the current account has a surplus. A deficit occurs if the opposite exists.

customs union An agreement between two or more nations to eliminate trade restrictions with each other and to adopt a common trade policy with other nations. There is, however, no effort to allow free movement of resources among the countries nor to adopt common monetary or fiscal policies. This is considered the second of four levels of integration among nations. See "common market," "eco-nomic union," "free-trade area" for the other three levels. See also "trading bloc."

cyclical unemployment Unemployment caused by business cycle recessions because demand for production is less than full-employment output. In other words, when the economy takes a downturn because businesses aren't able to sell all of the stuff they're producing, and they lay off some of their workers, then we get an increase in cyclical unemployment. Compare "frictional unemployment," "seasonal unemployment," "structural unemployment."

D

debt See "liability."

debtor nation A nation that owes more to foreign governments, businesses, and consumers than foreigners owe to domestic governments, businesses, and consumers. The United States, having been a "creditor" nation for many decades, has now achieved the status of debtor nation. This sort of thing happens when "exports" are less than "imports," creating a deficit in the "current account" of the "balance of payments" and thus a surplus in the "capital account."

deflation An extended decline in the average level of prices. This is the exact opposite of "inflation"—in which prices are rising over an extended period; it should be contrasted with "disinflation"—that is, a decline in the inflation rate. Deflation is a rare bird indeed in our economy and typically happens only when we're in a prolonged period of stagnation. We might see some deflation during a fairly lengthy "recession," but more than likely deflation saves itself for the occasional "depression" that dots our economic landscape. See "consumer price index," "GDP price deflator."

demand One half of the market exchange process (see "supply"). It's the willingness and ability to purchase different amounts of a good at different prices. The willingness part of demand comes from our unlimited wants and needs, while the ability is based on our limited income. Beyond the confines of academia, demand is sometimes used to mean the quantity of a good purchased at a specific price. Economists, however, prefer the term "quantity demanded" in this context and save the term "demand" for describing the willingness and ability to buy different quantities of a good at a whole range of current and potential prices. For example, a decrease in the price of a good causes an increase in the *quantity* of the good demanded by buyers. Thus, when a business wants to increase sales, it often needs to do little more than lower the price. See "demand price."

demand price The maximum price that buyers are willing and able to pay for a good. Buyers are always willing to buy a good for less than the demand price, but never more. The demand price depends on a number of things, like buyers' incomes and preferences, but a big one is the quantity being bought. The demand price tends to be lower when buyers buy more. Compare "supply price." See "demand."

deposit insurance A program of guaranteeing, or insuring, customers' deposits at a bank or similar institution. Since the 1930s, bank deposits have been insured by the Federal Deposit Insurance Corporation (FDIC). Other programs have insured deposits at credit unions and savings and loan associations. The FDIC works like this: If a bank is unable to pay back all or part of its customers' deposits because it has done something like go out of business, then the FDIC steps in to make up the difference—up to a pretty hefty limit. (This limit has been $100,000 in recent times.) The need for deposit insurance became most apparent in the 1930s, when thousands of banks closed their doors during the Great Depression, causing millions of dollars worth of deposits to simply vanish. (See "fractional-

reserve banking" for the whys and hows of this.) The disappearance of these deposits reduced the amount of money in the economy, put a big damper on consumer spending, and contributed to the length and severity of the "depression." Deposit insurance hasn't prevented bank failures, but it has kept people from losing their life savings.

depreciation A more- or less-permanent decrease in value or price. "More or less permanent" doesn't include temporary, short-term drops in price that are common in many markets. It's only those price declines that reflect a reduction in consumer satisfaction. While all sorts of stuff can depreciate in value, some of the more common ones are capital, real estate, corporate stock, and money. The depreciation of capital results from the rigors of production and affects our economy's ability to produce stuff. A sizable portion of our annual investment is thus needed to replace depreciated capital. The depreciation of a nation's money is seen as an increase in the exchange rate. This process is described in detail in the entry on the "J-curve." Compare "appreciation." See "devaluation."

depression An extended period—a decade or so—of restructuring and institutional change in an economy that's often marked by declining or stagnant growth. During this period, "unemployment" tends to be higher and "inflation" lower than a regular, run-of-the-mill "recession." Moreover, a depression usually lasts in the range of 10 years, often encompassing two or three separate shorter-run "business cycles." The most noted depression in the U.S. economy was the Great Depression of the 1930s. However, others occurred in the 1840s and 1870s. While a number of signs point to a depression from the mid-1970s through much of the 1980s, the jury's still out on that one. On the plus side, the more severe a depression is, and the more restructuring that's accomplished, then the greater the prosperity over the next few decades.

derived demand The notion that the "demand" for resources used to produce a good depends largely on the demand for the good being produced. For example, if a number of people buy hot-fudge sundaes, then ice cream stores will demand a lot of ice cream, hot fudge, nuts, and whipped cream. If, however, no one buys hot-fudge sundaes, then the demand for these ingredients will be less. As such, the demand for any and all resources—labor, capital, and natural resources—ultimately stems from the demand for the stuff they're used to produce. In more practical terms, if you want your labor resources to be greatly demanded and highly paid, then produce a good with great demand and high prices.

devaluation The act of reducing the price ("exchange rate") of one nation's currency in terms of other currencies. This is usually done by a government to lower the price of the country's exports and raise the price of foreign imports, which ultimately results in greater domestic production. The short- and long-run consequences of devaluation are described in the entry on the "J-curve." A government devalues its currency by actively selling it and buying foreign currencies through the "foreign-exchange market." Compare "revaluation." See "depreciation."

discount In financial terms, a bond or similar financial asset that sells below its face value. Discounting is done to equalize the interest rate attached to a bond with comparable interest rates in the economy. For example, a $100,000 bond that pays a fixed 10-percent interest on the face value (that is, $10,000 annually) would be discounted to $83,333 if comparable interest rates were above 12 percent. As such, the $10,000 annual interest payment works out to be 12 percent of a $83,333 price. Compare "premium."

discount rate The "interest rate" that the Federal Reserve System charges for loans to banks. To ensure that our nation's banks retain their liquidity and remain in business, the Federal Reserve System stands ready to lend "bank reserves" on a moment's notice to any bank. The discount rate is the interest rate the Federal Reserve System charges for these loans. Like any interest rate, when the discount rate goes up (or down) it discourages (or encourages) borrowing. In principle, the Fed can use the discount rate to control our nation's money supply. For example, a lower discount rate would make it easier for banks to borrow reserves and lead to a greater money supply. In practice, though, the Fed is more inclined to use open market operations to achieve changes in the money supply, with any discount rate changes playing a supporting role. See "bank panic," "fractional reserve banking."

discrimination Treating people differently based on some sort of group characteristic—like race, ethnic origin, or gender—rather than individual abilities. Discrimination is usually most prominent in employment and housing, but can filter into all aspects of life in many subtle ways. Discrimination tends to be inefficient because it limits the number of buyers or sellers that have access to a given market. Those who discriminate in this manner are, in essence, willing to pay extra for the privilege of associating only with "their own kind."

disinflation A decline in the "inflation" rate. While prices are still rising with disinflation, they're just not rising as fast as they once were. For example, disinflation would occur if the rate of inflation had been 5 percent for several years but dropped to 3 percent. Compare "deflation."

disintermediation A general deterioration in the profitability of a bank because it pays high interest rates on short-term borrowing, but earns relatively low interest rates on long-term lending. This was a big, big problem for savings and loans

(S&Ls) during the 1970s and ultimately caused many of them to fail in the 1980s. S&Ls were designed (by law) to make long-term (30-year) home loans to consumers, but to get the funds for these loans using standard savings accounts. When inflation and interest rates shot up in the 1970s, S&Ls found it necessary to pay savers higher rates to get the funds. But they still had a bunch of home loans—with low interest rates—that were 15, 20, or 25 years from being repaid. For several years, S&Ls received 6 percent on many of their loans, but paid out something like 12 percent. This gradually, but surely, eroded their profitability until many were forced to close their doors. Disintermediation is one reason why you see "very few quaint little buildings around your town with the term "Savings and Loan" in the title. See "bank panic."

disinvestment A drop in the total quantity of capital in the economy because the depreciation of existing capital is greater than investment in new capital. In other words, the capital we have is wearing out faster than we're replacing it with new stuff. This isn't good. At best, it limits "economic growth" and might even cause the economy's pie to shrink if increases in other resources don't kick in.

disposable personal income The total amount of income that consumers can use for either consumption or saving. This is the income left over after income taxes and social security taxes are removed and government transfer payments, like welfare, social security benefits, or unemployment compensation, are added. Because consumption and saving are important to our economy for short-run stability and long-run growth, economists like to keep a close eye on disposable personal income. Compare "national income," "personal income."

dividend The portion of a corporation's after-tax accounting profit that's paid to shareholders or owners. Corporate managers usually try to pay the shareholders some minimum dividend that's comparable to returns from other financial markets—such as the interest on government securities or corporate bonds—to keep the owners from selling off the company's stock. That portion of after-tax accounting profit that's not paid out as dividends is typically invested in capital. See "corporate income tax."

domestic Anything that has to do with activity within the boundaries of a nation. This should be directly contrasted with the term "foreign," which refers to anything beyond the boundaries of a nation.

Dow Jones averages These are the most widely used and recognized indexes of stock market prices in our economy. There are actually three separate indexes: for 30 industrial stocks, for 20 transportation stocks, and for 15 utility stocks. There's also a composite index for all 65 stocks. The Dow Jones Industrial Average is based on the stock prices of the 30 biggest, most important "industrial" corporations in the country, with a sampling that includes Alcoa, American Express, AT&T, Boeing, Coca-Cola, Disney, Eastman Kodak, General Electric, IBM, McDonalds, Proctor and Gambles, Sears, and Westinghouse. This index is the big one that leads off almost any news report on stock market activity for the day. The transportation average is based on the stock prices of such companies as American Airlines, Burlington Northern, Federal Express, Ryder, United Airlines, and Union Pacific. You can probably spot a "transportation" theme with these. The utility average includes some of the more important public utilities in the country, such as Arkla, Consolidated Edison, Pacific Gas and Electric, and Philadelphia Electric. The first Dow Jones average developed back in the 1880s was little more than a simple average of 11 stock prices: Add the prices, then divide by 11. Calculating the current averages are more involved. The summed stock prices are no longer divided by a simple number like 30, 20, or 15 stocks in the respective index. To correct for stock splits, dividends, and other stuff that have occurred over the years, these index "divisors" have been changed. For example, the industrial average divisor is something in the 0.44 range, rather than 30, while the utilities number is closer to 1.9 and not a straightforward 15. Compare "Standard & Poor's 500." See "big business."

dual labor market A proposition that our economy has two classes of workers: adult white males and other. The other includes, but isn't limited to, women, blacks, Hispanics, and teenagers. Based on the political and economic clout of whites and the traditional notion of men as the "breadwinners" of a family, white males constitute the primary labor supply and thus get the best, highest-paying jobs—like executive, physician, shop foreman, or U.S. Senator—with the greatest chance of advancement. The other groups, however, are left with secondary jobs—such as secretary, janitor, nurse, or convenience store clerk—that have very low pay and limited prospects to move up. Moreover, the way the system works, there tends to be little movement between these two labor markets. Oh sure, a black woman might become a physician or a white, Harvard-educated male might find himself employed as a migrant farm worker, but these are rare events. See "discrimination."

dumping Selling the same good to another country at a lower price, often below production cost, than that charged to the domestic buyers. Dumping usually occurs because: (1) producers in one country are trying to stay competitive with producers in another country, (2) producers in one country are trying to eliminate the producers in another country and gain a larger share of the world market, (3) producers are trying to get rid of excess stuff they can't sell in their own country, and (4) producers can make more profit by dividing sales into domestic and foreign

markets, then charging each market whatever price the buyers are willing to pay. See "export," "import," "free trade."

durable A good bought by consumers that tends to last for more than a year. Common examples are cars, furniture, and appliances. Durable goods play an important role in the "business cycle." During a business cycle "recession," consumers tend to put off buying durable goods, hoping that the ones they already have will last until the economy improves. This lack of durable-good purchases by consumers, though, contributes to the length and severity of a recession because durable-good producers are then forced to reduce output and lay off workers. An important part of a business cycle "recovery" is then an increase in durable goods purchases. Compare "nondurable."

E

easy money A term used when the "Federal Reserve System" pursues expansionary monetary policy. In other words, to stimulate our economy out of recession, the Fed increases the amount of money in the economy or makes it "easier" for people to get money (usually through bank loans). The number-1 way the Fed goes about this easy-money stuff is through what are termed "open market operations." This is where the Fed buys some government securities owned by corporations, banks, or whomever, which ultimately puts more bank reserves into the banking system. Banks use these excess reserves for making loans to the likes of you and me. The more bank reserves the Fed pumps into the economy, the easier it is to get a loan. It's just that simple. If we have more money, then we spend it on stuff, which tends to increase production, create jobs, and expand the economy. In principle, the Fed could also ease up on the money supply using the discount rate and reserve requirements, but these tend to be less reliable, less effective, and more difficult to use. Compare "tight money."

economic development The process of improving the economy's ability to satisfy consumers' wants and needs. Unlike "economic growth," which is concerned with year-to-year increases in production, economic development deals more with the basic fabric of society, especially the institutions that govern the way our economy and society functions. As such, a lesser-developed nation is not only likely to have a low level of production and limited amount of capital but also cultural beliefs and government practices that prevent more effective use of the capital.

economic growth The long-run expansion of the economy's ability to produce output. It is made possible by increasing the quantity or quality of the economy's resources (labor, capital, and natural resources). The quantity side of increasing resources is pretty straightforward. If we build more factories, expand our population, or discover new mineral deposits, then we're likely to see economic growth. The quality side, however, includes several less tangible components, especially technology and education. Economic growth is typically measured as the percentage change in "gross domestic product" from one year to the next. See "standard of living." Compare "economic development."

economic profit The difference between business revenue and total "opportunity cost." This is the revenue received by a business over and above the minimum needed to produce a good. In this sense, economic profit is a sign of inefficiency. If a business receives an economic profit, then society (the buyers) is spending more on a good than society (the resource owners) is giving up to produce the good. Some or all economic profit may be received by resource owners as "economic rent," rather than going entirely to the business owners. The two primary ways a business can get economic profit is (1) acquiring "market control" and (2) creating innovation and taking on some risk. When obtained through market control, economic profit creates inefficiency problems and redistributes wealth—with little or no benefit. When obtained through innovation and risk, the inefficiency of economic profit is typically balanced by economic growth. Compare "accounting profit." See "efficiency," "normal profit."

economic rent The difference between the payment received by a resource owner and the "opportunity cost" of the resource. This is the payment received by a resource owner over and above the minimum needed to produce a good. Many resource owners are able to extract a portion of the economic profit generated by a business as a economic rent. See "rent seeking."

economic union An agreement among two or more nations to eliminate trade barriers with each other, to adopt a common trade policy with other nations, to allow free movement of resources among the countries, and to adopt common monetary or fiscal policies. This is considered the fourth of four levels of integration among nations. See "common market," "customs union," "free-trade area" for the other three levels. See also "trading bloc."

efficiency Obtaining the most possible satisfaction from a given amount of resources. Efficiency for our economy is achieved when we cannot increase our satisfaction of wants and needs by producing more of one good and less of another. Competitive markets, absent of any "market failure," and especially "market control" by either side achieves the ultimate state of efficiency that's so highly prized by economists. In particular, this feat is accomplished when the price buyers are willing and able to pay for a good—based on the satisfaction obtained—is equal to the price sellers need to charge for a good—based on the "opportunity cost" of production. In other words, the value (satisfaction) of stuff given up to get a good is the same as the value (satisfaction) of the good produced. Satisfaction won't increase by producing more of either. See "demand price," "supply price."

embargo In general, any sort of restriction on foreign trade; in practice, the restriction of exports destined for sale in another country. Unlike "tariffs," import "quotas," and other "non-tariff barriers" that protect domestic producers from competition, embargoes are intended to punish the export destination country. One of the more famous embargoes in recent decades was the oil embargo that several Middle Eastern countries imposed on the United States in the 1970s. This caused higher gasoline prices in the United States, created all sorts of havoc for our economy, and pretty much achieved the punishment objective. The United States is also prone to throw up an embargo here or there when another country acts against our political wishes. See "trade barrier."

emigration Migration that leaves one country for another country. This is the other side of "immigration." While immigration is people moving *into* a country, emigration is people moving *out*. People emigrate for the same reasons they migrate in general, to improve their lot in life. Emigration can be a problem for a country that's not highly developed because those who leave are often the "best and the brightest." As such, a country that's struggling to advance often finds itself left with unskilled, uneducated labor: the poorest of the poor who can't afford to leave.

employment rate The ratio of people who are employed to the total civilian, non-institutionalized, working-age (16 years old or older) population. If, for example, our country has 190 million people who have reached their 16th birthday, are not in the military, and aren't in prison or mental hospitals, with 120 million of them working, the employment rate is then 63 percent. The employment rate corrects some of the problems with the more commonly used "unemployment rate." In particular, the unemployment rate goes up or down as people enter or leave the labor force—*even though they never find a job.* For example, suppose you're unemployed and looking for work, then decide to give up your job search and watch soap operas during the day. This decision to leave the labor force and drop your "official" unemployment status causes the unemployment rate to fall. However, nothing has really changed. You had no job before the decision, and you don't have a job after. The employment rate, in contrast, would not be affected in the least. If you work, then you're part of the employment rate. If you don't work, regardless of why you're not working, then you're out of the employment rate. Compare "labor force participation rate."

entrepreneurship A special sort of human effort that takes on the risk of bringing labor, capital, and natural resources together and organizing production. In that production necessarily occurs before consumption, an entrepreneur who starts production never knows for certain that people will want it. Herein lies the risk of entrepreneurship. A successful entrepreneur, one who correctly guesses what consumers want, is very likely to make oodles and oodles of profit. This dangling carrot of profit is what motivates entrepreneurs to search out new products, expand into new markets, and seek new ways of satisfying our wants and needs. This is one of the key driving forces behind "economic growth" and a higher "standard of living."

environment All of the naturally occurring stuff that came with the planet, before it's been altered, extracted, transformed, or used up for production. It includes air, water, land, vegetation, and wildlife. See "natural resources" for further explanation.

equity This has two, not totally unrelated, meanings in our wonderful world of economics. The first means ownership, especially the ownership of a business or corporation. As such, if someone questions your equity share in Omni Conglomerate, Inc., they want to know how much of its corporate stock you own (see "equity market"). The second meaning of equity is the "fairness" of our income or wealth distributions. Of course, this idea of "fair" is difficult to pin down. A totally equal distribution (that provides no rewards for extra effort because everyone gets the same stuff) and a totally unequal distribution (one person has everything, so there's also no reason to do anything) are both likely to be "unfair." What gives us a "fair" distribution has been, and probably always will be, a source of philosophical and political debate.

equity market A market that trades the equity of companies— in other words, a "stock market."

estate tax A tax on the value of a deceased person's estate, or all of the property and assets owned. This should be compared to an "inheritance tax," which is a tax on that portion of the estate that an heir actually receives.

excess reserves The amount of "bank reserves" over and above those that the Federal Reserve System requires a bank to keep. Excess reserves are what banks use to make loans. If a bank has more excess reserves, then it can make more loans. This is a key part of the Fed's ability to control the "money" supply. Using "open-market operations," the Fed can add to, or subtract from, the excess reserves held by banks. If the Fed, for example, adds to excess reserves, then banks can make more loans. Banks make these loans by adding to their customers' checking account balances. This is of some importance, because checking account balances are a major part of the economy's money supply. In essence, controlling these excess reserves is the Fed's number -1 method of "printing" money without actually printing money. See "easy money," "fractional-reserve banking," "tight money."

exchange rate The price of one nation's currency in terms of another nation's currency. This is often called the "foreign-exchange rate" in that it is the price determined in the "foreign-exchange market" when people buy and sell foreign exchange. The exchange rate is specified as the amount of one currency that can be traded per unit of another. For example, the price of one U.S. dollar might be 100 Japanese Yen: 100 Yen per dollar. An interesting thing about an exchange rate is that it's really two prices in one. That is, the price of a dollar, 100 Yen per dollar is also the price of Yen (0.01 dollars per Yen). The reasons people trade the currency of one nation for that of another is to engage in all sorts of international transactions, such as "foreign trade" and "foreign investment." The exchange rate, though, is not only affected by these transactions, it also acts on them. If the exchange rate goes up, then domestic goods become more expensive, and foreign goods are less expensive. This encourages imports and discourages exports. For more on this, check out the "J-curve." See "fixed exchange rate," "floating exchange rate," "managed float."

excise tax A tax on a specific good. This should be compared with a general "sales tax," which is a tax on all (or nearly all) goods sold. The most common excise taxes are on alcohol, tobacco, and gasoline. Excise taxes are used either to discourage consumption of socially undesirable stuff (like alcohol and tobacco) or to raise some easy revenue because the government knows buyers will keep buying regardless of the tax (like alcohol and tobacco).

excludability The ability to keep people who don't pay for a good from consuming the good. For some goods, it's very easy (that is, the cost is low) for owners or producers to keep others from enjoying the benefit of a good. Examples of this abound, like candy bars, shoes, houses, computers, and, well, a bunch of other stuff. Other goods, however, prove more difficult to keep the nonpayers away. Examples of these include oceans, national defense, and fireworks displays. Excludability is one of the two key characteristics of a good (see "rival consumption") that distinguishes between "common-property goods," "near-public goods," "private goods," and "public goods."

expansion One phase of the "business cycle." A general period of increasing economic activity. During an expansion, "real gross domestic product" increases by 2 to 5 percent each year, and the "unemployment" rate settles into its full employment level around 5 percent. "Inflation" might become a problem if an expansion goes too fast or continues for several years. Expansions typically last from 2 to 3 years, but have ranged up to 6 or 7 seven years. Compare "contraction." See "prosperity."

export The sale of goods to a foreign country. The United States, for example, sells a lot of the stuff produced within our boundaries to other countries, including wheat, beef, cars, furniture, and, well, almost every variety of product you care to name. In general, "domestic" producers (and their workers) are elated with the prospect of selling their goods to foreign countries—leading to more buyers, a higher price, and more profit. The higher price, however, is bad for domestic consumers. In that domestic consumers tend to have far less political clout than producers, very few criticisms of exports can be heard. On the positive side, though, exports do tend to add to the multiplicative, cumulatively reinforc-ing expansion of production and income (whew! see "multiplier"). Overall unrestricted trade between nations is good for both sides. Compare "import." See "comparative advantage," "balance of trade," "free trade."

externality Any cost or benefit that's not included in the market price of a good because it's not included in the supply price or the demand price. Pollution is an example of an externality cost if producers aren't the ones who suffer from pollution damages. Education is an example of an externality benefit when members of society other than students benefit from a more-educated population. Externality is one type of "market failure" that causes inefficiency. See "efficiency."

F

federal deficit An excess of federal government spending over tax collections (see "budget deficit"). The federal deficit has been the subject of on-again, off-again debates among vote-seeking politicians and pointy-headed economists for a number of years. The main points of the debate are: (1) the potential crowding out of investment in capital goods, (2) the use of borrowed funds for either "consumption" or "investment" government purchases, and (3) the constraints imposed on "fiscal policy." The jury of pointy-heads remains undecided on these issues. See "taxes."

Federal Deposit Insurance Corporation (FDIC) A program established by Congress in 1933, during the worst of the Great Depression, to insure the deposits of failed banks. The FDIC operates much like any private insurance company. It collects insurance premiums from its customers—the banks—in return for the assurance that it will stand behind, or be ready to pay off, any deposits that the banks can't. In other words, if a bank goes under, then the FDIC whips out its own checkbook and begins returning money to the bank's customers. There are limits, however, to the amounts that the FDIC will pay back. In the 1980s the limit was raised to $100,000, which is sufficient for the deposits of most over-worked, underappreciated members of the third estate. However, keep an eye on this limit because it is subject to change. In that the FDIC guarantees bank deposits, it also has the authority to inspect the books and make certain that the banks are properly managed. Originally only banks chartered by the federal government, so-called "national" banks, were required to be insured by the FDIC. Other banks could: (1) voluntarily join the FDIC, (2) be insured in other ways, or (3) carry no insurance at all. Savings and loan associations (S&Ls) were once insured by the Federal Savings and Loan Insurance Corporation (FSLIC), but after hundreds of S&Ls failed and depleted FSLIC funds during the 1980s, it has been merged with the FDIC. Most credit unions have their insurance through the National Credit Union Share Insurance Fund. The FDIC has been pretty successful. While untold numbers lost their bank deposits when thousands of banks failed during the first few years of the Great Depression, this wasn't a problem when banks began failing in large numbers in the 1980s. Some banks and S&Ls closed their doors, but customers got their deposits back. See "bank panic," "deposit insurance," "fractional-reserve banking."

federal funds market The market used by banks to borrow and lend "bank reserves." In particular, a substantial part of the reserves held by banks are deposits with the Federal Reserve System. On many occasions, some banks will have more deposits than they need to meet the Fed's "reserve requirements," while other banks find themselves a little short. It's a simple matter then for one bank to lend some of these extra reserves to another, usually for no more than a few days. Working on instructions from the

banks, the Fed electronically switches funds from one account to another, and a federal funds market loan has been completed. The interest rate tacked on by the lending bank is termed the "federal funds rate."

federal funds rate The interest rate that banks charge each other when loaning "bank reserves" through the "federal funds market." This is a key interest rate in the economy because it helps to determine banks' minimum cost of getting funds. If the federal funds rate is higher, then banks are likely to raise the interest rates they charge, like the prime rate, home mortgage rate, or rate on car loans. Compare "discount rate."

Federal Open Market Committee (FOMC) A part of the Federal Reserve System that's specifically responsible for directing "open-market operations," and is more generally charged with guiding the nation's "monetary policy." The FOMC includes the 7 members of the Fed's board of governors and 5 of the 12 presidents of Federal Reserve District Banks. The chairman of the Federal Reserve System is also the chairman of the FOMC. By design, the 7 members of the board of governors can always outvote the 5 district bank presidents. The FOMC meets every 45 days to evaluate monetary policy (except when emergencies like a stock market crash require more timely get-togethers). Is the money supply growing too fast? Not fast enough? Are interest rates too high? Too low? These are some of the questions they ponder.

Federal Reserve Note Paper currency issued by each of the 12 Federal Reserve District Banks in denominations of $1, $5, $10, $20, $50, $100. Unlike paper currency of the past that was issued by the U.S. Treasury, these notes are backed by the "Federal Reserve System." Specifically, each of the 12 Fed District Banks supplies notes within its district. Each district bank puts its own personal number and stamp (literally to the left of the portrait) on the notes it issues. For example, the number for the Boston District Bank is 1; for the San Francisco Bank, 12. See "gold certificate," "money," "silver certificate."

Federal Reserve System *The* central bank of the United States. It includes a board of governors, 12 district banks, 25 branch banks, and assorted committees. The most important of these committees is the "Federal Open Market Committee," which directs "monetary policy." The Fed (as many like to call it) was established in 1913 and modified significantly during the Great Depression of the 1930s. Its duties are to maintain the stability of the banking system, regulate banks, and oversee the nation's money supply. The Fed is a relatively independent federal agency, meaning that it is financially self-sufficient and doesn't have to answer to Congress for funding. This independence is helped by the structure of its board of governors, the policy making head of the Fed. The board includes seven members, each appointed for a 14-year term, with one term expiring every 2 years. While the President appoints and Congress confirms each board member, these staggered terms prevent any President from stacking the board with political hacks and cronies. The chairman of the board of governors, who is invariably one of the two or three most powerful players in the economy, is appointed by the President for a 5-year term. While the chairman and the board set the policies, they're carried out by a total of 37 Federal Reserve Banks: 12 district banks and 25 branch banks. The Federal Reserve System divides the country into 12 districts, with a district bank overseeing banking within it's particular district. In most of the districts, especially the larger ones in the west, the district banks are helped out by two or three branch banks. In addition to carrying out the policy wishes of the board, these Federal Reserve Banks also provide numerous services to the commercial banking sys-

tem. For example, using an extensive system of bank reserves, they offer check-clearing services, making it easier for one bank to collect payment from a check written on another bank. Federal Reserve Banks also stand ready to make emergency loans to any bank that is experiencing financial problems. See "discount rate," "Federal Reserve Note," "reserve requirements."

Federal Trade Commission (FTC) An independent federal agency run by a five-member commission that's charged by Congress with preventing unfair and deceptive business activities and other various "monopoly" practices that tend to inhibit competition. The FTC was set up in 1914 to help the Justice Department enforce a growing number of "antitrust laws." It has the authority to restrict assorted market monopolizing practices, such as mergers, false or misleading advertising, price discrimination, and price fixing. Since the time of it's formation, the FTC has grown into an important third-estate, consumer protection agency. If you think that you've been "had" by a big-time, second-estate business, then this is one place to go for help. See "unfair competition."

financial market A market that trades financial assets. Financial assets are the legal claims on the real assets in our economy and include such notable items as corporate stocks and bonds, government securities, and money. Examples of financial markets are stock markets, bond markets, commodity exchanges, the so-called "open market" (which trades government securities), and markets that trade futures and options. Other less formal transactions are also considered part of our array of financial markets. All of the lending and borrowing that consumers, businesses, and banks do through the banking system is a part. Insurance, as a legal claim on an uncertain future, is yet another dimension of financial markets. And not to be overlooked, foreign-exchange markets are critical financial markets for anyone engaging in the exciting world of foreign trade. Without financial markets our economy would find it almost impossible to accumulate the funds needed for investment in big, expensive capital projects. See "interest rate," "rate of return."

first estate In past centuries, this included the religious leaders and clergy. In modern times, it is the politicians and government leaders who can exert a great deal of control over resources through the coercive powers of government. One of the primary functions of the first estate is to protect the less-powerful consumers, taxpayers, and workers of the "third estate" from the market control typically held by the business leaders of the "second estate." It is not uncommon, however, for an unhealthy degree of cooperation between the first and second estates, which often ends up with the enslavement (figuratively and literally) of the third estate. At times, help is forthcoming from the watchdog journalists of the "fourth estate," unless they too have been overtaken by the ruling elite.

fiscal policy Use of the federal government's powers of spending and taxation to stabilize the business cycle—at least that's the general idea. The term "fiscal" comes from government's annual preparation of it's *fiscal* budget, which itemizes expenses and tax collections. Fiscal policy itself tends to be separate from these yearly budget chores, usually consisting of special legislation that enacts a change in taxes or spending. If the economy is mired in a "recession," then the appropriate fiscal policy is to increase spending or reduce taxes, termed "expansionary policy." During periods of high "inflation," the opposite actions are needed: contractionary policy. The consequences of fiscal policy are typically observed in terms of the "federal deficit." The federal deficit tends to increase with expansionary policy and decline with contractionary policy. In fact, expansionary policy is most effective if the government has a budget deficit (see "full-employment budget"). There are a few notable concerns with fiscal policy: (1) The time to get a policy working may be counterproductive. It takes so long to get a bill through Congress that the "business cycle" may have corrected its own problems. Fiscal policy may then end up doing the wrong thing at the wrong time—that is, contractionary policy during a recession, or expansionary policy during an expansion. (2) Short-run fiscal policy can cause long-run problems. In particular, expansionary policy can cause higher interest rates that inhibit investment in capital (see "crowding out"). (3) Given the politics of government, greater spending and lower taxes are easy to achieve. However, less spending and higher taxes aren't. This means the federal government, given a green light to pursue fiscal policy, is more than likely to run up a big "budget deficit" than a "budget surplus." (4) Along similar lines, the greater inclination for expansionary over contractionary policy tends to increase the overall size of government. Compare "automatic stabilizer," "monetary policy."

fixed exchange rate An "exchange rate" that's established at a given level and maintained through government (usually central bank) actions. To fix the exchange rate, a government must be willing to buy and sell currency in the "foreign-exchange market" in whatever amounts are necessary. A fixed exchange rate typically disrupts a nation's "balance of trade" and "balance of payments." If the exchange rate is fixed too low, then a government needs to sell it's currency in the foreign-exchange market and may end up expanding the money supply too much, which then causes inflation. If the exchange rate is fixed too high, then export sales to other countries are curtailed and the economy is likely to slide into a recession. Compare "floating exchange rate," "managed float."

floating exchange rate An exchange rate determined through the unrestrictive interaction of supply and demand in the "foreign-exchange market." A floating exchange rate means that a nation's government is *not* trying to manipulate currency prices to achieve some change in the exports or imports. Compare "fixed exchange rate," "managed float."

Food and Drug Administration (FDA) An agency of the U.S. Department of Health and Human Services that deals with the safety and effectiveness of food, cosmetics, drugs, and medical implements. It was formally established in 1906 to investigate and test what turned out to be some pretty dangerous and disgusting food additives that were being fed to an unaware public. During this wild and woolly era, for example, copper was added to green beans to keep them "green," chalk was mixed into watered-down milk to maintain its "milk-like consistency," and cocaine was a popular ingredient in soft drinks. The FDA is now charged with the task of keeping food and drugs free of hazardous additives and to ensure that they perform as promised. Drugs must undergo rigorous, lengthy tests on animals and humans to prove they're safe and effective. Critics argue that this testing is too long, too expensive, and prevents the timely introduction of new products. However, it has also prevented devastating problems caused by (whoops!) unanticipated side effects. Compare "Consumer Product Safety Commission." See "regulation."

foreclosure A legal move to acquire possession of mortgaged property when the borrower is unable to pay off the loan or make payments according to the conditions of the loan. In other words, if you can't make your house payments, the bank (or lender) can boot you out and take your house. The house can then be sold to pay off all or part of the loan.

One of the more notable things about foreclosure for members of the third estate is that the rules and procedures differ from state to state. If you anticipate foreclosure activity, it might be worth your while to find out the specifics in your locale.

foreign aid Gifts, loans, technical assistance, and other assorted transfers from one country to another that are intended to improve conditions in the receiving nation. The U.S. has been a major player in this foreign-aid game throughout much of the twentieth century. However, most of the more-developed countries of the world give aid to the lesser-developed ones. The stated objective of foreign-aid payments is to promote "economic development," but political considerations are often part of the process. During the Cold War years, for example, the United States was often inclined to provide ample foreign aid to countries with strategic military importance relative to Communist countries. The Soviet Union acted in a similar manner. While foreign aid is often criticized for "giving our money to other countries when we have problems here," we do obtain more than strategic military benefits. When foreign aid improves the development of other nations they (1) buy more U.S. exports, which creates jobs and stimulates our economy, and (2) produce stuff that we can then import, which improves consumer satisfaction. See "foreign trade," "International Monetary Fund," "World Bank."

foreign exchange Any financial instrument that gives one country a claim on the currency of another country and that is used to make payments between countries. The most important type of foreign exchange is currency itself, that is, the currency of *other* countries. However foreign exchange also includes things like bank checks and bills of exchange (a sort of contract that's paid for with the currency of one nation which can then be traded for the currency of another country). See "exchange rate," "foreign-exchange market."

foreign-exchange market A market that trades "foreign exchange." The currencies of the advanced nations, and many of the lesser-developed ones, are at the top of what's traded in this market. The price at which one currency is traded for another in this market is the "exchange rate." Like many "markets," this one is not located at any particular place but includes transactions around the globe. As you might expect, banks handle a lot of these transactions.

foreign investment The purchase of financial and physical assets in one country by businesses and residents of another. Business that call one country their home, especially those from more-advanced nations, have found it advantageous to construct factories, establish distribution centers, buy corporate stock, or otherwise invest in the assets of another country. The U.S.A. has bits and pieces owned by foreign investors, but we also own bits and pieces of other countries. In general, foreign investment, which seeks out the highest return as does any other investment, is a healthy sign for an economy. It indicates that an economy is relatively productive and worthy of investment by others. However, foreign investment also represents a return flow of funds that another country got through a balance-of-trade surplus. For example, the goods sold by Japan to the United States during the 1980s gave it a bunch of U.S. dollars, which it then used to buy some U.S. assets. See "balance of payments."

foreign trade Exchange of goods and services between countries. The inclination for one country to trade with another is based in large part on the idea of "comparative advantage," which says that any country, no matter how technologically disadvantaged it might be, can always find some sort of good that will let it enter the game of foreign trade. In this sense, foreign trade is just an extension of the production, exchange, and consumption that's a fundamental part of life. The only difference with foreign trade is that producers and consumers reside in separate countries. The cost of engaging in foreign trade depends on the quality, efficiency, and availability of transportation. Foreign trade has increased tremendously over the past few decades as the cost of transportation has declined. The "exchange rate" for foreign currency is also pretty important to foreign trade in that it effects the relative prices of "imports" and "exports." Although many reasons have been given to throw up a wide assortment of "trade barriers," the free flow of foreign trade is more often than not beneficial to all countries involved. See "balance of trade," "trading bloc."

Fortune 500 A list of the 500 largest (in terms of sales) publicly held corporations in the U.S.A., as compiled and published by Fortune magazine. While other business-oriented magazines publish similar lists, this one has come to symbolize the largest, most powerful bastions of the second estate. For a business to achieve ranking on the Fortune 500 is a mark of success. For consumers, the Fortune 500 is often a mark of powerlessness. If you're interested, Fortune also provides a list of the 500 largest foreign companies, and separate lists of the 50 largest banks, utilities, and retail, transportation and diversified financial companies. See "big business," "blue chip," "Dow Jones averages," and, just for the fun of it, "second estate," "market control."

fourth estate The journalist who keep a watchful eye on the evil doings of the first and second estates and hopefully provide valuable information to the consumers, workers, and taxpayers of the third estate. However, in that news and journalism have become, along with other businesses, a megagadzillion-dollar industry, many fourth-estate watchdogs have become card-carrying members of the second estate (or even the first estate). As such, some journalists are more concerned with protecting and promoting business and government interests than consumer interests.

fractional-reserve banking A system in which banks keep less than 100 percent of their deposits in the form of "bank reserves" and use the rest for interest-paying loans. Banks in the U.S.A., as well as those in most other modern countries, practice this system of fractional-reserve banking. Banks have long recognized that, on a given day, their customers withdraw a relatively small proportion of deposits. As such, banks need to keep 5, 10, or maybe 20 percent of deposits on hand to satisfy any of the day-to-day withdrawals. The bulk of these deposits is then used for loans that return an interest payment and generate revenue for the bank. Fractional-reserve banking creates a sometimes dangerous balancing act. On the one hand, a bank gets more revenue and earns more profit if it keeps fewer bank reserves and makes more loans. On the other hand, if it makes too many loans and keeps too few bank reserves, then it runs the risk of failing to meet the withdrawal demands of its customers. If the events of this "other hand" are realized, a bank is forced to close it's doors. Another part of this problem, one with a direct bearing on most hardworking, taxpaying consumers, is that banks add to the nation's total of checking account balances when they make loans. In that these balances are a large part of the nation's money supply, the practice of fractional-reserve banking gives banks the ability to "create" money. When banks are forced to close up shop, they take with them a portion of the money supply. With enough banks closing down, as was the case during the Great Depression of the 1930s, the money supply shrinks, and all sorts of devastating problems result. On a positive note, though, our government has recognized the potential dangers of fractional-reserve banking and has created numerous checks and balances, including the "Federal Reserve System," the "Federal Deposit Insurance Corporation," and an assortment of other federal and state regulatory agencies.

free enterprise A term that's often used, erroneously I should note, in reference to capitalism. In principle, free enterprise is an economy in which businesses and consumers are "free" to engage their resources in any desired production, consumption, or exchange without government restriction, regulation, or control. "It's my stuff; I'll do what I damn well please with it." This notion of free enterprise is championed by second-estate businesses and capital owners who do not want the government to limit their rather extensive market control. Of course, this market control can be used to take unfair advantage of workers and consumers in the third estate, by charging exorbitantly high prices, collecting obscene amounts of economic profit, and thus perpetuating second-estate wealth, market control, and political influence. Contrary to what some proponents would have you believe, free enterprise has never existed in the good old U. S. of A. at any time, nor has it ever existed in any other society or economy. Government has always played a central, and necessary role, in an economy's attempt to reduce the problems of "scarcity."

free-rider problem The inclination to enjoy the benefit of a good without paying for it if you don't have to. This is the main reason "public goods" are produced by government. Most people won't voluntarily pay for a public good, because "excludability" means they can get it without paying—a free ride. With a large number of free riders—perhaps everyone—voluntary payments like those occurring in markets won't provide enough revenue to pay production costs. The only way to finance public goods is to force free riders, and everyone else, to pay through taxes.

free trade The absence of "trade barriers," or restrictions, on "foreign trade." Based on the notion of "comparative advantage," unrestricted trade is generally beneficial to a trading country. However, while consumers benefit through a greater selection of products and lower prices, producers in a country are on the receiving end of lower prices and stiffer competition. In that producers tend to have more political clout than consumers, completely, unhindered free trade is seldom seen in the real world. Numerous trade restrictions such as tariffs, nontariff barriers, and quotas are usually the rule of the day (also the rule of the week, year, decade, and century).

free-trade area An agreement among two or more nations to eliminate trade barriers with each other. There is no attempt, however, to adopt a common trade policy with other nations, to allow free movement of resources among the countries, or to adopt common monetary or fiscal policies. This is considered the first of four levels of integration among nations. See "common market," "customs union," "economic union" for the other levels. See also "trading bloc."

frictional unemployment Unemployment caused by temporary job changes. In the absence of "cyclical unemployment," a significant amount of unemployment is still likely to exist as people leave one job in search of a better one. Frictional unemployment occurs because it takes a little bit of time before a person finds a new job. This sort of unemployment is an inherent and healthy part of any economy. Compare "seasonal unemployment," "structural unemployment."

full employment In principle, this is when all of our economy's resources are being used to produce output. In practice, however, our economy is considered to be at full employment when the "unemployment rate" is around 5 percent, and the "capacity utilization rate" is about 85 percent. This 5-percent unemployment rate includes structural and frictional unemployment. Historical evidence tells us that 5-percent unemployment is consistent with an expanding, growing economy that has very little inflation. If the unemployment rate drops much below 5 percent, then the inflation rate increases, suggesting that we're trying to produce more stuff than we're capable of doing. In other words, our resources are fully employed.

full-employment budget A hypothetical federal budget that would exist if the economy were at "full employment." Differences between the actual federal budget and the full-employment budget result from taxes and expenditures that depend on gross domestic product. While the full-employment budget may seem like another economist's excursion into fantasy land, it does serve a useful purpose. The full-employment budget indicates whether any of the federal government's "fiscal policy" is over- or understimulating the economy given our current position in the "business cycle." From a fiscal policy view, the federal budget should be balanced if the economy is at full employment. In this way, there is no "federal deficit" to stimulate us into inflation, nor a surplus to contract us into a recession. However, a budget deficit is the proper policy during a recession, and a surplus is the tune to sing during inflation. But how much of a deficit or surplus is desirable during these nonideal periods? During a recession the federal deficit should be just enough to generate a balanced budget at full employment. The same result is desirable if we're running a surplus with inflation. If the full-employment budget is *not* balanced, however, then we're doing too much or too little by way of fiscal policy, and changes are in order.

futures An agreement to complete the sale of a commodity at a predetermined price on some future date. Much of the real stuff that consumers buy is what is usually termed a "spot" transaction. You buy the stuff, pay the price, and take it home with you. While financial markets have a substantial number of these spot transactions, they are also heavily into futures transactions. For example, you can get a futures agreement to buy or sell 100 tons of soybean meal 1 year from today at $200 a ton. Why on earth would you want to do that? Why not just do your buying or selling now? Here are a few reasons: (1) If you're a soybean farmer, then you might want to insure, or hedge, against *lower* prices for your output (see "hedging"). In particular, if you're planning to harvest 100 tons of soybean meal in 1 year, then you can lock in the $200 price now. Even if the (spot) price goes below $200 a ton at that time, you get to sell your stuff for $200. Sure you don't get as much if the price ends up more than $200, but you're willing to forego the big potential profit for the guaranteed sales. (2) If you're a soybean buyer, using soybean meal as an input in food products, then you might want to insure yourself against *higher* prices and maintain a continuous supply of soybean meal. If you fix your supply price at $200 next year with a futures contract, then you can worry about your own business and not the ups and downs of the soybean market. (3) If you're a speculator, then you might be try to take advantage of the ups and downs of the soybean market. You would have a futures contract to sell soybeans at $200 next year if you thought the spot price was going to be less than $200. In this case, when that future date rolls around, you can buy the soybean meal on the spot market for less than $200, then immediately resell it for $200 using your futures contract, making a tidy profit in the process. Of course, if you guess wrong, then you lose your shirt. But that's the nature of "speculation." Those who speculate in futures actually help producers and buyers to hedge. The speculators are usually willing to buy futures when hedgers are selling, and sell when they're buying. See "insurance," "leverage," "option."

G

GDP price deflator A price index based on the calculation of "real gross domestic product" that's used as an indicator of average prices in the economy. Those lovable economists who spend their days and nights compiling and estimating the size of our economic pie, provide estimates of gross domestic product in both "nominal dollars" and "real dollars." To accomplish this seemingly miraculous statistical feat, they measure all of the stuff that makes up GDP in current prices—that is, the prices paid. Then they recompute the value of everything produced using prices that existed during some "base year" in the past (usually within the past decade). In that real GDP and nominal GDP are both calculated using the same production numbers, their only difference is the change in prices from the base year to the present. In particular, the GDP price deflator is calculated as the ratio of nominal GDP to real GDP. "Inflation" is measured by calculating the percentage change in the GDP price deflator from one year to the next. For example, if the deflator had a value of 150 last year and 160 this year, then the rate of inflation is 6.7 percent, which is (160 - 150)/150. Although less well known, the GDP price deflator is generally considered more accurate than the "consumer price index" because: (1) it includes the prices of *all* production in the economy, rather than just those purchased by urban consumers, and (2) it measures the prices of current production, rather than some market basket consumers purchased years earlier. However, the GDP price deflator gets less publicity because it's published only once every 3 months, compared to the monthly release of the consumer price index.

General Agreement on Tariffs and Trade (GATT) A treaty, signed in 1947 by 23 countries including the United States, that was designed to reduce "trade barriers." It now carries the signatures of about 100 countries, and over the years has been pretty darn effective in reducing tariffs, eliminating some import quotas, and getting member countries to extend "most-favored nation" status to each other. For example, tariffs that were 30 to 50 percent of the value of imports in the 1930s and 1940s are now less than 10 percent. GATT (as the acronym folks like to call it) conducts its business through "rounds" of negotiations among member countries that last several years. A total of eight rounds were conducted between 1947 and 1994. During each round, a few more trade barriers were chiseled away, usually over the screams and protests of producers and other "special-interest groups" back home. See "foreign trade," "free trade."

gift tax A tax on the transfer of assets from one person to another. The gift tax is different from "estate" and "inheritance taxes" in that it applies to people who are still alive. In fact, the gift tax was created because people sought to avoid estate and inheritance taxes by giving their stuff away *before* dying. But all gifts are not taxed. There are both annual and lifetime exemptions on gifts subject to this tax. These exemptions are changed from time to time, so you might want to investigate further if you happened to hit the big jackpot on a television game show. Some, but not necessarily all, of that prize is likely to be taxed.

Gini index One of the most common measures of "income" or "wealth distributions." It indicates how equal, or unequal, income, wealth, or similar stuff is distributed among the population. If you happen to come across a Gini index, you'll see that it falls in the range of 0 to 1. A value of 0 tells you that the distribution is *perfectly equal;* that is, everyone has exactly the same amount of income,

wealth, or whatever. A value of 1, however, tells you that the distribution is what we could call *perfectly unequal;* that is, one person has everything and everyone else has nothing. The Gini index for income in the United States tends to be in the 0.2 to 0.3 range, while the index for wealth is noticeably higher. A few countries have lower Gini indexes than the U.S.A., but most tend to be higher, some with an index well over 0.5. If you're concerned about the ongoing battles between the second and third estates, this is a handy little measure to watch. Victories by the consumers of the third estate cause the Gini index to decline, while increases in political and economic power of the second estate are often reflected in higher values.

gold certificate Paper currency issued by the U.S. Treasury from the Civil War until 1933 which could be exchanged for an equal value of gold. Gold certificates were used as part of a "gold standard." With the exception of collectors, gold certificates have long been out of circulation, replaced first by "silver certificates," then in the past few decades by "Federal Reserve Notes." See "money."

gold standard Use of gold as the standard for valuing a nation's currency. A gold standard can take at least three different forms, most of which have been part of the American economic landscape: (1) Gold is used as the money in circulation. As documented by many old cowboy movies, this was common in the U.S. West in the 1800s. (2) Gold is used to back up paper money in circulation. This involves the use of something like a "gold certificate," such that the number of certificates in circulation is the same as the amount of gold stored some place like Fort Knox. We had this for awhile in the late 1800s and early 1900s. (3) Gold is used to fix the exchange price of paper currency in circulation. In this case, the currency could, in principle, be exchanged for some predetermined amount of gold. In other words, the price of gold is fixed in terms of dollars. Up to the early 1970s, the United States fixed the price of gold at $35 an ounce.

government debt The total amount of all government securities outstanding. This is also frequently termed the "public debt."

government security A financial instrument used by the federal government to borrow money. Government securities are issued by the U.S. Treasury to cover the federal government's "budget deficit." Much like consumers who borrow money from banks to finance the purchase of a house or car, the federal government borrows money to finance some of its expenditures. These securities include small denomination ($25, $50, or $100), nonnegotiable Series EE savings bonds purchased by consumers. The really serious money, however, is borrowed using larger denomination securities ($100,000 or more) purchased by banks, corporations, foreign governments, and others with large sums of money to lend. Government securities are classified by length of maturity, with "Treasury bills" paid off in 1 year, "Treasury notes" in 1 to 10 years, and "Treasury bonds" in 10 to 30 years. While Series EE savings bonds are *not* negotiable, meaning that the original buyer is the only one who can "cash" a bond, larger denomination securities are negotiable and regularly traded in what is often termed the "open market." The total amount of government securities outstanding, or remaining to be paid off, is the "government debt." See "open market operations" for an interesting use of government securities.

graduated tax A type of progressive tax in which the tax rate is higher as the value of the taxed item increases. For example, a graduated sales would be one with a 5-percent tax rate on the first $10 of sales, 10-percent tax rate on the any sales between $10 and $50, then a 15-percent rate for anything above $50. Our personal income tax system uses graduated taxes.

group of seven (G-7) Seven of the most advanced and industrialized nations of the world—the United States, Britain, France, Italy, Canada, Germany, and Japan—that meet regularly to coordinate "fiscal" and "monetary policies." Their actions are based on the proposition that our global economy and the individual countries are better off through cooperation than conflict. See "exchange rates," "managed float."

gross domestic product (GDP) The total market value of all goods and services produced by an economy during a given period of time, usually 1 year. This is the federal government's official measure of how much output our economy produces. It's tabulated and reported by the Bureau of Economic Analysis, which is part of the U.S. Department of Commerce. Gross domestic product, often abbreviated simply as GDP, is one of several measures reported regularly (every 3 months) by the pointy-headed folks at the Bureau of Economic Analysis. Other common measures include "national income" and "personal income." GDP has replaced a perhaps better-known measure of output, "gross national product" (GNP), in most official discussions of the U.S. economy. Compare "net domestic product," "real gross domestic product." See "GDP price deflator."

gross national product (GNP) The total market value of all goods and services produced by an economy during a given period of time, usually 1 year. This was once the federal government's official measure of how much output our economy produces, but it has been replaced by "gross domestic product." The two measures are almost the same, but differ in one regard: GNP measures the value of output produced by *resources owned by the citizens of a country*, regardless of where the production occurs. GDP, in contrast, measures all of the output produced *within the political borders of a country*, regardless of the citizenship of the resources doing the producing.

H

hedging Buying or selling "futures" contracts to protect against price changes. This is a common form of "insurance" used by those who produce various commodities—such as wheat, cattle, coffee, and natural gas—as well as those who buy these commodities as inputs. Here's how hedging works for a commodity producer. An orange grower, for example, who is still months away from harvest time, might be inclined to sell a futures contract to protect against a drop in the price of oranges. If the price is lower come harvest time, the orange crop is sold at the *higher* futures price. Of course, if the price has risen, the grower loses out on this higher price. The orange grower, though, is not really in the business of buying low and selling high, but rather of producing oranges. By eliminating the uncertainty of price changes, the grower can concentrate on growing oranges. Commodity buyers hedge for similar reasons. They also want to protect against price changes, in their case *higher* prices. As such, they contract for future delivery of their inputs to ensure certainty in their supply and production costs. Sure, they lose out if prices drop, but they avoid considerable problems of sharp price increases. See "commodity exchange," "financial market," "insurance," "option," "speculation."

horizontal equity A system of taxes that treats equal people equally. In other words, if you make the same income as someone else and pay the same personal income taxes, then you have horizontal equity. See "vertical equity."

horizontal merger See "merger."

household production The creation of satisfaction using both goods purchased in markets and the uncompensated efforts of consumers. In other words, while you might buy stuff from the store, you often need to do something to it before it's ready to use. Probably the most common example is cooking a meal. You buy some pasta noodles, a jar of alfredo sauce, and a frozen package of bite-sized shrimp at the store, then use a little bit of your time and effort to prepare a tasty Italian meal. This idea of household production is an often overlooked and undermeasured part of our economy. It's difficult to calculate the extent of this household production, and thus virtually impossible to include any part of it in measures such as "gross domestic product." But these household efforts have a big, and over time changing, influence on working, shopping, and other measurable parts of the economy. Women, for example, with improvements in the technology of household production (such as dishwashers and the like), have thrown away the shackles of their traditional "housewife" role to enter the labor force in large numbers.

human capital The sum total of a person's productive knowledge, experience, and training. The acquisition of human capital is what makes a person more productive. One of the most notable methods of stocking up on human capital is through formal education—from grade school to advanced college degrees. However, human capital is also effectively obtained through less formal training and highly informal on-the-job experiences. The key to human capital, as it is with the more common forms of physical capital, is "investment." Human capital is produced through the sacrifice of current consumption. And like investment in factories, equipment, and buildings, human capital investment has a big-time payoff in "economic growth."

hyperinflation Exceptionally high "inflation" rates. While there are no hard and fast guidelines, an annual inflation rate of 20 percent or more is likely to get you the hyperinflation title. Some countries in the past have been quite good at creating hyperinflation. An annual inflation rate of 1,000 percent has not been uncommon. On occasion, the *trillion* percent inflation rate mark has been achieved. (That is, something with a $1 price tag in early January would have a $1-trillion price in late December. We're talking serious hyperinflation.)

I

immigration "Migration" that enters one country from another country. Immigration is usually seen as a problem for existing citizens of nation because: (1) the supply of labor increases, which tends to lower wages; (2) there's a greater demand for public services, which causes taxes to rise; and (3) the culture of immigrants is usually different, which creates all sorts of social conflicts. However, immigration can also be beneficial because: (1) the additional labor is a source of economic growth, (2) the immigrants might be willing to do some jobs that wouldn't be performed otherwise, and (3) some goods can be produced at lower cost. Compare "emigration."

import The purchase of goods produced in a foreign country. The United States, for example, buys a wide variety of stuff produced in other countries, including cars, electronic equipment, bananas, coffee, shoes, and clothing. Domestic producers (and their employees) are highly critical of imports, and frequently seek restrictions on them. The reason is that imports offer competition for domestic producers, which tends to reduce any "market control" they might have. Restrictions on imports, however, limit the quantity and variety of goods available to consumers. Imports are good for consumers and bad for producers. The benefits obtained from restrictions on imports need to be carefully considered in light of the efficiency benefits to be had from the free movement of goods between countries. Compare "export." See "comparative advantage," "balance of trade," "foreign trade," "free trade," "trade barriers."

income distribution The manner in which income is divided among the members of the economy. A perfectly equal income distribution would mean everyone in the country has exactly the same income. The income distribution in the good old U.S. of A., while more equal than most nations of the world, is far from perfectly equal. A certain amount of inequality in the income distribution is to be expected because resources are never equally distributed. Some labor is naturally going to be more productive—better able to produce the stuff that consumers want—and thus get more income. The same is true for capital and natural resources. However, without government intervention, an unequal distribution of income tends to perpetuate itself. Those who have more income can invest in additional productive resources, and thus can add even more to their income. Compare "wealth distribution." See "Gini index."

income tax A tax on income, including wages, rent, interest, profit, and (usually) transfer payments. The income tax system in the United States includes both a "personal income tax" and "corporate income tax." In general, the U.S. income tax is progressive, but through a number of deductions and other loopholes, it's less so in practice that on paper. See "Internal Revenue Service."

industry regulation Government regulation of an entire industry. The most common industry regulation has been in airline, railroad, trucking, banking, and television broadcasting. The objective of industry regulation is for a regulatory agency to keep a close eye on an industry's prices and product to ensure that they don't start a monopoly and take advantage of consumers. Unfortunately, more than a few of the regulatory agencies have been prone to work *too* closely with those they regulate, in large part because regulators move freely between industry and agency. The agency often ends up working *for* the industry and running what is effectively a legal monopoly that raises prices, prevents competition, and gouges consumers.

inflation A persistent increase in the average price level in the economy. Inflation is a continual rise in prices that, not coincidentally, leads to a continual erosion of the "purchasing power" of money. This occurs because the amount of money in the economy is directly tied to inflation. Here's how it works. Our economy grows a little bit each year, and can produce more output, as the quantity and quality of resources increase. Money is what we use to buy that output. If the amount of money we have increases in proportion to the growth of the economy, then we have the right amount of money needed to buy the output. If the money, however, doesn't keep pace, then we often find ourselves unable to buy everything we could produce. This is the often-discussed problem of a "recession." Alternatively, if there's more money added to the economy than we need, then we have inflation. One problem with inflation is that it haphazardly redistributes income and wealth. While inflation is an increase in *average* prices, prices tend to increase at different rates. When this happens, those fortunate enough to produce goods with the biggest price increases also get more income. Those with smaller price increases (even declining prices) get relatively less income. Inflation tends to erode the value of financial assets more so than other stuff. As such, the second estate, with a bunch of wealth in financial assets, tends to fear inflation much more than the third estate. See "consumer price index," "GDP price deflator."

inflation premium The difference between the "nominal interest rate" and the "real interest rate." The role of the inflation premium is, quite simply, to adjust the interest rate for inflation. The nominal interest rate (the one on the loan contract) includes a real interest rate needed by the lender and a surcharge equal to the *expected* inflation rate used to maintain the purchasing power of the future payments. This expected inflation rate is the inflation premium. Compare "risk premium."

infrastructure Capital used for transportation, communication, and energy delivery. This is often termed "social overhead capital" because it provides the basic capital foundation needed by an economy before business capital can adequately do its job. A sundial factory, for example, can do little production if there are no railroads to bring in the needed concrete input, streets and highways to ship the sundials to market, electrical lines to power the machinery, and telephone lines for the sales force to place orders. The government plays a key role because infrastructure (1) needs to be in place *before* businesses can do their production thing, (2) needs to span the entire country to be effective, and (3) has many characteristics of a "public good," which means a business can't produce it profitably. Infrastructure is also important because of the length of time needed for production. A nationwide infrastructure, like the interstate highway system, usually takes decades to complete. Investment during this period of construction creates a multiplicative, cumulatively interacting stimulation of the economy (see "prosperity"). Moreover, once the construction is over, the economy can experience an extended slump (see "depression") if other investments aren't begun.

inheritance tax A tax on that portion of the assets of a deceased person that's received by another. This should be compared with an "estate tax," which is a tax paid on the value of all assets before they are distributed to heirs. See "gift tax."

insolvency The condition of a business when liabilities (excluding ownership equity) are greater than assets. In other words, a business can't pay it's debts. This is a first step on the road to "bankruptcy," but it doesn't guarantee that legal bankruptcy proceedings will be initiated. Compare "solvency."

institution An established method or way of doing something that's widely accepted throughout society. Common institutions include marriage, market exchanges, high school football on autumn Fridays, government, and Christmas gift giving. Institutions provide the rules and guidelines needed to carry out the day-to-day activities of our lives. With the rules, though, come rigidities that can prevent resources from being reallocated to more productive uses. For example, unions might try to keep their members employed at one job when they and the economy would be better off with a reallocation. If institutions become too rigid and prevent a needed reallocation, then the economy and its institutions might "snap." The consequence could be a pretty darned devastating "depression."

insurance Transferring risk to others. The need for insurance occurs because people tend to be "risk averse" in many circumstances. As such, most of us are willing to pay for certainty. Those who satisfy this need for insurance, insurance companies for example, do so because they can pool risk. If insurance companies know the chance of some loss (an accident, illness, or whatever) and its cost, then they can divide this cost among a large group of risk averse types. The insurance company agrees to pay the cost of the loss, and each of the risk averse types pays a "risk premium," but gets the peace of mind that goes with certainty. While private insurance is a healthy, booming business in our economy, a lot of insurance is actually provided by government. Welfare, social security, and unemployment compensation programs are all examples of government insurance. We pay our taxes (grudgingly), but do so knowing that we're protected against unforeseen layoffs or disabilities. In fact, you could go as far as to say that government itself is a form of insurance.

We let it do things that we don't like (taxes, laws, and the like) to make sure that it's there to protect us if something bad happens (foreign invasion, black plague epidemic, market control by the second estate). See "broker," "financial market," "risk loving," "risk neutral."

interest rate The price of funds expressed as a percentage of the total amount loaned or borrowed. This is the cost of borrowing funds and the payment received for lending. Interest rates are invariably expressed as an annual percentage of the amount borrowed/loaned. A 10-percent interest rate, to run through an easy example, tells us that the cost of borrowing $1,000 for 1 year is $100. A given nominal interest rate tends to have three parts: (1) the "real interest rate," which is the basic opportunity cost of the lender, (2) a "risk premium," which is compensation for the chance that the borrower might not make good on repayment, and (3) an "inflation premium," which is an adjustment for the declining purchasing power of money. As with other prices, the interest rate matches buyers and sellers, or in this case borrowers and lenders. The most important match that's made in this regard are business borrowers who seek investment funds for capital and consumers who can be enticed to save and lend part of their incomes if adequately compensated. The end result is that businesses are willing to pay an interest rate that's the same as the rate of return on their capital investments. See "dividend," "financial market," "prime rate," "yield."

Internal Revenue Service (IRS) An agency of the U.S. Department of Treasury with the responsibility of collecting taxes. It was established during the Civil War in 1862, but underwent a major overhaul in 1913 when the 16th amendment to the U.S. Constitution gave it the power to collect income taxes.

International Monetary Fund (IMF) An agency of the United Nations established in 1945 to monitor and stabilize "foreign-exchange markets." Close to 150 of the world's nations (which is just about all of them) belong to the IMF. The IMF was set up to keep countries from manipulating their exchange rates in such a way as to gain a competitive trading advantage over others (see "J-curve" for more on this). Their strategies of control have changed over the decades, but they currently use a "managed float" where exchange rates are allowed to fluctuate with changing market conditions, but only within certain ranges. If exchange rates go too high or too low, then the IMF and member nations take corrective action. The IMF also plays an active role in providing the "international" currency needed to participate in foreign trade through its system of "Special Drawing Rights." See "World Bank."

inventory Stocks of finished products, intermediate goods, raw materials, and other inputs that businesses have on hand. One big reason to keep inventories is to maintain a continuous stream of production by avoiding any supply shortages. Another big reason is to avoid the loss of sales because finished products are unavailable when a customer is ready, willing, and able to buy. The total size of these inventories, economywide, gyrate over time. These gyrations are an important part of "business cycles." When our economy begins to dive into a recession, one of the first signs of trouble is a buildup of inventories; demand for products tapers off and inventories start to accumulate. This usually occurs before workers are laid off and before anyone is fully aware of the problems. Likewise, as the economy begins its recovery, the first sign is a reduction in those inventories as demand picks up. Some economists even go as far as arguing that the periodic buildup and drawdown of inventories is the number-1 cause of business cycles.

investment The sacrifice of current benefits or rewards to pursue an activity with expectations of greater future benefits or rewards. Investment is typically used to mean the purchase of capital by business in anticipation of the profit. It takes, however, many forms in the economy. Businesses invest in research and development (to improve products) and advertising (to increase sales). Consumers invest in new houses, cars, furniture, and appliances (to improve future satisfaction). They invest in education and job training (to enhance future income). Government invests in public infrastructure capital, such as highways, streets, and bridges (to promote future growth of the economy). They invest also in research and development and education—to enhance the general productivity of the economy's labor and capital resources. By increasing the quantity or quality of resources, investment, in it's many varied forms, is a source of "economic growth." While investment, in principle, is diverse, the official government measure, as reported by the Department of Commerce, includes businesses' purchases of capital and consumers' purchases of new houses.

investment banking The process of wholesaling newly issued government securities, corporate stocks, bonds, and similar financial assets by purchasing large blocks and reselling them in smaller units to the public. In essence, investment banks "underwrite" stocks and bonds when they're first issued by guaranteeing to sell them at a preset price. Of course, if the public doesn't buy at the preset price, then the investment bank *must*. This tends to make investment banking a risky proposition. If the bank underwrites a "hot" new issue, then it can make a quick gadzillion or two overnight. However, if it has a real dud, then it can lose an equal amount just as fast. The role of the investment banker in the financial markets is just as important as any other wholesaler. By bringing the buyers and sellers together, investment bankers make the "financial markets" function more efficiently. While investment banks are called "banks", they aren't really banks in the sense that they have checking accounts and safety deposit boxes. This term is really a holdover of the European banks where a single bank provides most bank services including investment banking. See "broker."

J

J-curve An interesting relationship that exists between the "exchange rate" for a nation's currency and its "balance of trade." In principle, the drop in a nation's exchange rate, or price of currency, makes the currency less expensive to "buy." With "cheaper" currency, the price of domestic production is less and the price of foreign stuff is more, causing an increase in exports to other countries and drop in imports coming in from foreign producers. The economy thus moves in the direction away from a "trade deficit" and toward a "trade surplus." However, this change in the balance of trade doesn't occur immediately. In fact, the first few months after a drop in the exchange rate, the balance of trade goes in the other direction, with any existing trade deficit increasing or any trade surplus shrinking. This occurs because the quantities of stuff imported and exported don't change in the short run, but the prices do. Because you pay more for the same amount of imported goods and receive less for the same amount of exports, total spending on imports increases, total revenue received from exports declines, and you move in the trade deficit direction. Once those quantities start adjusting in the long run, then we see a movement in the direction of a trade surplus. See "depreciation."

job vacancy rate A simple little ratio of the number of job vacancies in our economy to the sum of employment and job vacancies. In essence, this measures the fraction of jobs in the economy that are open but haven't been filled. To be included as an officially vacant job, employers must be actively searching to fill it with a warm body, by advertising in the paper, contacting employment offices, etc. Like the more common "unemployment rate," the job vacancy rate is a useful indicator of the "business cycle." When the economy is booming, the job vacancy rate is likely to be relatively high. A low rate signals a recession.

L

labor One of the three general categories of resources, or factors of production (see "capital" and "natural resources"). Labor is the services and efforts of humans that are directed toward production. While labor is commonly thought of as those who work in factories, it is *all* human efforts (except entrepreneurship), such as those provided by clerical workers, technicians, professionals, managers, and even company presidents.

labor force In principle, everyone 16 years of age and over who is willing and able to work. In practice, it includes the sum of anyone over 16 years who is employed or unemployed but actively seeking a job. This notion of labor force is usually limited to the *civilian* labor force by excluding anyone in the military. The civilian labor force number is an important part of the "unemployment rate" calculation. A 6-percent unemployment means that 6 percent of the civilian labor force is without work. See "labor," "labor force participation rate," "employment rate."

labor force participation rate The ratio of the civilian "labor force" (16 years and older) to the total noninstitutionalized civilian population (16 years and older). This ratio indicates the fraction of the population that is willing and able to work. This "official" statistic excludes several groups: children under 16 years old, military personnel, and anyone who is institutionalized (prison, mental hospitals, and the like). The U.S. participation rate has risen significantly since the 1940s, largely because of the entry of women into the labor force. It's currently in the 67-percent range and still seems to be on the rise. While the old traditional male/female stereotypes are lessening, there remains a notable difference in labor force participation rates. Men have a rate of about 75 percent, but dropping. Women are approaching 60 percent and rising quickly. Compare "employment rate."

lagging economic indicator One of seven economic statistics that tend to move up or down a few months after the expansions and contractions of the "business cycle." These statistics can paint a pretty clear picture of what the economy was actually doing a few months back. "How can this be of any possible use?" you might ask. In the complexity that is our economy, we're never quite sure where we are in the business cycle at any given time. "Leading economic indicators" tell us what's ahead, "coincident economic indicators" say what we're doing, and lagging repeats what just happened. While lagging indicators are clearly after the fact, they reinforce what the other two told us, giving us (hopefully) greater confidence in them in the future. Moreover, a lagging indicator signals the move from contraction to expansion for the last cycle *before* a leading indicator signals the turning point from expansion to contraction for the next cycle. In other words, we know the next recession won't start until the lagging indicators tell us the last one is over. The seven key lagging indicators brought to you from the fine folks at the National Bureau of Economic Research are: unit labor costs, the prime interest rate, the amount of outstanding commercial and industrial debt, the annual change in Consumer Price Index, consumer credit as a fraction of personal income, duration of unemployment, and business inventories.

laissez faire A French term that translates into "leave us alone." It has become the rallying cry for many business leaders of the "second estate" who oppose government intervention, regulation, or even taxation. It's based on the erroneous belief that markets alone can achieve an efficient use of our resources. The not-so-hidden ulterior motive of this expression is to allow the second estate a free hand in maintaining and expanding its already extensive market control. See "free enterprise," "market failure."

leading economic indicator One of 11 economic statistics that tend to move up or down a few months before the expansions and contractions of the "business cycle." You can probably see some important uses for leading indicators. If you know a recession is about to come, then preparation can be made beforehand. These leading indicators are: manufacturers new orders, an index of vendor performance, orders for plant and equipment, "Standard & Poor's 500" index of stock prices, new building permits, durable goods manufacturers unfilled orders, the money supply, change in materials prices, average workweek in manufacturing, changes in business and consumer credit, a consumer confidence index, and initial claims for unemployment insurance. Compare "coincident economic indicator," "lagging economic indicator."

leverage The use of credit or loans to enhance speculation in the "financial markets." Suppose, for example, that you take the $1,000 in your bank account to your stockbroker and purchase $1,000 worth of stocks, bonds, or whatever. A 10-percent increase in the value of the purchase then gives you a 10-percent return on your investment, an extra $100. If, however, the value declines by 10 percent, then you lose 10 percent, a loss of $100. This is a pretty typical financial transaction. Leverage works a little differently, providing a much bigger amplification of any gains or losses. A leveraged purchase would let you use your $1,000 to buy, let's say, $10,000 worth of stocks or bonds. The remaining $9,000 of the purchase price comes from a loan. This, by the way, is buying on the margin (see "margin requirement"). A 10-percent increase in the value of the investment in this case—from $10,000 to $11,000—means that you've doubled your initial investment. You can sell the asset, pay off the $9,000 loan, and end up with $2,000 in your pocket Neat trick, eh? But a 10-percent drop means you stand to lose everything. In fact, if it drops more than 10 percent, the bank, broker, or whomever provided the $9,000 loan becomes exceptionally upset if you can't come up with the difference. The widespread use of leverage prior to the stock market crash of 1929 was one of the big reasons that the stock market crashed in 1929. Too many loans were used to leverage too much stock, which forced investors to sell widely when stock prices began dropping below their margins.

leveraged buyout A method of corporate takeover or merger popularized in the 1980s in which the controlling interest in a company's corporate stock was purchased using a substantial fraction of borrowed funds. These takeovers were, as the financial types say, heavily leveraged. The person or company doing the "taking over" used very little of its own money and borrowed the rest, often by issuing extremely risky, but high-interest, "junk" bonds. These bonds were high-risk, and thus paid a high interest rate, because little or nothing backed them up. See "investment banking."

liability Something that you owe. The biggest liabilities for most consumers are loans, including mortgages, car loans, credit-card balances, and installment accounts at stores. Compare "asset."

liberal A political view that favors: (1) paternalistic government; (2) correction of "market failure" with government intervention; (3) equal opportunities for all citizens regardless of race, age, gender, ethnic origin, or planet of origin; (4) redistribution of income and wealth; and (5) extensive regulation and control by government over the profit-grubbing evildoers of the second estate. Liberals tend to come from the ranks of the third estate, with limited ownership of and control over resources. As such, they support policies and first-estate leaders who give them a fighting chance against the second estate. Compare "conservative."

limited liability A condition in which owners are not personally held responsible for the debts of a firm. Corporations are the main form of business in which owners have limited liability. Compare "unlimited liability."

liquidity The ease of converting an asset into money (either checking accounts or currency) in a timely fashion with little or no loss in value. Money is the standard for liquidity because it is, well, money, and no conversion is needed. Other assets, both financial and physical, have varying degrees of liquidity. Savings accounts, certificates of deposit, and money market accounts are highly liquid. Stocks, bonds, and government securities are another step down in liquidity. While they can be "cashed in," price fluctuations, brokerage fees, and assorted transactions expenses tend to reduce their money value. Physical assets—like houses, cars, furniture, clothing, food, and the like—have substantially less liquidity. As a general rule, liquidity carries a price: the interest or satisfaction that you don't get when you hold money.

lockout A plant or factory that is closed temporarily because it's owners are trying to gain a negotiating advantage over the employees' "union." A lockout is commonly used by a company's management if it suspects the union is planning to "strike." A lockout by management before the union strikes is much like a preemptive military attack that tries to hit the enemy hard, fast, and *first*.

logrolling A systematic exchange of votes by politicians to obtain approval of specific legislation. That is, Senator Grapht agrees to vote for Senator Brybe's pet project if Senator Brybe votes for Senator Grapht's favorite piece of legislation. Such logrolling can be explicit or implicit. The explicit kind involves two separate bills, in which each politician is forced to "go on record" with a vote. The implicit kind, which many politicians favor, is where several separate programs are wrapped into a single bill. Every politician can then tell the folks back home that he or she really only wanted the "one thing" that helped constituencies the most but had to vote for "other things" as well. Logrolling is one big reason our government is big and prone to inefficiency. See "principal/agent problem."

loss leader Products sold below cost by a retail store in an attempt to attract buyers who are then likely to buy other, more expensive stuff. Stores are very fond of advertising and even selling popular products at very low prices. However, they hope that once customers have seen fit to enter their stores, then the suckers, er, customers will decide to buy other products that aren't so popular or so low priced. These popular, low-priced products are loss leaders. Sure, the store loses money on the products, but they make up these loses on other stuff.

M

managed float An "exchange rate" that (like a "floating exchange rate") is free to move up and down but is subject to government control (like a "fixed exchange rate") if it moves beyond certain boundaries. With managed float, the government steps into the foreign-exchange market and buys or sells whatever currency is necessary keep the exchange rate within desired limits. The logic behind managed float is that an unrestricted movement of exchange rates is usually pretty healthy, but serious problems in the balance of payment and balance of trade result if it floats too far in either direction. See "group of seven," "International Monetary Fund."

margin requirement The fraction of the purchase price of financial investments, like stocks and bonds, that the buyer must pay for in cash. The remaining part of the purchase price can thus be financed with credit. This "leveraged" use of credit can create high rates of return. It can also create a great deal of instability in the financial markets. The stock market crash of 1929 was helped along its way by extensive use of credit and low margin requirements on stock purchases. When the prices of some stocks dropped below their margins, investors sold off other stocks to cover the difference. With this widespread selling, stock prices dropped like an empty safe from a stockbroker's window. The "Federal Reserve System" has since been empowered to regulate margin requirements in an effort (successful thus far) to prevent similar devastating crashes. See "financial markets," "speculation."

market In principle this is an organized, voluntary exchange between buyers who want a good and the sellers who have it. The buyers are said to "demand" the good, and the sellers have what is termed the "supply." The mutual negotiations among buyers and sellers generate the market exchange price: the amount of money (or some other asset) that buyers give the sellers in exchange for the good. If there are a large number of buyers and sellers, we have a competitive market, one that efficiently uses our scarce resources to satisfy wants and needs. See "barter," "market control," "market failure," "private good."

market control The ability of buyers or sellers to exert influence over the price or quantity of a good, service, or commodity exchanged in a market. Market control depends on the number of competitors. If a market has relatively few buyers but a bunch of sellers, then the buyers tend to have relatively more market control than sellers. The converse occurs if there are a bunch of buyers but relatively few sellers. If the market is controlled on the supply side by one seller, we have a "monopoly," and if it is controlled on the demand side by one buyer, we have a "monopsony." Most markets are subject to some degree of control. Compare "competitive market."

market failure A condition in which a market does not efficiently allocate resources to achieve the greatest possible consumer satisfaction. The four main market failures are: (1) "public good," (2) "market control," (3) "externality," and (4) imperfect information. In each case, a market acting without any government-imposed direction does not direct an efficient amount of our resources into the production, distribution, or consumption of the good. Under some circumstances, such as an external pollution cost, the market produces too much of the good. Under other circumstances, like a monopoly, the market doesn't produce enough of the good. Much of what the government does—national defense, education, business regulations, police protection—is intended to correct a real or perceived market failure

market share The fraction of an industry's total sales accounted for by a single business. In general, market share is a "first-guess" indicator of a business's market control. If, for example, a company has a market share of 100 percent, then you can rest assured it has a substantial amount of market control. A company with a 25-percent market share has less, but still notable, market control. In fact, when you get right down to the bottom line, the term "market share" is only worth mentioning for companies that have some degree of market control. There really is no market control for a company with a 0.00000001-percent market share.

materials balance A hard-and-fast rule that the total amount of stuff removed from the natural environment will be eventually returned, probably as "pollution." This is based on a fundamental law of physics that says material can be neither created nor destroyed, but only transformed. Much of what our economy does is to remove "natural resources" from the environment to make valuable consumer-satisfying stuff. However, once this stuff has done its job, and satisfied wants and needs, we return it to the environment. In some cases, the returned materials can be easily incorporated back into the natural scheme of things; in other cases, the environment and the people who live in it are harmed. To lessen pollution problems we have to find a way to return these materials to the environment in the least-damaging manner.

maturity That date at which the principle on a bond or similar financial asset needs to be repaid. Maturity dates can be anywhere from a few hours to 30 or more years. For example, government securities are classified by their maturity dates, with Treasury bills maturing in 1 year or less, Treasury notes in 1 to 10 years, and Treasury bonds in 10 years or more. Financial assets with maturity dates of a year or less are traded in money markets, while those with longer maturity dates are traded in capital markets. Interest rates tend to be significantly affected by maturity dates. Under normal (nonrecessionary) conditions, shorter maturity periods carry lower interest rates, while longer maturities need higher interest rates to compensate for the uncertainty of tying funds up for longer periods.

mediation Intervention by an impartial third party to settle disputes between two others. The actions of this third party—the mediator—are *not* legally binding. Mediators are frequently used in "collective bargaining" negotiations when unions and their employers have reached an impasse.

Mediators help both sides work out a satisfactory agreement, but neither side is legally compelled to follow the mediator's advice. Compare "arbitration."

merger The consolidation of two separately owned businesses under single ownership. This can be accomplished through a mutual, "friendly" agreement by both parties, or through a "hostile takeover," in which one business gets ownership without cooperation from the other. Mergers fall into one of three classes: (1) *horizontal*—two competing firms in the same industry that sell the same products; (2) *vertical*—two firms in different stages of the production of one good, such that the output of one business is the input of the other; and (3) *conglomerate*—two firms that are in totally, completely separated industries. In that horizontal mergers tend to reduce the number of competitors in a market, the government keeps a close eye on them to see if they violate "antitrust law." Vertical and conglomerate mergers can reduce competition, but are less likely to do so than horizontal mergers. See "cartel," "collusion," "monopoly."

migration The relocation or movement of permanent residence from one place to another. This includes people who move from one city to another, one state to another, or one country to another. It also includes those who move from rural areas to cities. Migration, however, usually doesn't include those who move from one part of a city to another part. This distinction stems from the role migration plays in the supply of labor. Most cities and their immediate surrounding area contain what is termed a "local labor market." Those who work there also live there, and vice versa. As such, migration is concerned only with movements that change the amount of labor in any local labor market. In general, migration results from real or perceived differences between two locales—with people motivated to move to the better area. The

most important differences relate to employment, climate, consumption goods, government, and familiarity with an area. See "immigration," "emigration."

minimum wage A legally established "price floor" on the wage paid to labor. The minimum wage was initiated in the United States in 1938 at a rate of 25 cents per hour. It has been raised numerous times since then, reaching a level in the 1990s of $4.25. The logic behind a minimum wage is to ensure that workers obtain an adequate income for their efforts. Workers, and their supporters in government, are rightfully concerned that businesses will use their market control to offer embarrassingly low wages, especially to people who have few alternatives. The problem with the minimum wage, as with other price floors, is that it tends to be inefficient and create a surplus—in this case unemployment. However, the big struggle is not over labor market efficiency as much as it is over the second or third estate and which has the most political and economic clout. The second estate favors low wages and an ample supply of cheap labor, while the third estate hopes to reallocate some of the economic pie in its direction.

misery index The sum of the "unemployment rate" and the "inflation rate." For example, a 5-percent unemployment rate and a 3-percent inflation rate gives us a misery index of 8. This index was developed during the 1970s when inflation and unemployment were both moving in the upward direction. In previous decades, higher unemployment was usually accompanied by lower inflation, and vice versa. This index was thus developed to show just how bad things really were. Unfortunately, it doesn't have a whole lot of meaning. A misery index of 8, with a 4-percent unemployment rate and 4-percent inflation rate, describes an entirely different economy that one with a 7-percent unemployment rate and a 1-percent inflation rate. Use this index with caution.

monetary policy The Federal Reserve System's use of the money supply to stabilize the "business cycle." As the nation's central bank, the Federal Reserve System determines the total amount of money circulating around the economy. In principle, the Fed can use three different "tools"—"open-market operations," the "discount rate," and "reserve requirements"—to manipulate the money supply. In practice, however, the primary tool employed is open-market operations. To counter a recession, the Fed would undertake expansionary policy, also termed "easy money." To reduce inflation, contractionary policy is the order of the day and goes by the name "tight money." Unlike "fiscal policy" that requires some sort of agreement between Congress and the President, monetary policy is much easier to implement. It requires only the actions of seven people who serve as the Board of Governors of the Federal Reserve System (and hopefully those seven know what they're doing). Moreover, monetary policy is less subject to the political shenanigans that have created our large federal deficit over the years. And expansionary monetary policy, unlike expansionary fiscal policy, tends to reduce interest rates and thus promote, rather than inhibit, investment in capital and economic growth. See "Federal Open Market Committee."

money Anything (with emphasis here on the "any") that's generally accepted as payment for goods, services, and other stuff. In the good old U.S.A., money includes currency, coins, and checking-account balances, all of which are commonly used to make payments. The currency part is Federal Reserve notes issued by each of the 12 Federal Reserve Banks. Together with coins minted under the authority of the U. S. Treasury, paper currency constitutes about 25 percent of to the money supply. The remaining 75 percent comes from checking account balances at our nation's banks, credit

unions, and (the last few remaining) savings and loan associations. While checking accounts are technically under the jurisdiction of banks, they are indirectly controlled through the actions of the Federal Reserve System. (To see how this works, check out "fractional-reserve banking" and "monetary policy.") The total of currency, checking-account balances, and a few other minor items (like traveler's checks) constitute what the Fed officially labels "M1." The Fed also has an M2 and other M-numbers that include bank accounts and other financial assets. See "liquidity."

money market A financial market that trades Treasury bills, commercial paper, and other short-term financial instruments. This market is often used by businesses when they need short-term funds to bridge the gap between paying operating costs and collecting revenue from product sales. As such, the term "money" in "money market" indicates that businesses are using highly liquid instruments to raise the money needed for operating expenses. Compare "capital market."

monopoly A market with a single seller. The lack of competition for the seller gives it extensive "market control." When a monopoly seller exerts its control over a market, the price tends to be higher and the quantity exchanged is less than that achieved by a competitive market, resulting in an inefficient allocation of our resources. This is one type of "market failure." While a monopoly seller can control the market price, however, it can charge no more than the maximum "demand price" that buyers are willing to pay. Because profit tends to be higher for monopoly sellers than for businesses with little or no market control many businesses, especially "big business," are inclined to pursue monopoly status. Much of this pursuit, however, has been outlawed by "antitrust laws." Because of the problems they cause, examples of unregulated monopolies are not widespread in our economy. See "monop-sony," "natural monopoly."

monopsony A market with a single buyer. The lack of competition for the buyer gives it extensive "market control." When a monopsony buyer exerts its control over a market, the price tends to be lower and the quantity exchanged is less than that achieved by a competitive market, resulting in an inefficient allocation of our resources. While a monopsony buyer can control the market price, it can pay, however, no less than the minimum "supply price" that sellers need to receive to cover their production cost. A good example of a monopsony buyer is given by a large business that employs most of the workers in a small town. Compare "monopoly."

most-favored nation A condition, usually as part of a trade agreement among nations (see "General Agreement on Tariffs and Trade"), that ensures that one country will extend its least restrictive "trade barriers" to another country. Suppose, for example, the good old U.S. of A. makes the Republic of Northwest Queoldiola a most-favored nation. If the United States then eliminates tariffs on sundials imported from Brazil, it must also eliminate tariffs on imported Queoldiolan sundials. Because countries have generally followed this most-favored nation system for several decades, international bickering over trade barriers has been significantly reduced. See "foreign trade."

multilateral An action, often used in terms of an international trade agreement, that's extended to more than two parties. As such, a multilateral trade agreement is between several countries. For example, the United States might enter into a multilateral agreement with every country in North and South America that reduces trade barriers on the exports and imports of food products. The General Agreement on Tariffs and Trade is one of the more well-known examples of a multilateral trade agreement. Compare "bilateral," "most-favored nation," "unilateral."

multinational company A business that operates in two or more countries. With increased foreign trade, many businesses in the United States, as well as in other nations, have found it worthwhile to open offices, branch plants, distribution centers, etc., around the globe. Almost all of the "big boys," like General Motors, Sony, IBM, British Petroleum, Mitsubishi, and Exxon, are multinational companies. As multinational companies grow bigger and extend their operations worldwide, some people feel that they lose their sense of country loyalty or national identity. See "big business," "foreign investment."

multiplier The cumulatively reinforcing interaction (whew!) between consumption and production that amplifies changes in investment, government spending, or exports. In other words, if businesses decide to increase investment expenditures on capital goods, or if government decides to expand the size of the already bloated federal deficit by spending more on national defense, then our economy's production and income are likely to increase by some multiple of this spending. The amplified increase in production and income, usually from 2 to 5 times, is what gives us the term "multiplier." The process is based on the "circular flow" idea that the people receive income by producing goods and then spend this income on additional production. The multiplicative, cumulatively reinforcing interaction between consumption and production (whew!) is a primary source of "business cycle" instability. Because a drop in investment or government spending is amplified by this multiplier, a minor decline in gross domestic product can be transformed into a major recession. By the same token, once the economy begins a recovery, the multiplier amplifies this into a self-reinforcing expansion.

mutual fund A company that pools the funds of hundreds or thousands of individuals to purchase corporate stocks, bonds, or other financial assets. The objectives of pooling funds is to reduce transactions costs and provide professional management not otherwise available. The most common types of mutual funds are "open ended," so called because there are no limits on the number of shares issued. Others are "close ended" because they issue a fixed number of shares that are then traded around. Mutual funds give consumers the chance to get higher interest rates or returns on the financial investment than available through banks. They also provide the opportunity to participate in "financial markets" that are typically closed to smaller investors.

N

National Association of Securities Dealers A "stock market" in which corporate stocks are exchanged by dealers across the country using a computerized system of stock price quotes. This is often referred to as the "over-the-counter" stock market, because, unlike the New York Stock Exchange, the American Stock Exchange, and others, the dealers don't conduct their business at a single location. They match up their buy-and-sell orders through a computer network rather than through face-to-face contact. Transactions conducted by the NASD give rise to one of the more commonly publicized stock market price indicators, the NASDAQ (which stands for National Association of Securities Dealers Automated Quotation). The widely used NASDAQ composite index is based on the prices of 5,000 of these over-the-counter stocks. See "Dow Jones averages," "Standard & Poor's 500."

national income (NI) The total income earned by all of our economy's resources when they generate production. This is the broadest, most comprehensive measure of income available. Moreover, because it is the sum total of all income *earned* in production, it constitutes the sum total of our income pie available in a given year. Anyone who receives income, whether they've earned it or not, must be getting it from this pie. There is a great deal of redistribution of national income over the course of a given year. Of course, government taxes, especially income taxes and social security taxes, are a big part of the redistribution. Another big part is government transfer payments, including social security benefits and welfare. These assorted redistributions give us two other common measures of income: "personal income" and "disposable personal income." See "gross domestic product," "net domestic product."

natural monopoly A special type of "monopoly" that's able to lower its price when it produces and sells a larger quantity. This somewhat remarkable ability results because a natural monopoly uses a great deal of capital. In that capital carries an up-front cost that must be paid regardless of production, a natural monopoly can spread these costs over larger quantity—if it produces more. The larger the quantity sold, the lower the cost for *each unit.* A single natural monopoly is thus able to produce and supply a good at a lower cost, and price, than two or more firms. In other words, if two or more firms try to supply the same good, the market will "naturally" end up with just one. Common examples of natural monopolies are telephone companies, electrical utilities, natural gas distributors, cable television systems, and, to some degree, airlines, railroads, and other transit companies. Many natural monopolies, especially those that supply essential stuff like electricity, are heavily regulated, controlled, or even out-and-out operated by the government to prevent any of the abuses that monopolies are inclined to perpetrate on the consuming public. See "industry regulation."

natural resources One of the three general categories of resources, or factors of production (see "capital" and "labor"). It is the naturally occurring materials of the planet that are directed toward production—including land, water, wildlife, vegetation, air, climate, sunshine, mineral deposits, and soil nutrients. Natural resources provide the "stuff" that's used to produce all of the tangible products in the economy, including both goods used for immediate consumer satisfaction and capital used for further production. See "environment."

near-public good A good that's easy to keep nonpayers from consuming (see "excludability"), but use of the good by one person doesn't prevent use by others (see "rival consumption"). Examples include transportation, television broadcasts, education, libraries, and relatively small parks. The trick with a near-public good is that it's easy to keep people away, and thus you can charge them a price for consuming, but there's no real good reason to do so. From an efficiency view, the more people who consume a near-public good, the better off our society is: the more, the merrier. This mixture of nearly unlimited benefits and the ability to charge a price means that some near-public goods are sold through markets and others are provided by government. For efficiency's sake, none should be sold through markets. See "common-property good," "private good," "public good."

net domestic product (NDP) The total market value of all final goods and services produced by an economy during a given period of time, usually a year, after deducting the depreciation of capital. NDP needs to be directly compared with "gross domestic product"—the grand total of all production in the economy. The drawback with this grand total of GDP is that some of the production goes for replacing capital that wears out, breaks down, or just becomes technologically obsolete—that is, depreciation. If a great deal of our production goes for depreciation, then GDP might be large, but our economy is really spinning its wheels and going nowhere. By subtracting out depreciation, NDP gives us a measure of the net production that is, shall we say, moving the economy forward. Compare "disposable personal income," "national income," "personal income."

New York Stock Exchange The largest stock market in the United States, located on the famous Wall Street in New York City. This is the big daddy of all stock markets in the country, often referred to as the "big board." It was begun in the 1790s to help fledgling corporations in our fledgling country raise the funds needed for capital investment. All stock transactions (millions each day) are conducted by its members, making membership a pretty valuable commodity. It currently has slightly over a 1,000 members or "seats." The only way to get a seat on the exchange is from a retiring or deceased member. See "American Stock Exchange," "National Association of Securities Dealers."

nominal dollars The actual dollar price of stuff when it's bought or sold. Compare "real dollars."

nontariff barrier Any sort of "trade barrier"—other than a "tariff" or import "quota"—that restricts imports. Some of the more popular nontariff barriers are those that specify the content of a good or how it was produced. There are many valid and important safety, health, and environmental reasons for establishing these sorts of nontariff barriers. However, some barriers can be downright ridiculous. European countries have long played this game with sausages, wines, and other food. For example, France might say that the only wine sold in France must use French grapes. That pretty much keeps out any Italian wine. Likewise, Italy might say that the only sausage sold in Italy must use seasoning made only by Italian producers. So much for importing German sausage into Italy.

nondurable A good bought by consumers that tends to last for less than a year. Common examples are food and clothing. The notable thing about nondurable goods is that consumers tend to continue buying them regardless of the ups and downs of the "business cycle." Compare "durable."

normal profit The opportunity cost of using entrepreneurial abilities in the production of a good, or the economic profit that could have been received in another business. As with the opportunity costs of other resources, normal profit needs to be deducted from revenue to determine economic profit. It is, however, seldom included as an accounting expense when accounting profit is computed.

O

Occupational Safety and Health Administration An agency of the U.S. Department of Labor, established in 1970, that's charged with regulating workplace safety and job-related worker health. It has the authority to impose health and safety rules and, much to the displeasure of businesses, inspect workplaces to ensure that the rules are followed. Some (second-estate) critics argue that their rules are unneeded, overzealous, and counterproductive. Other (third-estate) critics say that their rules are neither stringent enough nor adequately enforced. See "workers' compensation."

Office of Management and Budget (OMB) An office of the executive branch of the federal government, established in 1970, that's designed to help the President prepare the fiscal budget and undertake an assortment of Presidential office-management tasks. The OMB staff are appointed by the President, but unlike other appointments, they do not need Senate confirmation. The duty of preparing the fiscal budget, and what this means

for "fiscal policy," has made the director of the OMB one of the more influential economic positions in the country, ranking just a notch below the chairman of the Federal Reserve System's Board of Governors and the chairman of the Council of Economic Advisors.

Old Age and Survivors Insurance (OASI) See "social security."

open economy An economy with a great deal of "foreign trade." At the extreme, a completely open economy is one that has no trade barriers (see "free trade"). Most of the world's 100-plus nations are relatively open, but much less than they could be because of a wide assortment of trade restrictions. The more an economy is open, the more dependent it is on happenings around the world. Compare "closed economy."

open market operations The Federal Reserve System's buying and selling of government securities in an effort to alter "bank reserves" and subsequently the nation's money supply. These actions, under the direction of the Federal Open Market Committee, are the Fed's number-1, most effective, most often-used tool of monetary policy. If, for example, the Fed wants to increase the money supply (termed "easy money") it buys government securities. The Fed pays for these purchases by adding reserves to the banking system. The reserves are then used by banks for loans to consumers and businesses, which results in an increase in the total of checking-account balances in the economy. In that checking accounts are three-fourths of the money supply, this is the Fed's method of increasing the money supply in lieu of printing money. If the Fed chooses to reduce the money supply, called "tight money," it sells some government securities, which reduces bank reserves, restricts the ability of banks to make loans, and thus puts a lid on the money supply. Compare "discount rate," "reserve requirements."

opportunity cost The highest-valued alternative given up to pursue any sort of activity. This is a hallmark of anything dealing with economics—or life for that matter—because any action that you take prevents you from doing something else. The value—expressed in terms of satisfaction—of the untaken activity is your opportunity cost. Because there are usually several alternatives that aren't pursued, opportunity cost is the highest-valued one. An opportunity cost is sometimes compensated with some form of payment, like a wage. However, the existence of an opportunity cost is independent of any actual cash outlay. See "accounting profit," "normal profit."

option A contract that gives the buyer an "option" to complete a transaction within a given time period. Options are used frequently in "financial markets." For example, you might purchase an option to buy 100 shares of Omni Conglomerate, Inc., stock at $50 a share within the next 30 days. Regardless of what happens to the price of Omni Conglomerate, Inc., stock, you can to exercise this option within the time allotted. Of course, you pay a price for this right, and if you don't exercise the option, then you lose this up-front fee. When would you exercise the option and when would you choose to lose the fee? If the going, market price of Omni stock in our example is above a $50 option price within the 30-day period, you can exercise the option, and resell the stock at the higher market price. If the price remains below $50, you don't exercise the option and forfeit the up-front fee. See "futures," "hedging," "speculation."

P

partnership One of the three basic forms of business organization (see "corporation" and "proprietorship"). It's a business that's owned and operated equally by two or more people. The owners and the business are legally considered one and the same. As such, each owner has "unlimited liability," which means that an owner is held personally responsible for any and all of the business's debts, including those made by a partner. An owner can lose personal property over and above the amount invested in the business itself. In that partners are legally responsible for each others' mistakes, partnerships tend to be relatively small, with only a handful of people involved. This form of business is common for professional types, like lawyers, accountants, dentists, and physicians. See "small business."

per-unit tax A tax that is specified as a fixed amount for each unit of a good sold. Federal excise taxes on gasoline and cigarettes fall into this per-unit tax category. Compare "ad valorem tax."

personal income The total income received by consumers. This includes most of the national income earned in the production of "gross domestic product," with two important modifications. First, income that's earned but not received by consumers is deducted. The best example of this is the social security tax on wages. Second, income that's received but not earned in the production of gross domestic product is added in. Examples of this include an assortment of transfer payments, like welfare and social security benefits. Personal income is one of the three official measures of income regularly published by the Department of Commerce. The other two are "national income" and "disposable personal income."

personal income tax A tax on individual income. This is the primary source of revenue for the federal government, a big source for many state and local governments, and the reason most people dread April 15th. In principle, personal income taxes are progressive, based on a graduated tax scale. However, it's much more proportional today than it was several decades ago.

pollution Any waste material from consumption or production that causes damages or otherwise imposes an "opportunity cost" when it's returned to the natural environment. Pollution is one of the more prevalent examples of an "externality cost" and "market failure" (see "materials balance"). Examples include, but by no means are limited to, car exhaust, municipal sewage, industrial waste, and agricultural chemical run-off from farms. Pollution waste can be classified as degradable, persistent, or nondegradable, depending on how easily it can be broken down into nonharmful form by the natural environment. Pollution problems can never be eliminated, but they can be handled with efficiency if the amount of pollution is such that the cost of damages is the same as the cost of cleanup.

potential gross domestic product The total output that the economy *could* produce if resources were at full employment. If the economy *is* at "full employment" (a 5-percent unemployment rate) then actual gross domestic product is equal to potential gross domestic product. Of course, if the unemployment rate is greater than 5 percent, then actual production is less potential production. By calculating potential gross domestic product, we can figure out exactly how far below this potential we are. This information then can be used by government economists to recommend appropriate "monetary" or "fiscal policies." See "full-employment budget."

poverty A condition in which a person lacks many of the basic necessities of life and the income needed to buy them. If this seems like a fuzzy concept, it is. Poverty is often a subjective notion, because the notion of basic necessities is also subjective. While everyone needs food for life, will a handful of wild grain do the trick, or do you need an evening of fine dining? While there are no once-and-for-all, clear-cut answers, our good

friends with the government have developed a so-called "poverty" line used as an official measure of who's in poverty and who's not. Most importantly, this poverty line is used to determine who's eligible to receive welfare and other forms of public assistance.

preferred stock See "corporate stock."

premium In financial terms, a bond or similar financial asset that sells above its face value. A premium is paid to equalize a bond's interest rate with comparable interest rates. For example, a $100,000 bond that pays a fixed 10-percent interest on the face value ($10,000) would sell at a premium of $125,000 if comparable interest rates were 8 percent. As such, the $10,000 interest works out to be 8 percent of the $125,000 price. Compare "discount."

present value The amount of money today that, after interest is added, would have the same value as an amount some time in the future. For example, $100 today, given a 10-percent interest rate, would have a value of $110 in 1 year ($100 plus $10 in interest). Conversely, $110 in 1 year, given a 10-percent interest rate, would be equivalent to $100 today. Here's a simple little formula that will let you find the present value of any future payment: $PV = FP/(1 + i)n$, where PV is the present value you want to find, FP is the future payment, i is the annual interest rate, and n is the number of years until the future payment. The process of translating a future payment into its present value, such an amount to be received when a bond reaches its date of maturity, is often termed "discounting." See "discount."

price ceiling A legally established maximum price. The government is occasionally inclined to keep the price of one good or another from rising too high. Examples include apartments, gasoline, and natural gas. While the goal is invariably a noble one—like keeping stuff affordable for poor people—a price ceiling often does more harm than good. First, it usually creates a shortage, meaning that many of the buyers who are being protected against high prices can't even buy the good. Second, as a consequence of this shortage, a price ceiling is likely to generate a "black market" where the good is sold illegally above the price ceiling. Compare "price floor."

price discrimination Charging different prices to different buyers for the same good. This is an age-old practice for suppliers who have achieved some degree of "market control," especially those with a monopoly. The reason for price discrimination, of course, is higher profit. To be a successful price discriminator you must do a couple of things: (1) identify two or more groups who are willing to pay different prices, and (2) keep the buyers in one group from reselling their stuff to the other. In this way, you will be able to charge each group what they, and they alone, are willing to pay. Examples of price discrimination abound in our economy, including electricity rates, telephone long-distance charges, movie ticket prices, airplane ticket prices, and assorted child or senior citizen discounts. In each case, the buyers can't trade back and forth, and they're willing to pay different prices.

price fixing An agreement by two or more firms in an industry to charge the same price and avoid competing with each other. This is one of the methods businesses use to practice "collusion" or form a "cartel." It is, by the way, against "antitrust law."

price floor A legally established minimum price. Pressured by special-interest groups, our beloved government is often convinced that the price of a good needs to be kept at a higher level. Examples of goods that have had price floors bestowed on them include farm products and workers (see "minimum wage). The argument in both of these examples is that suppliers aren't getting enough

income for the stuff they sell (food or labor). A higher price is then expected to generate more income to these deserving souls. Unfortunately, price floors tend to create as many or more problems than they solve. They create inefficient surpluses. For food, this often means tons of stuff rotting in warehouses. For labor, it means potential workers aren't employed. Price floors also encourage suppliers to continue supplying stuff inefficiently. This has kept farmers doing their farming thing when they should be in some other line of business. Compare "price floor."

price-earnings ratio The ratio of the current price for one share of corporate stock to the earnings (profit) per share of stock. This is used by many financial analysts and investors as an indicator of a company's performance and potential for future growth. A relatively high price-earnings ratio suggests that investors think the company has a great deal of future growth potential. It can also be a sign, however, that the company is seriously overpriced and due for a big drop. See "speculation."

prime rate The interest rate banks charge their best, most credit-worthy customers. This is one of the key interest rates in the economy, and it is watched closely by financial types, government policymakers, and businesses. It's also an interest rate that should be watched closely by consumers who have loans with adjustable rates, like credit cards, that are "pegged" to the prime rate. Any movement in the prime rate triggers an automatic change in these adjustable rates. Compare "federal funds rate," "discount rate."

principal/agent problem A source of inefficiency in the way large businesses and governments are operated that occurs because those making decision (agents) have different goals than those affected by the decisions (principals). A great example is that of a corporation's management and it's shareholders. The shareholders—the owners of the corporation—are the principals interested in earning a nice profit. The managers of the firm play the part of the owners' agents. As agents they're supposed to be doing what's best for the owners. The managers, however, might be inclined to sacrifice a little of the owners' profit by bumping up their own salaries, employing more staff than really needed, or padding their own expense accounts. Shareholders are probably unaware of what the managers are doing. The owners might not know that their profits could have been a few percentage points higher. The managers are able to get away with this because they make the decisions and they have the information. You can probably see a similar problem with elected politicians and voters. As voters, we're often in the dark concerning our leaders' activities. Politicians have the opportunity and usually the incentive to pad their own pockets at our expense. See "logrolling."

private good A good that's easy to keep nonpayers from consuming (see "excludability), and use of the good by one person prevents use by others (see "rival consumption). Examples include almost anything that you can buy at a grocery store or shopping mall. The reason for this is that private goods are privately owned and can be sold to others for a price. For efficiency, it's best for these goods to be traded through markets without any direct government involvement (except in cases of a market failure). See "common-property good," "near-public good," "public good."

producer price index (PPI) An index that includes the wholesale prices of finished products and the prices of raw materials, intermediate goods, and other inputs used by businesses to produce output. The news guys often refer to this as the "wholesale" price index. Like the "consumer price index," it's compiled by the Department of Labor using a fixed "market" basket of stuff. Each month, number crunchers calculate the cost of this market basket, which is then compared with the cost in a "base year." The ratio of the current year with the base year cost gives us the PPI. The PPI—as an indicator of input costs—is most often used to forewarn what's likely to happen to consumer prices within the next few months. See "inflation."

producers' surplus The price sellers receive for a good over and above their opportunity cost of production. This is the difference between the price actually charged and the sellers' minimum "supply price." Most producers, even those operating in efficient competitive markets, get some producers' surplus. Buyers can confiscate part of this producers' surplus for their very own if they have more "market control" than the sellers. Compare "consumers' surplus." See "economic rent," "efficiency."

product differentiation Making goods that are essentially the same slightly different to increase sales. Many of the best-known businesses in our economy practice this technique of product differentiation to gain an advantage on the competition. For example, Coca-Cola and Pepsi-Cola are very similar, but each has a few differences in terms of taste, packaging, and esteem. Product differentiation is usually achieved through advertising. With product differentiation, each producer gains a bit of "market control" and is able to charge a slightly (or even a whole lot) higher price for its product. (Do you prefer Coke or Pepsi, and would you be willing to pay more for your choice?) While some product differences are little more than the hot air of advertising, others are very real and let consumers satisfy the hidden nooks and crannies of their desires. In fact, if not for product differentiation, we would all have really boring lives.

product market A market used to exchange the finished goods and services. Such a market could exchange consumer goods, capital goods, or the stuff purchased by government. A product market, however, doesn't include raw materials, resources, or any type of intermediate goods. The total value of stuff that's exchanged in product markets each year is measured by "gross domestic product." Compare "financial market," "resource market." See "circular flow."

production The transformation of natural resources using labor and capital into consumer-satisfying goods or capital. When you get right down to it, this is pretty much what our life on this planet is all about. We use and improve the stuff that comes with the planet to maintain and enhance our lives. Our most noted and most official measure of production is "gross domestic product."

profit As a generic term, this is the difference between revenue and cost. There are, however, three specific sorts of profit, each with a different meaning. "Accounting profit" is the difference between revenue and accounting expenses. "Economic profit" is the difference between revenue and the opportunity cost of production. "Normal profit" is the economic profit that could be earned by an entrepreneur in another business and is thus an opportunity cost deducted from revenue when calculating economic profit.

progressive tax A tax in which people with more income pay a larger percentage in taxes. A progressive tax is given by this example: You earn $10,000 a year and your boss gets $20,000. You pay $1,000 in taxes (10 percent) and your boss pays $4,000 in taxes (20 percent). Our income tax system is designed to be progressive, but assorted loopholes and deductions keep it from being as progressive in practice as it is on paper. Compare "proportional tax," "regressive tax." See "graduated tax."

promissory note A written agreement to pay a specific amount of money at a specific time to a specific person with a specific interest rate charged until repayment

is accomplished. Promissory notes are the most common method of formalizing consumer loan contracts. If you've borrowed the money needed to buy a house or car, then you've undoubtedly signed a promissory note. Promissory notes are also frequently used by businesses and government to borrow money. See "corporate bond," "credit," "government security."

property rights The legal ownership of resources, which entitles the owner to receive the benefits or pay the cost of the resources' productive activities. The notion of property rights came originally from the ownership of land (and the natural resources of the land), but it's equally important for labor and capital resources. In other words, your labor ownership gives you the *right* to be paid for your work. When resource owners have clearly defined property rights, resource allocation tends to be relatively efficient. That's because the owners won't let others use their resources unless they get adequate compensation for their opportunity cost. I won't sell my car (transfer the property rights to someone else) unless I'm paid what I think it's worth. While it would seem as though property rights are a cut-and-dried issue, either you own a resource or you don't; controversy and conflict are always lurking around the corner. The most notable is "common-property goods," such as rivers, lakes, oceans, and the atmosphere. In that the "public" owns them, in effect "no one" really owns them. These resources have no clear-cut property rights and can't be efficiently bought and sold through markets. The result is over-use, pollution, and congestion. The solution would seem to be giving, selling, or otherwise assigning someone the property rights for these resources, who would then see to their efficient allocation. But there are two problems with this. First, who gets the property rights. An equal share for everyone? The wealthy get more? The poor get more? Would property rights

property tax A tax on property or real estate. This is a popular tax at the local level for cities, counties, and school districts. In many places, it has been a primary source of funding for public schools. Because this invariably leads to tremendous differences in school funding, with wealthy areas getting the most funding, schools have moved toward income taxes and sales taxes for revenue.

proportional tax A tax in which people pay the same percentage of income in taxes regardless of their incomes. Here's an example of a proportional tax: You earn $10,000 a year and your boss gets $20,000. You pay $1,000 in taxes (10 percent) and your boss pays $2,000 in taxes (10 percent). While a proportional tax would seem to make a lot of sense, very few taxes are designed to be proportional, and even fewer come out that way in practice. The reason is often attributable to the ongoing battle between the second and third estates. Each side wants the other to pay a larger share of taxes. Compare "progressive tax," "regressive tax."

proprietorship One of the three basic forms of business organization (see "corporation" and "partnership"). It's a business that's owned and operated by one person. The owner and the business are legally considered one and the same. As such, the owner gets any and all profit and has what is term "unlimited liability"—the owner is held personally responsible for any and all of the business's debts. The owner can lose personal property over and above the amount invested in the business itself. The majority of businesses in our economy are proprietorships, but because their size is limited by the resources of a single person, they tend to be relatively small. See "small business."

prosperity A period of sustained growth that often lasts for a decade or two. A prosperity usually includes several separate business cycles, each with relatively mild recessions and very vigorous,

healthy expansions. The United States enjoyed prosperity from the late-1940s into the mid-1960s, a period that many look fondly on as our "golden age." The prosperity of this period, as is often the case, was the direct aftermath of a severe depression. In particular, the restructuring needed to achieve a period of extended prosperity was a hallmark of the Great Depression of the 1930s. See "institution."

public debt See "government debt."

public good A good that's difficult to keep nonpayers from consuming (see "excludability"), and use of the good by one person doesn't prevent use by others (see "rival consumption"). Examples include national defense, a clean environment, and any 4th of July fireworks display. Public goods are invariably provided by government because there's no way a private business can profitably produce them. Private businesses can't sell public goods in markets, because they can't charge a price and keep nonpaying people away (see "free-rider problem"). Moreover, businesses shouldn't charge a price, because there's no opportunity cost for extra consumers. For efficiency, government needs to pay for public goods through taxes. See "common-property good," "private good," "public good."

purchasing power In general the quantities of goods and services that can be bought with a given amount of money. The notable feature of purchasing power is that it declines as prices rise. In particular, "inflation" is the number-1 nemesis of purchasing power. When inflation gives higher prices, purchasing power falls. Be careful, though, that you don't get too caught up in the purchasing power of just a single dollar. The real question is not how much stuff one dollar can buy, but how many dollars you have. In other words, while the price of a brand new car might have been $10 when you were a kid (in the good old days), the average annual income was also $20. That's the same purchasing power as a $10,000 car price and a $20,000 income. See "cost of living," "real dollars," "nominal dollars."

purchasing-power parity The notion that the exchange rate between two currencies should reflect the relative prices of goods purchased in their respective countries. Suppose, for example, that sundials sell for $50 in the United States and 100 queolds in Northwest Queoldiola. Purchasing-power parity then exists if the exchange rate is 2 queolds per dollar. While this parity tends to hold for goods that enter the foreign-trade game, it doesn't necessarily hold for the many goods that are produced and consumed without ever crossing a national boundary. Nor does this parity exist if governments are manipulating exchange rates (see "fixed exchange rate").

Q

quota A limit on the quantity of some sort of activity. Two of the more-noted quotas are for "employment" and "imports." Employment quotas have been used as a means of providing increased opportunities to blacks, Hispanics, women, and other groups that have been historically subject to discrimination. Such quotas, however, tend to anger other groups, especially white males, who don't get favorable treatment. While employment or similar antidiscrimination quota systems might help address historical problems, they are not without cost. In particular, our economy's efficiency is likely to suffer if a less-qualified member of an ethnic group is selected over someone who is more qualified. Import quotas have similar problems. They are one form of "trade barrier" (see "nontariff barrier," "tariff") that's usually intended to reduce the competition faced by a domestic producer. In that an import quota restricts the quantity of goods imported, domestic producers gain greater "market control" and can charge higher prices. This may be good for producers, but it's bad for consumers.

R

rate of return The ratio of the additional annual income or profit generated by an investment to the cost of the investment. Here's a simple example, although the calculations are usually a great deal more involved for actual investments: If the cost of constructing a new factory is $10 million, and it gives you an extra $1 million in profit each year, then its rate of return is 10 percent. If a business is pondering the possibility of constructing this factory, this rate of return needs to be compared with the rates of return on other investment projects or interest rates in the financial markets. The bottom line, quite literally, for a business is to direct that $10 million to the highest rate of return or interest rate. This decision is straightforward once you have the rate of return. Complications in calculating the rate of return, however, arise if (1) construction costs are spread out over several years, (2) the extra profit varies from year to year, or (3) the factory is used only for a given number of years before it's shut down. Moreover, the biggest complication in calculating any rate of return is our uncertain future. You never know for sure how much extra profit or income you'll get in the future. But of course, this uncertainty is what makes investing both exciting and nerve racking. The rate of return is not only an integral part of business investment in capital, it's also applicable to other sorts of investment, such as that in education, human capital, or government spending on infrastructure. Calculating the rates of return on these become even more difficult because "income" or other returns are difficult to measure.

rational abstention The decision *not* to do something because the cost of doing it is more than the expected benefit. While this is a common part of everyday life, it's particularly important for voting. During a given election, a number of potential voters are likely to choose *not* to vote because they expect to get little or no benefit from doing so. As our society becomes more complex, with people increasingly engaged in a myriad of valuable activities and politicians further removed from the mainstream lives of consumers, we can expect rational abstention, that is voter apathy, to become more common. The problem, however, with rational abstention is that those elected to office may not truly reflect the interests of the public. See "principal/agent problem," "rational ignorance."

rational ignorance The decision *not* to become informed about something because the cost of doing it is more than the expected benefit. In that information is costly, there's always some limit to how much anyone can know. The idea of rational ignorance, while popping up on a daily basis for most of us, is quite important come election time. Many voters decide, logically so, that it's not really worth their efforts to get *all* of the details on every candidate and issue on the ballot. Of course, the result is that candidates get elected and issues get passed that might not be best for the voters. If only they had known. . . . See "principal/agent problem," "rational abstention."

real dollars The value after adjusting for "inflation." Economists are frequently interested in comparing stuff (production, income, or whatever) in one year with similar stuff in another year. However, in that inflation can distort such a comparison, it's best made using a fixed set of prices that eliminate an inflationary change. In practice, this is accomplished by using the prices in an arbitrary "base year." Once the price differences have been eliminated, the numbers are said to be measured in real dollars. Compare "nominal dollars." See "real gross domestic product," "real interest rate."

real gross domestic product The value of our economy's "gross domestic product" after adjusting for "inflation." It's found by asking, then answering, this simple question: What's the value of our GDP if we use the prices charged for stuff during some other year? This "other year" is termed a base year. By calculating this year's GDP as well as last year's GDP using prices from the base year, we can eliminate any change in GDP resulting from changing prices. A comparison of real GDP between years gives us changes attributed exclusively to production. As such, real GDP is a much better indicator of the health and vitality of the economy than GDP that's not adjusted for inflation. For example, a 10-percent increase in prices, with no change in physical production, would give us an *apparent* 10-percent increase in GDP. But this 10-percent increase is in name only. Our economy isn't 10 percent better off. We don't have 10 percent more stuff to satisfy our needs. Real GDP is the measure to use if you're concerned about recessions, recoveries, and "business cycles." See "GDP price deflator," "nominal dollars," "purchasing power," "real dollars," "real interest rate."

real interest rate The market, or "nominal interest rate," after adjusting for "inflation." This is the interest rate lenders receive and borrowers pay expressed in "real dollars." There are two ways to think about the real interest rate: (1) the historical, after-the-fact interest rate and (2) the desired interest rate lenders and borrowers have in mind when entering into a loan. The first one is straightforward. If the market interest rate is 10 percent and the inflation rate is 3 percent, then the real, inflation-adjusted real interest rate is 7 percent, the difference between the two. This tells us the purchasing power of any interest payments received or paid. The second way of looking at the real interest rate is a little more subjective because it's based on expectations of the future. If lenders *need* to receive a real interest rate of 7 percent, and they anticipate that the inflation rate will be 3 percent next year, then they will charge a 10-percent nominal interest rate (see also "inflation premium"). Of course, the real, after-the-fact interest rate could be different from the desired real interest rate if the actual rate of inflation turns out to be different from the anticipated rate. Expectations of future inflation rates play havoc with market interest rates. They rise and fall for no other reason than that borrowers and lenders *think* the inflation rate might change. See "nominal dollars," "real gross domestic product."

recession The common term used for the contraction phase of the business cycle.

recovery A transition phase of the "business cycle" after a recession has ended and before a full-blown expansion begins. During a recovery, the unemployment rate remains relatively high, but the growth of real gross domestic product rapidly increases. The recovery phase tends to last from about 6 months to a year. However, because it tends to melt into an expansion, there's usually no clear-cut end to a recovery.

regressive tax A tax in which people with more income pay a smaller percentage in taxes. A regressive tax is given by this example: You earn $10,000 a year and your boss gets $20,000. You pay $2,000 in taxes (20 percent) while your boss also pays $2,000 in taxes (10 percent). Examples of regressive taxes abound (is this surprising given the political clout of the wealthy?), including sales tax, excise tax, and social security tax. Compare "proportional tax," "progressive tax."

regulation Government rules or laws that control the activities of businesses and consumers. The word "regulation" is usually uttered by leaders of the second estate through clenched teeth and followed by a barrage of profanity. The motivation for regulation is that businesses are inclined to do things that are harmful to the public—actions that need to be prevented or otherwise controlled. Regulation is really nothing more than an extension of government's authority to protect one member of society from another. It tends to take one of two forms: (1) industry regulation that's intended to prevent firms from gaining and abusing excessive "market control" and (2) social regulation that seeks to protect consumers for problems caused by pollution, unsafe products, and the lack of information (see "market failure"). Most regulation takes the form of government decree: "Thou shalt do this or not do that." Examples include pollution limits on car exhaust, technical specifications for building construction, and content labeling of breakfast cereals. However, other sorts of regulatory tools are also used, such as taxes, licensing requirements, and price controls. While there are any number of really, *really* dumb government regulations that tend to hurt more than they help, our economy could not function without government supervision. See "antitrust laws."

rent seeking The inclination of everyone who is alive and breathing to get as much as they can for themselves. This stems from the idea of economic rent, which is a payment over or above the "opportunity cost." People are said to be rent seeking when they try to get higher wages, more profit, or any other payment over or above the minimum they would be willing to accept. See "special-interest group."

reservation price The lowest price at which a supplier is willing to supply any amount of a good. This is usually based on the minimum cost of production. For labor, it's the lowest wage that makes it worthwhile to get up in the morning, miss your favorite daytime television shows, and go to work. See "supply price."

reserve requirements Rules by the Federal Reserve System governing the amount of bank reserves that banks must keep to back up their deposits. Legal reserve requirements came about because banks that practice "fractional-reserve banking" are sometimes inclined to make too many interest-paying loans and neglect to keep enough reserves on hand to pay their depositors. In the 1800s, this type of indiscretion forced many banks to close down and created several economywide bank panics. In principle, the Fed can alter reserve requirements to control the money supply. In practice, however, the Fed prefers to use "open-market operations" or the "discount rate." Reserve requirements tend to be in the range of 3 to 10 percent for checking accounts, and less for savings accounts, certificates of deposit, and other types of bank accounts.

resource Anything that falls into one of three general categories of inputs—labor, capital, or natural resources—used to produce consumer-satisfying stuff. A special category of human effort—entrepreneurship—is sometimes added to this list. Resources are often given the more descriptive term "factors of production," which you should work into any conversation you're having with a roomful of pointy-headed economists.

resource market A market used to exchange the services of resources: labor, capital, and natural resources. The value of services exchanged through resource markets each year is measured as national income. Compare "financial market," "product market." See "circular flow."

revaluation The act of increasing the price ("exchange rate") of one nation's currency in terms of other currencies. This is done by the government if it wants to raise the price of the country's exports and lower the price of foreign imports. This is an appropriate action if the country is running an undesired trade surplus with other countries. The procedure for revaluation is for the government to buy the nation's currency and/or sell foreign currencies through the "foreign-exchange market." Compare "devaluation." See "appreciation."

right-to-work A law preventing employers from making "union" membership a condition of employment. In other words, your boss can't force you to join a union if you don't want to. There are two sides to this argument. On the one hand, workers should have the freedom to join a union or not based on the benefit had from the union and perhaps their philosophical orientation towards unions. On the other hand, unions gain their strength by representing workers. Its negotiating position is hurt if it represents only a fraction of the workers. Moreover, any benefits a union gets for workers are enjoyed by its members (who pay dues) as well as nonmembers (who don't pay dues). This is another one of the big-time debates between the second and third estates.

risk The possibility of gain or loss. Risk, the calculated *probability* of different events happening, is usually contrasted with "uncertainty," the *possibility* that any number of things could happen. For example, uncertainty is the possibility that you could win or lose $100 on the flip of a coin. You don't know which will happen; it could go either way. Risk, in contrast, is the 50-percent chance of winning $100 and the 50-percent chance of losing $100 on the flip of the coin. You know (or think you know) that your probability of winning or losing is 50 percent because the coin has a 50-percent chance of coming up either heads or tails. The probabilities that we assign to different possibilities, as we turn uncertainty into risk, can be objectively or subjectively determined. An objective determination is based on historical information, some sort of statistical analysis, or perhaps the implications of a sophisticated theory. A subjective determination could involve nothing more than a "gut" reaction, hunch, or semieducated guess. See "financial market," "insurance," "profit," "risk averse," "risk loving," "risk neutral," "risk pooling," "risk premium."

risk averse A person who values a certain income more than an equal amount of income that involves "risk" or "uncertainty." To illustrate, let's say that you're given two options: (1) a guaranteed $1,000 or (2) a 50:50 chance of getting either $500 or $1,500. If you chose option (1), then you're risk averse. Both options give you the same "expected" values. In other words, if you select option (2) a few hundred times, then your average amount over those few hundred times is $1,000. The notable thing about risk averse people is that they're willing to pay something to avoid a risky situation. While you would not only take option (1) over option (2), if you're risk averse, you also might be willing to take option (1) if it only guaranteed $900. That is, you would be willing to pay $100, a risk premium, to avoid the risk of option (2). This willingness to pay is a basic need that makes "insurance" a profitable business. Compare "risk loving," "risk neutral." See "hedging," "risk pooling."

risk loving A person who values a certain income less than an equal amount of income that involves risk or uncertainty. Suppose that you have two options: (1) a guaranteed $1,000 or (2) a 50:50 chance of getting either $500 or $1,500. If you chose option (2), then you're risk loving. While both options give you the same "expected" values, you get more satisfaction from the risky option than the guaranteed one. In fact, risk-loving people are willing to pay for the opportunity to experience a risky situation. Such thrill is what lies at the heart of the gambling industry. It's also behind amusement park thrill rides, sky diving, bungee jumping, and entrepreneurship. Compare "risk averse," "risk neutral." See "speculation."

risk neutral A person who values a certain income the same as an equal amount of income that involves risk or uncertainty. Let's say that you're given two

options: (1) a guaranteed $1,000 or (2) a 50:50 chance of getting either $500 or $1,500. If you don't really care which option you chose, because both options have the same "expected" values, then you're risk neutral. Compare "risk averse," "risk loving."

risk pooling Combining the uncertainty of individuals into a calculable risk for large groups. For example, you may or may not contract the flu this year. It's the sort of uncertainty in life that can drive you crazy. However, if you're thrown in with 99,999 other people, then health care types, who spend their lives measuring the odds of an illness, can predict that 1 percent of the group, or 1,000 people, will get the flu. The uncertainty is that they probably don't know which 1,000 people; they only know the number afflicted. This little bit of information is what makes risk pooling possible. If the cost is $50 per illness, then an insurance company can insure your 100,000-member group against flu if the company collects $50,000 ($50 x 1,000 sick people), or 50 cents per person. By agreeing to pay the cost of each sick person in exchange for the 50-cent payments, the insurance company has effectively pooled the risk of the group. Risk pooling is also used extensively by financial investors. For example, some stock prices might go up and others down, but investing in dozens, hundreds, or even thousands of stocks can pool the risks. See "financial market," "mutual fund," "risk premium," "speculation."

risk premium This has two very closely related uses. First, it's what risk averse people are willing to pay to avoid a risky situation. For example, if you would be equally happy with a guaranteed $900 or a 50:50 chance of getting either $500 or $1,500, then you're risk premium is $100. Second, it's the extra percentage points added to an interest rate to compensate for the risk of a loan. As a general rule, each 1-percent chance of default on a loan adds a risk premium of about 1 percent to the interest rate. See "bankruptcy," "hedging," "insurance, profit."

rival consumption Consumption of a good by one person imposes a cost on, or prevents consumption of, the good by another person. Some goods, like food, have extremely rival consumption. One person, and only one person, gets the benefit. Other goods, like national defense, have no consumption rivalry; everyone can benefit simultaneously without imposing a cost on others. This is one of the two key characteristics of a good (see "excludability") that distinguishes between "common-property goods," "near-public goods," "private goods," and "public goods."

S

sales tax A tax on retail sales. This is a major source of revenue for many state and local governments. Because poorer people tend to spend a larger share of their income on stuff covered by sales taxes, it tends to be a "regressive tax." To reduce this regressiveness, some state and local governments exclude items like food and medicine.

scarcity A pervasive condition of human existence based on unlimited wants and needs, but limited resources used to satisfy the wants and needs. In other words, while we want a bunch of stuff, we can't have everything we want. In slightly different words, no one is completely satisfied. This problem of scarcity is extremely fundamental to the sorts of things that occupy the days and nights of economists. In fact, it's pretty darn fundamental to what occupies the waking, working, thinking, producing, and consuming lives of every human. We do the best we can to satisfy our needs with what we have available. An important offshoot of this scarcity problem is the concept of "opportunity cost." Given the unlimited things our resources could be used to produce, each consumer-satisfy-

ing use precludes hundreds, perhaps thousands, of other potential consumer-satisfying uses. See everything else in this guide, because it's all related to scarcity.

seasonal unemployment Unemployment caused by annual (and usually fully expected) changes in business activity. Unlike "cyclical unemployment," which could occur at any time, seasonal unemployment is an essential part of many jobs. For example, schoolteachers can expect 3 months of unemployment during the summer; construction workers can count on a few months of unemployment during the winter; and department store Santa's have a guaranteed 11-month layoff between jobs. While seasonal unemployment often enters into official unemployment measures, it's usually part of the job and shouldn't be considered a major hardship. Compare "frictional unemployment," "structural unemployment."

second estate In past centuries, this included kings, queens, dukes, and others of the ruling elite. In modern times, this means the leaders of "big business," who have extensive ownership of and control over resources, especially capital and natural resources. The interests of the second estate are usually in direct conflict with the consumers and workers of the "third estate." In that the second estate tends to have more economic and political clout, it also tends to get the upper hand in most conflicts. Help for consumers may come from the government leaders of the "first estate" or the watchdog journalists of the "fourth estate"—but don't count on it. The wealth and power of the second estate invariable infiltrates the first and fourth as well.

Securities and Exchange Commission (SEC) A federal government agency that regulates the trading of corporate stock to protect investors against unscrupulous practices. Like a number of other federal regulatory agencies, the SEC was established in the 1930s—1934 to be exact.

The impetus for its formation was to prevent investors from manipulating the stock market and to prevent other practices that contributed to the 1929 stock market crash. The SEC has all sorts of rules governing the stock market, including information disclosure, insider trading, speculation, and use of credit.

sellers' market A condition in a competitive market when there's a shortage, such that sellers force the price up. Note that a sellers' market is not the same as a market in which sellers have "market control" caused by the lack of competition. A sellers' market merely has an imbalance between the amount buyers are buying and the amount sellers are selling. Compare "buyers' market."

severance tax A tax on the value of raw materials, such as minerals and fossil fuels, when they are extracted from the environment. This is one of those hidden, unpublicized taxes on producers that is ultimately passed along to consumers.

silver certificate Paper currency issued by the U.S. Treasury from 1878 until the 1960s that could be exchanged for an equal value of silver. An occasional silver certificate will pop up in circulation, but for the most part they have been relegated to the storage vaults of collectors and have been replaced by "Federal Reserve notes" as the nation's paper money. Compare "gold certificate."

small business The businesses in our economy that individually produce very little output, have little or no market control, but collectively produce about half of our total production. Most small-business owners may aspire to the ranks of the second estate, but they're card-carrying members of the third. Compare "big business."

Small Business Administration (SBA) An independent federal agency that was started in 1953 to help small business. It provides a variety of assistance, including financial, technical, and managerial help. It helps other agencies in the federal government direct contracts and spending in the direction of proprietorships and small corporations. It also provides low-interest loans to small businesses that suffer from natural disasters.

social regulation Government "regulation" that addresses specific social problems, including pollution, product safety, worker safety, and discrimination. The late 1960s and early 1970s was a period of considerable social regulation. Within a 10-year period, the government established several regulatory agencies, including Equal Employment Opportunity Commission, Environmental Protection Agency, National Highway Traffic Safety Administration, Occupational Safety and Health Administration, and Consumer Product Safety Commission, to deal with social problems. Social regulation represents one of those divisive issues that tends to draw a line between the second and third estates. The goal of social regulation is, more often than not, to protect consumers and workers of the third estate against the considerable economic and political clout of the second estate. Compare "industry regulation."

social security A system for providing financial assistance to the poor, elderly, and disabled. The social security system in the United States was established by the Social Security Act (1935) in response to the devastating problems of the Great Depression. Our current social security system has several parts. The first part, Old Age and Survivors Insurance (OASI), is the one that usually comes to mind when the term "social security" comes up. It provides benefits to anyone who has reached a certain age and who has paid taxes into the program while employed. It also provides benefits to survivors or dependents of qualified recipients. In other words, a widow, widower, or orphaned child can qualify for monthly checks. The second part of the system is Disability Insurance (DI), which provides benefits to workers and their dependents in the case of physical disabilities that keep them from working. The third part is Hospital Insurance (HI), more commonly termed Medicare. Medicare provides two types of benefits: hospital coverage for anyone in the OASI part of the system and optional supplemental medical benefits that require a monthly insurance premium. The last part of the social security system is Public Assistance (PA), which is the official term for "welfare" and is covered under it's own heading. See "baby boomers," "poverty," "social security tax."

social security tax A tax on wage earnings that's used to fund the "social security system." In principle, the social security tax is divided equally between employer and employee: Your share is listed under the FICA heading of your paycheck. In practice, however, employees really end up paying both employee and employer contributions. The reason is that employers need to consider the *entire* cost of hiring an employee, including wages, fringe benefits, and assorted taxes. The more they pay in these nonwage items, like social security taxes, the less they pay in wages. In that the social security tax is only on earnings, and excludes profit, interest, and rent, it tends to be a "regressive tax."

socialism In theory, an economy that is a transition between "capitalism" and "communism." It is based on: (1) government, rather than individual, ownership of resource; (2) worker control of the government, such that workers, rather than capitalists, control capital and other productive resources; (3) income allocated on need rather than on resource ownership or contribution to production. As practiced by many countries around the world, however, socialism is a type of economy based on: (1) government ownership and control of the most crucial resources, like those for energy production, communication, transportation, and health care, and (2) a heavy dose of economic planning by government. The primary goals of modern socialism are to correct the inefficiencies of market failures to obtain more equal wealth and income distributions and to equalize economic opportunities.

solvency The condition of a business when liabilities (excluding any ownership equity) are less than assets. In other words, the business is doing fine and able to pay all of it's debts. This is most important when contrasted with the alternative, "insolvency."

Special Drawing Rights (SDRs) A system of accounts nations have with the International Monetary Fund that are used to settle any "balance of payments" deficits. In essence, SDRs are simply an international currency that makes it easier to conduct all sorts of international transactions. In decades past, when gold was used as the primary international currency, any balance of payments deficits was paid with gold. However, in 1967 this system of SDRs was established in lieu of sending gold all over the globe. See "money."

special-interest group A group that has more to gain or lose from some candidate, issue, or policy and thus tries extra hard to ensure that the political system is aware of their preferences. Some special-interest groups can be fairly tame, merely voting in elections for their chosen candidate, while others are quite active. The more active ones form political action committees and undertake all forms of lobbying (legal and illegal). The ultimate success of special-interest groups arises from the inclination of other people to choose "rational ignorance" and "rational abstention."

speculation Buying an asset with the intent of reselling it later at a higher price. The purpose of speculation is simply to buy low and sell high. Those who engage in speculation have no reason for buying the asset, other than resale at a later time. Such speculation is quite common in most financial markets (futures are a particular favorite), but it's also a motive for those who have "investments" in fine art, baseball cards, coins, and real estate. It's tempting to classify speculators as risk loving, those who enjoy the thrill of a risky future. While speculators might, as a general rule, be more risk loving than others, they can also be risk averse, using the practice of risk pooling, much like insurance companies, to translate risk into a calculable loss or gain.

spot The sale of a commodity for immediately delivery on the "spot." Most stuff that consumers purchase are what we could call "spot transactions." You give the store some money and go home with your purchase. Much buying and selling in financial markets is also of the spot transaction variety. For example, you give your stockbroker $100,000 and "take home" 2,000 shares of Omni Conglomerate, Inc., stock. To appreciate why it's necessary to have a name for these sorts of transactions, you need to examine "futures." See "hedging" and "speculation" as well.

stagflation High "inflation rates" at the same time the economy has high "unemployment rates." Throughout much of the economic history of the U.S.A., we've seen a tradeoff between inflation and unemployment. During an expansion, inflation is usually higher and unemployment is lower. The opposite has tended to occur during a recession. In the 1970s, however, inflation worsened at the same time the economy dropped into a recession. This led economists not only to coin the term "stagflation" (stagnation + inflation) but also to reevaluate the existing explanation of how the economy works. See "misery index."

Standard & Poor's 500 An index of the prices of 500 corporate stocks traded on the New York Stock Exchange. It includes an assortment of stocks for industrial, transportation, and utility companies. It also includes a larger number of stocks

than the comparable Dow Jones composite index (see "Dow Jones averages"), which means it's often considered a better measure of the overall performance of the stock market. Less commonly publicized are separate Standard & Poor's indexes for industrial, transportation, utility, and financial stocks.

standard of living In principle, an economy's ability to produce the goods and services that consumers use to satisfy their wants and needs. In practice, it is the average "real gross domestic product" per person—usually given the name "per capital real GDP." See "economic development," "economic growth."

stock market (stock exchange) A "financial market" that trades ownership shares in corporations—corporate stock. The three best-known national stock markets in the United States are the New York Stock Exchange, the American Stock Exchange, and the National Association of Securities Dealers. There are also a few regional markets—the Chicago, Philadelphia, and Pacific exchanges are the most notable—that trade stock on a smaller scale. Other countries that use corporations to produce stuff, all of the industrialized ones, also have stock markets. The biggest and most worthy of attention are in Tokyo, London, Toronto, Frankfurt, and Paris. Stock markets play a vital role in our economy, making it possible for businesses to raise the large sums of money needed for investment. See "Dow Jones averages," "Standard & Poors 500."

strike An agreement of workers, usually the members of a "union," to stop working. The objective of a strike is to encourage an employer to raise workers' wages or to improve working conditions. Strikes can be a powerful tool for unions to overcome the market control of employers or to gain a negotiating edge in "collective bargaining." They can also create frustrating production bottlenecks that are ultimately suffered by underappreciated consumers. Compare "lockout."

structural unemployment Unemployment caused by a mismatch between workers' skills and skills needed for available jobs. In other words, workers have the wrong training and experience. As strange as it may seem, this sort of unemployment is an inherent part of any healthy growing economy. As an economy expands, especially through technological progress, new (and, I might add more consumer-satisfying) products require different labor skills. For example, farming skills were important in the 1800s—manufacturing skills were needed for much of the 1900s—and now information-processing skills have moved to the top of our economy's list. Structural unemployment, however, rears its head when a worker is trained for a job that's eliminated by this progress. The only solution is a continuous program of investment in human capital. Compare "cyclical unemployment," "frictional unemployment," "seasonal unemployment."

subsidy A payment from government to individuals or businesses without any expectations of production. The best way of thinking about a subsidy is as a *negative* tax. Government extends subsidies for many different reasons. They go to students, unemployed workers, the poor, farmers, wealthy friends of political leaders, businesses trying to fend off foreign competitors, and the list could go on. Subsidies are frequently used to redirect resources from one good to another. Sometimes this is justified on efficiency grounds; at other times it's just the result of political power.

Supplemental Social Insurance (SSI) See "social security."

supply One half of the market exchange process (see "demand"). It is the willingness and ability to sell different amounts of a good at different prices. While willingness on the part of sellers to offer a good for sale can play a part in the supply of some goods, the ability to cover production cost is typically more important, especially for profit-seeking businesses. In most markets, an increase in the quantity of a good supplied is only possible with a higher price. This occurs because businesses need to purchase additional resources that are more expensive. See "supply price."

supply price The minimum price that sellers are willing and able to accept for supplying a good. Sellers are always willing to sell a good for more than the supply price, but not less. The supply price depends on a number of things, like production cost, but a big one is the quantity sold. The supply price tends to be higher when sellers sell more. Compare "demand price." See "demand."

T

tariff A tax that's usually on imports, but occasionally (very rarely) on exports. This is one form of trade barrier that's intended to restrict imports into a country (see "nontariff barrier" and "quota"). Unlike nontariff barriers and quotas, which increase prices and thus revenue received by domestic producers, a tariff generates revenue for the government. Most economists who spend their waking hours pondering the plight of "foreign trade" contend that the best way to restrict trade, if that's what you want to do, is through a tariff.

tax Any sort of forced or coerced payment to government. The primary reason government collects taxes is to get the revenue needed to finance public goods and pay administrative expenses. However, the more astute leaders of the first estate have recognized over the years that taxes have other effects, including: (1) redirecting resources from one good to another and (2) altering the total amount of production in the economy. As such, taxes have been used to correct "market failures," equalize the "income distribution," achieve "efficiency," stabilize "business cycles," and promote "economic growth." Taxes come in many shapes, sizes, and varieties. Here's a short list for your further consideration: capital gains tax, consumption tax, corporate income tax, excise tax, gift tax, inheritance tax, personal income tax, sales tax, social security tax, and value-added tax. Compare "subsidy."

tax avoidance A *legal* reduction in taxes. The complexity of our system of taxes, especially income taxes, makes it extremely worthwhile to identify the mix of spending, working, and assorted activities that reduce taxes. This has also created a major industry of accountants, lawyers, educators, public speakers, and others who spend their efforts uncovering legal tax loopholes. In terms of the big efficiency picture, this is a complete waste of resources. Our lives would, in general, be better off if this tax avoidance industry devoted its efforts to increasing "gross domestic product" rather than diverting it from one pocket to another. This, though, is not a fault of theirs but of the tax system itself. Compare "tax evasion."

tax evasion An *illegal* reduction in taxes. Tax evasion occurs when someone fails to pay his legal taxes. This is the sort of thing that leads to a prison sentence. Ethical considerations aside, it is also the sort of thing that's likely to happen if tax rates are high or unpopular. Compare "tax avoidance."

tax incidence The ultimate payment of a tax. Many taxes are initially paid by one person but passed along through production and consumption activities until it finally reaches someone else. An obvious example is the sales tax. While officially paid by the retail store (which writes the check to the government), the tax is tacked on to the prices paid by consumers. Consumers, thus, bear the lion's share of most sales taxes. The incidence of other taxes is not quite so obvious. Some taxes are paid by producers early

in production—such as severance taxes on oil extraction—without the knowledge of consumers, who end up paying through higher prices. As a general rule, taxes are passed through the system until they reach someone (usually consumers) who can pass it no further.

technology The sum total of knowledge concerning the productive use of resources. It has been one of the more important sources, if not *the* critical source, of economic growth in the United States. Similar to other sources of "economic growth," it requires a heavy investment, specifically in education, scientific research, and product development.

terms of trade The quantity of one good that's given up to get another. Terms of trade is usually applied to foreign trade, although it's just as applicable to any sort of exchange. Terms of (foreign) trade are said to improve when one country gives up a relatively smaller quantity of its stuff to get a relatively larger quantity of another country's stuff. Terms of trade depend on the relative productivity of two countries and is reflected by "exchange rates."

third estate In past centuries, this included the peasants, serfs, or slaves who performed the dirty deeds for the ruling elite. In modern times, the term refers to the workers, taxpayers, and consumers who have limited ownership of and control over resources—usually nothing more than their own labor. The third estate, which forms the backbone of any modern economy, is usually at odds with the business leaders of the "second estate." Help may come from the government leaders of the "first estate" or the journalists of the "fourth estate"—but don't count on it.

third-party payment Payments made on behalf of one person (party) to a second person (party) by a third person (party) for benefits received by the first person (party). Eliminating the person (party) language, these sorts of payments are a standard method of buying health care. Insurance companies and the government pay doctors for the medical care received by patients. Problems arise because the party with the checkbook (insurance companies and government) aren't getting any of the benefits, while the party getting the benefits (patients) don't have to be concerned about payment. As such, third-party payments give patients an incentive to buy too much health care. Let's not, however, place the blame entirely on their shoulders. The second party (doctors), knowing that (1) patients aren't concerned about the price and that (2) insurance companies and government are usually unaware of the treatment, has the opportunity and motivation to overcharge for services. Combining third-party payments with "market control" by physicians and throwing in a little "principal/agent problem" is a recipe for high health care costs.

third-world country A country with a relatively low "standard of living" and which lacks the "economic development" of more advanced industrialized nations like the United States. Most third-world countries are in Africa, Asia, and South America; they often rise to newsworthy prominence when they have a famine, are overthrown by a military dictator, or are invaded by a more-developed country. They tend to have high rates of population growth and limited success in doing what's necessary to achieve "economic growth." Their problems are a motivation behind the "foreign aid" extended by the United States and other advanced nations. The term "third world" is an outgrowth of the Cold War between the Capitalist countries of the "West" (first-world countries) and the Communist countries of the "East" (second-world countries). As first- and second-world countries try to spread their own brand of philosophy around the globe, these less-developed third-world nations often become the center of conflict and the recipients of politically motivated foreign aid. While the struggles of many third-world countries have continued over the decades, some like South Korea, Taiwan, and Poland have seen marked improvement.

tight money The pursuit of contractionary "monetary policy" by the Federal Reserve System. In other words, to reduce high rates of "inflation," the Fed decreases either the growth of the money supply or even the total amount of money in the economy, which "tightens up" the amount of money people can get (usually through bank loans). The number-1 way the Fed goes about this tight-money stuff is through "open-market operations." This is where the Fed sells government securities to the public, which takes bank reserves out of the banking system. With fewer reserves, banks aren't able to make as many loans to you or me. The more bank reserves the Fed takes out, the harder it is to get a loan. If we don't have any money, then we can't spend it, which reduces prices and inflation. In principle, the Fed could also tighten the money supply using the "discount rate" and "reserve requirements." These, however, tend to be less reliable, less effective, and more difficult to use. Compare "easy money."

trade barrier A restriction, invariably by government, that prevents "free trade" among countries. The more popular trade restrictions are "tariffs," import "quotas," and assorted "nontariff barriers." An occasional embargo will even be thrown into this mix. The primary use of trade barriers is to restrict imports from entering the country. By restricting imports, domestic producers of the restricted goods are protected from competition and are even subsidized through higher prices. Consumers, though, get the short end of this stick, with higher prices and a limited choice of goods. In that producers tend to have more political clout than consumers, it's pretty obvious why trade barriers are a "natural" state of affairs. There are a few notable, yet not all that valid, justifications for trade restrictions, including: (1) A young, emerging domestic industry needs protection from foreign competition until it gets more fully established. (2) Retaliation is needed to "level the playing field" because another country restricts imports. (3) An imported good doesn't meet the same stringent safety or environmental standards as domestic stuff. (4) An imported good is of such strategic military importance that its supply can't be left up to the production whims of some foreign country. See "foreign trade."

trade deficit Formally termed a "balance of trade" deficit, a condition in which a nation's imports are greater than exports. In other words, a country is buying more stuff from foreigners than foreigners are buying from domestic producers. A trade deficit is usually thought to be bad for a country. For this reason, some countries seek to reduce their trade deficit by: (1) establishing trade barriers on imports, (2) reducing the "exchange rate" (termed "devaluation") such that exports are less expensive and imports more expensive (see also "J-curve"), or (3) invading foreign countries with sizable armies. See "trade surplus."

trade surplus Formally termed a "balance of trade" surplus, a condition in which a nation's exports are greater than imports. In other words, a country is buying less stuff from foreigners than foreigners are buying from domestic producers. A trade surplus is usually thought to be a good thing for a country. However, every country in the world cannot run a trade surplus at the same time. Excessive trade surpluses can also lead to invasion by sizable foreign armies. See "revaluation," "trade deficit."

trading bloc A group of countries that are economically intertwined, share some common cultural background, are located close together, and coordinate their foreign-trade policies. There are three trading blocs of note—North America,

Europe, and Asia—although other portions of the globe aspire to this status. The North American bloc centers around the United States, with Canada and Mexico playing increasingly important roles. The European bloc contains most of Western Europe, with leading roles played by Germany, Britain, and France. Japan is the center of the Asian bloc that includes Korea, Taiwan, Hong Kong, Malaysia, and several other countries. The logic of trading blocs is a sort of "us versus them" mentality. The European trading bloc has gone as far as establishing a formal economic union that reduces trade barriers among member countries in an effort to compete with the other two blocs. The United States has made similar moves to formalize the North American trading bloc through the North American Free Trade Agreement (NAFTA). And Japan has worked hard in recent decades to integrate itself with the economies of other Asian countries. At the same time that countries are lowering trade barriers through the "General Agreement on Tariffs and Trade," they are raising others through these trading blocs. See "unilateral," "multilateral," "bilateral."

transfer payment A payment, usually by the government, without any corresponding production. The three most popular transfer payments in our economy are for social security, unemployment compensation, and welfare. The intent of these transfer payments is to redistribute income, and thus the goods and services that can be had with the income. If you're interested in numbers, transfer payments are part of the difference between national income and personal income.

treasury bill One kind of government security issued by the U.S. Treasury to obtain the funds used to finance the federal budget deficit. A treasury bill (or T-bill) has a maturity length of 1 year or less, with 90 days a common maturity. T-bills, together with short-term commercial paper issued by businesses, are traded in money markets. The interest rate on T-bills is one of the key indicators of short-run economic activity. See "treasury bond" and "treasury note."

treasury bond One kind of government security issued by the U.S. Treasury to obtain the funds used to finance the federal budget deficit. A treasury bond (or T-bond) has a maturity length of over 10 years, with 15 and 30 years common maturities. T-bonds, together with other long-term bonds issued by state and local governments and businesses, are traded in capital markets. The interest rate on T-bonds is a key long-run interest rate. See "treasury bill" and "treasury note."

treasury note One kind of government security issued by the U.S. Treasury to obtain the funds used to finance the federal budget deficit. A treasury note (or T-note) has a maturity length of between 1 and 10 years. See "treasury bill" and "treasury bond."

U

uncertainty The *possibility* that any number of things could happen in the future. In other words, the future is not known. This should be compared with "risk," which is assigning *probabilities* to alternative possibilities.

unemployment When resources that are willing and able to produce, or otherwise capable of production, aren't. "Unemployment" is most commonly used in regard to labor and measured by the "unemployment rate." However, capital and natural resources can also be unemployed. The best measure of capital unemployment is the "capacity utilization rate." The diversity of natural resources is so great that a single unemployment measurement is not really possible. One overwhelming problem with unemployment is lost production. Whenever resources are unemployed, our economy loses consumer-satisfying goods and services or capital that can

never be recouped. Another problem of unemployment is the income lost by resource owners, which tends to create the biggest hardship for labor, which unlike capital and natural resource owners, seldom has much income from other resources. While we also have some unemployment in the economy, it tends to become most severe during the recession of a "business cycle." See "cyclical unemployment," "frictional unemployment," "minimum wage," "seasonal unemployment," "structural unemployment," "unemployment compensation."

unemployment compensation A system of government-sponsored insurance, created by the Social Security Act (1935), that provides benefits to unemployed workers. Funding is obtained by taxes on employers. The system is mandated by the federal government but operated by each state. As such, the amount and duration of the benefits differ from state to state. See "automatic stabilizer," "social security," "transfer payment," "unemployment," "welfare."

unemployment rate In principle, simply the ratio of total unemployment to the total labor force. To be counted in the standard, official unemployment rate, you must be 16 years old or older and actively seeking employment. The labor force in this case includes everyone who is employed plus those who are unemployed but actively seeking work. There are, however, a few problems with this standard, official unemployment rate measure. Here are two: (1) To be counted as unemployed you must be actively seeking work. However, a bunch of unemployed people get discouraged and give up looking when they can't find a job. (2) To be counted as employed and part of the labor force you only need to be working a few hours a week, even though you might want a full-time job. The Department of Labor, which is responsible for compiling and publishing unemployment information, takes account of these and other problems by calculating seven separate unemployment rates; the standard, official one is number 5. See "capacity-utilization rate," "business cycle."

unfair competition A wide assortment of business practices that are deceptive and dishonest, and usually hamper competition. Examples of unfair competition include false or misleading advertising, price discrimination, bribery, and even industrial espionage. These practices and many, *many* more are illegal according to antitrust law, specifically the Federal Trade Commission Act (1914). See "Federal Trade Commission."

unilateral An action, often used in terms of an international trade agreement, that's extended to only one party. For example, the United States might enter into a unilateral agreement with Canada over the employment of Canadian hockey players in the United States. The agreement, though, would have nothing to do with U.S. hockey players in Canada. Compare "bilateral," "multilateral."

union An organization of workers or employees who act jointly to negotiate with their employers over wages, fringe benefits, working conditions, and other facets of employment. The main function of unions is to provide a balance for the "market control" exerted over labor by "big business." Unions have had a long and turbulent history in the United States. While the first unions appeared in the late 1700s, they struggled both on the streets and in the courts throughout most of the 1800s for the right to organize legally and negotiate with employers. The late 1800s saw unions gain ground, but it wasn't until the Great Depression of the 1930s, when political conditions became most favorable, that unions attained the full legal standing and economic clout enjoyed during the mid-1900s. While the 1950s saw nearly 30 percent of the labor force in unions, that percent had declined to about 15

percent by the 1990s. See "collective bargaining," "lockout," "strike."

unlimited liability A condition in which owners are personally held responsible for any and all debts created by a business. Proprietorships and partnerships are the two kinds of businesses in which owners have unlimited liability. Compare "limited liability."

user charge A tax that's disguised as a price—a charge for the use of a publicly provided good. Government produces and supplies a number of near-public goods, like education, libraries, parks, and transportation systems. The "prices" for these goods are user charges. The logic is that people who benefit from the good and are willing to pay should pay for them. While this helps pay production costs, it tends to be inefficient.

V

value Quite simply, this is the amount of consumer satisfaction directly or indirectly obtained from something. The more a good satisfies a person's want or need, then the more valuable it is, to that person. Furthermore, different people are likely to place different values on a good. Resources are valuable to the degree that they are used to produce stuff that consumers want. The bottom line is that value, like beauty, is truly in the eye of the beholder.

value-added tax A tax on the extra value added during each stage in the production of a good. Most of the stuff our economy produces goes through several "stages," usually with different businesses. In each stage, resources do their thing to the good to make it a little more valuable. For example, an ice cream store can take 50 cents worth of ice cream, fudge, and whipped topping and turn it into a hot fudge sundae that's valued at $1.50. The efforts of the ice cream resources thus add $1 in value. A value-added tax is based on this extra value. While it's been debated off and on in the United States, a value-added tax is commonly used in Europe.

vertical equity A system of taxes that treats unequal people unequally. In other words, if you make less income than someone else and pay fewer personal income taxes, that's vertical equity. See "horizontal equity."

vertical merger See "merger."

W

wealth The net ownership of material possessions and productive resources. In other words, the difference between physical and financial assets that you own and the liabilities that you owe. Wealth includes (1) all of the tangible consumer stuff that you possess, like cars, houses, clothes, jewelry, etc.; (2) any financial assets, like stocks, bonds, bank accounts, that you lay claim to; and (3) your ownership of resources, including labor, capital, and natural resources. Of course, you must deduct any debts you owe. The wealth of the economy falls along similar lines. Our total wealth is the combined sum of material possessions and productive resources for everyone in the economy. Financial assets cancel out for the economy because they are an asset for one person but a liability for another. For example, money is part of your individual wealth, but not part of our economy's wealth—an asset for you, but a liability for the U.S. government. Individual wealth can be acquired either from others (see "wealth pyramid") or through investment of current income. In contrast, the wealth of the economy can be increased only through investment in the quantity or quality of resources.

wealth distribution The manner in which wealth is divided among the members of the economy. A perfectly equal wealth distribution would mean that everyone in the country has exactly the same wealth. In reality, wealth is unequally distributed. A few people have a great deal of wealth and most others have less. Any well-functioning economy that's doing a pretty good job of satisfying consumer wants and needs will have some degree of inequality in the distribution of wealth. This occurs because some people have done a good job of producing what people want, and thus grow wealthy. However, wealth tends to perpetuate itself, over and above what is justified by valuable production. Along with wealth comes market control, political power, and the ability to accumulate more wealth at the expense of others. Compare "income distribution." See "Gini index."

wealth pyramid A handy technique that many get-rich-quick schemes use to transfer a little wealth from a lot of people into the overflowing pockets of a few. It works in this manner: A person or business establishes a multilevel pyramid of investors, employees, or "distributors." Each level is responsible for recruiting the next level beneath it. The trick is that each distributor at one level recruits several distributors into the next lower level in an ever-expanding fashion. Each recruit transfers a little, teeny, tiny bit of his own wealth to the next higher level. In that each higher level has fewer members, that little, teeny, tiny bit of wealth accumulates rapidly, making those at the top incredibly well-off. No wealth is actually created, nor is anything of value produced. The few merely get a transfer ("steal" might be more appropriate) of wealth from the many. This pyramid ultimately crumbles when the bottom level of the pyramid runs out of prospective recruits. Most people in a wealth pyramid are then left with smaller bank accounts and bags of empty promises.

welfare An assortment of programs that provide assistance to the poor. The cornerstone of our welfare system is Aid to Families with Dependent Children (AFDC), which was created by the Social Security Act (1935). It provides cash benefits to assist needy families with children under the age of 18. Funding comes partly from the federal government and partly from states. Because states also administer their own programs, benefits, and qualification, criteria differ from state to state. A second part of the welfare system, one that's run entirely by the federal government, is Supplemental Security Income (SSI). This program provides cash benefits to elderly, blind, and disabled in addition to any benefits received through the social security system. Our welfare system includes a whole bunch of additional benefits, including Medicaid, food stamps, low-cost housing, school lunches, job training, day care, and earned-income tax credits. See "poverty."

workers' compensation A government-run insurance program that provides benefits to workers injured on the job. Funding for these benefits comes from premiums paid by employers. The federal government mandates the program, but it's administered by each of the states. This creates a great deal of diversity, with some states having good benefits and high premiums (sort of pro labor), while others have lousy benefits and low premiums (pro business). In addition to differences among states, premiums also differ based on a business's historical record of accidents. Those companies with a higher number of industrial accidents pay more in premiums than those with fewer accidents. Workers' compensation runs into controversy, in large part because it's another part of the ongoing conflict between the second and third estates.

World Bank (International Bank for Reconstruction and Development) An agency of the United Nations that was established in 1945 to promote the "economic development" of the poorer nations in the world. It pursues this goal by providing low-interest loans to less-developed countries and by offering technical assistance on the best ways to use these loans. Funds for the loans are obtained by the World Bank by selling bonds on the world's "financial markets."

Its long-run economic development orientation is usually coordinated with the shorter-run efforts of its sister U.N. agency, the International Monetary Fund.

X

X-inefficiency Cost that is higher than it needs to be because a firm is operating inefficiently. This is most often seen for firms that have a great deal of "market control," especially "monopoly." The lack of competition allows a business to pad its expenses, hire unneeded employees (like relatives), goof off instead of working, and all sorts of other things that lessen production and increase cost. The business is not penalized for these actions, because market control allows the company to extract whatever price is needed to cover cost. See "economic rent," "profit."

Y

yield The rate of return on a financial asset. In some simple cases, the yield on a financial asset—like commercial paper, corporate bond, or government security—is the asset's interest rate. However, as a more general rule, the yield includes both the interest earned from an asset plus any changes in the asset's price. Suppose, for example, that a $100,000 bond has a 10-percent interest rate, such that the holder receives $10,000 interest per year. If the price of the bond increases over the course of the year from $100,000 to $105,000, then the bond's yield is greater than 10 percent. It includes the $10,000 interest plus the $5,000 bump in the price, giving a yield of 15 percent. Because bonds and similar financial assets often have fixed interest payments, their prices and, subsequently, yields move up and down as economic conditions change.

Z

zoning Legal restrictions on where different activities can locate within a city. Most cities regulate the location of industrial, commercial, and residential activities. The underlying motivation behind zoning is to keep less desirable, but perhaps more profitable, activities from encroaching on residential areas. The economic rationale of zoning rests with the idea of "externality," often termed "neighborhood effect" in this context. In a nutshell, this tells us that the quality of an entire neighborhood depends on the quality of each house—and any other activities located nearby. A rundown, dumpy house, with an unkempt, weed-infested yard, can reduce the value of other houses in the neighborhood. Anything done to one house creates an externality for other houses. If an adult book store, smoke-belching factory, or all-night honky-tonk saloon opens up in a nice, peaceful residential neighborhood, property values drop, and so too drops the wealth of the homeowners. Zoning seeks to prevent this.

SECTION 4

INDEX

A

Accounting profit, 175–76
Advertising, 16, 63–66
    benefits of, 63–65
    control of information
        through, 65–66
    problems with, 65
American Stock Exchange, 195
Arbitration, 202
Athlete salaries, 67–70

B

Baby boomers, and social
    security, 190–91
Balanced budget, 109. *See also*
    Budget deficit
Balanced–budget amendment,
    108
Banking, 113
Benefits, net, 7
Big business, 72
Bonds, 153
Booms, 57
Budget deficit, 106–9, 111, 149
Budget surplus, 149
Business
    competition in, 73–74
    cooperation in, 74
    equality in, 71–72
    market control in, 74
    political power in, 74
    risk in, 74
Business cycle, 108–9
    booms and busts in,
        57–58
Business ownership, types of,
    72–73
Business savings, 149
Business structures, as invest-
    ment, 147
Busts, 57

C

Capital, 4, 92
    human, 4, 8, 94–96
    nurturing, 21–22
    working, 148
Capital markets, 113
Certification of physicians, 128
Circular flow, 53–60
    consumption in, 55
    markets in, 55

multiplicative, cumulatively
    reinforcing interaction of
    the, 56–57
    production in, 55
    resources in, 54
Commodities, 154
Common property goods, 39
Comparative advantage,
    23–24
Competition, 73
    advertising as restriction
        on, 65
    and athlete salaries, 68
    and negotiation, 16
Competitive markets, 100
Competitors, 14
Conservative Republicans, 160
Consumer price index (CPI),
    135, 136
Consumer satisfaction, and
    demand, 13
Consumer sovereignty, 16
Consumers savings, 149
Consumption
    in circular flow, 57
    rival, 38
Contractions, 57
Control
    and ownership, 19
    politics of, 19–20
Cooperation, 74
Corporate profits, taxes on,
    197–98
Corporate stock, 193
Corporations, 73, 194–95
Cost, 5–6
    of free goods, 6
    of information, 48
    of production, 14
Cost/benefit analysis of crime,
    80–84
Credit, 113
Credit cards, 76
    interest rates on, 78
    market control in, 78–79
    preapproved limits on,
        77–78
    tips for, 79
    wonders of, 76–77
Crime, 80–83
    business of, 82
    cleaning up, 82–83

cost/benefit analysis in,
    80–84
    and morality, 82
    opportunity cost in,
        81–82
    tips for avoiding, 83
Crop reduction, 103–4
Cultural change, 93
Customer satisfaction
    opportunity cost of fore-
        gone, 14–15
    supply and, 14

D

Deficit, federal, 106–9, 111,
    149
Deficit spending, 106–9
Deflation, 137
Demand, 12, 28
    and consumer satisfac-
        tion, 13
    for funds, 112
Demand–side, athlete salaries
    in, 68–69
Democrats, liberal, 160–61
Depressions, 57, 109
Direct payments, 104
Discrimination, 84–86
    cost of, 85
    definition of, 84
    reasons for, 85–86
    tips for, 86
Diversification, 152–53
Dollars
    nominal, 136
    real, 136
Downturn, 57, 58
Durable equipment, as
    investment, 147–48
Durable goods, 151

E

Economic forecasting, 87–90,
    183
    cautionary tips on,
        89–90
    extrapolation of trend, 88
    theories in, 88–89
    uncertainty in, 89
Economic growth, 7, 8,
    91–93

role of education and
human capital in,
96–97
tips for, 93
Economic profit, 176–77
Economic rent, 177
Economy
importance of information
to, 45–47
limitations on, 3–9
limits on efficiency of,
51–52
redistribution of
resources, 8
Education, 94–97
responsibility of
government for, 37
Efficiency, and advertising, 64
Emigration, 131
Employment, and
immigration, 133
Entrepreneurship, 4
Equality, 37–38
Equity
horizontal, 40
vertical, 40
Exchange rates, 98–100
Excludability, 37
Expansions, 57
Exports, 99, 119, 120–21
Extracurricular events, 183

F
Farm subsidies, 101–5
categories of, 103–4
good and the bad of, 104
Federal deficit, 106-9, 111, 149
benefits of, 107
problems with, 107
reducing, 107
Fees and user charges, 198
Financial markets, 110–13
uncertainty and risks in,
51
Forecasting, economic, 87–90
Foreign exchange, 115
Foreign investment, 114–17
Foreign trade, 118–21
Free goods, 5–6
consumer tips for, 6–7
cost of, 6
Funds

demanders of, 112
suppliers of, 112
Future, information as critical
in, 49
Futures markets, 113

G
Gambling, 122–26
Goods
common property, 39
durable, 151
financing of through
advertising, 64–65
free, 6–7
government, 39–40
near public, 38–39
private, 38
public, 335–44
Government, 36
and the exchange rate,
99–100
fighting inefficiency in,
43–44
functions of, 36–38
as public good, 35–44
role of, in economy,
58–59
sources of money, 40
Government goods, 39–40
Government savings, 149
Government securities, 106
Government taxes, 181
Great Depression, 109
Gross domestic product
(GDP), 5, 107, 135, 180
health care in, 127
price deflator, 136
Growth periods, 57

H
Health care, 33, 127–30
preventive, 130
Health insurance, 128–29
national, 129
Horizontal equity, 40
Human capital, 4, 8, 94-96

I
Immigration, 91, 131–34
Import quotas, 120
Imports, 99, 119, 120
Incentives, 16

Income, 13
correlation with
production, 5
national or personal, 180
taxes on, 197
Industry, regulations for,
185–86
Inflation, 58, 99, 109, 135–38,
145
Inflation premium, 145
Information, 186
challenge of searching
for, 47–48
control of
and advertising, 65–66
and health care, 128
costs of, 48
as critical in future, 49
importance of, to the
economy, 45–47
limited, 47
and product safety, 173
tips in searching for,
49–51
usefulness of, 48
Infrastructure, investment in,
149
Inheritance, taxes on, 198
Innovations, 178
Insurance, 113, 139–42
Interest rates, 143–46
Inventories, investment in,
148–49
Investment, 92, 147–51
education as, 96
foreign, 114–17
nurturing capital with, 22
promotional, 6
J
Job displacement, 92–93

L
Labor. *See also* Human capital
quantity side of, 91, 92
Land, 21
Laws and restrictions, 186
Leading economic indicators,
183
Legal system, responsibility of
government for, 36–37
Liability
limited, 194

unlimited, 194
Liberal Democrats, 160–61
Licensing, of physicians, 128
Limited liability, 194
Limited production, 4
Limited resources, 4, 5
Lockout, 203

M
Market, 12
    in circular flow, 55
    futures, 113
    options, 113
    product, 55
    resource, 55
    spot, 113
    stock, 113
Market control, 74, 167, 177,
    178
    consumer tips on, 31–34
    for health care, 127–28
    of politics, 33
    politics of, 32–33
Mediation, 202
Medical school accreditation,
    128
Migration, 131
Money, 113
Money market, 113, 153
Monopoly, 26
    buy low and sell high,
    27–28
Morality, 82
Mutual funds, 152–54
    bonds, 153
    commodities, 154
    growth, 153
    growth and income,
    153–54
    income, 153
    international, 154
    liquidity, 153
    selected industries, 154

N
NASDAQ index, 195
National defense
    as example of public
    good, 38
    responsibility of
    government for, 36
National health insurance, 129

National mood, 182–83
Natural resources, 4, 91,
    155–59
    conservation tips, 158–59
    nonrenewable, 156
    perpetual, 156
Nature, 20
Near public goods, 38–39
Needs, wants and, 13–14
Negotiation, and competition,
    16
Net benefits, 7
New York Stock Exchange,
    195
Nominal dollars, 136
Normal profit, 178
Nurture, 20

O
Occupational Safety and
    Health Administration
    (OSHA), 214
Opportunity cost, 5, 176
    and athlete salaries, 67–68
    of foregone satisfaction,
    14–15
Options markets, 113
Ownership
    and control, 19
    politics of, 19–20

P
Partnership, 73, 194
People, 4
Personal wealth, 5
Political power, 74
Political views, 160–64
Politics, 183
    and market control, 32–33
    of regulation, 187
Pollution, 92, 165–69, 177, 186
Preventive health care, 130
Price differences, 48
Price supports, 103
Price volatility, 48
Principal/agent problem, 128
Private goods, 38
Production
    in circular flow, 55
    contribution to, 14–15
    effect of resources on, 5

income correlation with,
    5
    limited, 4
    value of foregone, 15
Production cost, 14
Productive resources, invest-
    ment in, 8
Product markets, 55
Product recalls, 173
Product safety, 170–74
Professional sports, 33
Profit, 175–79
    accounting, 175–76
    economic, 176–77
    normal, 178
Progressive taxes, 199
Promotional investment, 6
Property, taxes on, 197
Proportional taxes, 199
Proprietor resources, 177–78
Proprietorship, 72–73, 194
Prospectus, 154
Prosperities, 57
Public debt, 107
Public goods, 38, 106
    government as, 35–44
Purchase, frequency of, 48

Q
Quotas, 120

R
Real dollars, 136
Real return, 145
Recession, 57, 58, 107, 109,
    180–84, 183, 184
Recoveries, 57
Redistribution, of resources,
    6–7
Redistribution program
    costs of, 7
    long–term effects of, 7
Regressive taxes, 199
Regulation, 185–88
Renewable, 156
Rent, economic, 177
Republicans, conservative, 160
Residential structures, invest-
    ment in, 148
Resource depletion, 92
Resource markets, 55
Resources, 4–5, 91

capital, 92
in circular flow, 54
distribution of, 52
effect of, on production, 4–5
labor, 91–92
limited, 4, 5
natural, 91
quantity of, 18–19
redistribution of, 6–7
Retail sales, 180–81
Risk, 74
Risk averse, 50, 122, 139
Risk loving, 50-51, 123, 139
Risk neutral, 50, 123, 139
Risk pooling, 140–41
Risk premium, 145
Rival consumption, 38

S
Safety
product, 170–74
worker, 212–15
Safety standards, 173
Salaries, athlete, 67–70
Sales, taxes on, 197
Satisfaction, 13
Saving
business, 149
consumers, 149
government, 149
Scarcity, 10–12, 54, 92, 156
definition of, 3
Second estate, 75
Small business, 72
Social, regulations, 186
Social security, 189–92
Special–interest groups, 42

Specialization, 23, 24–25
Spot markets, 113
Standard of living, 156
Standards, 186
Stock, corporate, 193
Stock market, 113, 193–96
Strike, 202–3
Subjective values, 10–16
Subsidies
farm, 101-5
in insurance, 141
tips on, 104–5
Subsidization, 6
Substitutes, 13
Suppliers, of funds, 112
Supply, 12, 28
and customer satisfaction, 14
Supply–side, athlete salaries in, 67–68

T
Tariffs, 120
Taxes, 186, 199–201
corporate profits, 197–98
fees and user charges, 198
on income, 197
on inheritance, 198
and pollution, 168
progressive, 199
on property, 197
proportional, 199
regressive, 199
on sales, 197
on wages, 197
Technology, 14, 92
Third estate, 75
Third–party payments, 129

Total expense, 48
Trade, foreign, 118–21
Transactions costs, 152
Transportation, responsibility of government for, 37

U
Underpayment, in athlete salaries, 69
Unemployment, 58, 109, 182
and inflation, 137
rate of, 180
Unions, 202–4
Unlimited liability, 194
Used–car market, information in, 47

V
Value
subjective, 10–16
tips on, 15–16
Vertical equity, 40
Voluntary exchange, 12

W
Wages, taxes on, 197
Wants, and needs, 13–14
Waste, 7
Wealth
creating, 205–8
personal, 5
restrictions on, 5
Welfare, 209–11
Women, working, 216–18
Worker safety, 212–15
Working capital, 148
Working women, 216–18

WANT MORE?

Enjoyed our pedestrian trek through the economy? Don't want to stop? Craving for more? Have I got deal for you! PEDESTRIAN *Footnotes*! It's the newsletter of the *Ambling Institute of America*, the foremost authority in the pedestrian study of all things economic. PEDESTRIAN *Footnotes* has insights into intriguing issues, timely consumer tips, and updates on the unscrupulous doings of government and business.

Four issues of PEDESTRIAN *Footnotes*, that's a whole year's worth, can be yours just for the asking. All you have to do is rip out the form below, write legibly, then mail it to the *Ambling Institute of America*. In short order, you will receive your first issue filled with information essential to every overworked, underappreciated, taxpaying consumer.

But that's not all. By reading *Economic Literacy* and correctly answering the FINAL EXAM question given below, you will receive a prestigious Doctor of Pedestrianism (PeD) degree. Your diploma will accompany your first issue of PEDESTRIAN *Footnotes*. To paraphrase the Wizard of Oz: *the only difference between you and the "experts," they have a diploma.*

Well, what are you waiting for? Rip out this form and mail it to me as fast as you can.

3 STEPS FOR 4 FREE ISSUES OF PEDESTRIAN *Footnotes*

FILL IN THE BLANKS

Name:

Street Address:

City: State: Zip Code:

ANSWER THE QUESTION

Q. IS OUR ECONOMIC PIE LIMITED?

☐ YES
☐ NO

RIP IT OUT AND MAIL TO

Ambling Institute of America
P. O. Box 2045
Stillwater, Oklahoma 74076